DIANA'S NIGHTMARE

The Family

CHRIS HUTCHINS
AND PETER THOMPSON

NEVILLE NESS HOUSE

This edition published Neville Ness House Ltd 2015

www.nevillenesshouse.com

nevillenesshouse@sky.com

www.chrishutchins.info

A CIP catalogue record for this book is available from the British Library ISBN: 978-0-9933566-4-3

Layout by EBooks by Design

wwww.ebooksbydesign.co

CONTENTS

PROLOGUE

THE LAST CHANCE SALON

'The royals don't want the fairy-tale anymore'
Andrew Morton

LAUGHING in the rain, a soaking wet Diana, Princess of Wales, sheltered from a downpour at her sons' school sports day as a new star took her place in the royal firmament. Though she had no wish to usurp Diana's place, the Honourable Serena Alleyne Stanhope found herself being presented to the public from the balcony of Buckingham Palace as very much one of the Family. Her presence between the Queen and the Queen Mother in the traditional line-up after Trooping the Colour on Saturday, 12 June, 1993, owed as much to the plummeting ratings of the House of Windsor as to her engagement to Her Majesty's nephew, Viscount Linley.

The Windsors had run decidedly short on glamour following Diana's acrimonious separation from Prince Charles the previous December and the earlier exodus of Sarah, Duchess of York, in a flurry of scandal. Considering the voices noisily raised against her family, the Queen needed every vote-catcher she could muster. Like the seasoned campaigner she was, she had eagerly seized upon the forthcoming union of the Armani public relations girl and Princess Margaret's carpenter son to win a few popularity points.

In themselves, the couple presented a paradox typical of Britain's contradictory class system. For one was the daughter of a viscount, though still a commoner, and the other, though the son of a commoner, was a viscount who stood twelfth in line to the throne. Only the Windsors, however, rated as real royals and their position was threatened as never before.

Serena, a twenty-two-year-old ash blonde, might not have possessed Diana's magnetic attraction for the cameras which were recording the occasion, nor Sarah's extrovert charm which had enlivened proceedings in the past, but she symbolized a positive start in a new direction. The young heiress was a welcome addition to

1

royal ranks and she accepted the compliment as modestly as she could. Noted for her sweet, friendly nature and her preference for casual dressing, it was just possible that the aptly named newcomer might bring a touch of serenity to Europe's most troubled royal household. Newly slim and neat in a navy designer suit, she looked up from under the broad brim of a straw hat swathed in matching blue material. 'Half a duvet,' someone had unkindly called the generous trimming.

Overhead in the leaden skies, RAF jets zoomed past in a salute to their sovereign on the official date of her sixty-seventh birthday. In one of them was Sarah Kennedy, who was broadcasting live to listeners of the BBC's Radio Two. 'It's like that quote from Gilbert & Sullivan, "Everybody's somebody when nobody is anybody," ' opined Ms Kennedy, a self-confessed republican, after her jet had landed. 'The royals have lost the mystique and they'll never get it back. I don't want to get rid of them, although at times I wanted that balcony to disintegrate.'

David Linley stood just behind his bride-to-be, smiling wryly at the events which had suddenly propelled him to the forefront of royal life. His days as one of the country's most highly eligible young men might be numbered, but he could be proud of the fact that he was fulfilling a role which had cruelly eluded his princely cousins. Among the Queen's children, only Princess Anne, who had remarried after her divorce, had managed to restore order to her private life and, although she had chosen to spend this gloomy day elsewhere, the Queen knew she could count on her total support. Her three sons were an entirely different story. Not one had managed to find a wife suited to the peculiarities of royal life.

Although the Windsors' right to rule is enshrined in an Act of Parliament, the law could be changed to alter the line of succession. Twice in its history, Parliament has removed monarchs who have displeased it, one of them ending his reign on the scaffold. Only a handful of rabid republicans seriously want to remove the Queen, but quite a few people seem anxious to deny Prince Charles his birthright.

Charles, the Windsor heir who had taken a mistress during his marriage, was a seriously worried man as he stood next to his father, the Duke of Edinburgh. He appeared neither comfortable in his ceremonial rig nor in himself. Resting his hands on the parapet, he surveyed the scene across the Palace forecourt and down the long leafy boulevard known as the Mall. Beyond the gilded bronze figure of Victory atop the marble pedestal of the Victoria Memorial, the glass and steel tower blocks of the City of London rose mockingly on the horizon.

Everything he cherished and despised about the kingdom, the worthy old and the tacky new, was directly in his line of vision. But Charles's comments on the failings of the world had counted for little since his affair with Camilla Parker Bowles had become public. He had been exposed as an adulterer in a six-minute taped telephone call and the consequences were horrible.

After a millennium of monarchy, Charles had desperately wanted to take the Crown into the twenty-first century – to boldly go where no other king had gone before. Many thought he was struggling in this objective even before the latest electronic devices known to mankind had exposed one of its oldest vices. Once Camillagate and Squidgy had entered the language of Shakespeare and Milton, the prospect of divorce represented a personal disaster for an heir more errant than apparent.

The British sovereign is not only head of state, the judiciary, the armed forces and the Commonwealth, but also head of the Church of England. As a divorced man, it would be impossible for Charles to become Defender of the Faith, leading a church which, while accepting the ordination of women priests, still forbids divorce. The Coronation Oath would have to be changed solely for his benefit and some senior clerics seriously questioned the wisdom of such an irrevocable step.

If his thoughts weren't on Camilla at that moment, reminders of her were all around him. The stone balcony on which he was standing had been constructed by her family as part of the Palace's new East Wing 143 years ago. The Caen stone that Camilla's forebear, the builder Thomas Cubitt, had chosen for the work, had begun to crumble soon afterwards and the balustrade, dressed for this ceremonial occasion in burgundy-and-gold velvet, had been replaced with more durable Portland stone. Some wondered just how durable the House of Windsor itself might be now that Diana was no longer its star performer.

So few royals were present this overcast summer's day that the ribbed columns of the Palace showed between gaps in the line-up.

There was no Prince Andrew, who had been helping his estranged wife with her emotional problems since her disgrace at St Tropez. No Prince Edward, still a bachelor by choice, who was aboard the QE2 for a luncheon celebrating the fortieth anniversary of his mother's coronation. No William or Harry of Wales, who were enjoying a picnic hamper between showers with Diana at Ludgrove School near Wokingham in Berkshire. No Beatrice or Eugenie of York. No Master Peter Phillips or his sister Miss Zara Phillips.

All six of the Queen's grandchildren were missing from the celebrations marking her official birthday. On this showing, it seemed that the Windsors might have reached the end of the lineage. But anyone who believed that the monarchy was about to fall, and some were even taking bets on it, had drastically underestimated the Queen. Her Majesty had recently made some fiercely contested concessions towards paying income tax on her private wealth and, as a further gesture to public opinion, she had dropped members of her family from the Civil List. Republican sympathisers who scanned the line-up looking for fresh scalps were to be sadly disappointed. Serena Stanhope, for one, could afford to pay her own way in any company. She stood to inherit millions from the estate of her grandfather, the Earl of Harrington, who had wisely removed himself to the Republic of Ireland, where tax rates were far more reasonable.

In just twelve months, the Windsors had succeeded in bringing more grief to loyalists than in any comparable period since Edward VIII had stepped aside fifty-seven years ago. Most deplorably, its critics claimed, it had failed in its fundamental obligation to uphold traditional family values. The monarchy, wrote Sir Antony Jay, scriptwriter of the 1992 BBC documentary *Elizabeth R,* 'can set a consistent moral standard which people can look to as a guide and example.' He added: 'Even when some members of the Royal Family do not behave as well as people expect them to, they are still contributing to the process of reviewing and revising the nation's behaviour patterns.'

This interpretation provided ample scope for rewriting the rules in a society which had been firmly instructed before 1992 – the Queen's *annus horribilis* – that royal proclivities towards adultery and other high jinks were just figments of a lurid tabloid imagination. The Press, particularly the tabloids, had been proved right time and again despite the robust denials of Buckingham Palace.

Diana's nightmare in the royal world was just one symptom of a far-reaching malaise affecting the Windsors. Her decline and fall from grace in the eyes of the Family had, perversely, consolidated her place in the hearts and minds of ordinary people. They had watched her royal progress and sympathised as though she was one of their own.

'It was terrifying,' Diana the archetypal girl-next-door had said, referring to her wedding at St Paul's Cathedral on 29 July, 1981.

'Being a princess isn't all it's cracked up to be,' she had ventured a little later when the tiara began to slip.

In 1993, Diana the Defiant was openly talking about the agonies of women locked into loveless marriages and enslaved by addictive illnesses.

Laughing in the rain that gloomy Saturday was one of the joys of her new freedom outside the Family.

AT 10.15 on a Monday morning two weeks later, the clouds had cleared and bright sunlight spilled down on a lone figure walking along Drummond Street in a cosmopolitan neighbourhood near Euston Station. He was tall and fit, broad shoulders clad in a white T-shirt and long, tanned legs stretching from a patterned pair of shorts down to the unfashionable pavement. He was carrying a bottle of milk for the tea he liked to drink as he worked. He looked straight ahead, no longer fearful of the tap on the shoulder or the prying eyes of the security forces. Opposite Joe's Cafe, the man, younger in appearance than his forty years and thoughtfully bespectacled, entered a door beneath the blue canopy of the Haandi Tandoori Restaurant and climbed the carpeted stairs to his well-equipped office.

Only the blue lettering on the T-shirt gave any outward sign that his life had changed perceptibly. The wording read: *Recently at the Regent Beverly Wilshire.* ($395 per night for a deluxe room.) Andrew Morton, scourge of the royals and a very New Money millionaire, was about to start work at his one-man operation known as Palace Press.

Morton's biography, *DIANA: Her True Story* – written, most people believed, with the Princess's co-operation – had sold five million copies in twenty languages since its publication exactly a year earlier. The book had alerted the world to the hopeless state of the Waleses' marriage, to Diana's bulimia and her supposedly suicidal cries for help, and to Charles's friendship with Camilla Parker Bowles. Ever since, it had been the catalyst for a lot more besides. Its publication had probably been the lowest point of the *annus horribilis*, both a milestone in royal reporting and a millstone around royal necks.

'It's a phenomenon,' said Andrew Morton, serving tea on a circular pine table in his office. 'I no longer consider myself as the author. It has a life of its own. I have scratched the surface and got some way in, probably a bit further than other people. But nonetheless there is still a lot there – it's a mine shaft with many unexplored corridors.'

The worst, it seemed, was not over yet for the Windsors, a view confirmed by one of their number. Shortly after he returned from a holiday on Mustique with Princess Margaret, Lord Linley had taken his new fiancée to a dinner party at the home of friends in West London. 'Let me tell you,' he said, meaningfully, 'something's going to come out that makes everything else look like nothing.' 'He wasn't joking,' said one privy to the secrets of that dining table. 'Everyone got excited but he wouldn't explain what he meant.' Royal scandal, once a taboo subject in polite society, was now both *aperitif* and *digestif* in even the smartest households.

Nor was he referring to a photograph of Serena, tights ripped and curled up on a floor, which was published on the front page of the *People* newspaper a short time later. The paper's graphic description of her affair with a former boyfriend was passed off as nothing more serious than the amorous adventures of any graduate of the figurative Sloane University. But for the real royals, any bad publicity was potentially dangerous now that the traditional screens of secrecy had been removed. More than their mystique, they had lost the unquestioning veneration that had protected them for generations. The party was almost over. To vary a favoured metaphor of the age, the royals were drinking in the Last Chance Salon. The caste system that typified British royalty might still be in place, but some of its members were like the targets in a fairground coconut shy.

'The decline is very serious in the sense that the ideological framework which has sustained them as the idealised family has basically been undercut,' said Andrew Morton. 'The royals themselves don't want the fairy-tale anymore. They have decided, Okay, the myth and the mystique have gone, let's just be ordinary people. We're paying our tax now and we are essentially private people and we have the same rights as private people. They will become really quite aggressive about invasions of privacy in the future. There won't be as many of them doing the job of being royal and they won't sacrifice themselves for the job in the way they have done in the past. They are retreating from their public personae and re-inventing themselves as private people.'

The Queen, however, carries on very much in the style to which she has grown accustomed. While the monarchy debate raged even on the fortieth anniversary of her coronation, she did what she enjoyed doing most. It was Derby Day and Her Majesty went to the races.

PART ONE

THE NIGHTMARE

PART ONE

1

ANGEL IN EXILE

'This may sound crazy, but I've lived before'
Diana, Princess of Wales

THERE was a mischievous spring in Princess Diana's step as she strode across the Knightsbridge pavement to lunch with her sons at San Lorenzo. Smartly dressed in jackets and ties, William and Harry entered their mother's favourite restaurant in this select part of London for a holiday treat. The schoolboy princes were due to fly to Scotland after the meal to join their father, Prince Charles, at Balmoral for what remained of the Easter holiday. But for the next hour at least, the boys were Diana's to show off in the one public place where she felt entirely safe.

San Lorenzo is situated at No 22, Beauchamp Place, a short thoroughfare of *bijou* shops which include two other stylish landmarks in the greatest royal scandal since the Abdication. Flanking the restaurant on one side is Kanga, the salon of Charles's friend Lady Tryon, and on the other the showroom of couturier Bruce Oldfield. For very good reason, Diana no longer wears clothes with the Kanga label, but Oldfield – creator of the 'Dynasty Di' look in a previous life – remains high on her list of approved designers. Many people in the royal circle found it either expedient or necessary to take sides once the Prince and Princess of Wales had set up rival courts at St James's and Kensington.

Inside San Lorenzo, Diana could relax, confident in the knowledge that the natives were friendly. Considering the knife-grinding at Buckingham Palace, this was a reassuring point. It was fair to say that she was now perceived as an enemy among those dogmatically loyal to the House of Windsor. At San Lorenzo, the Italian owners, Mara and Lorenzo Berni, made her feel nothing if not wanted, needed and loved. Besides, Diana had just seen the new photographs and they had boosted her confidence even more.

Dressed in a figure-hugging navy suit with a skirt short enough to be called eye-catching, the Princess clutched a son in each hand as she descended the nine stairs to the basement level. They were greeted by Mara, a motherly figure who, among other services, collected private mail for her most famous though often troubled friend. On her way to the familiar corner table beneath the giant potted palms, Diana made a point of stopping whenever she recognised a diner to exchange a greeting, giving the impression that the two princes, aged ten and eight, were the most important young men in her life. 'My small ones,' she called the Heir and the Spare. James Gilbey, her former escort on nocturnal visits to San Lorenzo, referred to them cutely as 'the Lovebugs'.

Four traumatic months had passed since the Prime Minister announced the official separation of the Prince and Princess of Wales and his suggestion that Diana could rule as queen had seemingly disappeared into the mists of antiquity. But Diana knew that, barring a divorce, there was still a possibility. Queenship, though, was something she had been prepared to sacrifice to gain her freedom from the nightmarish life she had lived as a royal.

'The extraordinary and ironic thing is that Charles did choose right,' said a well-placed royal observer. 'He chose the perfect future queen. The trouble is that, unlike other royal wives, she wouldn't look the other way while he two-timed her.'

Even before John Major had spoken, Diana had been made aware that the notorious Squidgy tape-recording of her intimate conversation with Gilbey had jeopardised her position. At first, she had found it difficult to come to terms with the likelihood that she would go down in history as the best queen Britain never had. But since that dreadful time, she had worked hard to build the image she presented this spring day: that of a winner, self-assured and as beguiling as she ever had been before Squidgy tarnished some of the lustre.

As she said, 'I'm just myself – and that was really something. But this, it seemed, wasn't enough to satisfy her once Squidgy had finally exploded the convenient myth of 'Shy Di'. Very deliberately, she was changing every facet which didn't comply with her confident new self-image. Even her old voice and its whining Squidgy accent, heard by millions on a play-back telephone line which the *Sun* had helpfully installed for its readers, was in the process of disappearing. For the past four weeks, she had been receiving speech therapy to help in the public speaking that was part of her new agenda. The new accent, a cross between *Howard's Way* and *Howard's End,* added a modern, composed touch to her outwardly calm exterior.

If 1993 turned out to be *Horribilis II* for Her Majesty, Diana was well-placed to survive whatever traumas might befall the Family. By sheer self-will, she had reclaimed her place as the unchallenged darling of her mother-in-law's kingdom and she was, indisputably, a force to be reckoned with. Since the Court Circular had been divided to separate the Waleses' engagements, Diana had attended only half as many functions as Charles, but easily drawn four times the crowds. More significant was the number of photographers' metal stepladders present on each occasion, a true indication of media interest in the royal combatants. The ratio stood at twelve-to-one in Diana's favour. In an age of cosmetic politics, she was a clear winner in the image war being fought between the rival courts. Diana had long been the patron saint of the paparazzi.

At a time of her choosing, her fans among the incalculable millions following every scene of the royal drama would see the new pictures. For now, the San Lorenzo diners made an adequate preview audience for yet another facet of her performance as a liberated woman.

'How are you today, Terry? Did you enjoy the motor racing?' she asked the photographer Terry O'Neill, who she had seen at Donington Park a few days earlier. Later, he could hardly remember how he had replied, but he had no difficulty recalling the stir Diana's entrance had caused. 'She took everyone's breath away,' he said. 'She looked so beautiful; she looked like a million dollars, she was radiant – and she knew it.'

As she passed Andy Warhol's portrait of Marilyn Monroe, one diner whom Diana did not recognise, or chose not to acknowledge, was her husband's one-time biographer Anthony Holden, who sat at a table directly in her path. San Lorenzo was *her* territory; her husband and his followers past and present had no place within its cool white walls.

The royal trio moved past hanging baskets of fern and tasteful water colours which added freshness to the interior's spot-lit ambience. Diana's favourite table was on a slightly higher level, where she sat with her back to a mural depicting a bus tootling along a Sardinian landscape. It had been painted to remind Mara of her childhood homeland. Under the watchful eye of her personal detective, Inspector Ken Wharfe, Diana, William and Harry ate a hearty lunch. The armed detective had been removed from Diana's side after the Squidgy tapes revealed that he was involved in setting up a secret rendezvous between her and Gilbey. He had been transferred to office duties until, at the Princess's insistence, he was reinstated, his name cleared.

According to friends, Diana was winning her battle against the eating disorder *bulimia nervosa,* which had plagued her teenage years and resurfaced in virulent form before her wedding. 'I've had bulimia for ten years,' she told a worker at Turning Point, the drug abuse and mental health charity, long before the break-up. Diana had been desperately sick throughout the worst decade of her life. The pictures would show the world how far she had moved along the road to recovery.

For their part, William and Harry were the perfect extras in this cameo of a woman re-emerging from the clamour of a marital break-up which had riveted the world as no other could. Charles and Diana were the biggest talking point from Belgravia to Boston and those who dined at San Lorenzo were networkers, just the right sort of people to spread the word that whatever else was wrong with the Royal Family, Diana was in sparkling form and her sons were with the one they really loved.

Directly below the restaurant's foundations runs the San Lorenzo Fault, an invisible flaw that stretches from Kensington Palace to the Throne Room at Buckingham Palace. Considering the tremors which were rocking the monarchy, it could be said to imperil the Crown itself. So serious did Prince Philip regard the threat that he had exchanged heated words with his daughter-in-law. But Diana had few regrets. She had learned the secrets of the Windsor dynasty with every painful year she had spent as its most valuable if not most valued asset. Rejecting the attitude that she should have been 'grateful for the goodies that came with her title', as one former Sloane Ranger friend put it, she had already lashed out once. It was no exaggeration to say that any further seismic activity on her part could be fatal to all involved. 'She struck the royals a blow from which they are going to find it hard to recover,' said one close to her entourage.

Not that her plan was to destroy the monarchy, although she had arguably done a great deal to damage it. Now that the ugly shadow of Squidgy had passed from her face, her primary concern was who should occupy the throne after Her Majesty's death: Charles III or William V. She had once hated Charles as only a woman scorned could and it was widely felt in her circle that she believed he was unsuited to rule. If she couldn't be queen, she saw William as the deserving heir apparent. 'She doesn't want to wreck any chance of being the power-behind-the-throne as far as William goes,' said a titled Chelsea lady who knows the royals well.

The Queen, fully briefed on the Diana Problem by her advisers, had seized upon a chance encounter to take some of the heat out of the situation. Spotting the estranged Princess outside a shop in Knightsbridge, Her Majesty instructed her chauffeur to blow his horn. 'The Princess was standing with her bodyguard when he noticed the Queen's Daimler approaching,' said eye-witness Jason Fraser, a royal photographer. 'He said something to her because she turned round and looked.' Her mother-in-law gave her a friendly wave through the window of her Rolls-Royce. Diana smiled, waved and blew a kiss back. 'I have the best mother-in-law in the world,' Diana had stated not so long ago. They were still on speaking terms even if they hardly ever spoke anymore.

The day before she lunched at San Lorenzo, the Princess had presented a very different face to the world in this operatic phase of her life. She took Wills and Harry to Thorpe Park, the adventure centre in Surrey to which she had introduced them two summers earlier as her shaky marriage continued its helter-skelter descent. In San Lorenzo, she was at her smartest. At the fun park, she was Daredevil Di, wet hair slicked back as she thundered down the rides in black trousers, leather jacket and suede ankle boots.

While other pleasure-seekers had been astonished to find the royal trio in their midst, the half-dozen freelance photographers and a television crew showed no such surprise. Nor were the newsmen restrained by the usually protective Inspector Wharfe as they filmed Diana and the boys, clad in jeans and bomber jackets, shooting down Thunder River and getting soaked in the process. As the boys clambered aboard the Hudson River Rafters for more excitement, the cameras clicked away unimpeded and it was the same when Diana and her sons rode the Flying Fish Roller Coaster and the twirling Giant Tea Cup before rounding off the day with a Super Soaker water-gun shootout. The Princes revelled in it, but the question remained: who tipped off the Press? 'I don't want to risk money-in-the-bank jobs like this by ratting on my source,' said one cameraman when the pictures had been plastered over acres of newsprint. 'Let's just say no one from Thorpe Park told me, and Diana wasn't surprised to see us.'

It was clear from the start of the princes' leave from Ludgrove School that Diana intended to meet the challenge of separation head-on. The holiday agenda was packed with go-kart racing, the European Grand Prix at Donington Park and simulated aerial dogfights at the Flying Aces Virtual Reality Centre. Charles could take his sons fishing for salmon on the banks of the Dee where he had once wooed her, but she had indulged their spirit of adventure.

'I wouldn't say that she is completely devoid of manipulative qualities at all,' said Georgina Howell, one of the most perceptive writers on the royal scene, if you go on manipulating somebody, eventually they will become manipulative as well because they see how it's done.' Diana had learned her manoeuvres from some highly qualified exponents at the very heart of the Royal Family. The danger was that she would not be able to sustain the cracking pace she had set. As one of Charles's advisers had cautioned him: 'This is a marathon, not a sprint.'

NOTHING summed up the new royal era better than attendance at the Easter Sunday service in St George's Chapel, Windsor. Ticking off the arrivals, royal watchers noted that Diana and her princes were not the only regulars to go missing. The Duchess of York and her children, Princess Beatrice and Princess Eugenie, had stayed behind at Sunninghill Park House, their former home, while Prince Andrew joined his mother and father for the traditional devotions. He would be joining them for lunch, re-creating the family circle which had been torn apart by the announcement of the Yorks' separation a year earlier. He spent so much time helping his disturbed wife that there was talk of a reconciliation. Any prospect of that was dimmed, however, by Andrew's new posting in the Royal Navy. He would soon be taking command of HMS *Cottesmore* and could expect to serve in the plastic-hulled minehunter, one of Her Majesty's so-called 'Tupperware fleet', for a year at least.

Prince Edward, deliberately the least high-profile of the royals, was absent as well, but he was attending to official family business, presenting awards bearing his father's name at a ceremony in Canada. Onlookers were delighted to see Princess Anne with her new husband Commander Tim Laurence, who was making his first appearance as a royal consort at this annual event. Although no substitute for Diana, or Fergie for that matter, he had some novelty value and a refreshingly boyish grin. Anne, for one, had completely lost patience with her two sisters-in-law, referring to them, it was said, as 'those silly girls'.

Prince Charles arrived with the Queen Mother and Princess Margaret. His London address was now York House, a large apartment at St James's Palace which held some unfortunate memories of a previous occupant: Edward VIII. After Charles moved in, removal vans took loads of personal belongings, including wedding gifts, from Kensington Palace to Highgrove. There they were smashed up and burned in a bonfire.

Charles would have been distressed to know that, up in Leicester, his wife and sons were watching the Formula One racing from a VIP suite only yards from where James Gilbey worked in the Lotus pit. When Gilbey was tipped off that Diana was so close, he jumped on a motor scooter and disappeared into the crowds. After Squidgy, he needed to distance himself from any fresh scandal. But it didn't stop speculation about his relationship with Diana. Breaking his silence for the first time, James Gilbey told the authors: 'I've done my time, really, in terms of being a sort of punchbag for a lot of the various things that have been happening.'

Despite innumerable headlines and a million words, the real story behind Squidgy remained known only to Diana and a handful of others privy to the secret. The truth formed a big part of her recurring nightmare.

'I think there was a plot, yes,' says Stuart Higgins, the journalist who found Squidgy a place in the *Sun*.

The other character central to this drama, Mrs Camilla Parker Bowles, stayed close to her two teenage children, Tom and Laura, that Easter. After her love affair with Prince Charles became public, she had remained in seclusion behind the stone walls of Middlewick

House, an eighteenth-century manor fifteen miles from Highgrove. When she emerged briefly to prune some shrubs in her garden, a posse of photographers sent her dashing for cover. No royal edict could protect her from the consequences, much as Charles wished to distance her from scandal. As well as the taped telephone call which lead to what was known as Camillagate, there was the eyewitness account of PC Andy Jacques, who claimed he had seen the couple smooching on a sofa at Highgrove. Asked how Camilla was coping, a friend replied: 'How do you think? She's absolutely shattered.'

While she had waited tensely for John Major's announcement, Camilla had been observed pacing up and down her drawing room. As the Prime Minister began to speak, she sat bolt upright in front of her TV set to take in the news. She was, she said later, 'very sorry for the royal couple'. In tweed jacket and blue jeans, her face lined with worry, she cut an unlikely figure as a scarlet woman.

Over Easter, she and her husband, Brigadier Andrew Parker Bowles, known to Army jokers as 'the man who laid down his wife for his country', entertained a small group of friends to lunch. One of them was Lady Tryon, who had rallied to her friend immediately the scandal broke. 'Monarchy is a wonderful institution,' she said. 'The events of the past year have been very, very sad.' Parker Bowles was no longer describing his wife's entanglement with Prince Charles as 'pure fiction'.

Many considered that the House of Windsor was getting a long overdue, and richly deserved, come-uppance. 'The royals are behaving as they've always done,' said a royal historian. 'Jet-set, or the period equivalent, is their normal behaviour. We were lulled into a false sense of security when George VI and Queen Elizabeth did such a good job during World War II. What's happening now is nothing new. Since William the Conqueror, you can practically count the periods of respectability among the royals on the fingers of one hand.' Prince Philip had once declared: 'Only a moral imperative can persuade husbands and wives to be faithful to each other.' If this were meant as a bench mark for royal marriages, it had failed miserably. Somewhere along the line, the moral imperative had been mislaid.

By the time Diana was ready to leave San Lorenzo after the Easter treat, a crowd big enough to warrant police supervision had gathered around her car, which was illegally parked in the street. After a farewell hug from Mara, she stepped out into the sunlight to a sound other royals rarely heard any more: gales of unrestrained cheering. Blue eyes sparkling, the People's Princess waved to the well-wishers and disappeared from sight. She was never really out of the limelight, though. Even in her off-stage moments, her name was on someone's lips in some corner of the globe. The Royal Family had unwittingly made Diana the most famous woman alive.

PATRICK Demarchelier, the ruggedly handsome French photographer, had smiled to himself when he received his second summons from Diana. The first had come in the late summer of 1991 when she had personally telephoned his New York apartment from Kensington Palace. She needed some photographs, she explained, for her Christmas card and one or two other purposes she had in mind. Would he take them? The Frenchman was flattered to be asked and readily agreed to keep the project secret.

Diana knew that she was breaking an important rule of the royal code by making direct contact with an unapproved photographer. If word reached her enemies at the Press Office at Buckingham Palace, she would have to explain her action to the Queen. To make sure she was undetected, she even bypassed her trusted Private Secretary, Patrick Jephson, in setting up the picture session. Like Demarchelier, the hair stylist and make-up artist were sworn to secrecy. The deception had worked amazingly well.

When Diana coyly produced her snaps over lunch with Liz Tilberis, the editor of British *Vogue,* the journalist was instantly hooked. Demarchelier had captured a Diana the world had never seen before. Gone was the heavy makeup and the trademark blue eyeliner; her hair was cropped gamine-like and an understated black cashmere jumper gave the subject a sophisticated new appeal. The two women struck a deal: *Vogue* could publish one picture on the cover of its Christmas issue in return for publicising the Royal Ballet, a cause the Princess patronised. It was a notable coup for Diana in her struggle for independence, one made even sweeter because the Palace bureaucrats knew nothing of it until the magazine arrived on the newsstands. One of the photographs in particular, Diana had reasoned, would make the perfect illustration for a book jacket.

Now Diana was sure that the new pictures would receive the same reaction – and re-create her sense of victory over the Palace and the Highgrove Set. Emerging from a dark winter, Diana's purpose was to show that she was stronger and happier than she had ever been. Once again, she and Demarchelier had slipped off to a secret studio session and the results were even better. 'The Princess would make a natural picture editor,' the photographer enthused. 'She has a great eye for spotting the saleable points as well as the faults of any photograph.'

In the presence of Christy Turlington, Linda Evangelista and Naomi Campbell, whom he was using in a series of car advertisements, Demarchelier would have had to admit that the thirty-one-year-old mother of two would not have qualified had she been other than the Princess of Wales. But inside his studio for the second time, Diana was content to know that, though she mightn't be in the supermodel class, she was her own best image-maker and publicist. The adroitly successful 'Selling of a Princess' thus far had been all her own work. Her skilful manipulation of her image to remain the most popular member of the Royal Family despite the separation from its heir had succeeded to great effect.

Great, too, was the pleasure it gave Diana to compare her efforts with those of her former best friend, her sister-in-law Sarah, the Duchess of York. Stumbling from one public relations disaster to another after she was photographed topless in St Tropez with her financial adviser and pedicurist Johnny Bryan, Fergie had tried to land the cover of *Harpers & Queen* a few weeks earlier. The result had been catastrophic and earned her a stinging rebuke from the magazine's editor, Vicki Woods.

Instead of a discreet lunch with the editor, Fergie instructed her Private Secretary, Jane Ambler, to dictate terms under which the Duchess would agree to grace the magazine's cover. Her Royal Highness, Ms Ambler told the editor, would be bringing along her own personal manicurist, her personal dresser and her personal photographic agent. When Ms Woods suggested top fashion photographer Michael Roberts for the shoot, the Duchess, unaware of his reputation, demanded a list of the celebrities in his portfolio; worse, she wanted to know if he matched up to Demarchelier's qualifications. Her motive, it was patently obvious, was to outshine Diana.

To make the project even more unworkable, Johnny Bryan took over the negotiations with an indelicacy which would have embarrassed a rhinoceros. Things went so badly that the day before the shoot, Ms Woods finally withdrew her offer of a cover after Bryan insisted that Fergie retain the copyright of Roberts's pictures, an unheard of demand in the world of professional photography. Nor would there be any interview to accompany the pictures. Nevertheless, the session went ahead with Fergie confident of salvaging something from the wreckage. The result was four pictures, mainly of the Duchess's Rita Hayworth-like hair, which failed to attract an immediate buyer at the asking price of £10,000. Ms Woods reconciled herself to the loss of an exclusive cover by filling four pages of the magazine with a swingeing attack on the Duchess and her so called courtiers for their ineptitude. Fergie had been furious about the collapse of the deal, which she interpreted as another example of royal favouritism.

Bryan had told Ms Woods that much of the reason the Duchess wanted the cover was that 'the Big D might be coming out with a cover too.' Fergie put it more personally, it's always me who has to carry the can; it's always me who gets the blame for this kind of thing; it's always MY fault, and I've had enough of it; that's why I want OUT of the whole thing so I can get on with my own life and stop being blamed for everything,' she moaned to the exhausted editor. 'I'm SO tired of carrying the can for all of them. I have been the scapegoat for the Waleses for four years.'

The Big D smiled when she heard about the debacle. She didn't like Johnny Bryan and she no longer trusted Fergie. Her comments merely confirmed the Duchess's paranoid attitude towards her. The two women, once so close that Diana had acted as matchmaker in Fergie's romance with Prince Andrew, had grown apart, although they were on speaking terms again. The disintegration of Fergie's marriage had given Diana some breathing space in trying to resolve her own marital difficulties. The spotlight, and the criticism, had swung in Fergie's direction. But the denouement at St Tropez had been so final that Diana no longer wished to be associated with Fergie's crass efforts at self-aggrandizement. Fergie, the Princess concluded, was a loser, and a bad one at that.

One big difference between the two royal superstars was money. Quite apart from what Charles paid for her upkeep, Diana had recourse to virtually unlimited funds of her own. She received the income from Spencer family trust funds worth £20 million. Diana was one of the richest women in Britain, while Fergie's fortunes at this stage continued to be more problematical. She received money from Andrew under the terms of their separation deal, but her future was largely tied into the marketing fate of her children's storybook character Budgie the Little Helicopter. So far, the Budgie millions remained pie in the sky.

As her sons headed north to join Charles in Scotland, Diana flopped down in a comfy chair in her empty nest at Kensington Palace and flicked through the new Demarchelier portfolio. She was also trying to decide whether to move out of this royal village to a home of her own.

IN the months prior to the Palace's admission that the Waleses were finished, it seemed that Diana's secrets had all been laid bare. Reacting to the powerful forces ranged against her, she and her brother Charles, the ninth Earl Spencer, were reputed to have orchestrated many of the revelations in Andrew Morton's book *DIANA: Her True Story*. But they had been unable to control the coverage to their liking. Much of it had rebounded and what emerged was Diana's pitiful dilemma as a woman who, although brave, was more victim than heroine. She was presented in the Press as a suicidal hysteric, a weak-willed bulimic, too sick and vulnerable to stand up for her rights. If Charles felt aggrieved by unflattering descriptions of himself, Diana saw her portrayal as a grotesque distortion of the truth. But the notion persisted that she was unwell, and it was said that constantly seeking public adoration was one of the symptoms of her food addiction; that she desperately needed to be the heroine.

Georgina Howell, however, added a more political element to the equation: 'The Princess has become the recipient of an establishment backlash in the United Kingdom, the reaction of powerful and aristocratic sections of society that recognise — whatever the extent of her acquiescence in the book that exposed the state of the Waleses' marriage – that she has rocked the system that supports them. Over dinner tables on country estates, her one-time tendency to bulimia is being used to stamp her as hysterical and unstable.'

These words appeared in the American edition of *Vogue*, hardly a forum of radical dissent. But its very publication showed that the media were taking sides in a global propaganda war. Nor is Ms Howell's view an aberration. 'The establishment', a term coined by the writer Henry Fairlie to define a phenomenon peculiar to the British class system, consists of aristocrats, political grandees and their Civil Service mandarins, senior figures in academia, the Church and law enforcement, and top military brass. They are the country's unelected rulers, its real lords and masters. At their centre is the Queen, not only constitutional Head of State, but also head of the judiciary, the armed forces and the Church of England. Unaccountable to Parliament, and thus immune from any electoral censure, the establishment orbits around the monarch. In times of trouble, their sole objective is to defend the sovereign. 'Defence of the Realm' justifies just about anything.

Any fears that people in high places might have had about Diana reached fever pitch when it was revealed that she had taken an interest in Catholicism, 'the Church of Rome', as Buckingham Palace prefers to call it. Strenuous denials failed to shake the belief that Diana might convert. Many of her best friends were Catholics, including James Gilbey and the Honourable Rosa Monckton, who introduced her to Father Antony Sutch at a Belgravia dinner party. The Benedictine monk said that the Princess was 'looking for an answer' but the Palace replied frostily: 'There is no question of the Princess of Wales moving in the direction of the Church of Rome.' In fact, Father Sutch was just one in a succession of doctors, psychiatrists, therapists, theologians, spiritualists and astrologers she had sought to help her.

Charles's friendship with Camilla had been only the first shock-wave to hit Diana even before the wedding at St Paul's Cathedral in July 1981. Day by day, she discovered new and painful secrets about Charles and the Family until the situation became unbearable not only for the Princess but also for her husband. Life with Charles, she told James Gilbey, was 'just so difficult, so complicated.' While she was 'doing God's work on earth,' Diana believed that Charles, his mistress and the Highgrove Set had contrived to drive her away.

One insoluble problem between them was that Charles resented finding himself consigned to a walk-on role whenever he and Diana stepped out. 'I used to like Prince Charles, but I went off him,' said

Mike Lawn, the award-winning royal photographer. 'He used to have quite a good sense of humour, but it disappeared when Diana started to get all the attention and he just became the Man in the Grey Suit. Men in grey suits make very boring pictures. The only time he comes alive is when we get him in a hot country and he puts on a tropical outfit. Even then, he was no match for the Princess once she started to happen. When Diana was around, he didn't exist and he knew it.'

When Diana discovered the depth of the feeling against her at Highgrove, she turned to her brother for support. 'He is a very quick-tempered young man who dotes on his sister,' said an American friend. 'Her distress made him furious. It was Charlie Althorp's unseen hand that guided many of Diana's actions.'

At the time of the Royal Wedding, Diana's father, the eighth Lord Spencer, had said tearfully: 'I've lost her. She's gone and she won't be back.' Later, he was heard to mutter: 'Poor, poor Diana. It's too, too awful.' He had tried to smooth out some of the difficulties by discussing them with his monarch. At Sandringham, he ventured to tell the Queen: 'Diana is a very single-minded girl.' 'The Princess of Wales,' Her Majesty corrected him, 'is a very stubborn woman.'

Quality or defect, Diana's determination to live life her way was to become her saving grace. Part of her obstinacy, she tried to explain to a friend, was due to a powerful sense of destiny; a deeply held conviction that she had been placed on earth for a purpose. 'I know this sounds crazy,' she said, 'but I've lived before.' Diana believed implicitly that, since her father's death in March 1992, he was still guiding her from the spirit world. Through an Irish medium, Diana contacted him during seances set up in the privacy of London hotels. The medium, Mrs Betty Palko, claimed that Earl Spencer had appeared before her while Diana was present and she relayed messages between them.

For so long isolated by the rest of the Royal Family, Diana had been stranded on a pinnacle which, nevertheless, left her with enough room to manoeuvre. Far from diminishing her standing, the separation from Prince Charles – and thereby the family that had propelled her to such heights – added to Diana's public following. That children and the poor had taken her to their hearts, while showing deep dissatisfaction with the wealth and privilege of her husband and his family, was a paradox even members of Her

Majesty's secretariat found perplexing. Diana understood her appeal better than anyone else and she had learned to use it. 'I understand people's suffering, people's pain, more than you will ever know,' she told a bishop, it's not only AIDS, it's anyone who suffers.'

Her understanding of the political game she was playing was illustrated perfectly during a private trip she made to the Kingdom of Nepal. She arrived just as previously unpublished parts of the Squidgy Tapes were published, including this incriminating exchange:

Diana: I don't want to get pregnant.

Gilbey: Darling, that's not going to happen, all right?

Diana: Yeah.

Gilbey: Don't think like that. It's not going to happen, darling, you won't get pregnant.

Diana: I watched EastEnders today. One of the main characters had a baby. They thought it was by her husband. It was by another man.

Gilbey: Squidgy, kiss me. Oh God!

Diana was unfazed. She was received in the 'kingdom on the roof of the world' like a living goddess. 'Wreathed in marigolds and cornflowers, she moves on to be greeted by Crown Prince Dipendra and the prime minister,' recorded Georgina Howell. 'Head and shoulders above the crowd, she swims briefly into focus, the most famous woman in the world, the honey-coloured hair and skin, the demure sweep of eyelashes, the swoony, brilliant gaze familiar from a billion photographs.' If Squidgy were on her mind, she chose to ignore it by throwing herself into what she called 'the Work'. In a mountain village, she visited a mud hut that served as home to a Nepalese family. There was no electricity, water or sanitation. 'I'll never complain again,' she vowed. On a visit to a leprosy mission, she stroked diseased limbs with her bare hands. When she sat on a leper's bed and touched his stumps, she was fully aware of the cameras clicking behind her. She knew the pictures would be compared with the one taken a few days earlier of Prince Charles carrying a polo trophy in Mexico.

'The Princess has helped show that leprosy is not a curse from God but an illness like any other and one that can be treated,' said Dr Des Suares, who showed Diana around the Red Cross leprosy mission.

What he did not know was that it was helping the Princess just as much. 'If you want to be like me, you have got to suffer,' she had told James Gilbey. 'And then you get what you deserve – perhaps.'

'I met Diana at a Press reception in Kathmandu and she was totally mistress of the situation,' said Georgina Howell. 'She worked the room independently and she was perfectly capable of dealing with anything that was thrown at her. You have to give her credit for having changed and matured and grown a lot not only wiser but a lot more manipulative. We talked about the Work and it is absolutely, genuinely close to her heart. There's no question about it. She has turned into a modern woman in the most triumphant and delightful way. It's tragic for the royals that she's no longer in their midst because she would have been a very valuable ally.'

Diana saw the Work as neither callous nor cynical despite suggestions that it was both. Her mentor was not the Queen or her own mother Frances Shand Kydd, but Mother Teresa of Calcutta, whom Diana was fond of quoting. She told a story about a nun who asked to be excused from her duties helping the poor 'because I have flu and the day is so hot'. 'Better to burn in this world than the next,' Mother Teresa replied. This statement incited Diana to pronounce: 'I will never cancel an engagement again because I have a cold.'

The Work showed Diana many sides of life, including case studies of marital infidelity at Relate, the marriage guidance service. Dressed in an inexpensive jumper and skirt, and wearing little make-up, Diana had turned up with eight others to learn how Relate works. She was already patron of the organisation but she was anxious to become a counsellor as well.

It was, she reasoned, a fair exchange: Relate needed her name and she needed their experience. Her staff were surprised. This, after all, was the same Diana who had exasperated them during the earlier years of her marriage by refusing even to read briefing notes before official engagements.

Her fellow pupils at the Relate headquarters in Rugby saw how much she was prepared to give in dealing with unhappy personal relationships. 'Even princesses cry,' she told a woman who accused her of not understanding misery. Diana had known what she faced when she volunteered her services but she also recognised something within herself: that the very suffering of others drove her on. The pain of an AIDS victim, the craving of a drug addict and the desperation of the homeless all served to distract her from a husband she could not stand and courtiers who would crush her if they could.

'When I see suffering that is where I want to be, doing what I can,' the Princess said after comforting a dying AIDS patient and his family at a hospital in South London. The comment had its effect on her detractors at the Palace and finally stopped their efforts to steer her away from what they saw as 'the inappropriate AIDS issue'. Diana had made her point. *She* would decide which causes she supported – not her husband's advisers.

She had long since made the discovery that showing concern for others made her own troubles pale into insignificance. As she put it to the Duchess of York: 'The best way to deal with low self-esteem is to do something estimable.' At the height of her bulimia, Diana had such an uncontrollable temper that she could wreck a bedroom in a tantrum. Wise counselling had taught her that this was no way for a young mother to behave, let alone a princess. So losing herself in the troubles of others was both a useful and therapeutic solution and Diana applied it with remarkable success.

As a result, organisers of the charities she supported found that she was far from just a decorative figurehead designed to attract donations. They saw in her a woman who not only wanted to become involved in the policy-making that affected those who were helped but also one who *needed* to make contact with the sufferers: to get her hands dirty when necessary. Starting from a basic belief in the causes with which she empathised, Diana made a decision to get involved and then followed through with direct action. Either that, she was told, or her self-obsession could cost her her life.

Eleven years at the top had taught Diana not only how to handle fame but how to use it against the forces that wished to drive her into oblivion. 'On that day (in January) when the boys went back to school and Diana walked back into Kensington Palace alone for the first time, she rang me,' said a friend. 'She said she knew what people would be thinking and what the papers would be saying — that she was weeping and in a desperate state of loneliness. Well, I can tell you that she was really happy on that day. She felt free and she sat down to plan – not the rest of her life in some dramatic fashion, but the next few months for herself. She was free of the husband she had loathed and out of the deal whereby she had to make sure she was pleasing his family every waking moment. Do you know she even got a ticking-off once for going to San Lorenzo so often? For goodness sake, she only eats there about once a month, but the way Prince Philip went on about it being a place for show business hangers-on, you'd think she was putting in nightly appearances at a house of ill-repute.'

One of the earliest pieces of advice Earl Spencer had given his youngest daughter was never to bear a resentment. He told her: 'Resentments kill everything in their path.' So, Diana might have pointed out, does adultery. Even the Prince's most loyal supporters had to concede that she had a point about Camilla.

Diana was once grateful to the brigadier's wife for having positively vetted her as a potential royal. But her annoyance at supposedly discovering that her husband's double C-engraved cuff links stood for 'Charles and Camilla' turned to anger when the other woman's photograph allegedly fell out of his diary. The fate of the marriage was sealed when she heard him whispering sweet nothings into a portable telephone from his bathtub, her friends claimed.

To the outside world, Diana might be the clichéd 'caring princess and loving mother'. But inside Buckingham Palace she was regarded as a neurotic woman who held a dangerous weapon. The courtiers knew she could rock the monarchy again by suing for divorce — and that she had the ammunition in the Camillagate tape. None of the Queen's advisers could deny that the recording of Charles's passionate utterances to Camilla were as good as an admission of adultery. To Diana, his intimate expressions demonstrated that he was as besotted by Camilla as he ever had been before their marriage. 'He makes my life real, real torture,' she confided to James Gilbey. It is hard for outsiders to realise how difficult Diana's dealings with the Royal Family have been since all the animosity became public,' said her confidante. 'But however hard the Highgrove Set try to woo Prince William, Diana will ensure that they can never match the love that he and his little brother get from their mother.' Her enemies might make slighting references to Diana's lack of academic achievement and, curiously, she had encouraged this view. 'I'm as thick as a plank,' she would say. 'Brain the size of a pea I've got.' Somewhere along the line, however, she had learned joined-up thinking and it showed. For the first time in history, a royal matriarch-in-waiting was shaping the future of the monarchy from outside the future monarch's bedchamber. Ironically, her nightmare has become the bedrock of the power she wields today.

There are many examples of Diana's charisma but none more telling than her box office appeal in the United States. When the English National Ballet, one of her charities, received an offer to stage a new production of *Sleeping Beauty* in big American cities during summer 1994, one important stipulation was made. 'An American benefactor promised to underwrite everything provided Diana attended the premieres in San Francisco and New York,' said a ballet source, if Diana showed up, the costs were sure to be covered, but without her, it was no deal.'

But Diana needed to consolidate her power base closer to home. She stepped up her attendance at high society events without sacrificing the Work. By living life to the full she wanted to dispel a belief that followed publication of *DIANA: Her True Story* that she was suicidal. 'Let's face it, most books have got three facts in them really,' said Andrew Morton. 'This one's got Camilla, bulimia and suicides. They are the three headlines.' It was the third one that had returned to haunt Diana because it challenged her sanity.

'She didn't throw herself down the stairs at Sandringham although she might believe she did,' said a well informed royal sleuth. 'A witness who actually saw it happen says she slipped two or three steps and fell on her bottom. She was found by a Royal Protection Squad officer. She was not concussed and not unconscious. The Prince of Wales insisted a doctor be called. Yet I am sure she genuinely believes it to be true now.'

Coupled with the emotional stress of the break-up, the strain of living the legend had exacted a heavy price.

WHEN the Princess stared into the dressing table mirror on what turned out to be her last morning at Highgrove, she did not like what she saw. Diana later admitted that she had cried much of the previous night away and she was prepared for the puffy eyes which confronted her. What troubled her were the fine lines emanating from the corners of her eyes. To Diana, the flawless image she had cultivated was extremely important. The thought of her looks fading was as awful as the prospect of the clock striking midnight for Cinderella. Others seized on the cosmetic factor as well. 'She will be diminished, especially when she loses her youthful looks,' claimed John Casey, a Cambridge don well disposed towards the monarchy.

The greatest health and beauty experts in Britain had worked their magic to create the Princess who turned heads even among Hollywood's fairest. The women at *Vogue,* where her sister Jane had worked, had played their part. Style queen Anna Harvey waved her wand over the Princess's wardrobe and make-up experts Barbara Daly and later Mary Greenwell created the masterstrokes of colour that shaped her face. Fitness expert Carolan Brown moulded her figure during hour-long workouts three times a week at Kensington Palace or the LA Fitness Centre in West London. Diana even inspired others to keep fit. When she visited a gym and saw Marje Proops, the *Daily Mirror's* evergreen agony aunt, working out on an exercise bike, she said encouragingly: 'Keep going, Marje, we'll soon be on Page Three.'

Sam McKnight cut her hair every six weeks and she visited Daniel Galvin's salon in Mayfair to have her highlights touched up. The therapist improving her speech was Peter Settelen, an actor who once played Edward VIII. Her 'working clothes', either for daytime or evening wear, were styled by Catherine Walker, Victor Edelstein, Bruce Oldfield and Bellville Sassoon. 'Clothes are for the job – they've got to be practical,' she said. 'Sometimes I can be a little outrageous, which is quite nice, but only sometimes.'

But there is more to Diana than this dazzling glamour. At home, she is happy to loaf about in a threadbare tracksuit. Unlike her husband, she possesses the ability to behave naturally. She offered a splendid example of this when she took her sons into a corner shop to buy them sweets. When they visited Thorpe Park, Diana queued with other families to buy two thirty-five pounds Supersave tickets for her party, which included the two young sons of her butler, Paul Burrell. This was the common touch in action. Few could imagine the Prince of Wales crammed into an economy seat close to the lavatories of a long-haul flight, swapping stories about children with an Antiguan woman – as Diana did during her ten-day New Year break with the young princes on the Caribbean island of Nevis.

'Her Royal Highness has replaced what one might call wifely duties with good works,' said a supporter. 'But it would be wrong of anyone to think that this has softened her resolve. HRH has become very skilful at using those around her. She is inclined to pick people off one at a time, win them over with her enormous, girlish charm and then play them off against each other. This way she gets exactly what she wants without ever having to ask for it. In all my years in royal circles I have never come across one so adept at playing palace politics – even with John Major. I would hate to be on the other side.'

Charles and Diana had been playing separate courts for six months when they met up on *Britannia* at its Merseyside berth to attend the same public function. They joined forces for the fiftieth anniversary of the Battle of the Atlantic at Liverpool Cathedral. The Prime Minister greeted them with equal enthusiasm. After the service, the Waleses smiled at each other and worked the crowd together for the first time in years. If the smiles lacked any particular warmth or conviction, they at least proved that the couple were on speaking terms. They also flew back to London on the same flight but, once there, Charles headed for Highgrove and Diana returned to Kensington Palace.

The only significance in the reunion was that the Queen wished the Waleses to be seen once more as people liked to remember them: as royals doing their duty in a civilised fashion and not the war-torn adversaries of the tabloid headlines.

When an onlooker in the crowd complimented them on how well they looked, Charles couldn't resist one of his cryptic one-liners which, in this case, needed little translation: it's all done by mirrors,' he said wryly.

2

DEVIL IN DISGUISE

'It's amazing what ladies do when your back is turned'
Prince Charles

SET in spacious grounds on the edge of a West Country village, the Victorian mansion that had been the setting of several highly confidential tete-a-tetes about Diana looked a picture of elegance in the morning sun. Parking on the gravel drive, the visitors knew that the only important person who had not been present at these meetings was the Princess of Wales herself. Not once had she entered the stately Georgian doorway nor set foot in the splendid oak-panelled hall beyond. In this quiet corner of rural England, she was *persona non grata*.

The visitors were ushered into the drawing room and left alone to admire the sheaves of early summer flowers while the butler disappeared down a long corridor to prepare drinks. But it was the mantelpiece and a Regency sideboard rather than the flower displays that caught the attention. Closer inspection confirmed that no brief was held for Diana here. Among a collection of family photographs, there was one of the Queen and Prince Philip in their Garter robes, and another of the Queen Mother. Pride of place, however, was given to a small portrait of a youthful Prince Charles mounted in a frame bearing his personal three-feathered crest. There was not a single picture of Diana in this or, apparently, in any other room.

Through the French windows, the lawns swept down to a river where geese nested on the grassy banks. Drinks duly served in tumblers of the finest crystal, the visitors stepped out on to the patio. At that moment, the sound of a car beyond the border hedge signified the return of the owner of the house, who had been attending to business in a nearby village. The royal friend swept into view with a characteristic flourish to greet the guests. Chatting animatedly, they adjourned to the dining room, where the shining mahogany table had been set for lunch. Even on this warm day, a log fire burned invitingly in the hearth.

After the first course of mushrooms *en croute* had been served, the friend paused until the butler had withdrawn, silently closing the double doors behind him. Alone now, the guests listened in astonishment as the talk turned to what had gone wrong in the marriage of Charles and Diana. The most unfair thing, it transpired, was that Charles had been cast as the villain of the piece and his wife as the innocent victim of a heartless conspiracy. There was a completely different side to the story, according to the friend.

First, there was that picture. It had been taken twelve years ago and a recent event in faraway Nepal when the Princess of Wales had worn a transparent skirt on a visit to a Ghurka regiment had revived the memory. Prince Charles, the friend explained, had been staying with the Queen at Balmoral when his valet, Stephen Barry, delivered the morning papers on 18 September, 1980. Barry had served his master for more than a decade of bachelor life and, if Charles noticed a mischievous glint in his eye, it was only to be expected. The arrival of Lady Diana Spencer had already signalled the beginning of the end of Barry's royal service.

Plastered all over the front pages he held out was a picture of Diana in a thin cotton skirt patterned with romantic floral hearts. She had taken care to put on gold loop earrings, a lilac blouse and purple sleeveless pullover, but she had neglected to slip into a petticoat. The skirt was transparent in the autumn sunlight and the pictures revealed her showgirl legs in glorious silhouette. As an added quirk of nature, the sunshine had placed a golden halo around her blonde head. She was half Lolita, half angel. The photograph had been taken outside the Young England kindergarten, attached to St Saviour's Church in the Pimlico district of London, where she worked as a child minder. Diana had posed with two decorative tots, Louise and Scarlett, one tucked under each arm. She had also talked. 'You know I cannot say anything about the Prince or my feelings for him,' she confided in a most telling way. 'I am saying that off my own bat. No one has told me to stay quiet.'

Previous accounts all suggested that Charles had found Diana's performance fetching, the picture flattering. But the friend, who was with him that day, revealed that his reaction was very different. He was 'angry and worried' as he contemplated the implications of

Diana's first exercise in media manipulation. Was she naive beyond belief or was she an opportunist?

'Charles telephoned her almost immediately and asked, "Why did you do it?"' said the friend. 'When he got off the phone, he said she had replied: "I thought they (the Press) would go away if I did a picture for them." In hindsight, it seems that Diana knew exactly what she was doing. She wanted the limelight even then. What better way to get a vaguely sexy yet virginal image for herself than to pose for national newspapers in a see-through skirt surrounded by innocent children?'

Diana's subsequent remark – 'I don't want to be remembered for not having a petticoat' – cut no ice with those in the Prince's camp. Indeed, his Balmoral companion added that if Diana had meant either of the things she said, her next move was even harder to comprehend: 'She went out and bought a new car, a Mini Metro, in the most notice-me colour available – red.' While she could truthfully tell Charles that she always tried to give newsmen the slip, she had made it remarkably easy for them to pick up the trail after she had parked to visit a friend or go shopping.

The Prince believed that the two episodes marked the birth of a media star, one his friend described as 'self-centered and egotistical – a woman who did the most selfish thing possible when she left her husband, to pursue her own personal happiness.'

There was a pause while the butler dished breasts of chicken *supreme* on to the Royal Doulton dinner plates and proffered a selection of mashed potatoes, creamed swede and garden peas. The picture that had been painted was so alien from the accepted image of the Princess of Wales that, in the sunlit dining room, it was like watching a hologram of Snow White turn into a devil in disguise.

'One of the reasons the marriage failed is that she would not make any effort to share his hobbies or his other recreational activities,' the friend related. 'She made it clear that she was not interested in fishing or polo, yet she had been more than happy to join him on the banks of the Dee and to cheer him on from the edge of the polo field when he was considering asking her to marry him. Towards the end of the marriage she refused to let him have the boys when they were apart. But once they were officially separated she had to abide by an agreement which gave him access on an equal number of days. For the first time, he was able to get quality time with his sons. Even so, she chided him with newspaper stunts like the highly publicised trips at Easter. When the princes then went to Scotland to be with their father, so did the photographers. He had plenty of opportunity to be photographed with them, with his arms around them, with them smiling at him just as they had smiled at her. But he wouldn't play Diana's game; he's too much of a gentleman. When he came in from fishing one day, I asked him how it had gone and he said, "Terrible! I only got twenty minutes in because the Press were so awful." He had William and Harry with him and he could have taken the chance to turn it into a photo call, but he's not like that and he never will be by choice, no matter how powerful Diana gets by using the media.'

The butler returned briefly to present the cook's special dessert, pears marinated in wine and served beneath a nest of crystalised sugar. When he had gone, the friend resumed: 'Look at that time when she went on the big PR exercise to France just before the separation. She made a tremendous thing of posing with President Mitterand, but what was she talking to him about – frocks? I can feel genuinely sorry for Fergie; she's just — well, stupid. But Diana is mean and calculating and the people who suffer are the man who married her and their sons, especially the sons. How can you put two boys through that? No marriage is perfect, but we make them work just so we don't cause pain and suffering. Not Diana, she thinks only of herself and her amazing publicity campaign.'

Unknown to Charles's supporter, even at that moment Diana was preparing to set off on another expedition that would guarantee her a place on the front pages.

THE Princess slipped out of Kensington Palace and flew across the Channel in the company of two friends, Hayat Palumbo and Lucia Flecha de Lima. She had met Lucia, the fifty-two-year-old wife of the Brazilian ambassador to Britain, during a tour of Brazil two years earlier. The two women sometimes met for a chat behind the pink geraniums at the Kaspia restaurant near Berkeley Square. Lady Palumbo is the wife of Lord Palumbo, a controversial figure in property development who has openly clashed with Charles. At the small airport at Le Bourget, a Renault Espace minibus, hired in her name, was waiting for the visitors. With Ken Wharfe at the wheel, they headed for the shops and the sights of Paris.

The purpose of Diana's trip five months earlier had not, of course, been to discuss frocks with the President. She had been invited to attend the Lille Arts Festival, which was featuring Paul McCartney's Liverpool Oratorio. This had been Diana's first tour as an independent woman after the Squidgy Summer, and it had come only a week after she had returned from a lacklustre trip to Korea with her husband where, with the marriage well into injury time, the couple had studiously ignored each other, much to the embarrassment of their hosts.

Varying her usual routine of 'doing the job' and flying straight home, Diana started the French tour with two days in Paris. As she strode through Orly Airport in a Catherine Walker suit of emerald green, no one could have been oblivious to her new status. No fewer than eight members of the new court arrived with her in a British Aerospace 146 of the Queen's Flight. Her sister, Lady Sarah McCorquodale, had taken over as lady-in-waiting, and Geoffrey Crawford joined Patrick Jephson to deal with protocol and the Press. Detective Inspector Ken Wharfe and Sergeant Dave 'Razors' Sharpe looked after security while Helena Roach, dresser, and Sam McKnight, hairdresser, took care of Diana's appearance. Mr Ron Lewis, of Kensington Palace, was in charge of the baggage.

Straight into the Work, she visited a centre for handicapped children in southern Paris and told an official: 'I can see their souls in their smiles.' The French could see the change in Diana, and they liked what they saw. She was, they reasoned, very similar to Danielle Mitterand who, although the President's wife, led an entirely separate life from her husband. At the Elysee Palace, Madame Mitterand stood in the freezing cold to greet Diana and once inside, they talked privately through an interpreter. It was after this meeting that President Mitterand made his entrance to welcome the Princess in person. The trip boosted Diana's self-esteem so much that she vowed to return as soon as possible for a more private visit.

Ostensibly no one was supposed to know about her second visit, let alone have access to her itinerary. Photographer Daniel Angeli, however, had been tipped off in the same manner that the British paparazzi had been given advance notice of her outing to Thorpe Park. Angeli was the man who had been guided to a hillside above St Tropez the previous August and provided indisputable proof of Johnny Bryan's affair with the Duchess of York. Suitably equipped, he was positioned outside the Houses of Chanel and Dior while the Princess shopped inside. He did not follow, however, when Diana went to inspect a Left Bank apartment on the Rue de l'Universite which her mother was keen to buy. Frances Shand Kydd had fallen in love with the abode during a dinner party at which she had been a guest the previous December. It was for sale at around £400,000, but after Diana had viewed it, she dropped negotiations.

The following day Angeli was in place outside the Marius and Janette restaurant off the Champs-Elysees to witness Diana's arrival for lunch with the French film star Gerard Depardieu. They ate lobster and sea bass and sipped Perrier water as the photographer waited patiently outside to record their separate departures. Diana went on a brief shopping expedition before accompanying Hayat and Lucia to Notre Dame, where Angeli had all the time he needed to photograph her as just another face among a crowd of ordinary mortals. He testified later that she left the tourist track to spend twenty minutes at the Roman Catholic Chapelle Notre Dame de la Medaille Miraculueuse, a detour that Mother Teresa would have applauded.

That night, Diana was out on the town once more to dine at the modestly-priced Brasserie Balzar and again the cameraman was on hand to record that Diana was with no one other than her girlfriends and detective. Her weekend to the City of Lights continued with a Sunday morning trip to the Pompidou Centre, where she viewed an exhibition of Matisse masterpieces before being driven by a British Embassy chauffeur on a sightseeing tour. That night she dined at the Ritz, exchanging pleasantries with movie-maker Steven Spielberg, before disappearing from even Angeli's view.

The need for apparent secrecy over, she returned to London on a scheduled British Airways flight. Angeli's rolls of film followed on a later plane, already bought by the *Daily Mirror* for £12,000, a modest sum compared with the estimated £1 million he made from the St Tropez pictures. But as the *Mirror* was well aware, this time it was buying no scandal, just another set of look-at-me pictures twelve years on from that first session in a kindergarten playground.

Back in the Royal Borough of Kensington and Chelsea, a titled lady of the Royal Family's closest acquaintance was drawing an interesting new comparison. Diana, she had decided, reminded her of the former American First Lady, Jackie Kennedy Onassis: 'The trouble with Charles is that he has some brains and he's got some bright ideas but he lacks his wife's allure. If he and Diana had carried on as they were halfway through the marriage, it would have been Camelot all over again. They'd have been unbeatable; it would have been like the Kennedys.

Everybody knew what was going on with Jack but so long as they stayed together, it was all right. He was the brain and she was the beauty. After Jack was assassinated, Jackie became the most desirable woman in the world. The Princess of Wales has taken over from Jackie Onassis; she will sell a magazine in Peru if she is on the cover.'

WITH such lucrative newsstand appeal, a new menace inevitably surfaced: the unscrupulous hoaxer out to make a killing. Fleet Street calls the summer months the Silly Season because, in the absence of hard news, frivolous stories are often printed. In May 1993 the Silly Season got off to an early start when readers of the *Sun* were astonished to discover details of an apparent row between Charles and Diana which, the paper claimed, had been transcribed from a recording made by MI5 at Highgrove the previous November. The couple were reported to have been arguing about the futures of their children, particularly where the princes would spend Christmas. Readers were invited to believe that 'the tape' was especially embarrassing to the authorities because the couple were talking not on the phone but face to face in their own home.

One passage of dialogue read:

Diana: For once stop being so self-centred. You still think of me as the person you married.

Charles: I stopped thinking like that years ago.

Diana: Yes, I suppose that would be a good indication of why we drifted apart, my dear.

Charles: Can I say anything right? Tell me what is it you want me to say?

Diana: Say something I want to hear.

Charles: I'm leaving.

Diana: Oh, don't be so bloody childish.

Charles: Oh God.

The embarrassment, as it turned out, was all that of James Whitaker, the *Mirror's* royal correspondent, who had secured the alleged transcript from a source he refused to name. He had tried to keep the contents secret for a book he was writing, *DIANA v CHARLES*. The so-called transcript was ridiculed by the Palace, which took the rare step of denouncing it as a fake. Senior Palace sources went further: they let it be known that reports of the royal couple being bugged by the security services were based on a hoax, clearly signalling the Royal Family's belief that the conversation never actually took place, it's completely made up,' the source told the *Sunday Times*, it's laughable. But the Prince is very angry at being a pawn in a tabloid circulation war.'

Some took it less seriously. TV scriptwriter George Evans described it tongue-in-cheek as 'dialogue any scriptwriter would be proud of', it is well constructed, flows beautifully and has lots of dramatic impact,' he said, if anything, it is almost too perfect. It reads like a script that has been honed to perfection after two or three rewrites, rather than an emotional argument.'

Although the *Sun* had published the 'transcript' first under the headline *MIS BUGGED CHARLES & DIANA BUST-UP*, billing it as a world exclusive, it transpired that the paper had carried out what Whitaker called 'a pretty successful spoiling tactic'. The *Sun* had obtained an advance copy through an American source 'by a piece of skulduggery'. The *Mirror* had planned to serialise the book a few weeks later but, seeing their rival's cheeky spoiler, they rushed into print with the authorised version the same night. The paper's thunder had been stolen and it was very much a lost cause. The Palace's categoric denial only added to a fiasco, which was labelled Tomatogate after Diana's unkind nickname for the somewhat florid Whitaker, The Red Tomato.

The royal reporter found himself struggling against a tide of disbelief when Sir Antony Duff, a former director-general of MI5, said he had been authorised to say that the stories of MI5 being involved in bugging members of the Royal Family were absurd. His statement followed a meeting between the current Director-General, Stella Rimington, and the Home Secretary, Kenneth Clarke. Whitaker's original claim that the 'row' had been recorded the previous November had been rebutted by a Palace statement that at no time during November, or early December for that matter, were the royal couple and their children in residence at Highgrove at the same time – making a nonsense of Charles's alleged quote: 'Quiet, you'll wake the children.' The author subsequently changed the fix on the date of the 'row' to October 28, but on that date it transpired that the Prince was in Manchester and Diana in London. When it was revealed that Whitaker hadn't actually heard 'the tape', it became clear that he had been misled. The reporter, not the royals, was the real victim of the hoax. As if psychic, he had entitled the bugging chapter in his book 'Dirty Tricks'. Tomatogate fizzled out when the *Mirror* ended its serialisation just three days after it had begun, in the final resort, all we could mount was a damage limitation exercise,' admitted Amanda Platell, managing editor of Mirror Group Newspapers in its post-Maxwell recovery.

The irony wasn't lost on those who had heard a genuine tape of a conversation between Whitaker and Major Ron Ferguson at the time it was disclosed that the Duchess of York's father was visiting the Wigmore Club, a West End massage parlour which offered the services of prostitutes to its clients. The call was picked up by a radio scanner tuning in to a mobile phone network in exactly the same manner as the Squidgy and Camillagate tapes:

Whitaker: All this animosity is calming down now, Ron. Soon it will be all over, and the pressure will come off. You have done brilliantly taking the advice I gave you on the first night and saying absolutely nothing. That is the only way, Ron.

Major Ron: I was not sure at the time, I confess.

Whitaker: It was the only way. Do you know, Ron, what has happened to you has made me feel ill – and I'm a journalist. Certain newspapers have behaved disgracefully.

Not only for the royals are taped phone calls an occupational hazard. Andrew Morton wisely uses a scrambler.

THE real Season, the one that carries By Appointment on it, began with the royals putting on a brave face. Fewer in number, they worked harder to keep up the myth that nothing had changed. This is the time of year when the Royal Family, either solo or en masse, lend their support to Britain's blue-ribbon sporting and social events. Starting with The Rose Ball at the Grosvenor House Hotel in April, the Season takes in the Derby, Royal Ascot, Wimbledon and the

Henley Regatta, ending with Queen Charlotte's Ball in late September.

No longer the exclusive preserve of the well-bred and the well-connected, it has become a season for all men and their womenfolk. New Money values and corporate entertainment have chipped away at the elitist gloss. This is one of the things that rankles with the upper classes about the changing face of Britain. 'The Deb of the Year was so *declasse* – just a meat rack,' sighed a young Chelsea socialite. 'Many of the girls had come to London to buy some class, not to look for a husband which used to be the whole point. The *nouves* only have to pick up a copy of *Hello!* to see where to go these days.

'Henley was such a disappointment – there was a real outbreak of trogomania. Nobody obeys the dress code any more. You are supposed to wear skirts below the knee and have your arms covered. But I saw so many people wearing non-regulation outfits that it was disgusting. I thought, "My God, you're paying to be exclusive and it's not. You might as well pay the punter's price and just go in anything." All you needed to get into the Royal Enclosure at Ascot was for someone to put your name up and you got a pass. But it was so grotty that most of the people I know weren't there. It was full of company people trying to impress their clients. It used to be incredibly chic and now it's rubbish. This is why the whole thing about royalty has gone so down market. Looking to them to set a certain standard is a joke. It was common knowledge among the upper middle classes that some of them screw around, but now it's common knowledge on a daily paper basis. You don't have to be up there to know that Charles is having a leg-over or that Diana is seeing James Gilbey.'

It really hurt that readers of the *Sun* were just as well-informed about royal high jinks as the man in the top hat drinking Pimms at the Ascot bar. The millionaire rock star Phil Collins, a true son of the proletariat and a friend of Charles's through his work for the Prince's Trust, understood this perfectly. 'What's going on in the monarchy is nothing new,' he said, it's just that nowadays you can read about it.'

On Coronation Day, tumultuous cheers greeted the Queen and the Queen Mother as they arrived for the Derby at Epsom racecourse in Surrey. It was the Queen Mother's first public appearance after an operation to remove a piece of fish from her throat. 'She looked frail but she hardly sat down all day,' observed one racegoer. 'Those Scottish legs of hers just keep on going.' The Queen waited anxiously with her trainer Lord Huntingdon for the result of the two forty-five in which her horse Enharmonic shared in a photo finish. She gave a whoop of joy when Enharmonic was declared the winner by a head. At the rewarding odds of twelve to one, Her Majesty was starting to enjoy herself again.

Prince Charles, in topper and morning suit, looked around distractedly. Everywhere there were newspapers headlining a speech his wife had made the previous day at a Turning Point conference on women and mental health. *WOMEN WHO SUFFER ALONE,* said the *Daily Mail,* reporting that, 'The Princess of Wales drew on the darkest days of her own life to bring hope to millions of women yesterday. In what seemed like a reference to the end of her own marriage, she said women should not have to sacrifice everything for their loved ones and live in the shadow of others "at the cost of their health, their inner strength and their own self-worth". She spoke of the "haze of loneliness and desperation" that drove women to tranquillizers, sleeping pills and anti-depressants and used the phrase "anxious zombies" – a description she has privately applied, half-jokingly, to herself,' said the *Mail.* 'Health and happiness taken at the cost of others' pain and suffering cannot be acceptable,' said Diana, possibly referring to Prince Charles. 'Women have a right to their own peace of mind. Each person is born with very individual qualities and potential. We as a society owe it to women to create a truly supportive environment in which they too can grow and move forward.'

This was Diana's most powerful speech yet and, through no fault of her own, its coverage completely upstaged the Queen on the anniversary of her coronation. Only the *Daily Mirror* devoted its front page to the monarchy. It presented an unflattering caricature of Elizabeth by Charles Griffin, which showed her as an aged, bespectacled figure hunched beneath an enormous crown. The headline in the previously loyal newspaper read unapologetically: *HOW LONG TO REIGN OVER US?*

'Forty years ago today Elizabeth Alexandra Mary was crowned Queen of the United Kingdom, head of the Commonwealth and Defender of the Faith,' the paper editorialised. 'The *Daily Mirror* congratulates Her Majesty on this latest milestone in her reign. But it is not a happy anniversary. It is no coincidence that she has insisted there shall be no official celebrations. There will be gun salutes at Hyde Park and the Tower of London. And that is all. The Queen will visit the Derby, as usual, and will spend the evening alone at Windsor Castle. Not even her family will be with her. Some anniversary.'

Enharmonic had brought home the royal racing colours of purple, scarlet, black and gold, but it seemed that Her Majesty just couldn't win. When she guarded her money, she was miserly but if she had thrown a lavish party for herself, she would have been accused of extravagance. It was no fun being a monarch anymore.

NOR was it much fun being the Prince of Wales. One of the cushions at Kensington Palace when Charles had been in residence was embroidered with the legend: it's tough being a prince'. It was even tougher being 'a trainee king', as the Goon Show comedian Spike Milligan called his friend. After Camillagate, Charles found out just how tough it could be. He had to wake up every morning to the unpalatable fact that, already a two-time loser, he faced the prospect of losing the Crown as well. He had lost his wife and, for the forseeable future, his mistress. He simply couldn't afford to lose his birthright.

Spurred on by his Palace advisers, he set out to repair some of the damage. This meant fighting his wife in the highly volatile arena of popular acclaim where Diana, not only taller than him in stature but more visible in every other way, was a winner. Charles furrowed his brow, tugged his earlobe and, sucking air between clenched teeth, sallied forth. His first sortie was an embarrassing flop.

The Prince visited Warrington to comfort victims of an IRA bomb blast which had killed one small boy, mortally wounded a twelve-year-old and injured many other people. He smiled throughout a tour of the hospital where victims were recovering from their injuries. 'Your courage has made my day,' he told a woman who had lost a leg. This made it seem as though he was more concerned about himself than the wounded bomb victims. It was an off-key performance and one he deeply regretted.

When a memorial service was held for the two murdered boys, Jonathan Ball and Tim Parry, the Palace vetoed a request from Diana that she should be allowed to attend. Prince Philip, as the senior royal, would represent Her Majesty, who only attended memorial services for close friends, said a spokesman, confirming that protocol was still the deciding factor. Stung by the rebuff, Diana telephoned the families of the two victims to express her condolences. 'She said she was terribly sorry about what had happened to the family,' said Tim's father Colin Parry. 'She was just very, very sympathetic. She was talking to us as another mother rather than as the Princess of Wales.' it is a great comfort that someone in her position should take the time to think of us,' said Maria Ball.

Charles, wearing the full-dress uniform of a Royal Navy captain although he ceased being a serving officer in 1976, spent the day in Spain. He attended the funeral of King Juan Carlos's father, Don Juan, Count of Barcelona, his first cousin twice removed. This took place in a gloomy granite monastery at San Lorenzo (no relation). Diana did not lunch at her favourite restaurant that day. She stayed alone at Kensington Palace while her sons remained at Highgrove. The result was more critical headlines.

Embittered and middle-aged, Charles could not escape the conclusion that he wanted for nothing, yet lacked something. If he had suffered a mid-life crisis after breaking his arm at polo three years earlier, the collapse of his marriage had induced an outbreak of anger and resentment. Above all, he suffered from wounded pride, a deadly emotion in one surrounded mainly by sycophants.

Filled with self-pity, Charles apparently demanded that Diana apologise to him over her suspected collaboration with Andrew Morton. She refused and, considering the indiscretions of Camillagate, she was quite within her rights. Perhaps Charles should have remembered something he noted early in his marriage: it's amazing what ladies do when your back is turned.'

He had been used to every woman in his life, except the most important, his mother, doing exactly what he wanted. Nannies, governesses and a variety of surrogate mothers, including one of his grandmothers, had led him to believe that women would always be at his beck and call. But Diana, chosen for her youth and compliance, had rebelled against the controls he had sought to impose.

'When Charles gave in to the pressure to marry Diana, Prince Philip probably said to him, "Conduct the marriage carefully and properly and see Camilla on the side,"' said Harry Arnold, the reporter who brought Camillagate to the world, it follows his line. He married the Queen, fathered some heirs and spares and then flitted around the world enjoying the company of other women. I tend to think that this might have been an arrangement with father and son, not father, mother and son. The Queen was probably distraught when she heard about Camilla and probably angry that he got caught. But the Queen has so many regrets at the moment that that may not be on the agenda. You cannot dismiss her role in all this. She failed to recognise the change in the twentieth century.'

Ostensibly searching for a bride, the Prince had turned his own back on quite a few women in his time. 'Girlfriends with whom Charles had affairs had to remember to call him Sir even when passing his underpants,' claimed royal author Sally Moore. Better known ones were invited to call him Arthur, his favourite given name. They might be sharing a bed with Arthur the alter ego, but the heir to the throne remained unsullied. 'He was spoon-fed an Arthurian legend in the nursery that Arthur would return when things were going wrong for Britain,' said the royal historian. 'He'd always identified with that and it explains a lot, but he was actually named after Prince Arthur, Duke of Connaught, who was Queen Victoria's favourite son.'

Elizabeth's first-born had been christened Charles Philip Arthur George in the Music Room at Buckingham Palace on 15 December, 1948. After a family lunch, the royals leafed through Victoria's photo albums to decide who the month-old Prince most resembled. Queen Mary was adamant: he looked just like Prince Albert, she declared. Much as he grew to admire Victoria's husband, Charles became more intrigued by his Welsh connections. When he was nine, his mother announced she intended to create him Prince of Wales. He studied Welsh history for years and discovered that he had more Welsh ancestors than many previous holders of the title. One was Cunedda, a fifth-century King of Gwynedd, kinsman of the warrior Owain Ddantgwyn – the legendary King Arthur. Charles was related to his boyhood hero.

As Charles/Arthur grew accustomed to getting his own way, his amorous flings confirmed the view that he didn't really understand the opposite sex very well. This failing came across in his infamous phone call to Camilla. Time and again, she had to reassure him that he was truly loved and madly desired. For a man who had just turned forty-one when the conversation took place, he displayed a disconcerting lack of confidence in his masculinity. Camilla had to play the double role of lover and nanny. His 'dirty talk' clearly gratified his lust while her equally suggestive responses stroked his ego.

When Charles said, 'My luck to be chucked down a lavatory and go on forever swirling around the top, never going down,' psychiatrists had a field day. 'Prince Charles has one particularly significant hobby: collecting lavatory seats,' opined Dennis Friedman in his book *INHERITANCE: A Psychological History of the Royal Family.* 'To use a lavatory seat it is necessary to turn one's back to it. The lavatory seat becomes a metaphor for his wish to retaliate against all those who, at one time or another, have turned their backs on him – his parents, and now, finally his wife.' This was an interesting theory but what was manifestly true was that his self-worth, one of Diana's buzz words, appeared to be dangerously low. Now forty-four, Charles had come to realise that titles and uniforms were merely disguises which hid his true identity. While people respected his rank in society, he began to doubt that they had much respect for him.

'Once you get out of bed, or before you get into bed, you have to talk about something,' summed up Harry Arnold. 'Charles is interested in culture and nature, he speaks fluent French and he's a man of cultivated tastes who could have taken up many professions. Yet he was married to a woman who rings up Capital Radio and requests songs. I think Camilla gave him what he wanted. Here is a woman saying, "I can never marry you and, in fact, we can never acknowledge our relationship. But I still think you are Mr Wonderful." That is what she did for him.' But Camilla is no longer available and he is wracked with guilt about the humiliation she silently endures. For a time, Charles lapsed into melancholia.

His relations with men are equally fraught. As a noticeably shy boy, he had been terrified of bullies whenever he ventured outside the protective walls of Buckingham Palace. At prep school, he had been called 'Fatty' and 'Big Ears' and ragged about his family. But he had learned to fight back at Gordonstoun and carried a more assertive attitude into the Royal Navy.

His mentor on the manhood issue had been Tricky Dickie Mountbatten, so named because of his duplicity. At Cambridge, Mountbatten had befriended Prince Albert but quickly transferred his affection to his brother Edward, the Prince of Wales. He was a much more glamorous companion than the shy, stammering Bertie. When Edward abdicated, Mountbatten had swung back unashamedly to Bertie, the new King George VI. He had influenced Prince Philip during his formative years and, when the young Charles became a better prospect, traded the father for the son. Dickie's scandalous 'open marriage' to Edwina Ashley, granddaughter of Edward VII's financier friend Sir Ernest Cassel, had wrecked any confidence he had in himself as a husband. He turned into a ladies' man of a different kind and gravitated towards men with whom he felt comfortable. Many of them were either bisexual or homosexual, like Stephen Barry, the man chosen as Charles's valet.

Mountbatten knew it was vital for Charles to marry well but before his marriage he encouraged him to experiment sexually with girls from the upper classes. Stephen Barry confirmed privately that his master led an active sex life, but said publicly: in all those twelve years that I worked for him, if he was meant to be in his bed in the morning when I went in to wake him up, he was in bed – alone.'

Charles's key adviser is Commander Richard Aylard, who replaced Sir Christopher Airey, becoming his fifth Private Secretary since 1978. Airey's departure was announced after an embarrassing mix-up showed the lack of co-operation between Charles and his wife. The Prince made a speech on education on the same day that Diana spoke about the AIDS issue, one cancelling out the other in terms of publicity. Charles was furious and Sir Christopher tendered his resignation after barely a year in the post. He declined to elaborate on the real reasons.

One departing aide told friends: 'The man (Charles) is totally disorganised. I used to sit in the corridor for three hours just waiting for him.' 'Charles is very difficult to advise because he takes advice from every other crank who pins him up against the wall,' said another disgruntled insider. 'However, he never sacks anyone. He simply freezes them out.' The truth was that it had taken Charles some time to assemble a team of like-minded advisers around him at

St James's Palace. He encouraged them to stop looking over their shoulder at Head Office, as Buckingham Palace is known.

After the Warrington fiasco, Charles reassessed the situation with those closest to him. One of his strategists explained that Charles no longer saw himself as competing with the Princess of Wales. Rather, their roles were considered to be complementary. 'Richard Aylard shares an office with Patrick Jephson and they work closely together trying to make sure that they aren't both making major speeches on the same day or going to the same part of the country,' he said. 'They are trying to get the best value from their separate programmes.

'Charles is an extremely robust individual and, of course, he's used to being under pressure, but he's certainly putting a great deal into his work now as he always has. His approach to his work and his very real understanding of his role has developed over a number of years. The Prince is not someone who believes in short-term, quick-fix solutions to achieve popularity. What is important is the long-term worth of what he is doing. Even if he were attracted to the quick-fix solution, he's got all this very worthwhile work going on with the Prince's Trust and the Youth Business Trust, which has created 25,000 jobs so far. He's very committed to that kind of work. He's not going to give up those things. In the same way, he's established a very good *modus operandi* for his foreign tours. He undertakes tours such as the ones to Mexico, Poland and Bosnia on the advice of the Foreign Office – he goes wherever they feel he can do most good. He wants to do everything he can to help what he calls Great Britain plc. Clearly the concentration on his private life had been unhelpful and a distraction from his work. But he wouldn't say he was at a crossroads at all.'

When things bother him, Charles turns to dangerous sports, particularly polo. 'Polo helps keep me sane,' he said, it's the only team sport I play.' His exertions in the saddle show that he is a highly competitive player. He plays to win even if it hurts. An old back problem struck him after only twelve minutes into a game at Windsor on 13 June, 1993, after he tried to turn his pony one way and it insisted on going the other. Charles stormed off the field, crashed his polo helmet to the ground and told worried aides who advised medical attention: I don't want a bloody doctor.' The Prince, his face twisted in agony, lay down at full stretch behind the wheels of an ambulance until the pain eased. At Highgrove, he called in Sarah Key, his Australian physiotherapist, to massage and manipulate his spine. Friends revealed that Charles suffered from a crumbling disc which put pressure on the spinal nerve. The man who had made his wife's life 'real, real torture' was exposed as tormented, crippled and disturbed himself. Despite every conceivable warning, he was back in the saddle again within a couple of weeks.

The vagaries of Charles royal birthright troubled him so much that he was once compelled to explain himself to complete strangers. 'I've had to fight to have any sort of role as the Prince of Wales,' he told a group of editors at Kensington Palace. 'I am determined not to be confined to cutting ribbons.' One editor who dined with Charles mused: 'I sometimes wonder what he does in the morning. Does he wake up and say, "I think I'll be an admiral today" and the valet fetches the right uniform out of the wardrobe?' According to Stephen Barry, the wardrobe contained no fewer than forty-four uniforms. After the break-up, Diana sent them all over to St James's Palace on a mobile clothes rail.

Charles had, in fact, been given at least one excellent opportunity to play an active role. When James Callaghan was Prime Minister, he put Charles on the Commonwealth Development Corporation, but he quickly lost interest. 'He should stop pretending that he has never been given a chance to test himself to the ultimate,' one of his critics remarked at the time.

At the core of Charles's problem is what he sees as his rejection by his parents as a child. Wanting for nothing in material terms, he had yearned for parental approval. While his father was a technocrat and pragmatist at heart, he had turned into a dilettante. Even at Highgrove he couldn't settle. 'He loves his garden, but as soon as he's finished sorting out every inch of it he will get bored and take up something else,' said Diana. 'Like most men he does what he wants to do.'

Moreover, his search for a Holy Grail with such spiritual sherpas as the writer Sir Laurens van der Post has met with only limited success. He described Sir Laurens, with whom he went meditating in the Kalahari desert, as 'the most formative influence on my life'. Another guru, the violinist Sir Yehudi Menuhin, taught him the relaxation and meditation techniques of yoga. But neither has equipped him for his role as the stereotyped but wholly human component of an everyday eternal triangle. 'There are very few relationships, certainly in Western society, that can survive that sort of triangulation,' said Andrew Morton. 'Three into two doesn't work.'

Infidelity, Charles discovered after the full Camillagate transcript was published in Australia on 13 January, 1993, was a great leveller. He now ranked uncomfortably alongside the milkman, the window cleaner and the travelling salesman as the butt of dirty jokes. He had cuckolded a friend and although it might be argued that the circumstances were different, the morality was the same. Never again could the Prince of Wales take the moral high ground.

3

THE CAMILLA CONSPIRACY

'Your greatest achievement is to love me'
Prince Charles

CAMILLA Parker Bowles's father, Major Bruce Shand, was known more for his bravery than his imagination. But he was, in his own way, quite a ladies' man. 'When I met him, he was a single man in his twenties, a dashing cavalry officer who was considered rather good looking,' said Lady Edith Foxwell, then a beautiful debutante of nineteen. 'He rode well and looked good on a horse. He was considered to be a ladies' man but, to be honest, I thought he was rather dull. I was a bit naughty myself and I always liked unusual people. We went to lots of parties together and Bruce was always a very nice escort.'

Major Shand's eldest daughter was far more direct in matters of the heart. Camilla, it was said, had been introduced to Charles at a polo match and taking the bit between her teeth, had teased him: 'My great-grandmother was your great-great-grandfather's mistress – so how about it?' Alice Keppel, Camilla's great-grandmother, had indeed been the courtesan of Albert, Prince of Wales, later the bearded lothario Edward VII known to the masses as 'Good Old Teddy'. When Diana heard about this opening gambit, she marvelled at the woman's audacity. Such a full-frontal approach to any man, let alone the heir to the throne, was beneath her dignity. This was only the first of many occasions that caused her to wonder about Camilla's barefaced cheek.

At twenty-five, Camilla had been a year older than the Prince, a lively, confident, well-endowed young debutante with an unsanitized sense of humour that matched his own. Above all, she was a blonde and the Prince adored blondes. Charles, whose self-deprecating manner masked a highly active libido, didn't think too deeply. He accepted the invitation. History was about to repeat itself.

Camilla's confidence stemmed in no small measure from the fact that her family were not only extremely well-connected but exceedingly rich. Alice Keppel had two children, Violet by her husband, and Sonia, it was believed, by Edward VII. Violet married Denys Trefusis in 1919, but it emerged from letters and diaries published after Violet's death that she had been the lesbian lover of Mrs Harold Nicolson, better known as the author Vita Sackville-West. Sonia married the third Baron Ashcombe, a member of the Cubitt dynasty, who, as well as projects for royalty, had built most of Belgravia for the Duke of Westminster's Grosvenor Estate. They had two children, Harry, the present Lord Ashcombe, and Camilla's mother, Rosalind. Bruce Shand, born on 22 January, 1917, went to Sandhurst after Rugby and won the MC twice during World War II. After the war, he built up his own business as a Mayfair wine merchant. He and Rosalind were married in 1946.

The first of their three children was Camilla Rosemary, born at King's College Hospital, London, on 17 July, 1947, a Cancerian like Diana. With her sister Annabel and brother Mark, she was raised at The Laines at Plumpton in Sussex, and whereas Diana excelled at swimming and tennis, Camilla thrived on blood sports. She was hooked, so to speak, fox, stock and barrel. After a bracing introduction to school life at Dumbrills near her Sussex home, Camilla was educated at the Queen's Gate School in South Kensington. This private academy attracted girls from well-to-do families whose main interest was procreating an upper-class lifestyle. More energetic and shapely than beautiful, Camilla was never as ravishing as Alice Keppel, who had completely captivated Charles's philandering forebear.

It hadn't mattered that Alice was already married to an Army officer, Colonel George Keppel. Marriage was more a useful cover than a hindrance in the louche society Edward frequented. 'No woman was safe in his company,' said the royal historian. To the despair of his mother Queen Victoria, Edward maintained a string of mistresses, the most famous of whom was 'The Jersey Lily', Mrs Lillie Langtry. Alice started a passionate, twelve-year affair with him, which ended only on his death in 1910. 'There was a twenty-seven-year age difference between them,' said the royal historian. 'She made no secret of their affair and they often went out as a couple. She used to say, "Curtsy first – then leap into bed". But it can't have been easy. Edward became so gross from over-eating that he had to be strapped into a hanging harness, complete with footrests, to enable him to make love.'

If Alice's daughter Sonia, Camilla's grandmother, were actually the King's illegitimate child, then Charles and Camilla were second cousins several times removed. By all accounts, they were soon doing more than kissing.

Their affair began after Charles led Camilla on to the dance floor at Annabel's, the nightclub synonymous with the latest in Mayfair chic. Other guests saw that the newly graduated naval officer was enchanted by the vivacious blonde in his arms, although they arrived down the wrought-iron staircase separately. Camilla's 'fairly steady' boyfriend, Captain Andrew Parker Bowles, had been posted to Germany with his Household Cavalry regiment, the Blues and Royals. She arrived accompanied by her sister Annabel. When Charles asked her to dance, the young debutante eagerly accepted. Even then, she and Andrew had 'an arrangement'. Charles and Camilla seemed to be made for each other. He found that not only was he immensely attracted to her, but he could speak openly to her on subjects closest to his heart. They talked the same language in more or less the same accent. House was 'hice' and nice was 'neece'.

Although physical contact was first made at Annabel's, its Champagne Charlie atmosphere was a far cry from the habitat in which love started to blossom. Camilla's passion for outdoor country pursuits more than matched the Prince's own. She was an expert rider who loved to hunt with the Belvoir or the Beaufort, and her upbringing enabled her to share Charles's pleasure in fishing and shooting, not as a spectator but as a highly competitive participant. 'She's quite happy sloshing across a windswept field with her hair in a scarf,' said a friend. 'But she dresses up beautifully when the occasion demands it. She would have made a tremendous daughter-in-law for the Queen; unlike Diana, they have a lot in common.'

Their rapport completely unnerved Charles, who was only twenty-three and young for his age. if Camilla had played the long game, it might have been a different story,' said the friend. 'But it happened so quickly – little more than six months from start to finish. I doubt if Charles could believe his good fortune. But he wasn't mature enough to handle a relationship properly so he dithered. It's said that

Camilla "wasn't keen on queendom", but I'm sure she could have been persuaded if that were the only obstacle. It wasn't, of course. Other things were involved.'

For one thing, Camilla wasn't a virgin and, despite the sexual liberation of the permissive Sixties, it was expected that the next Queen of England should go into her husband's bed *virgo intacta.* To complicate matters, Andrew Parker Bowles had been a close friend of Princess Anne and only his Catholicism had prevented their relationship from going further. These two facts alone would have given royal moralists, and the Press, a field day. it would have been preferable for all concerned if this had been faced realistically at the time,' said the Palace insider, it could have been sold to the public as a modern love story. The romantic element would have overshadowed any bad publicity very quickly. Heaven knows, the mood was right for a change in social attitudes. Charles could have married Camilla and saved everyone from years of hypocrisy.'

But the prevailing mood in the House of Windsor at the time was not receptive to such a radical departure. 'Charles was frightened of his father at this stage of his life,' said a friend. 'I'm not saying there was an argument or that Prince Philip vetoed the relationship. But it would not surprise me if Charles decided it was easier to simply cut and run.'

To a large extent, the decision was taken out of his hands. He joined HMS *Minerva* and spent most of 1973 far away in the West Indies, hardly conducive to a romance in England. Soon after Charles bowed out, Camilla accepted a proposal from Andrew Parker Bowles, now a major with an assured military career in front of him. By some accounts, Charles was devastated. The couple were married at the Guards Chapel in July 1973. Princess Anne was among the congregation to see her former boyfriend walk down the aisle with her brother's loved one.

At Park House adjacent to the Sandringham estate in Norfolk, Diana had just celebrated her twelfth birthday. The biggest event in her life that year was her sister Sarah's coming-of-age party at Castle Rising, a Norman castle. Diana has her eye on Prince Andrew, not his big brother.

As Camilla settled down to married life in Bolehyde Manor in Wiltshire, Charles threw himself into his naval career. Having gained his pilot's licence, he trained to fly helicopters at the Royal

Naval Air Station at Yeovilton, Somerset. When her first child, a son, was born he attended the christening and became a godfather. The child was given the names Thomas Henry Charles.

AS a bachelor conducting an affair with a married woman, Charles would turn to Lady Tryon for advice. The Australian blonde, born Dale Elizabeth Harper, hailed from Melbourne, not far from where the Prince had spent six months at Timbertop, the character-building, up-country adjunct of Geelong Grammar School. He preferred her nickname, Kanga.

Of all the women Charles ever met, she was the most immediately endearing. 'They hit it off from the start,' said a friend. 'Dale was very attractive, but it was her personality that appealed to him. She is completely natural and unaffected. She was a school friend of Barry Humphries, but she didn't turn out remotely like Dame Edna.' She was also extremely brave. Dale had been born with spina bifida and the crippling illness was undetected at birth. Her father, Barry Harper, a wealthy magazine publisher, noticed the problem when he saw his daughter, aged seven, walk crookedly across a beach. As a result, she spent years of her childhood in a hospital for crippled children. 'She has never let her illness slow her down,' said the friend. 'She's a terribly energetic workaholic and Charles adores her.' 'My life is work, work, work,' said Kanga, who turned her hand to fashion designing. 'I work for the money – and because that's the way my father brought me up.'

They became friends after Dale arrived in London and started going out with one of his chums, Lord Anthony Tryon, the six-foot-four son of the Queen's Treasurer. Dale was working in public relations for Qantas, the Australian airline. The day she was due to return home, Lord Tryon, who coined the nickname Kanga, invited her to a farewell lunch in the City, where he worked as a merchant banker. Before the bill arrived, he had proposed to her and she had accepted. Kanga and 'Ant' as she called her fiancé were married in the Chapel Royal at St James's Palace.

Lady Tryon soon became one of the more delightful additions to the higher echelons of the London social scene. Charles was a frequent visitor at her home in Walton Street, Knightsbridge, and the family's manor, Ogbury House, set in 700 acres of prime shooting and fishing country in a Wiltshire valley. The trio started a yearly ritual: an expedition to the Tryons' unpretentious lodge on the Hoffsa River in the ruggedly beautiful north-east of Iceland, where the salmon fishing is the best in Europe.

Kanga already knew about Camilla and Charles and, as they were now rural neighbours, the two women talked about him constantly. Both realised that Charles's years in the Navy had changed him from the cavalier young beau who had first flirted with them into a more mature man. When he talked about marriage, he said more or less the same thing he said in public: if I'm deciding on whom I want to live with for the next fifty years – well, that's the last decision in which I want my head to be ruled entirely by my heart.' Much as it troubled him, he knew that his heart was already taken.

Charles was due to leave the Navy after taking his first command in the coastal minehunter, HMS *Bronington*. His need to find a challenging role outside the services was uppermost in his mind. To that end, he set up the Prince's Trust to help young go-getters make a start in life and became its hands-on president. He displayed a gift for organisation by raising £16 million for the Queen's Silver Jubilee Appeal in 1977. But none of this was enough without approval. Like Edward the previous Prince of Wales, Charles wanted his father to acknowledge his accomplishments. 'Camilla understood this need and gave her unstinting, unselfish praise,' said a friend. The insider revealed that the relationship resumed in earnest after the birth of Camilla's second child, a daughter named Laura Rose, in 1978.

'It seemed like a workable arrangement at the time,' said the friend. 'Andrew Parker Bowles spent most of his time in London, where he had other interests of his own, and Camilla lived close to mutual friends. Her marriage provided the perfect cover for their meetings.' Like the two Edwards before him, Charles saw nothing wrong in having an affair with someone else's wife. Some things didn't change.

Andrew Parker Bowles had connections of his own. He was related to the Duke of Marlborough and the Earls of Derby and Cadogan. He rose to brigadier of the Royal Horse Guards and First Dragoons and later became director of the Royal Army Veterinary Corps. In 1987, he was appointed Silver Stick in Waiting to the Queen, a largely ceremonial post which, in previous times, required the holder to lay down his life for the sovereign in the event of an assassination attempt. He lived in a four-story pied-a-terre in South Kensington.

'There was a fair amount of sexual activity of the heterosexual variety,' said one privy to the household's comings and goings.

When the Queen pressed Charles about marrying, he consulted Camilla and Kanga. The Twin-set Twins would, they promised, scout around for a suitable prospect. They had, in fact, already started looking because Camilla had a personal interest in Charles's choice. Thus the Camilla Conspiracy was hatched to find a bride for Charles.

Wallis Simpson, her predecessor as lover of a Prince of Wales, had no real desire to marry Edward VIII. Her intention had been to see him settle down with a homely, complaisant spouse who dared not challenge her position as the King's mistress. She wanted power, not duty. It was only after Edward sacrificed his throne for her, and the option disappeared, that she finally agreed to marry him. 'She is a nice woman and a sensible woman – but she is hard as nails and she doesn't love him,' said the Cabinet Minister Sir Alfred Duff Cooper. Camilla's dilemma was different. She loved Charles but knew that, even if she divorced her husband, marriage to him was out of the question. They had to find another way.

WHEN Charles flew off for a well deserved holiday in April 1979 to do some serious thinking, he knew he was living on borrowed time. His destination was the Bahamas, where, ironically, the Duke and Duchess of Windsor had been banished during the war years. 'The St Helena of 1940,' the Duchess called it. The big difference was that, unlike Napoleon, the Windsors got out alive. Edward was forty-one when Wallis eventually married him on 3 June, 1937 at the Chateau de Cande at Tour in France, but Charles had already been 'rash enough' to declare that thirty was a reasonable age for a man to wed. As he was now in his thirty-first year, his days as the world's most eligible bachelor were numbered.

His birthday party six months earlier had been a roisterous affair at Buckingham Palace, the dynamic black singers, the Three Degrees, starring his friend Sheila Ferguson, providing the up-tempo glitz which had become associated with his bachelor style. His date that evening was the fresh-faced blonde actress Susan George, star of the explicit movies *Straw Dogs* and *Matidingo*. Her profession disqualified her as a future queen. Previously dated by tennis star Jimmy Connors, Ms George had also been a girlfriend of the sentimental singer Jack Jones who, Charles was later to confide mischievously, spent more time crying on her shoulder than cooing in her ear. As always, Camilla and Kanga were present to monitor the royal progress; to be consulted, to encourage and to warn.

Watching Charles dance to the thumping disco beat was Lady Diana Spencer, who had been surprised to receive an invitation. The Queen Mother and her grandmother, Ruth, Lady Fermoy, had taken a hand in that although they didn't seriously consider Diana as a possible bride at this stage. Most of what Diana knew about Charles and his tangled love life came from Sarah, her feisty, red-headed sister who had been his previous girlfriend. Like any other teenage girl in the country, Diana seized every morsel Sarah cared to drop about her famous escort.

Diana was changing. While staying at her mother's home in Chelsea, she had started visiting Headlines, the salon of a young hairdresser called Kevin Shanley in South Kensington. He saw distinct possibilities in this lanky, hunched country girl. 'She was a natural blonde right into her mid-teens, but then her hair got darker until it was light brown,' he said. He persuaded her to put blonde highlights through her fine, mousy tresses. The effect was electrifying. She sparkled as a blonde. Looking in the mirror, Diana straightened her shoulders and marched out of the salon a new woman. The Spencer family speculated that she might marry Prince Andrew, who knew her as the girl next door at Sandringham. She had kissed him under the mistletoe one New Year's Eve. 'I'm saving myself for Prince Andrew,' she told friends. His big brother was, after all, far too old. Her family's nickname for her was The Duchess, 'Duch' for short.

The first time Prince Charles had actually set eyes on her was when he called at Park House and baby Diana was playing happily in her nursery. She was, her father proudly told the world, 'a superb physical specimen'. Sarah formally introduced Diana, not at all glamorous in country rig of jeans, jumper and wellies, to Charles during a pheasant shooting weekend at Althorp while she was on leave from West Heath school. This famous encounter in a ploughed field near evocative Nobottle Wood in the winter of 1977 had left Charles with the impression of 'a very jolly and amusing and attractive sixteen-year-old – I mean, great fun, bouncy and full of life'. Diana was less articulate about this milestone in her life. 'Just amazing,' was all she could say about Charles.

Lady Sarah, who suffered from the unpredictable effects of *anorexia nervosa*, the compulsive starving illness, made a fatal mistake after Charles invited her to accompany him on a skiing trip to Klosters. 'Our relationship is totally platonic – I think of him as the big brother I never had,' she said. 'I wouldn't marry anyone I didn't love whether it was the dustman or the King of England. If he asked me, I'd turn him down.' After that astonishing gaffe, Charles swiftly transferred his attentions elsewhere, although some believed that Sarah dumped him after rejecting his proposal. Diana observed the break-up and learned an important lesson in the ways of the Prince.

By this time she too had begun to suffer from the effects of an eating disorder, which later developed into bulimia. At West Heath she regularly binged on four bowls of All-Bran at breakfast. 'We used to throw up together,' said a titled young lady who knew Diana in her teens.

Her problems originated at home. She had been brokenhearted when her father divorced her mother Frances in April 1969 over her admitted adultery. Frances had married her lover, Peter Shand Kydd, but that marriage also ended in the divorce courts. To his children's deepest distress, Johnnie Spencer fell in love with Raine, Countess of Dartmouth and married her despite their open hostility. The children called her 'Acid Raine' and prayed for her to go away but when Earl Spencer suffered a cerebral haemorrhage, he survived largely because of his new wife's constant presence at his bedside. 'Raine did a lot more than will him to live,' said a friend. 'She simply refused to let him die.'

After this trauma, Sarah and Diana were relieved to be invited to join a shooting party at Sandringham in January 1979. Jane, the quieter, more homely, middle sister, had married Robert Fellowes, the Queen's Assistant Private Secretary, and she had put their names forward. Charles noticed Diana again. She made him laugh and, soon after she returned to London, he started to invite her to join his circle of friends on occasional nights out.

Diana already knew that the one thing Charles would not tolerate in a prospective bride was loose talk about his intentions. It ran counter to everything he believed about his right to make up his own mind. He simply would not be pressured into a match because the Press wanted him to wed. 'Charles was secretive — no, furtive — about his girlfriends,' said the Palace insider. 'He was furious if word leaked out, even about quite innocent stuff.' Charles expressed it thus: 'I trust my friends implicitly and they know that. The more discreet they are the better.'

Sometimes the parents of his lovers conspired in the secrecy, as the former beau of a society beauty discovered to his astonishment. When he turned up at the family mansion to pay his respects, he was met at the front door by the young lady's mother. 'She's up there with Him,' she whispered, pointing skywards. 'I thought for a moment she was indicating that the Almighty had taken her daughter to heaven,' said the jilted suitor, the son of a baronet. 'Then I realised she was speaking in code. She was telling me that her daughter was upstairs with Prince Charles. Quite amusing, really.'

NO ONE knew Charles better than his great-uncle, Earl Mountbatten of Burma. In this reworking of the Arthurian Legend, he played Merlin. 'I'll make this prophecy,' said Uncle Dickie, who was due to meet Charles on the Bahamian island of Eleuthera. 'When Charles finds someone he wants to marry, he will not ever be seen with her in public. Very privately he will try hard to win her round like any other suitor.' Uncle Dickie, as usual, was right. Even Prince Philip did not know his son as well as the Prince's HGF (Honorary Grandfather).

Marriage was high on the agenda for the sessions Charles looked forward to with Mountbatten in the peace and quiet of Windermere Island, Eleuthera, where the Earl's two sons-in-law kept holiday homes. Charles was to stay in the villa of Lord Brabourne while Mountbatten was ensconced in the palatial residence of the interior designer David Hicks across the road. Brabourne, who was married to Lady Patricia Mountbatten, was a noted film producer, his works up to that time including *Othello, Romeo and Juliet, Sink the Bismarck, Murder on the Orient Express* and *Death on the Nile*. He moved easily around the celebrity circuit, sometimes accompanied by his daughter, Lady Amanda Knatchbull. Uncle Dickie had big plans for Amanda. He hoped she might link the Windsor and Mountbatten names in the most propitious way. The matchmaking Merlin had, he thought, conjured up a Guinevere.

As the prime mover in the Queen's marriage to Prince Philip, Mountbatten had often discussed the succession with Her Majesty over tea at Buckingham Palace and during her visits to his Broadlands estate in Hampshire. The mother of Charles's heir was a matter of abiding concern to them both. While a Windsor-Mountbatten union would have thrilled Uncle Dickie to the core, neither the Queen nor her son was quite so convinced. Mountbatten's ruthless ambition seriously worried Her Majesty.

As strict security had been enforced to confine journalists to the far side of a causeway in the northern section of the island, Charles was confident that this much needed break from active royal service would pass peacefully. He was half right.

Travelling with Prince Charles was Chief Inspector Paul Officer of the Royal Protection Squad, who had guarded the Prince on many foreign assignments. A tall, lean vegetarian dedicated to the personal well-being of his royal charge as well as his physical safety, Officer approached Chris Hutchins in the lobby of the Windermere Island Club while checking the identities of guests to ensure that none represented a threat. The writer and the policeman struck up a rapport and agreed to dine together in the club's restaurant that evening, as they did on more than one occasion.

'HRH has a great deal on his mind at present,' Officer ventured over the meal they savoured that first night. He would not elaborate on what precisely it was that preoccupied his employer, but another member of the Brabourne party was more forthcoming: 'Dickie believes that Charles might well fall in love with Amanda on this trip and I think the Prince has a bit of a conscience about that.' The writer, who was acting on a tip-off that 'things were moving on the Charles front', put a question mark besides Amanda's name on his list of 'possibles', but he didn't rule her out entirely. Mountbatten was noted for his cunning.

When Hutchins suffered from a sore throat the next day Officer mentioned it to the Prince, who recommended a herbal remedy he sometimes used himself and which could be bought on the island. On at least two other occasions, Officer greeted Hutchins by announcing: 'HRH wants to know if the medicine is working.' The writer mused aloud that he would appreciate an opportunity to thank His Royal Highness for his consideration. The policeman carefully considered his answer. 'I'm not suggesting anything, but you might like to know that he will be jogging along the beach at six a.m. tomorrow,' he said.

At five a.m. the writer made his way to a point the bodyguard had indicated as Charles's resting place on his morning run. He promptly fell asleep and was awoken by the sound of the Prince's advance along the wet sand. 'He ran a few yards past me and sat down on the beach,' Hutchins recalled. 'He stayed there for almost half an hour just staring out at the wreck of a ship on the shoreline. I did not engage him in conversation because what I saw in front of me was a man who carried the worries of the world on his shoulders. Although we sat so close to each other for so long on such a desolate beach, I left him alone with his thoughts and Officer later told me he had appreciated that.'

If Charles had reflected honestly on the women in his life, he would have had to confess that he was guilty of a particular kind of male chauvinism. 'I've been in love with all sorts of girls,' he admitted frankly on one occasion. 'And I hope to fall in love with lots more.' But he had, he conceded, abdicated the role of royal rake in favour of his younger brother. Charles said that he and Prince Andrew had been walking together when 'a small teeny-bopper – a girl about fifteen – came running up to my brother and said, "Hooray, it's Prince Andrew". I thought, "My days are numbered", and I walked round to the back of the car. Then an elderly lady of about sixty walked up to me and said, "Hooray, it's Prince Charles". So I leave the field to him.' Andrew, hunkier than his brother, needed no encouragement to start accumulating numbers in his little black book.

Having survived the public school system in England, Scotland and Australia with his virginity intact, Charles had found to his relief that his fascination for exciting women was eagerly reciprocated. All he lacked was experience. One of his earliest loves was Lucia Santa Cruz, the daughter of the Chilean ambassador to London. Their dalliance, conducted with the connivance of Lord 'Rab' Butler, master of Trinity College, Cambridge, added lustre to the Prince's studies in kingship. At twenty-three, Lucia was three years older than Charles and she was the first woman to make him conscious of his sexual potential. The shy, Goonish youth parodied as Big Ears quickly learned to stop apologising for what he was and to enjoy the power of being who he was.

After what Lord Butler termed 'the Lucia Experience', Charles put many girls to the test and found that his sexuality was just as much an aphrodisiac as his position, even if some of his conquests regarded *him* as a trophy.

But of all the young women Charles courted in those carefree years, Camilla was the one he couldn't get out of his system. When he visited Rhodesia, Camilla was at hand to welcome him to Salisbury. Her husband had been appointed aide-de-camp to Lord Soames, the last Governor-General before the British colony gained its independence as the Republic of Zimbabwe. Although Camilla spent most of his tour of duty raising their children back in Britain, she managed to turn up in Africa in time for Charles's visit.

Andrew Parker Bowles was almost killed while preparing part of the itinerary. Charles was supposed to ride an African buffalo through the street, rodeo-style, and the intrepid aide decided to road-test the beast to make sure that it was safe. The buffalo, Ziggy, threw him to the ground and badly gored him. During his tour of duty, Parker-Bowles befriended Lord Soames's daughter Charlotte, the disco-loving great-granddaughter of Sir Winston Churchill.

On Eleuthra, Charles and Uncle Dickie had faced up to the problem that he had to marry a virginal Protestant of acceptable, if not exactly regal, birth, it's nothing to do with class; it's to do with compatibility,' the Prince said, defensively. Still, he was drastically limited in his choice and the older he became the less chance he seemed to have of finding a suitable partner. 'Marriage is a much more important business than falling in love,' he mused. 'I think one must concentrate on marriage being essentially a question of mutual love and respect for each other, creating a secure family unit in which to bring up children. Essentially, you must be good friends, and love, I'm sure, will grow out of that friendship. I have a particular responsibility to ensure that I make the right decision. Having tried to learn from other people's experiences, other people's mistakes – yes, in one's own family and in other people's – I hope I shall be able to make a reasonable decision and choice.' Sitting on the beach, his knees drawn under his chin, it is possible that his mind turned to jolly, bouncy Diana.

THE unthinkable happened while Charles was enjoying his annual fishing trip with the Tryons at their Icelandic lodge. Mountbatten had been holidaying with his family at his Irish home, Classiebawn Castle, County Sligo. He had been going there for so many years that he had stopped worrying about security. One of his favourite pastimes, much to the delight of his grandchildren, was to catch lobsters in the pots he placed just out to sea. Soon after eleven-thirty a.m. on 27 August, 1979, the Mountbattens were clearing Mullaghmore harbour wall in his thirty-foot boat, Shadow V, to retrieve the night's catch. At that moment, IRA terrorists triggered a fifty-pound bomb on board by remote control. Charles's HGF, who was as old as the century, was killed instantly.

When Charles heard the news at the Tryon chalet, he returned to London dressed sombrely in black – the clothes he always carried with him in case of such an eventuality. As a matter of form, he kept black-edged notepaper with him on which he was able to write letters of condolence to all members of the Mountbatten family. He wept at the funeral.

It does seem a bitter and cruel irony that a man who served in both wars, who was torpedoed, mined and sunk by aerial bombardment, who helped defy the scourge of tyranny and oppression, a man of such passionate concern, should suddenly be blown to bits through the agency of the most cowardly minds imaginable,' he said at a memorial service in St Paul's. 'He was a man for whom blood was thicker than water. He was the centre of the family, a patriarchal figure. I adored him and I miss him so terribly.' It was the most traumatic event in his life.

As gently as he could, Charles had let his great-uncle know on Eleuthera that marriage to Amanda was a non-starter. 'There was a story that Charles sounded her out during that holiday and she replied, "What a funny idea,"' said the Palace insider. 'He had given her a bracelet as a present but all of this was Mountbatten's doing. He knew they weren't in love but he believed that an arranged marriage could work. He even sent Amanda to Paris with the Duchess of Abercorn to spend £3000 on designer clothes.' Sharing their grief, Charles became very close to Amanda after Mountbatten's death, but only as a friend.

'He continued to include Diana in his circle, but there was nothing between them,' said the Palace insider. 'Her youth gave her one distinct advantage: she could move in royal company without attracting attention. People thought she was far too young for him.'

Charles had more wild oats to sow and, in the process, he was confronted with disquieting evidence of his failings. He had met Anna Wallace, the beautiful daughter of a millionaire Scottish landowner, while hunting with the Belvoir on the Duke of Rutland's estate in November 1979. Their affair was so sudden and explosive that Charles was smitten. His usual caution seemed to desert him; it was even said he proposed to her. She was still thinking it over when he squired her into the Queen Mother's eightieth birthday ball at Windsor Castle. Charles felt so sure of himself that he neglected his sweetheart for long periods of the evening while he mingled with his grandmother's guests. The fiery Anna stood there, boiling, until she could take the humiliation no longer. She was not known as Whiplash for nothing. 'Don't ever ignore me like that again,' she chastised him loudly. 'I've never been treated so badly in my life. No one treats me like that – not even you.'

The romance was rekindled after Charles apologised even though it was revealed that two other men had shared her affections before they became an item. This should have ruled her out immediately, but Charles sallied on. Camilla realised he had become besotted, posing a threat to her own privileged position. Anna, she knew, would stand for no nonsense. When Charles brought his loved one to a polo ball at Lord Vestey's home, Stowell Park in Gloucestershire, Camilla worked her magic spell and succeeded in monopolising him to such an extent that Anna stormed out in a fury. As she roared away into the night in a borrowed BMW, Charles and Camilla were locked in each other's arms on the dance floor. 'Was it a set-up? Hard to say,' said the Palace insider, it certainly worked.'

The message Camilla imparted to Charles that night concentrated his mind wonderfully: finding a suitable bride was no longer merely desirable, it was extremely urgent. Charles did the sensible thing. He consulted his grandmother.

The Prince could not have known that a young Chelsea girl had already made up her mind that she was destined to be his bride. In Bahrain, a wealthy Scottish stockbroker, newly returned from a trip to London, told friends eager for news that he had been to St. Paul's Cathedral in the company of Lady Diana Spencer. 'We were walking through the Whispering Gallery when she suddenly turned to me and declared, "One day I'm going to marry Prince Charles in this church".'

4

ENGAGING THE ENEMY

'I've got to get it right first time'
Prince Charles

FORTY-EIGHT hours before her apotheosis into a royal goddess, Diana almost called the whole thing off. She was led away from a reception at Buckingham Palace in a state of collapse. It was touch and go whether she would marry Prince Charles at St Paul's Cathedral on Wednesday, 29 July, 1981. The breakdown was kept secret from all but the closest members of Diana's family, who had been among the Queen's guests two nights before the wedding. 'Diana looked ravishing in a red dress, but rather wild,' said Reinhold Bartz, who was married to Diana's cousin Alexandra. 'By eleven p.m., her eyes were swollen as if she had been crying. Then she suddenly disappeared. Apparently, she cracked under the strain. She nearly had a nervous breakdown.'

Diana was immediately driven back to Clarence House, the Queen Mother's home in the Mall, put to bed and expertly nursed through the next twenty-four hours. She recovered in time, but it had been a near miss. Before she had even joined the Royal Family, Diana's nightmare had driven her to the brink. Part of the problem was that Charles had arrived at her by a process of elimination – and it had not been a simple process.

With the encouragement of Camilla and his grandmother he had rung Diana at her new home, a three-bedroom apartment she had just bought for £60,000, 60 Coleherne Court in Brompton Road, Earl's Court. Her three flatmates, Carolyn Pride (later the talkative singer Carolyn Bartholomew), Anne Bolton and Virginia Pitman, longed to meet him once they started dating. Charles, however, wouldn't take the risk of being spotted. To avoid being photographed together, he made her drive herself alone to meet him at secret rendezvous of his choosing. When the relationship became more serious, Stephen Barry drove her to Highgrove several times and returned her to

Coleherne Court at daybreak so that it appeared she had spent the night at home, I would frequently collect Lady Diana and whisk her away,' said Barry. 'She would ring and say, "It's Diana". She would give me the address where she could be found and we would drive off for her meeting with the Prince.'

Charles did, however, invite her to watch him play polo for his team, Les Diables Bleus, at Cowdray Park in Sussex. It was after polo one evening that she met a redheaded extrovert who reminded her in some ways of her sister Sarah. This Sarah, however, was called Sarah Margaret Ferguson and they met at the home of her mother and stepfather, Susan and Hector Barrantes. Charles dropped in to talk about polo with Hector, a bear-like Argentinian known as El Gordo who came to England to play for Lord Vestey. Diana started chatting to his stepdaughter.

Wide-eyed at the possibilities, Fergie instantly befriended the newcomer. Her own world was shaping up nicely after the heartbreak of her parents' divorce. She was working as an assistant at Durden-Smith Communications, a public relations outfit based in Knightsbridge. The two trainee Sloanes agreed to meet for coffee (black, no sugar for Fergie; sugarless white for Diana) in the cafeteria of their favourite store, Harvey Nichols. They talked about parents, divorce, men in general, and Prince Charles in particular. There seemed to be a lot of common ground. Fergie, more experienced with the opposite sex, told Diana to stand up for herself. 'She urged Diana to be more assertive,' said a friend. 'She's a great team player like that. Her attitude is, "You do your bit and I'll back you up". Diana liked what she heard.' This was the start of a long, painful journey for both young women.

Charles found that, despite the age gap of twelve-and-a-half years, he could talk to his new partner. Although she cheerfully confessed to reading nothing more challenging than escapist Mills & Boon novellas, Diana had a deeper, more serious side which the receptive Charles found appealing. Her main aim in life, she told him, was to marry happily and to help others less fortunate than herself. Her father's behaviour which had driven her mother away from Park House had left painful emotional scars. The healing process would be helped by finding true love.

She had explained this need to one of her nannies, Mary Clarke, when she was nine years old. 'I can see her now, this child with fair hair down to her shoulders, rosy cheeks and downcast eyes, talking about love,' Mrs Clarke told Geoffrey Levy of the *Daily Mail*, i remember her saying, "I shall only get married when I am sure I am in love so that we will never be divorced". The abiding ambition of this child was simply to marry happily and have children.'

Charles's heart started to rule his head. He responded positively. Many of his own efforts to act as a catalyst, 'to send ripples across the pond to see how far they go', had been unfairly criticised. People laughed at him. Diana sympathised. He missed his great-uncle terribly. Diana comforted him. His spiritual quest had brought nothing but derision of a particularly boorish kind. Diana understood. They began to tune into the same wavelength, even if the music was a confusing mixture of modern and classical. 'Diana realised she had a chance and she was determined to make the most of it,' said a friend. 'But it was more than that; I'm sure she was falling in love and she started to believe Charles might love her.' She was three-quarters right. Charles very nearly fell for her.

An invitation to join the Royal Family on board the Royal Yacht Britannia during the Cowes Week regatta in August 1980, presented Charles with the perfect chance to size up the intriguing young blonde. When she donned the more revealing garb of a figure-clinging swimsuit, he liked what he saw. She was still 'a superb physical specimen'. He became attentive; she encouraged him, laughing at his jokes and treating him like a younger man, but always with respect. She continued to call him Sir.

It was on the banks of the River Dee during a trip to Balmoral, ostensibly to see her sister Jane, that the Press first zeroed in on Lady Diana Spencer. She was spotted watching Charles fish for salmon and the *Sun* reported gleefully on 8 September, 1980: *HE'S IN LOVE AGAIN! Lady Di is the new girl for Charles.* Her nickname had made its first appearance in print, and she hated it from the start. 'She cringes at the very mention of "Di",' said Kevin Shanley. The writer of the story was Harry Arnold, the paper's royal correspondent, who was noted for his Palace contacts. His source on this occasion, however, was Arthur Edwards, the paper's royal photographer. 'A very good friend of mine called Arthur saw this friendship going on at Balmoral,' said Arnold, 'and delivered the immortal words, "She follows him around like a lamb". I took the story from there.'

Charles was perplexed. When he flew to India in the autumn, he sought out the reporter, who was covering the tour. 'I had written that Diana had stayed with him at his new home, Highgrove in Gloucestershire,' recalled Arnold. 'At a reception on the lawns of the British High Commission in New Delhi, the Prince astounded me by walking over and striking up an extraordinary conversation about Diana. "Why do you think she is the girl I want to marry?" he asked me in a tone that was curious rather than aggressive. He went on, "What you don't understand is that just because a girl stays in the same house overnight, it isn't a case of 'Here we go, hooray and whoopee!' In my position I have to live an old-fashioned life." Then he added the prophetic words, "You can afford to make a mistake. I've got to get it right first time."'

'I have since thought long and hard about whether I misinterpreted the meaning of his words,' said Arnold. 'I thought then that he was saying, "How do you know she's the one I'm serious about?" In other words, "How did you rumble me?" I think now that he was very, very unsure – unsure to the point that she was nothing more than another girlfriend at the time and we rather railroaded him. He wanted to know why was I pressing her upon him.'

When Diana visited Sandringham in the New Year, the Royal Family were besieged by newsmen anxious to spot her. Diana knew every twist and turn of the lanes that criss-crossed the Sandringham estate and she used her local knowledge to give newsmen the slip. Her West London home was subjected to a stakeout from eight each morning until after midnight. She was followed to and from the Young England kindergarten in Pimlico. Newsmen were given a merry runaround as Diana became adept at switching cars, jumping red lights and using girlfriends as decoys. Once, she was almost run over. 'Diana was dashing across the road and she and the bonnet of my car ended up making contact,' said Sarah Kennedy. 'She wasn't hurt but it was a near thing.'

Once her initial fright at being followed had been overcome, she worked out a strategy based on a variant of the principle, 'If you can't beat them, join them'. To Diana, it became: If you can't beat them, use them.' She soon learned to manipulate the Press with great skill. This was the aspect of her character that had first concerned Charles over the see-through dress. The pattern now became more obvious. Eyelashes flashing coyly, Diana encouraged journalists to propagate the image of Shy Di, the innocent shrinking violet. Once her uncle, Lord Fermoy, vouched for her virginity ('Diana, I can assure you, has never had a lover'), they stopped looking for previous boyfriends, although a chap called George Plumtre was given the onceover. Young James Gilbey, who lived nearby, barely rated a second glance.

Instead, the Press concentrated on publicising her in a positive way, helped along by little nudges and winks. When her photograph started appearing in print, Diana, naturally enough, took greater care with her appearance. She was more than willing to learn from her mistakes. Thus she started a lasting love affair with her greatest ally, the camera.

'The royal photographers call her Blue Eyes,' said Arthur Edwards. 'She has her eyelashes tinted and it works wonders, giving her a wide-awake look. She has long, long legs and that means she looks good in everything from jeans to a ballgown.' Edwards had endeared himself to Diana one day when photographers blocked her car with empty beer barrels to delay her departure. She promptly burst into tears. The East Ender rolled the kegs away to clear a path and warned her: 'Don't let them see you crying.' 'Diana is a great flirt,' said Mike Lawn, who got to know her well, if you make eye contact with her, she'll start to giggle. She gets this rapport with men like us who she sees around a lot and it's obvious she knows that it makes them feel good. I can't think of any newsman who has met her and doesn't fancy her.'

For Charles, it was time to make up his mind. 'He was under great pressure to get married,' said Harry Arnold. 'The papers were calling him the Clown Prince, he was thirty-something and looking like a bachelor. I believe the Queen said words to the effect, "What's wrong with this one? You've got to marry some day and she seems very likable and attractive and the nation like her already". After a suitable period of vetting, which definitely goes on to see if there are any boyfriends to come out of the woodwork, let alone lovers, it was almost a *fait accompli.* She was crazy about him, but whether she was crazy about the Prince of Wales or Charles Mountbatten-Windsor, we shall never know. Film stars like Robert Redford have experience to fall back upon before they were famous to know if they are attractive to women. But in the case of royalty, they are born to it and it must be a great problem for a man in particular.'

Two days after Charles returned from a skiing holiday in Switzerland in February 1981, he formally proposed to Diana after dinner in the blue sitting room of his *pied-a-terre* at Buckingham Palace. It was the second time he had raised the subject of marriage. Nervously, he had made a trial run when Camilla and her husband arranged a secret meeting at Bolehyde Manor. Legend has it that the Prince of Wales, 'strangely stifled', in Diana's words, first broached the subject in the cabbage patch there, if I were to ask you, do you think it would be possible?' he said. It wasn't a formal proposal, and Diana told friends: 'I couldn't help giggling.' A little prematurely, Camilla opened the celebratory champagne, which was chilling in readiness on the ice. She had known the game plan all along. The Conspiracy had produced a result.

Diana had selected her engagement ring from a tray of rings at a dinner given by the Queen at Windsor Castle. 'The Prince had never been shopping in his life,' said Stephen Barry. 'After dinner, the Prince said to Lady Diana, "Here is the tray". She chose the largest ring on the tray and the Queen's eyes nearly popped out of her head.'

When Diana swanned into Headlines on Monday, 23 February, she found it hard to contain her excitement. Sitting in her usual cream leather chair away from the window, she blurted out to her hairdresser: 'By the way, Kevin, I'm getting engaged tomorrow.' She showed him the engagement ring. He kept her secret, but *The Times,* in a rare breach of protocol, pre-empted the official announcement which was made at eleven a.m. the following morning. An hour later Diana, wearing the sapphire-and-diamond ring (valued at £28,500 in the Garrard & Co catalogue), posed with Charles on the garden steps at Buckingham Palace. She stood one step below him to disguise the one-inch difference in height. The hem of her blue engagement suit from Harrods had been hastily lowered and the crease showed. Charles said that he was 'absolutely delighted and frankly amazed that Diana is prepared to take me on'. Were they in love? 'Yes,' Diana replied swiftly. 'Yes, whatever that is,' murmured Charles.

The Prince had his first row with his fiancée a few days later. After the see-through skirt episode, he thought he had made it plain that she had to dress becomingly. He was absolutely dismayed and frankly appalled when she chose a strapless taffeta ballgown for her first official function on the Court Circular. While the black dress contrasted nicely with her English rose complexion, the plunging neckline drew excited comment from other guests at an opera gala in the City of London. Flashlights exploded like Guy Fawkes' Night as she alighted from a Rolls-Royce outside Goldsmiths Hall and bent down to accept a pink rose from a well-wisher. 'She's been elevated to the cleavage,' quipped one headline writer. If this was the shape of things to come, Shy Di was more intriguing than anyone had thought possible. Charles was furious and he told her so.

This skirmish proved to Diana, still only nineteen, that she was expected to dress, and behave, in a manner acceptable to her future husband. Her own wishes came a poor third after the very particular needs of Charles and the intrusive demands of Palace advisers. Reluctant as she was to become simply an accessory on his arm, or a 'Throne Clone' to suit royal protocol, she was even more terrified of blowing her big chance. Her sense of destiny told her she was the Chosen One, her illness told she wasn't worthy of it.

The situation was saved by the timely intervention of Princess Grace of Monaco, one of the guests that night. Her Serene Highness drew Diana to one side at a Buckingham Palace reception which followed the performance. They chatted privately for a few minutes. 'What shall I do?' Diana asked Grace, according to one of her friends. 'Don't worry, dear,' Grace replied, it'll only get worse.'

Diana relaxed and smiled. Her sense of humour was one of her most attractive qualities. Even though she had been the actress Grace Kelly beforehand, Princess Grace knew all about the problems of switching to the royal stage. 'Sensing the young girl's timidity, Grace went out of her way to put her at ease, an act Diana never forgot,' recalled Steven Englund, Grace's biographer. The feeling was mutual. 'Grace told me over dinner in Monte Carlo that Diana was the daughter she wished she had had,' said an American friend. 'When Grace smiled, you got wobbly — the same effect Diana has on men.' Just over a year after Diana's wedding, Princess Grace was killed in a car crash in which her daughter Princess Stephanie had been injured. Diana represented the Queen at the funeral in Monaco.

Charles's bride had moved into the nursery section at Buckingham Palace not only to be near him, but to be protected from harmful outside influences. When Charles was away on solo royal duties, Diana felt cut off and abandoned. When he was at home, her isolation was even more deeply felt because he often dined alone with the Queen. When she strolled into the Palace kitchens, she was searching not only for between-meal snacks but some company as well. When she ventured outside the Palace walls, Paul Officer never left her side. This stifled any inclination she may have had to share her joy with other people.

Gradually, Diana withdrew into herself, her weight dropped alarmingly, and she began to feel trapped, a prisoner in the Palace that was supposed to protect her. She contacted Fergie, who made the first of several visits to the Palace. The situation had become tricky. Diana, naturally cautious, had hoped Charles would get to know her better during the course of a long engagement. The Queen, however, had told the couple that the wedding should take place without delay. She and Prince Philip were fed up with the fuss. It was disrupting more serious business. By tradition, royal engagements are short, but Diana felt that Her Majesty's advice sounded like an ultimatum. She asked Fergie if she would serve as her lady-in-waiting once she started her duties as the Princess of Wales. Her staunch new friend eagerly agreed, but the Palace vetoed the suggestion. At twenty-one, Miss Ferguson was considered too young, and probably too unruly, to undertake such a responsible position. Her reputation as a Sloane who loved 'going on the toot' was already established in the Chelsea wine bars.

Diana bowed to the pressure and the wedding date was set for Wednesday, 29 July. But it was still not too late to back out.

THE more theatrical side of the Prince's nature now came into play. A frequent guest at other people's weddings, he had spent years planning his own nuptials. 'My marriage has to be forever,' he reminded himself. As a milestone in his life, the wedding eclipsed even his investiture as Prince of Wales, which took place at Carnarvon Castle, coincidently, on Diana's birthday. She was only eight but she had watched the ceremony on the family TV. The investiture was primarily an historical set piece. This was his own show. Above all else, he intended to use the occasion to focus on the role he had struggled so hard to carve for himself.

Charles, and his beautiful bride, would be centre stage in the kind of richly regal tableau Hollywood directors could only dream about. As a piece of theatre, the ceremony would have a rare quality which would not only celebrate England's musical and religious heritage, but express his own aspirations as well. It would be Charles's Triumph, 'I think I shall spend half the time in tears,' he said. At that point, he did not realise that Diana would completely steal the show.

The Lord Chamberlain and other dignitaries whose duty it was to plan the enterprise found the Prince's mastery of stagecraft truly impressive. He selected St Paul's Cathedral as the venue, he explained, because it was more spacious and less gloomy than Westminster Abbey and because the acoustics beneath Wren's vast dome would give greater clarity to the rousing sounds that would accompany the service. As a modern man, he chose the works of twentieth-century composers from Elgar and Walton to Vaughan Williams and Benjamin Britten. The ceremony would reflect his concern for family values; there would be grandeur, and simplicity, in equal measure.

There was another, more sentimental reason behind the choice of the huge cathedral squatting foursquare between the thundering presses of Fleet Street and the mercantile and business heart of the City of London. St Paul's might be Sir Christopher Wren's masterpiece, but it was Charles II, so often portrayed as a squandering womaniser, whose warrant had guided this jewel of English baroque into existence. The Prince knew of his namesake's dedication to the arts and science and, mindful that he would one day rule as Charles III, he turned his wedding into a showcase of everything he cherished about the country he was born to rule. The bells, Great Tom and Great Paul, would ring out the chimes.

'Charles sees himself as a latter-day Renaissance Man,' said the Palace insider. 'He is, in fact, a well-rounded person. He paints well, reads extensively, writes easily and plays the cello passably. He's a romantic, but never forget that he's tough, too.'

Her nerves on edge as the wedding day approached, Diana tried to match the spirit of this enthusiasm. But she was frightened. Her biggest performance to date had been in school plays, nonspeaking roles preferred. If Buckingham Palace overawed her with its silent miles of red-carpeted corridors, creeping footmen and sanctified calm, the prospect of walking down the aisle of that vast amphitheatre in front of 2,500 guests filled her with stomach-churning panic. Other people's expectation of her were so great that she realised she must feel part of the event before it happened or risk the consequences. Her biggest fear was that her father, handicapped since the stroke that nearly killed him, would stumble during the long walk down the aisle, bringing them both crashing down.

Diana desperately needed friends and allies. She drew great strength from the encouragement of Elizabeth and David Emanuel, the twenty-eight-year-old designers she had chosen to make the wedding dress after wearing an Emanuel skirt and blouse for a *Vogue* fashion session with Lord Snowdon. The designers operated from a cramped salon in a tall, narrow building off Brook Street, Mayfair. It was there that they worked on their one-off creation for 'Miss Deborah Smythson Wells', as they code-named the bride.

'We had a meeting with Lady Diana and promised total secrecy – as far as was in our power,' said Elizabeth Emanuel. 'Naturally the project tied in with a lot of people, but we tried to arrange it so no one knew more than they needed for their section. Not even our machinists knew entirely what was happening. They all worked on various dresses so they may have worked on *the* dress and not known it. There wasn't even a sketch. The one we submitted to Lady Diana was torn up immediately and we worked from what was in our heads.' The dress would make the Emanuel label synonymous with the most glamorous wedding for years. Diana may have felt slightly unnerved if she had known that the couple were secretly estranged.

The bride quietened her wedding day nerves by eating an enormous breakfast and, after seemingly endless preparation, stepped into the Glass Coach for the journey from Clarence House to St Paul's. 'My dear, you look simply enchanting,' the Queen Mother had told her. As the Emanuels folded the twenty-five-foot long train into the coach, Diana threw back her head and serenaded them. 'Just one Cornetto,' sang the bride, in the words of a TV ice-cream commercial. 'Give it to me ....' The coach door closed and she and her father set off for St Paul's through streets packed with a million well-wishers, the waves of cheering reaching a crescendo as they approached the cathedral.

The night before, Charles had assured Diana in a note: 'I'm so proud of you and when you come up the aisle I'll be there at the altar for you. Just look 'em in the eye and knock 'em dead.'

ROW upon row of guests craned to catch a glimpse of the bride. To the soaring brass and booming drumbeat of the Trumpet Voluntary, she appeared at the West Door in the Emanuel dress, a crinoline of ivory-silk taffeta embroidered with mother-of-pearl sequins and pearls. Crumpled in the coach, the dress had survived in all its glory. Lace flounces, meeting stylishly in a bow, set off the V-shaped neckline. For good luck, a shiny new horseshoe and a blue bow had been sewn to the waist. The 'something old' on the bodice was Carrick-ma-cross lace, which had belonged to Queen Mary. The 'something borrowed' were diamond earrings belonging to her mother. Right on cue, Earl Spencer moved unsteadily forward, his youngest daughter on the arm of his grey morning suit. Following cautiously in the wake of the twenty-five-foot-long train came her friend Lady Sarah Armstrong-Jones, three other bridesmaids and two pages dressed as midshipmen.

As Diana walked slowly down the nave, her head bowed briefly beneath the Spencer family's diamond tiara and, through the tulle veil, her eyelashes began to flutter. She tried to 'look 'em in the eye' and Fergie, for one, beamed back brightly. Princess Grace and Lady Tryon smiled encouragingly. No one knew enough to check Camilla's reaction.

The ivory-silk wedding slippers gripped the red carpet and it appeared more than once that Diana was in charge, guiding her brave father on the longest journey of his life. For strength, her right hand gripped the bridal bouquet, a fragrant array of gardenias, freesias, stephanotis, white orchids, lilies-of-the-valley, a sprig of myrtle from a bush planted at Osborne House from Queen Victoria's posy and, in his memory, golden roses named after Lord Mountbatten. A world-wide television audience of 750 million was gripped by this moving picture of youthful elegance. In Charles's words, she knocked 'em dead. To those closest to her, Diana appeared even more beautiful: a vision drawn from the misty hues of a Gainsborough palette.

At last, she reached Charles, resplendent in the full-dress uniform of a Royal Navy commander, on a raised dais at the foot of the chancel steps. Smiling, he said: 'You look wonderful.' 'Wonderful for you,' she replied. If she had rehearsed that bit, it had the desired effect. Her nerves calmed down, but only momentarily. When she had to repeat Charles's names after the Archbishop of Canterbury, she fluffed her lines. She called her groom Philip Charles Arthur George by mistake, causing Prince Andrew, who was acting as supporter to Charles along with Prince Edward, to quip: 'She's married my father!' Charles showed that he, too, was not immune to the tension by saying: 'And all thy goods with thee I share' instead of 'And all my worldly goods with thee I share'. Significantly, Diana did not promise to obey her thrifty husband.

'Here is the stuff of which fairy-tales are made,' the Archbishop, Dr Robert Runcie, told the congregation. 'All couples on their wedding day are royal couples. Let us pray that the burdens we lay on Charles and Diana be matched by the love with which we support them in the years to come.'

To Elgar's Pomp and Circumstance and Walton's Crown Imperial, the Prince and Princess of Wales walked out of the cathedral, coincidently a temple to the goddess Diana in Roman times. Until that moment, they had been distant cousins through many generations of their family trees. He was her seventh cousin once removed through William Cavendish, third Duke of Devonshire; tenth cousin twice removed through King James I; eleventh cousin through Queen Elizabeth of Bohemia; and fifteenth cousin once removed through King Henry VII.

Charles had become the first Prince of Wales to marry on the sacred site since 1501. To Diana went the distinction of being the first Princess of Wales to be married in the present St Paul's. But she had surrendered her Christian name in the process. Her correct form of address was now Her Royal Highness the Princess of Wales. The 'Princess Diana' title was just an honorary accolade from Fleet Street. In terms of royal precedence she ranked third to the Queen and the Queen Mother among women throughout the United Kingdom. It was a moment to savour.

Queen Victoria had described Princess Alexandra, her predecessor as Princess of Wales, as 'one of those sweet creatures who seem to come from the skies to help and bless poor mortals and to brighten for a time their path'. The words would prove a fitting epitaph to Diana's marriage.

CAMILLA Parker Bowles had lived rent free in Diana's head in the five months between the engagement and the wedding. She had the unnerving knack of turning up unexpectedly, always *au fait* with what was happening. Diana's faith in Charles had become touchingly naive once the sapphire ring was on her finger. She believed that he would forsake his former girlfriend and learn to love her instead. But the Curse of Camilla continued to blight Diana's life; it seemed to follow her everywhere. Her presence at almost every royal social occasion was an affront that she was powerless to combat. When she blurted out her suspicions, her sisters Sarah and Jane told her she was on edge; her imagination was exaggerating the importance of the other woman.

Diana stifled her doubts and carried on bravely, but her Cancerian instincts had been correct. Just before the wedding, according to Andrew Morton, Diana opened a parcel to find a gold bracelet with a blue enamel disc and the entwined initials 'F' and 'G'. She knew they stood for 'Fred' and 'Gladys', said Morton, the pet names secretly used by Charles and Camilla. Others said it stood for 'Girl Friday', the Prince's term of endearment for his mistress. There was an outside chance that both were right. Certainly the bracelet activated Diana's alarm system. When she challenged her fiancé, he reacted in exactly the same dismissive manner as he had over other incidents. Diana was left to guess whether his relationship with Camilla was still alive and, in the absence of any firm assurance to the contrary, she concluded that it was. Her bulimia resurfaced and she was frequently ill and tearful. This was the reason she had nearly cracked up at the Queen's reception in front of her own family.

Unknown to her, though, Charles had also been anguishing over his decision. Proud of her though he undoubtedly was, he knew in his heart that he did not love her. if they had been honest with each other, they could have saved themselves from so much pain,' said a friend. But so committed were the Windsors and the Spencers to this union of the heir and his fair lady that there could be no turning back.

Arthur may not have found his Guinevere, but the Professor had married Eliza. Not before some hesitation, the couple sealed this royal version of *Pygmalion* with a kiss on the balcony of Buckingham Palace. As the crowd chanted: 'Kiss her, kiss her,' Prince Andrew nudged his brother to comply.

'Go on,' he urged. 'Kiss her!'

'I'm not getting into that caper,' replied Charles, embarrassed. He turned to his mother.

'May I?' he asked.

Her Majesty gave her blessing. The audience cried for an encore.

The honeymoon began with a three-day break at Broadlands, which Diana hoped would give her and Charles a chance to relax in each other's company. She knew that the great mansion held many painful memories of Lord Mountbatten for her husband; perhaps she could reach him there. After weeks of hectic, late-night planning and partying, the newlyweds virtually collapsed during the ninety-mile ride from Waterloo Station to Hampshire in the Royal Train. Diana had scored one small, but symbolic victory: neither Camilla nor Kanga had been invited to the wedding breakfast at the Palace. They lunched elsewhere, Kanga with friends at San Lorenzo.

Diana sipped her champagne and cheered up. But the Royal Train was, in itself, a painful reminder of an assignation which had taken place between Charles and an unidentified blonde eight months earlier. Diana told friends she had been astonished when the *Sunday Mirror* reported that she had joined Charles while the train was standing overnight in a siding at Holt in Wiltshire on 5 November. She claimed she was at home, nursing a hangover after attending a party thrown by Princess Margaret at the Ritz. 'I am telling you the absolute truth,' said Diana. 'I stayed in all that evening with my three flatmates, Virginia, Carolyn and Anne. I had some supper and watched television before going to bed early. I don't even know what the Royal Train looks like.'

Reporters who worked on the story, based on a tip-off from a reliable informant, were reluctant to admit they got it wrong, but one finally conceded: 'Right train, wrong girl. I thought it might have been her sister Sarah,' he said. The story had tormented Diana ever since. She now believed that Charles had, indeed, received a late-night guest: Camilla Parker Bowles.

At Broadlands, the Prince and Princess of Wales slept in the Portico Room, overlooking the lawns that ran down to the River Test and shaded from the westering sun by massive columns. The past crowded in. The Queen and Prince Philip had slept in this four-poster during their honeymoon in 1947. So had Lord Louis and Edwina. Guests like to search the curtains for a motif woven into the 1854 chintz fabric. It traced the profiles of young Queen Victoria and her beloved Prince Albert. The intimacy Diana had prayed for was difficult to capture in the excited bustle of the great mansion. They rarely seemed to be alone. By day, Charles went fishing while she sat silently on the bank.

One of the most treasured heirlooms at Broadlands was a fragment of the wedding dress of Mountbatten's twenty-first great-grandmother, Saint (no less) Elizabeth. Just weeks before his murder, Lord Louis told the legend behind it to Chris Hutchins.

'The ruler whom Elizabeth married was a very hard man on his subjects, and it was in defiance of his strictest instructions that she carried bread to the poor in her apron when he went out hunting,' said Mountbatten. 'He suspected she was doing this and returned one day to catch her out. "What have you got in your apron?" he asked, and she replied, "Roses, sire". "Roses in winter? A likely story. Show me." "Oh God, let it be roses," she prayed, and as she opened her apron, roses fell out. She was canonised by the Pope.'

At Broadlands, Diana learned that her own struggle was just beginning. When she later declared: 'My husband has taught me everything I know,' the compliment was like a double-edged sword aimed straight at his heart.

5

KENSINGTON PALLAS

'It was as if he was married to them, not me, and they
were so patronising it drove me mad'
Diana, Princess of Wales

BEFORE the House of Wales was irrevocably split by divided royalties, Charles and Diana proved that they could be a world-beating team. When they placed their differences on hold, the myth of 'the perfect couple' became momentarily real and the effect was dazzling. They were able to achieve far more than anyone else on the royal payroll, and that included the Queen and Prince Philip.

Diana's charisma and her husband's title had great pulling power among members of the Big Hitters' League, the unofficial name for the rich benefactors who funded many royal charities. 'She was seen as a cross between Cleopatra and Cinderella, and he was the luckiest man alive,' said one big player. 'Everyone wanted to meet them, and they were prepared to pay handsomely for the privilege.' There was no more graphic example of this than the occasion Charles and Diana raised £1.2 million for charity in a single night. For a short period, Wales Inc. was a going concern and it prospered.

At the time of their marriage, Charles had promised, at Diana's insistence, that he would cool his relationships with Camilla Parker Bowles and Lady Tryon. He refused to freeze them out completely, but he agreed with Diana that she must rate as the most important woman in his life. In return, she promised to fit in with royal life as best she could. The pact seemed to work for the first three years, during which Prince William and Prince Harry were born. But Charles, according to his wife's friends, never really honoured his side of the bargain. His heart wasn't in it once the arguments started. When Diana found out that he was still secretly in touch with the Twin-set Twins, particularly Camilla, she exploded. She felt betrayed and she lost her temper.

Even as early as their extended honeymoon, a bedroom was wrecked and there were highly disagreeable arguments at Balmoral. 'They came down to breakfast one morning as though everything was all right,' said a guest. 'But both side tables to the bed in their room had been knocked over and both lamps were smashed. When this was discovered, they said they had had a pillow fight. But I think it was a proper fight.' 'Diana started to give voice to the screams that had been mounting inside her for months,' said a friend. 'She more or less forced a deal out of Charles.'

In the face of this domestic disharmony, the Prince reacted in character. He put some distance between himself and the problem. He moved out of the marital bedroom, first into a dressing room at Balmoral, and then into a spare room in Kensington Palace. He made excuses to spend more time at Highgrove, which the Duchy of Cornwall had bought for him to use just before his engagement.

The Gloucestershire estate became his Shangri-La, a haven where he could retrace the lost horizons of his bachelor days. 'I have put my heart and soul into Highgrove,' he declared. His landscaping, gardening and farming activities there were 'the physical expression of a personal philosophy'. It was also a place where he could express himself physically and personally with Camilla. She would later act as hostess at his dinner parties.

'Mrs Parker Bowles behaved just as though she and the Prince were married,' said one familiar with the household. 'She chose the menu, supervised the cooking and helped select the dinner guests. When they arrived, they treated her with all the respect you would expect them to give the Princess of Wales. They did everything but curtsy to her. Many of the staff felt disloyal simply by being there when Mrs Parker Bowles was granding it over everyone. There was very strong feeling about the way the Prince was behaving in humiliating his wife.'

Charles's friends claimed that it was Diana's bulimic behaviour and her irrational tantrums that drove him back into Camilla's arms. The truth was somewhere in the middle, in every marriage break-up, there are three stories: His, Hers and the Truth,' said one friend.

Yet at the mid-point of their married life the Waleses had come to identify the influences that were driving them apart. If they couldn't resolve their differences, they could at least 'keep it between themselves' for the sake of the children. Diana consulted several doctors and psychiatrists about her bulimia and the post-natal depression which had followed each birth. The result was a shaky stalemate which signalled a let-up in hostilities if not exactly the outbreak of unconditional peace. After a very unpromising start, things began to get a little better.

It was during this brief reprieve that Wales Inc. went into action to spectacular effect. Harry Goodman, the East End-born holiday tycoon, was serving a term as Chief Barker of the Variety Club of Great Britain in 1986 when he received an unexpected call. 'My secretary told me Prince Charles was on the line and I said, "You're kidding!" I'd met him socially at film premieres and that sort of thing, but you still don't expect to get that kind of phone call. It came right out of the blue. Charles said he'd been introduced to the Rev Ted Noffs, an Australian clergyman who was visiting England after being voted Australia's Man of the Year. He ran this church in Kings Cross, Sydney, right in the middle of the city's drug culture. He had launched a programme called Life Educational to teach children about the dangers of drug abuse. Special caravans drove around giving animated shows to children and the results had been so successful he wanted to introduce the same sort of thing in Britain. Charles asked me to meet him to see if we could raise the money to get it off the ground. I saw Ted Noffs at my office, he was a terrific guy, and we had a series of meetings with the Prince and Princess of Wales and other members of the Variety Club.

'One evening, Ted and I turned up at Kensington Palace for a meeting and found Diana playing with the kids in the garden. I'd never been there before and it was incredible to see how normal it was. Diana was wearing a pair of jeans and, as we sat down inside, she said, "Would you like some tea?" She actually poured the tea. It was a small thing, but I was absolutely gobsmacked because I thought there would be liveried flunkeys to do it. She was still in her jeans and there was a lovely atmosphere; it was terrific, just fabulous. I sat there thinking, "The Princess of Wales poured me a cup of tea" and I realised that's how you fall in love with the woman. That's the charm.

'The mobile units cost £60,000 each to put on the road and we discussed the best way to sponsor them. I told the Prince that we would need his backing and he and the Princess agreed to do a dinner. It was up to us what sort of dinner we did. We could either do the traditional thing and get a thousand people at £50 a head or try something quite different. Myself and one or two other people decided the best way would be to do a very select dinner for twenty Big Hitters who would each pay £60,000 for the privilege. Charles and Diana said it couldn't be done, no one would pay that kind of money, but they agreed to take part. We booked it at the Dorchester Hotel: twenty couples at sixty grand a couple. It wasn't easy, but it took no more than a month to set up and we raised £1,200,000 in one night.

'We took adjoining suites, one with a balcony for a cocktail reception, and next to it a huge dining room with five tables laid out. Ted Noffs was there and it was a tremendous success – a warm, caring evening. I won't name the guest list, but they were either very rich individuals or people sponsored by major companies. Everyone made a thing about it being very anonymous, but they paid £60,000 to go.

'Charles and Diana both looked terrific – they *were* terrific – and they seemed very happy. If there were any problems in their relationship, it didn't show. It's said the marriage was bad from the beginning but I don't believe it. She's a lot of fun, obviously, and his sense of humour is a lot drier, but they were a lovely couple. They chatted to everyone and Charles made an anti-drug speech. Diana was the star but she wasn't the confident lady she is today. She was quite nervous and I did think, "It can't be easy to marry someone with his background. How do you marry into the Firm?"'

The Firm, of course, was one of the key symptoms of Diana's real problem. When she inadvisedly called the other royals 'this f***ing family' a few years later, she was speaking from bitter experience. She had found out that, in her own words, 'being a princess is not all it's cracked up to be'.

DIANA had to put her natural home-making flair to one side while she perfected her new role as the Princess of Wales. The 'double apartment' she and Charles were to occupy at Kensington Palace presented great possibilities for imaginative design. Really a three-storey house with twenty-five rooms, Apartments Eight and Nine had been derelict since they were firebombed during the Battle of Britain in 1940. Restoration work had been completed inside and out just before the engagement. The grace-and-favour residence Prince

Charles called 'the perfect present-day home in London' still needed to be decorated. He was happy to leave it to Diana, who eagerly responded to the challenge. But she found that her consultations with Dudley Poplak, the interior designer, had to be fitted in between other, more pressing, engagements.

Diana was now a working royal and she had promised Charles that this would be her main priority. From the moment she stepped outside their temporary home in his bachelor quarters at Buckingham Palace, she was on show until the wrought-iron gates closed behind her late at night. When she collapsed into their four-poster bed, she was aware that she was sleeping under her mother-in-law's roof. Even more off-putting for a newly-wed, she suspected Charles had shared the same bed with Camilla and other girlfriends. There was the added discomfort of having to live in the presence of courtiers and staff committed to running the Sovereign's household. She felt that even the lowest footman was smirking behind a gloved hand. They had been there before her; they knew Charles's secrets. Diana was made painfully aware like others before her that, even inside the Palace, she was regarded as an outsider.

The same applied whenever the royal roadshow moved to Windsor, Balmoral or Sandringham with as many as two hundred retainers in tow. The Windsors could never be called a close family, although they were close-knit in the most tribal way. Diana found the atmosphere in the Queen's circle stifling to the point of suffocation. When she complained to Charles, he told her bluntly that she would have to adapt. To escape the tedium of Balmoral, she once flew to London to go shopping for a few hours and was roundly criticised. Nothing so far remotely resembled the intimate married lifestyle she had longed for as a child searching for true love. She had been warned about the pressures of royal life, but the reality was much more demanding. An unending cycle of packing, unpacking, hairdressing, clothes-changing and briefings to meet rigid Palace schedules began to exact a high price on her health.

She was fortunate that, instead of Fergie, her chief lady-in-waiting was Anne Beckwith-Smith, a cheerful woman and a very capable organiser. Fergie, however, continued to call and her advice rarely varied: 'Stand up for yourself.' Diana was always on the go and her weight kept falling. 'I'm exhausted, but I can't let people down,' she told a friend.

Her initiation as a fully-fledged royal had been a three-day tour of Wales a few weeks after they returned from the three-month honeymoon, which had included a Mediterranean cruise in *Britannia* and a trip to Egypt. Diana had just become pregnant with William and morning sickness, coupled with outbreaks of bulimia, left her drained and frightened. Even Charles, who had been carrying out royal duties for most of his life, found it difficult to accept his altered status. For a start, he had to think in the plural, the 'royal we' now meaning precisely that. Yet the understandable, though selfish, habit of thinking mainly of himself was so deeply ingrained that he began to have regrets. Unless he was travelling with his parents, Charles had always been the centre of attention, the unchallenged Number One. Proud as he was of his new wife, he was more than a little jealous of her instant fame. He was, he found, now definitely Number Two.

Diana's star quality had been evident on their wedding day and if Charles had any doubts that he had been relegated to second place, they were soon removed. In wet and windy Wales, the crowds made it patently clear that they had turned out to see Diana. Her appeal was overpowering. People who had seen the film now wanted to meet the star. Among ordinary folk, she rated higher than Elizabeth Taylor, Barbra Streisand or any of the Hollywood icons she watched so avidly in *Dallas* or *Dynasty*. Sick as she was, she gave great value. 'Poor you! I feel cold myself,' she told one shivering woman. 'My hands are freezing – and you must be much worse. Thank you for waiting for us.' The common touch was genuine and heart-warming.

If people admired Charles, they adored Diana. She developed an instantaneous street cred that crossed the barriers of sex, age, race and class. No one ever got close enough to Madonna to ask for a kiss, let alone get one. From early on, Diana kissed children, their grandparents and everyone else in between. People reached out to touch her. She embraced them by the thousand and laid her healing hands on the crippled and the sick. Through the media, she became the most recognisable image in world popular culture. She brought joy to complete strangers, but she was suffering inside. Since her engagement, she had lost twenty-eight pounds in weight.

'Diana was brilliant because she's got an obsessional personality which is just right for the job,' said the titled Chelsea lady, it's a pity she had to marry anybody, but that was the thing that got her into the limelight.'

At first, Charles seemed bemused. 'Over here, Darling,' he called out to guide her to yet another cluster of well-wishers. When this wasn't enough, he said awkwardly: 'I haven't get enough wives; I've only got one.' Very quickly Charles found that he had been marginalised and it hurt his vanity. 'We want Di!' the expectant crowds chanted wherever they went. He had never expected to have to compete with his wife for the affection of his future subjects. It took him some time to work up a joke good enough to save face. When people groaned if he left the royal car on their side to start a walkabout, he quipped: it's not fair, is it? You'd better ask for your money back.' Initially, he sent her love gifts as tokens of his appreciation, but he was hurt and the gulf between them widened.

Diana kept reassuring herself that things would be different once they moved into 'the KP condo'. Her bulimia was now a serious problem. At official dinners, she chased food around her plate with her knife and fork, i cut it up, move it around, and bring my fork to my lips without taking a mouthful,' she told a friend. This is a strategy commonly used by people with eating disorders. 'They do it so that others cannot tell precisely how little or how much they are eating,' said a counsellor in food addiction.

Secretly, Diana binged on Frosties, sliced apple and caster sugar covered in cream. Chocolate cakes and tubs of ice-cream were other favourites. Her drugs of choice, in the addict's vernacular, were sugar and white flour, which gave her an artificial 'high', if they are abused, they are as lethal and mood-altering as other drugs,' said the counsellor. 'Compulsive vomiting to avoid obesity is also very dangerous – it can cause internal haemorrhaging.'

Just five weeks before her baby was due, Apartments 8, 8c and 9 had been finally converted to a single home, but by this time the damage had been done. 'Diana should have had her own place from the beginning,' said a friend, if the Queen hadn't pushed for an early wedding, everything could have been made ready. A home of your own wasn't much to ask in a family like that. As it was, Diana was worn out by the royal routine and very unsettled in herself.'

'Do I really look that thin?' she asked another friend after seeing one set of pictures in the papers. 'I'm not starving myself — I eat what I want.' The adulation, however, was feeding only her ego; the illness was gnawing away at her self-worth. She was deeply aware of what she later called 'the quest for perfection' which left her 'gasping for breath at every turn'. She admitted to friends that some stories in the Press upset her so much that she wanted to lock herself away for days, 'I get an awful feeling deep down inside,' she said miserably. Later, she described this 'disease' as 'feelings of guilt, self-revulsion and low personal esteem'. Even something as relatively harmless as criticism of her clothes could have a depressing effect on her morale. One barb among a thousand bouquets caused pain.

Isolation, however, wasn't an option. She had to show up and show willing. 'There were times when she was close to tears,' said the friend. 'She was unhappy with the constant, relentless demand of public duties.' She 'ate' these uncomfortable feelings of self-doubt and uncertainty by heavy bingeing, then purged herself by induced vomiting. Bulimia had become her 'shameful friend' once again.

SO it was that the Prince took the unhappy mother of the unborn heir he wanted to call Arthur to his Kensington Camelot. Through the white Georgian front door, they entered the hall and walked across the green and grey carpet patterned with his three-feathered crest. The beautifully restored, hand-carved staircase led to a huge drawing room, its walls a shade of soothing yellow, and to a dining room, complete with a circular mahogany table big enough to seat sixteen. This was where Charles planned to run the social side of Wales Inc. in the egalitarian manner of King Arthur himself. The highest and the lowest would sit side by side at the round table and discuss the projects closest to his heart.

'My trouble is that I feel very strongly about things,' he said, 'I can't help it. I don't know where it comes from.' His determination to change society certainly did not stem from the previous holder of his title. When Edward VIII said 'something must be done' about poverty among the Welsh miners, he had already decided to abdicate and promptly did so, abandoning the miners and everyone else.

Edward had called Kensington Palace 'the Aunt Heap' because so many of his elderly relatives lived inside its seventeenth-century brick walls. The modern-day residents were Prince and Princess Michael of Kent, the Duke and Duchess of Gloucester and Princess Margaret. As a newcomer, Diana soon found out that the neighbours could be just as difficult as those in any other tight-knit community. She discovered that she was not in Camelot at all but a daily soap opera which might be called Coronet Street or, better still, Kensington Pallas. Each episode centred around some facet of life among the royals.

When a wrought-iron gateway at the end of Princess Michael's garden was bricked up for security reasons caused by the Waleses' arrival, she was duly annoyed. After that, relations between the two households were more than a little strained. Charles had cause to tell his glamorous neighbour not to remonstrate with his staff, one of whom had sworn within her hearing. The Princess had told the servant to mind his language. Charles told her to mind her own business.

On top of the palace, Diana and Charles had a roof garden big enough to hold a sizable party. Charles became the chef, cooking salmon steaks, corn on the cob and potatoes baked in foil on a barbeque. The smells wafting into Princess Michael's home were so tempting that she built a roof garden for herself. Unfortunately, it only had room for two people and it overlooked the Waleses' bedroom.

'Diana and Princess Michael don't get on, one gathers,' said the titled Chelsea lady. 'Princess Michael was born an Austrian baroness and, although she was raised in Sydney, she's just too forthright for the British – much too pushy, bossy and obvious. But if you look at her, she's a stunning woman and Prince Michael is obviously crackers about her.'

Eventually, a truce of sorts was declared, at least between Charles and the former Marie-Christine von Reibnitz. They found that they shared a mutual love of opera, it has become a custom for them to go together to the Royal Opera House in Covent Garden,' revealed Father Charles Roux, a spiritual confidant of Princess Michael. 'As Princess Diana is not so interested in opera, she is happy to stay at home. They are keen for their evenings out to stay secret so they never use the Royal Box. Instead, they wait until the lights go down and quietly enter another box nearby. Just before the lights go up, they leave as discreetly as they arrived.'

If things were rocky for the Waleses, they were even more turbulent at times for Princess Michael and the Queen's bearded cousin. She had been arranging discreet meetings with a divorced property tycoon, J. Ward Hunt of Dallas, Texas. Word of the assignations was passed to the *News of the World* by a friend who was dismayed at her husband's distress. When the liaison became headline news, Princess Michael returned to the family fold, crestfallen and repentant.

A mutual dislike of Princess Michael gave Diana and Princess Margaret a stimulating talking point. Marie-Christine had never been invited to dine with Princess Margaret, who lived in Apartment 1A at the end of a long passage which ran to the opposite side of the palace. A full-scale feud erupted after Lord Linley, Margaret's furniture-making son, insulted his unpopular relative. Asked what he would give his worst enemy for Christmas, Linley replied: 'Dinner with Princess Michael of Kent.' Prince Michael confronted Linley and demanded that he 'explain himself. Princess Michael told him: 'Don't ever speak to me again, you disgusting boy.' She turned the tables neatly by saying that she would give her worst enemy some of Linley's handmade furniture.

The truth was that Margaret had refused point-blank to accept Princess Michael, a divorcee, into the Family. The explosive issue of divorce had been used to prevent Margaret from marrying Peter Townsend, although he had been the innocent party in his marital breakdown. Margaret, a devout Anglican, had bowed to the Church's wishes. She resented the fact that Marie-Christine, after divorcing her first husband, stockbroker Tom Troubridge, by mutual consent, had had the marriage annulled. In the eyes of the Catholic Church, she was then free to marry Prince Michael. 'Margaret has not had a happy life herself and has become rather bitter,' said Father Roux. 'She feels she is losing some of her ground to Princess Michael and sees her as a rival, a challenge. As well as the age difference, Margaret does not like Catholics.'

After her marriage broke up, Margaret entertained a wide circle of friends from the Arts, the theatre and the New World. One of her American guests was Lynn Wyatt, socialite wife of the Texas oil tycoon, Oscar Wyatt Jnr. She was the mother of Steve Wyatt, who was mixing with a fast crowd in New York in the company of his Houston buddy, Johnny Bryan. Lynn hoped he would move to London, where he might acquire a little gentility. 'Lynn was very anxious to see Steve get married and settle down,' said a friend in her home town of Houston. 'Princess Margaret knew Steve from her visits to Allington (the Wyatt home) and they talked about finding the right girl for him.'

The glamorous Lynn, who held themed birthdays parties every year at La Mauresque, the Wyatt villa at Cap Ferrat, collected royalty wherever she went. She moved with ease from the Palm Beach polo pitch via the Ascot turf to the green baize of Monte Carlo. A particular friend had been Diana's saviour, Princess Grace. Through polo, and later her royal connections, Lynn got to know Sarah Ferguson. One day she would invite the next Duchess of York to Houston for a meeting with her son that would change their lives.

For the time being, however, Fergie was enjoying life to the full. She called at KP to visit Diana in between trips to Verbier, the Swiss resort known to regulars as Chelsea-on-Skis. Excitedly, she told Diana she had moved in with the Grand Prix millionaire Paddy McNally at his chalet, Les Gais Lutins, the Gay Gnomes. This was the hub of the Verbier social scene, her first taste of Jet-set life, and she dazzled Diana with gossip about the Verbier bon vivants. Her plan was to marry McNally, a widower with two young sons, and share his life in Formula One motor racing.

Of the senior royals, Diana felt most comfortable with Princess Margaret, whom she referred to as Auntie Margo. She also got along well with her daughter, Lady Sarah Armstrong-Jones. Margo was a heavy drinker and an even heavier smoker, neither of which was condoned inside the wholesome Wales household. When Margo came to dinner, she made her own rules. She knew about Diana's behaviour at Balmoral during the honeymoon and, Scotch and Malvern water in hand, offered some worldly wise advice. To her credit, Margaret tried to help, but she could see problems ahead.

Only the Gloucesters seemed to lead a life approaching domestic bliss. Richard, the Duke of Gloucester, had married Birgitte Eva van Deurs and raised three children with a minimum of fuss. 'She was a secretary at the Danish Embassy and they met when she was attending the Bell School in Cambridge,' said the titled Chelsea lady. 'He was at Magdalene doing architecture and he fell hook, line and sinker for her. They got married in a very quiet wedding at Barnwell Manor, the family house at Peterborough. The Queen relies on Birgitte to do some of her spadework, and she has done it so successfully that she's been given the Royal Victorian Order. She takes precedence over Princess Alexandra, the Duchess of Kent and

Princess Michael, but you wouldn't realise it. She keeps a very low profile and just gets on with her work.'

Birgitte was the secret royal. At times, Diana envied her role outside the limelight. She also envied Fergie's freedom in the Swiss Alps.

BEHIND the white Georgian door of numbers 8 & 9, the arguments took on a more serious tone. Diana's addictive illness played havoc with her emotions. No matter how Charles responded, Diana always returned to the central theme: 'Prove that you love me.' Nothing he did was ever enough. Baffled and hurt, he retreated into his soundproofed study to play opera at full volume while Diana brooded in front of the TV in her private sitting room. But he didn't always back down. When Diana issued instructions to staff one morning without telling him, he was livid, and he let her know in no uncertain terms. Shouting, he marched into her pastel green dressing room while she was having her hair done. Sitting at her white, kidney-shaped dressing table in front of a gilt mirror, Diana remained unruffled as Charles complained vigorously.

'It was rather awkward for me, to say the least,' said the hairdresser, Kevin Shanley, who was caught in the middle of the furore. 'So I turned my hairdryer on to full blast to try to drown them out. When Charles had made his point, he stormed out of the room. Diana wasn't at all bothered – in fact she joked, "A good job it wasn't something serious." ' In fact, Diana had enjoyed the outburst in front of a witness because it proved that Charles wasn't the mild-mannered paragon of popular myth. Most of these semi-public tiffs were described by an insider as 'heated words, not blazing rows'. They were still calling each other Darling, if only for the sake of appearances. Soon after Prince William's birth in the Lindo Wing at St Mary's, Paddington on 21 June 1982, Charles left his home to play polo, saying fondly: 'I'll try to score for you and Wills, Darling.' Once again, a witness was present so it was possible that Charles was only playing to the gallery.

To visitors, Diana seemed to have it made according to every maxim in the Sloane Ranger manual. After William's birth, she had regained her figure by strenuous exercise with the Jane Fonda workout and her diet seemed healthy. Nearly every day, she drove herself to Buckingham Palace to swim in her mother-in-law's pool.

She was spotted dancing along the corridors, a Sony Walkman blaring music into each ear. At home, she was very informal, cherishing her moments of freedom off the royal rota. She didn't mind if staff saw her walking around in a calf-length dressing gown of pink or white towelling, matched by open-toed slippers. In summer, she wore a brightly-coloured silky kimono.

While Charles was away, she filled the apartment with the loud pop sounds of Neil Diamond, Supertramp and Spandau Ballet. Another favourite was the ballad singer Barry Manilow. 'He's gorgeous but he needs a wife to look after him,' she decided after meeting him backstage following a concert, i would have said she was enjoying life,' said one visitor to KP. 'It's still hard to believe that it was a parody.'

Word began to creep out that all was far from harmonious in the Wales household. Below stairs, Diana, not Charles, was referred to by some servants as 'The Boss', and it was claimed that she was 'an arrogant tyrant'. When staff began to resign in embarrassing numbers, she was accused of driving them away. This hurt her so much that she declared: 'I want you to understand that I am not responsible for any sackings. I just don't sack people.'

The impression, however, gained credence when her brother said: 'She is an exceptionally kind and thoughtful person, but nobody is saying she is a fool. She has weeded out quite a few hangers-on that she has found round her husband and his family in a subtle way.' Althorp was, in fact, referring to some of Charles's friends, not to members of the staff, a point which was hastily clarified. The distinction only served to alienate those in the Prince's camp who found Diana far from subtle. She made it plain that she had little time for many of the men Charles had collected in what one observer termed 'the Class Menagerie — both the people in his service and the ones in his set.' 'Noddies,' Diana called them. Yes-men.

At polo, Charles had only to hold out his hand between chukkas and a glass of water would instantly materialise. He had been waited on, literally hand and foot, since birth. He never needed to change a razor blade or put the cap on the toothpaste, 'I was astonished by some of the men I met at Highgrove,' said a visitor from London. 'He surrounds himself with buffoons.'

Despite her earlier denial, Diana admitted that she had resented Charles's original staff, it was as if he was married to them, not me, and they were so patronising it drove me mad.' The first to depart after the wedding was Stephen Barry, who had served at Buckingham Palace for sixteen years, rising from a humble footman to the elevated rank of Charles's personal valet. Surrounded by a world rich in privilege and possessions, Barry began to develop expensive tastes far beyond his Palace income or station. 'Stephen worshipped the Prince – he did everything for him and gradually started to imitate him,' said Philip Benjamin, a former steward on the *Britannia*. 'He became a Prince Charles clone. He was an ordinary working class lad but developed a taste for classical music, expensive clothes, foreign travel and the finest things in life. Whenever he went shopping for the Prince, he bought himself exactly the same. He wore the same shirts, the same suits and he even had his shoes hand-made like Charles.'

Diana realised she had to make a stand after Barry barred her from the Prince's study just before the engagement. He told her Charles was too busy to see her, but she swept past him and confronted Charles about the valet's proprietorial manner. After the wedding, she insisted that Barry would have to go. He had been punched in the eye at a gay club and photographed wrestling with a male model during a function to promote the American pop group Village People at the Royal College of Art. 'He used to say he resigned but he was pushed and she did the pushing,' said a friend. 'He called her a spoiled brat.' As her later work with AIDS sufferers showed, Diana was far from homophobic. She just didn't want Barry, a snobbish poseur, anywhere near her while she tried to settle into royal life.

Charles Althorp, for one, did not envy his sister's lifestyle. 'I've never been the slightest bit jealous because I can see exactly what she has to put up with,' he said, it's very easy for somebody who's nowhere near Diana to think, "God, I'd like a life like hers". But all of us who are close to her are not so envious.'

The couple's outward display of happiness impressed guests staying at Balmoral during the final stages of Diana's pregnancy with her second child. They walked through the grounds hand in hand and spent hours playing with Prince William.

There was a slight tremor one Sunday as the royals were gathering to go to church. Diana, beautifully turned out, was waiting patiently for the others in the hall when the Queen said to her: 'Oh Diana, you needn't come.' The Princess brightened visibly at the prospect of spending the time with William, but Charles was taken aback. 'Oh my goodness, she's spent all morning getting ready,' he said in aggrieved tones, it was a very husbandly remark,' said one privy to the secrets of Balmoral. 'But apart from that, they seemed absolutely happy.'

Charles had been delighted to learn that Diana was pregnant again, and he prayed for a daughter. 'He was very good-humoured about it,' said a friend. 'He knew she had had a terrible time with William and he teased her and made silly jokes.' It was his rather clumsy way of trying to share the burden. In fact, it only emphasised the distance between them. As at William's birth, he stayed by her side in the Lindo Wing, giving her lumps of ice to suck and cream for her dry lips.

Prince Henry, or Harry as he instantly became, was born at four-twenty p.m. on Saturday, 15 September, 1984. Straight away, Charles phoned the Queen and Prince Philip at Balmoral, Earl Spencer at Althorp and Mrs Shand Kydd in Scotland. The next day, he brought an excited William to see his brother and, when Diana and the baby left hospital, Charles drove them home in a blue Daimler. He had, he felt, done everything possible to make them comfortable.

Piling his polo gear into the back of his Aston Martin, he dashed off to Windsor Great Park, where his team mates feted him with champagne and cigars. He was away for only three hours, but his enemies seized on this as an example of his selfish attitude towards Diana. The sad truth was that Charles had done everything in his power, but it wasn't enough and never would be. Diana's needs were insatiable; as long as she was in the grip of the illness, she would always want more. Sick and depressed, she said she 'felt something die inside me'.

Filled with self-pity, Diana stalked off during a recuperative skiing holiday in Lichtenstein and her bewildered husband was heard to mutter: 'I suppose I'll get it in the neck now.' Charles knew the time had come for him to stand up for himself, and not only to his wife. The Press were starting to annoy him intensely.

THE Fergie Follies opened before a glittering audience, including a full house of royalty, at Windsor Castle in the summer of 1985. The visiting star, Miss Sarah Ferguson, of Lavender Gardens SW11, had already played the Farm Club at Verbier, the Palm Beach circuit and the Hippodrome in the West End to mixed reviews. She was still trying to forget one performance as a cocktail waitress at a party after which one guest was able to confirm: 'She's a natural redhead.'

This, however, was by far the biggest role of her life and she came on stage smartly dressed in a cream silk suit. Her friend the Princess of Wales had written the script in which Prince Andrew, the best the Royal Family could offer in the way of a playboy, had been cast as the leading man. But Fergie couldn't resist the temptation of ad-libbing. The moment she and Andrew indulged in a friendly scuffle over a plate of profiteroles, this grand lunch in the State Dining Room at Windsor Castle before Royal Ascot reverted to pure slapstick.

'We were made to sit next to each other at lunch,' said Andrew later, when Sarah was wearing his £25,000 ruby-and-diamond engagement ring. 'Yes, and he made me eat chocolate profiteroles which I didn't want to eat at all,' complained Sarah. 'I was on a diet.' Andrew had tempted Fergie to eat some of the rich pudding by saying that he would have some only if she did so first. After she had eaten her portion, he told her he was joking. Sarah did the only reasonable thing: she gave him an unscripted whack on the shoulder. 'I didn't have it so I got hit,' he said.

Fergie's debut at Windsor Castle, which she admitted 'scared me witless', might have lacked decorum, but as a portent it was uncannily accurate. Andrew found that he enjoyed romping around with this roly-poly girl whose idea of a good time matched his own. Their repertoire ranged from cream-bun fights and mustard squirting to a particular after-dinner game played trouserless with ice-creams. But though they shared an interest in filthy jokes and high jinks they had little else in common. She loved riding and skiing, he was interested in flying and the Navy. 'Let's face it, they were totally unsuited,' said a friend. 'She should never have been there and she knows it.'

Fergie came into Andrew's life just as he was resting between romantic engagements. A performance of a more professional kind in *The Adventures of Emily,* an erotic film, had placed the actress-turned-photographer Koo Stark, off limits. Missing Koo, he pursued a bevy of blonde beauties until his double act with baronet's daughter Vicki Hodge in a Caribbean one-nighter, widely reviewed in the Sunday papers, convinced Her Majesty that it was time he stopped playing away from home and settled down.

As Sarah's romance with Paddy McNally was going nowhere, Diana seized the chance to introduce an ally into the royal ranks. 'Be delightful, but be discreet,' Diana cautioned her friend. This was like asking Pavarotti to break dance. Fergie's whole *raison d'etre* was 'to be myself', even if it meant treading on sensitive toes. The problem was that she wasn't quite sure who she was.

Andrew decided that, if he had to marry, Fergie would be far preferable to the grasping Sloane Rangers and outdoorsy blue bloods of his acquaintance. To everyone's immense relief, they became engaged on Wednesday, 19 March, 1986.

The Fergie Follies returned on the night of Andrew's stag party. Pamela Stephenson and Elton John's wife Renate turned up at a friend's flat in Belgravia dressed as policewomen. Fergie and Diana slipped into wigs and hired two WPC uniforms. The intention was to gatecrash the all-male preserve and arrest the bridegroom, but they found security at the venue, Aubrey House, a walled mansion in Holland Park, too tight to penetrate. Undaunted, they proceeded to Annabel's in Berkeley Square where patrons were treated to the sight of four giggling policewomen drinking Buck's Fizz at the bar. 'The wig was hot and uncomfortable and my feet were killing me – the shoes were two sizes too small,' said Diana. 'But you have to have a laugh sometimes.' Charles did not share the sentiment.

After the Yorks' wedding at Westminster Abbey, Fergie tried to adapt to married life at Buckingham Palace while Andrew went back to the Navy. Diana, fighting her own battles, initially welcomed her friend's presence. They swam together in the Palace pool, went shopping in Knightsbridge and arranged skiing trips to Klosters. But it became obvious to Diana that Fergie, a deeply insecure woman beneath the bravado, was 'doing all the wrong things'. She saw that the courtiers, not her favourite people, 'were giving the Duchess enough rope to hang herself'. Charles told Diana just how seriously wrong it was going after the royal superstars Diana and Fergie were photographed at Royal Ascot, not chatting to friends in the Royal Enclosure but jabbing men's bottoms with their rolled-up umbrellas. Always conscious of how other people's behaviour reflected on her, Diana stepped back and let Fergie get on with it.

Charles had taken to Fergie in the first phase of her married life, hoping that she would provide Diana not only with company but inspiration as well. 'Diana always said that Sarah was intent on ingratiating herself all over the place, and certainly in the early stages she made a deliberate attempt to get Charles on her side,' said a friend of the royals. 'Charles did take to her and, on her first birthday as the Duchess of York, he gave her a very expensive piece of jewellery.' Moreover, the Prince began to compare Diana unfavourably with the outgoing Duchess and, more than once, suggested to Diana that she should be 'more like Fergie — fun to be with'. This drove an even deeper wedge between the two royal superstars. Diana was friendly to Fergie's face, but she harboured a deep mistrust.

Yet another folly was enacted when Prince Edward organised a royal version of the popular TV show *It's a Knockout* as a fundraising venture with the BBC. He persuaded his mother to agree to the Duke and Duchess of York, the Princess Royal and himself acting as team leaders in a medieval contest entitled The Grand Knockout Tournament. In her sitting room at Kensington Palace, Diana watched with a mixture of horror and fascination as Fergie, dressed as a Tudor wench, swaggered on to the battlefield. When the 'games' were over, Fergie and the others were widely criticised for rubbing the Royal Family's good name in the mud.

Diana quietly sought other remedies for her troubles. Through an intermediary, she booked an appointment to see Betty Palko, an Irish clairvoyant based in a semidetached mock Tudor house at Surbiton, Surrey, 'I was recommended to her – I never advertise,' explained Mrs Palko. 'My clients, you see, are higher as well as lower class people. They include people suffering bereavement and emotional and business problems. I counsel and advise, but I don't tell people what to do. I just give them what I see. I don't want to do this work but I've been chosen by a spirit to do it.'

As Diana wanted to keep the meeting secret, she met Mrs Palko in a discreet hotel. Betty read tarot cards for the Princess and held a seance during which she passed on the advice of Lin Foo, a long-dead Chinese philosopher. Diana was so impressed with the medium's insight into her life that she started to see her once a month. Initially, she wanted to get in touch with her paternal grandmother, Cynthia, Countess Spencer, who died of a brain tumour in 1972 when Diana was eleven.

Diana's belief in spiritualism and reincarnation was strengthened in the most uncanny way when she holidayed in Majorca in 1990. For holiday reading, she chose *Afterlife*, an investigation into evidence concerning life after death by Colin Wilson, the English writer on the occult and paranormal. Sunbathing in a red bikini on *Fortuna,* the yacht of King Juan Carlos, she soaked up Wilson's true case histories of people involved in psychic experiences.

The very first example concerned a young woman called Sarah Worthington, who was being treated for moods of depression during which she was tempted to commit suicide. During therapy, the nervous young woman suddenly started speaking in a completely different voice. 'When they (the psychiatrists) asked the woman what she wanted to do, she replied, "Help Sarah,"' wrote Wilson. 'She identified herself as Sarah's grandmother. According to the grandmother, she had "taken possession" of Sarah Worthington when her granddaughter was playing the piano – both of them loved music. She was able to give the psychiatrists invaluable information about Sarah's family background. And although Sarah was at first astonished to realise that her grandmother was speaking through her, she gradually learned to accept it, and began to achieve deeper insight into her problems. At the end of two months she was cured.'

Diana was an accomplished pianist who often sat for hours playing on a Broadwood grand piano at Kensington Palace. Moreover, she had been very close to Lady Spencer, whom she resembled not only in looks but also in personality. Lord Spencer had comforted her at a memorial service for her grandmother at the Chapel Royal with the prophetic words, 'The living and the dead are never quite separable'. Diana had believed in the afterlife ever since.

She was also consulting two astrologers, Penny Thornton and Debbie Frank, for guidance from the stars. Astrology, Ms Thornton explained to her royal client, was 'a spiritual path that can only lead to growth.' 'You are getting a panoramic vision of your own life instead of just looking one step at a time,' she said. 'Your canvas is spreading out so that you start to see more and more things. Your life is evolving, your awareness is expanding and your connection with your soul, your spiritual centre, is more and more acute.'

But none of the cards, crystal balls or zodiac charts proved infallible. No one, it seemed, warned Diana against making telephone calls to single male admirers on New Year's Eve.

WHEN Charles later surveyed the wreckage, exactly the same thing stood out as a symbol of his own downfall: a telephone. He had bought the portable phone to make private calls, but it became an instrument of his destruction.

At Highgrove, he took it with him on long walks to phone Camilla and Kanga. Sometimes he spoke to his forbidden friends from the privacy of his walled vegetable garden or from the middle of a field. Surrounded by organic greenery, he chatted freely with the two women who made him feel needed. But some of the calls were not so innocent. Diana told friends that she caught him one day, in his mahogany-sided bathtub, speaking softly into the receiver and telling Camilla: 'Whatever happens, I will always love you.' From that moment, the flimsy charade was over.

The first prop to go was Diana's *entente cordiale* with Kanga, who had made the peace by inviting the Princess to her Knightsbridge salon and lunching with her at San Lorenzo. Diana had been pleased enough to buy several outfits, which she wore for a time. But her suspicions were revived after she started to avoid going on holiday with Charles to Balmoral or Sandringham, or to watch polo at Windsor. 'Whenever Kanga went to Balmoral or Sandringham, she was spotted with Charles, but Diana knew that her husband Anthony was there as well,' said a friend. 'Diana suspected that Kanga was acting as a decoy for Camilla, who was keeping well out of camera range.'

In country rig of tweeds and green wellies, Kanga went deer stalking, shooting and fishing with Charles, sports that she genuinely loved. When concern was expressed about the Prince's health, she leapt to his defence. 'I see him all the time and he's as fit as a fiddle,' she said. 'His farming, skiing and polo make him one of the healthiest men in the country.' This only confirmed the impression, albeit misleading, that Kanga the old friend was the new woman in Charles's life. Diana wasn't present when Charles grabbed Kanga by both arms and she kissed his cheek after a polo match at Windsor, but she saw the picture in the papers.

The couple's separation stretched to five weeks during the autumn of 1987, the longest estrangement in their six-year marriage. Charles stayed at Balmoral Castle or Birkhall, the Queen Mother's residence on Deeside, while Diana moved between Kensington Palace and Highgrove.

'October is a busy time on the Scottish estates and in the absence of the Duke of Edinburgh, the Prince has had to take charge,' explained an aide at Balmoral. 'He also has many business meetings in connection with the Prince's Trust, the Duchy of Cornwall and other projects which do not receive publicity.' He had time to go deer stalking with Kanga, though, and the decibel level rose in the phone calls he received from Diana.

Kanga was back at Birkhall the following Easter when she fished with Charles on the Dee while Diana stayed with her sons at Highgrove. On all of these occasions, Lord Tryon and other friends of Charles, either married couples or well-connected singles, were house guests as well.

Diana's response in public was to play the incidents down. 'When we first got married, we were everyone's idea of the world's most ideal, perfect couple,' she said. 'Now they say we're leading separate lives. The next thing I know I'll read in some newspaper that I've got a black lover.'

IN Oxfordshire, a balding royalist called Cyril Reenan handed in his keys and left the Abingdon branch of the Trustee Savings Bank for the last time as manager. For thirty-two years, he had listened to people talk about overdrafts, interest rates and mortgage repayments. He had been a good listener.

In retirement, he visited a studio equipped with electronic monitoring devices and overheard a private telephone conversation. It concerned plans to redesign an aircraft. Cyril was intrigued. 'I couldn't believe how easy it was or how clear,' he said. 'But it was just innocent entertainment, nothing more than that.'

He bought a small radio scanner and he and his wife Phylis began to listen in to other people's phone calls from the breakfast room of their neat, red-brick Victorian home. He never dreamed that he would one day become notorious as Cyril, the Squidgy Squirrel – the man who would lead an unsuspecting world to believe that Diana had indeed taken a lover.

6

LIVING DANGEROUSLY

'Diana has suddenly realised what she's been missing'
Lucy Acland

DIANA always managed to conceal her anger from the world during her marriage. Although she was capable of shenanigans which raised eyebrows at private functions, she never completely lost her temper in a public place. It was only after the marriage had ended in separation that she finally cracked and, in a moment of madness, disclosed a side of her character that was all too familiar to Prince Charles.

Five days after their twelfth wedding anniversary in 1993, she took William and Harry to see *Jurassic Park,* the Steven Spielberg movie about dinosaurs. When photographer Keith Butler snapped her picture as she left the Empire cinema in Leicester Square, she dashed up to him and, standing on tiptoe to confront the six foot three inch tall cameraman, she screamed: 'You make my life hell.' Passerbys gazed in amazement at the sight of the Princess of Wales, in black blazer and silk trousers, brushing tears from her eyes as she stormed off down the street ahead of her sons and their detectives. The mask had slipped.

'I have never known anything like it — she raced across and put her nose right up to mine,' said Butler, one of the paparazzi's shrewder operators. 'A sign of her anger was that she had both fists tightly clenched. I thought she was going to punch me. She was clearly very stressed about something. I think I was the target of a deeper anger.'

The outburst had been building up ever since Diana had spent the previous weekend with an old friend, the merchant banker Willie van Straubenzee, at Floors Castle, the Scottish home of the Duke and Duchess of Roxburghe. Staubenzee had been spotted when he arrived at Heathrow airport for the flight north and Diana's dream of an idyllic break suddenly collapsed in ruins. Newsmen staked out the castle, famous as the scene of Andrew's proposal to Fergie, for the duration of her stay, even secretly photographing her playing tennis while 'Straubs' watched from a bench on the sidelines. The intrusion made Diana furious and reminded her that every one of her friendships with men, no matter how innocent, had been destroyed by the glare of publicity.

The problem had initially surfaced during a particularly turbulent stage of her marriage, damaging her standing in the eyes of the Queen. Her Majesty, Diana suspected, had reached quite the wrong conclusion about the innocent night she had spent at Gatley Park, the Midlands home of the Lord Lieutenant of Hereford and Worcester, Thomas Dunne and his wife Henrietta. True enough, the Dunnes had not been in residence on the occasion early in 1987 as they were away skiing in France. Diana had been there with their son, the darkly handsome Philip Dunne, a twenty-eight-year-old senior manager with a merchant bank. She had, by all accounts, invited herself. Dunne's sister Camilla was one of Diana's closest friends but if she was there on the night in question then she made no public declaration of it. The Prince of Wales was certainly not there. He had his reservations about Philip Dunne.

With Charles spending more and more time in the company of Camilla and Kanga, Diana was not merely turning to a group of young male friends for companionship. At this critical point in her life, she was living downright dangerously. Knowing that she was getting a reputation for being flirtatious – or 'a terrible tease' as one of her titled girlfriends put it – she even fuelled the gossips by disappearing from Highgrove for a mysterious weekend that winter after Charles had left for Africa to walk through the Kalahari desert with Sir Laurens van der Post. She turned up close to tears at Kensington Palace after being pursued in her Escort Turbo by a car filled with high spirited Arabs.

The year had not begun well. Diana had been accused of flirting her way through a tour of Portugal after Charles had embarrassed her by making a joke in public about keeping a mistress. They asked for, and were given, separate bedrooms during the tour throughout which she cold shouldered her husband. At a banquet in their honour she played the vamp by making eyes at the host country's good-looking Prime Minister, Cavaco Silva. He responded by inviting Diana to use his villa for a holiday with William and Harry.

But there was worse to come. In the wake of criticism that at official functions she paid particular attention to the men while ignoring their wives, she twanged the braces of Portugal's President, Mario Soares. He blushed the colour of the Royal Box's crimson decorations but Diana, looking ravishing in an off-the-shoulder dress, piled on the agony by asking him coquettishly: 'If I get cold will you warm me up?'

Harry Arnold offered a seasoned opinion of her behaviour: 'It was a tease in the old-fashioned sense,' he said. 'I think she took the view that while she could not be unfaithful to Charles and she had never had another guy, she nevertheless thought, "I wonder what it would be like with somebody else". She was also aware that her husband knew exactly what it was like with others.' 'Mobbing-up' was the term Diana and her friends had coined for flirting in their Sloane Ranger days, although one offered a different explanation: 'She only does it when she's insecure. It means she's had a row with Charles.'

The couple were showing signs of strain when they returned to London to prepare for an almost immediate departure for Switzerland. Along with Andrew and Fergie they were to spend a week skiing in Klosters with the brewery heir, Peter Greenall. Charles had stayed with Greenall, who was third in line to Lord Daresbury's title, on previous holidays.

The royal quartet were ensconced in a rented chalet at Wolfgang along with four detectives and equerry Richard Aylard. Philip Dunne was also a member of the party, but he flew home after just two days when rows erupted among the group. One of the banker's friends said: 'There was a terrible atmosphere there surrounding the party so Philip decided to get out quickly before it got even worse. He told me it had been a very bad-tempered trip and he just couldn't stick it out for a full week.'

Determined to have fun, Diana left Charles behind in the chalet and went disco dancing with Greenall and his wife Clare. Wearing a slinky white blouse and tight black leather trousers, she rocked for two late-night hours at the Casa Antica discotheque. Disc jockey Martin Melsome said she was dressed to kill and was easily the most attractive woman in the club. The DJ said that the Princess had asked him to play her favourite record, Diana Ross's *Chain Reaction*, adding: 'She didn't look lonely or sad that her husband wasn't with her. She drank red wine and did fantastic rock 'n roll solos to my records.'

Fearing that perhaps she had gone too far in the alpine resort, Diana took some short-term action through the media to reverse the damage. She went to some lengths to get a message to Harry Arnold asking him to make it known that 'just because I go out without my husband, it doesn't mean my marriage is on the rocks'. For his part Charles, while seemingly bemused by his wife's reckless behaviour, let it be known that he was becoming increasingly irritated by the way his marriage, his private life and his state of mind were being 'misrepresented by the Press'. A member of his entourage was instructed to convey this to a reporter from the Press Association after he had spent three days among the crofters on the Outer Hebridean island of Berneray, only to find a report of his mission in the *Sun* was headlined *A Loon Again*. Charles also sought the counsel of men more worldly than himself and turned up one evening at the home of comedian Spike Milligan for supper. Spike said: 'I had to insist that he should not wash up and he explained to me that he just wanted to be a normal person.'

Any hopes that Diana had learned to conform were dashed when she resumed her prince-teasing at the society wedding of 'Bunty', the Marquess of Worcester, to the actress Tracy Ward, a star of the *C.A.T.S. Eyes* television series. Other guests at Cornwell Manor in Oxfordshire were astonished at the intimate manner in which Diana danced with Philip Dunne while her husband looked on. They said she ran her fingers through the bespectacled Clark Kent lookalike's hair and planted a kiss on his cheek.

To some measure, Charles was consoled by the companionship of his old flame, Anna Wallace, but at two a.m. his anger boiled over and he strode across to exchange a few well-chosen words with his wife. Her reaction was to laugh in his face, leading one guest to conclude: 'Someone must have spiked her drink. She was out of control. She was almost falling out of her dress.' Whatever her condition, Charles left Diana to dance until dawn and drove himself to Highgrove.

The episode was repeated a few nights later when she again refused Charles's entreaties, this time to leave a barbecue for the polo fraternity hosted by Susan Barrantes at a house near Cowdray Park. The Queen and Prince Philip had been among the guests but

Diana waited until they had left before amusing others with a wild new dancing style, it was like watching a windmill in action,' said one who watched her dance to records which included the obligatory Diana Ross offering, *Chain Reaction.* Once more, Charles left alone. Then, while he visited his regiments in Germany, he learned that the mother of his children had accompanied her sister Sarah to yet another all-night party in Lincolnshire.

Her friend Lucy Acland, the heiress granddaughter of wealthy businessman Cyril Kleinwort, said: 'Diana has suddenly realised what she's been missing all these years married to Prince Charles, surrounded by fuddy-duddy philosophers and elderly businessmen. Fergie has introduced Diana to a whole new crowd who like to go to nightclubs, down bubbly and have a good time. Naturally some of them are handsome young men like Philip Dunne. They are elegant, charming and full of fun. They pay her nice compliments and Diana responds.'

It had not escaped Charles's attention that it was his sister-in-law who had brought both Dunne and his friends the Greenalls into Diana's life. Fergie had also introduced her to Major David Waterhouse, a Household Cavalry officer who had been another member of the skiing party in Klosters. Waterhouse received a telephone call from Diana asking him if he would escort her to a David Bowie concert at Wembley. She told him she had the tickets and that the concert would be as great a treat for her as it would be an endurance test for her husband. He had his own treat fixed up — a performance of Vivaldi's work he had arranged to attend with the Archbishop of Canterbury. At the Bowie concert, with no visible encouragement from the army officer, Diana perfected her teasing technique by nestling her head on his shoulder. Photographs suggested they were cuddling, but Waterhouse explained them away saying: 'The unfortunate thing about those pictures is that at a concert like that, the noise is simply astronomical and you have to lean towards the person next to you to make yourself heard.'

The experience did not faze her companion and Waterhouse, a cousin of the Duke of Marlborough's drug-addicted heir Jamie (the Marquess of) Blandford, became something of a regular escort, taking her to the cinema and to restaurants whenever she tired of royal life. One of her girlfriends was usually on hand to act as a chaperone and it was Julia Samuel who made it a threesome when

Diana and Waterhouse went to see Dustin Hoffman in *Rain Man* at the Kensington Odeon. Later they went back to Kate Menzies' mews house, enjoying what witnesses described as 'an especially merry night'.

Merry, that is, until Diana and Waterhouse stepped from Kate's doorway and into the viewfinder of Jason Fraser's paparazzi camera. Fraser resisted threats from Diana's detective but agreed to hand over his film when the Princess herself tearfully pleaded with him. He regretted the decision almost immediately. 'As soon as I gave her the film, she stopped blushing and her tone became clipped,' he said. 'Her tears were turned off and I had the distinct feeling that it had all been an act.'

THE Queen was growing increasingly alarmed about Diana's most unroyal acts. But the crux of Diana's dilemma was loneliness of a particularly feminine kind. As she told one of her *confidantes* over a Chinese meal at the Tai Pai restaurant in Knightsbridge, she had produced an heir and a spare and, in the light of her loveless marriage, she faced a stark choice: to enjoy some pleasure with the bankin', shoppin' and dancin' set, or to stay at home and turn into a Palace couch potato.

At close quarters, she had seen Princess Anne, once her marriage had turned sour, promptly enjoy the advances of a handsome replacement for Captain Mark Phillips in the young naval officer, Commander Timothy Laurence. Diana had no need to be taught that royal dalliances were not in themselves forbidden, only royal scandals. It was acceptable for one to cavort as long as one was not caught.

She came close to stepping over the line however, when her fondness for Major James Hewitt, an athletic Life Guards officer, caused her to be generous to the point of carelessness. She had met the major at a friend's party in St John's Wood and he became one of three of the officers in the Sovereign's bodyguard regiment who would accompany her on picnics when Charles was away. Hewitt quickly became her favourite. The ginger-haired officer's tendency to blush easily was an endearing trait and he was entrusted with the task of teaching William and Harry to ride. Initially, Diana took her sons to Cobermere Barracks on the outskirts of Windsor for their lessons but the instructor so charmed the trio that his face was soon familiar at Highgrove. No one could quite remember the circumstances or even the date on which Diana decided that she would also like to learn to ride properly and duly placed herself in the horseman's hands.

Hewitt had acquired the services of an attentive (and, as it turned out, inquisitive) valet and groom, one Lance Corporal Malcolm Leete, who started to make careful note of Diana's comings and goings, what she wore and what she brought with her. His record subsequently showed that the Princess would arrive for instruction on Monday, Wednesday and Friday mornings, more often than not accompanied by neither her detective nor a lady-in-waiting. Furthermore, he observed, she would often bring the Major presents of expensive clothing carried in highly distinctive green Harrods bags. She was later to boast to Gilbey of her generosity to Hewitt on the Squidgy tape:

Diana: I've decked people out in my time.

Gilbey: Who did you deck out? Not too many, I hope.

Diana: James Hewitt. Entirely dressed him from head to foot that man. Cost me quite a bit.

Gilbey: I bet he did. At your expense?

Diana: Yeah.

Gilbey: What, he didn't even pay you to do it?

Diana: No.

Gilbey: God, that's extravagant, Darling.

Diana: Well I am, aren't I? Anything that will make people happy.

Gilbey: No, you mustn't do it for that, Darling, because you make people happy. It's what you give them ...

In addition to clothes, the gifts HRH showered on her instructor to make him happy included a diamond-studded tiepin from Asprey's and a gold-and-silver clock from Garrad & Co. She did not itemise them in the Squidgy call nor did she mention the name she used to sign the cards which accompanied her expensive gifts to him: Dibbs.

Exhilarated though she appeared after more than twenty months of living dangerously, Diana was reaching a low ebb. So much so that before the year ended a caring friend gave her the unlisted telephone number of Stephen Twigg, a therapist who did not advertise but whose techniques had achieved spectacular results, especially for women who were close to rock bottom in their emotional lives.

With the arrival of the cold autumn weather, Diana's riding lessons were transferred from the park to the indoor riding school. The disloyal servant Leete claimed that one November morning he stood on a mounting block to peer in through a window and saw his master cuddling the Princess. Hewitt could, of course, have been soothing a bruised arm Diana was known to have strained, possibly from a fall. But the bigger bruising was taken by the gallant officer's girlfriend, Emma Stewardson.

Ms Stewardson said she ended a four-year relationship with the officer after he had ended a passionate bedroom session with her in ungentlemanly fashion by talking about Diana. After that, she said, 'he wouldn't even discuss it'. Bitter about losing his undivided attention, she told her story to the *News of the World* in 1991, declaring emotionally: 'I felt threatened by his crush on her. How could I compete with that? Diana's beautiful, she's fabulously rich and she lives in a completely different world from me.'

In her memoirs, Emma recalled how James had first talked to her about the Princess when they went for a meal in a village pub. 'All through the meal he was being very light and entertaining, but I knew he wanted to get something off his chest,' she said. 'It was then that Jamie told me of his feelings for Diana. He said, "By the way, the Princess of Wales is a close friend of mine ... a very close friend of mine." He seemed to think he could tell me as a friend about this crush without damaging our relationship.' She said he had even stood her up to keep a lunch date with Diana at Highgrove and then told her that she shouldn't feel threatened by such events as they changed nothing. Charitably, Emma concluded that Hewitt, who colleagues called The Iceman but she nicknamed Winkie, had merely helped Diana to overcome her fear of horses.

'The relationship is entirely innocent,' Hewitt maintained strenuously. At the beginning of September 1992 he launched a libel action against *News International.* His solicitor, Mark Stephens, said his client 'felt it necessary to bring this action because of the scandalous nature of the false allegations about him'. But when experts on defamation explained that Diana could be subpoenaed by the defence and cross-examined in the witness box, Hewitt dropped his action even though he said the Princess had vowed to stand by him. 'If she had been called as a witness the court ordeal would have been horrendous for her,' he said. 'The whole case would have turned into a media circus. It would have caused too many people too much distress.' Besides, he admitted, there was always a chance that he would lose: 'I was told costs could have topped £300,000. Even though the truth is on my side, nothing is clear cut when it comes to libel cases.'

HEMMED in at Kensington Palace by her in-laws, attended by servants who were plugged in to their counterparts at Buckingham Palace and constantly watched by the protection service, Diana was aware that nothing but nothing escaped Her Majesty's notice. The network, however, could feed intelligence in both directions. It was in this way Diana learned that, although Her Majesty understood her daughter-in-law's dilemma, she very much disapproved of the open gossip.

To escape the royal network, Diana joined the Vanderbilt Racquet Club in Shepherd's Bush, ostensibly to play tennis, and found herself plugged into another network. Other members included Mick Jagger, Charlton Heston, the Harold Pinters and Richard Branson's mother, Eve. She especially endeared herself to Charles Swallow, the club's director and a former history master at Harrow, by insisting that she pay the £650 entrance fee and annual subscription of £550. Furthermore, she made no objection to photographs of herself chatting with other members being included in the montages which lined the club hallway.

Her court manners were impeccable. She became known for clapping a hand over her mouth and blushing when she missed an obvious shot. Her court partners included Swallow, her friend Antonia, the Marchioness of Douro, the former tennis professional Annabel Croft, the Conservative MP William Waldegrave and tennis writer April Tod, who observed: 'She is not a particularly good player. She is fairly competitive but her main object seems to be to keep the ball in play.'

But her regular visits to the nine converted hangars in an unfashionable area of West London did not release her from the pressures that were closing in on her at Buckingham Palace. There, at a musical evening, she said she found herself being regarded by her mother-in-law in what she could only describe as an unnerving manner. It was to her father that she turned for advice.

Earl Spencer sought to comfort his daughter by pointing out that Her Majesty had also formed a circle of male friends when she was about the same age and at a similarly troubled stage in her own marriage. What, for example, would a disrespectful Press have made of the Queen's highly private visit to Lord Porchester at the Savoy Hotel in 1959 had the likes of Jason Fraser been around to capture her coming and going on film? Once the Queen's teenage dancing partner and sweetheart, Porchester was admired by her every bit as much as James Hewitt was by Diana three decades later.

Although nothing had appeared in the newspapers, royal gossip had linked the Queen's name with Old Etonian Porchester, who was later appointed as Her Majesty's racing manager and who succeeded his father as the Earl of Carnarvon in 1987. When her second, and preferred son, Prince Andrew, was born in February 1960, royal observers hoped that the rift between the Queen and her husband had been healed in the bedchamber. But as Andrew grew up to resemble Porchy's children rather than Charles, Anne or Edward, false rumours took root and spread. 'Prince Andrew's paternal grandfather?' a baronet's son queried. 'You don't mean Prince Andrew of Greece, you mean the late Earl of Carnarvon.' Ironically, when Andrew once needed to conceal the identity of a real girlfriend in his pre-Fergie days, it was Porchester's daughter — Diana's friend and lookalike Lady Carolyn Herbert – who he enlisted as a decoy, often escorting her in public. After Andrew himself had confided in a woman with whom he became deeply attached, she subsequently remarked to a later lover: 'He knows who his real father is and it's not Lord Porchester.'

The Queen had other close male friends including her equerry Patrick, the seventh Baron Plunket, who was Deputy Master of her Household. Eton and Cambridge educated, Lord Plunket had been equerry to King George VI. A slender and handsome man with thinning dark hair and an aristocratic profile, he worked with Sir Anthony Blunt in the Queen's Gallery. Despite the assertion of a Palace source that she was in love with him, the Queen knew that Patrick Plunket, like Blunt, was not interested in women. Safe in his company, she would apparently slip out of the Palace on Monday evenings, driving her Rover car, a scarf over her head, and travel to the cinema – usually the Odeon in the King's Road, Chelsea. Together with the man she referred to as 'my beloved Patrick', she would go on to Raffles Club for supper, dining at a table towards the darkened back of the wood-panelled room, enduring what one member described as 'particularly nauseating food' at the time in return for the anonymity on offer. She was distraught when her friend died of cancer.

The Queen's fondness for Patrick Plunket was something Diana was able to relate to when she formed what could never be anything more than a purely platonic relationship with the art consultant Adrian Ward-Jackson. Introduced to her by Princess Margaret in his one-time role as governor of the Royal Ballet, Ward-Jackson dined regularly with Diana at Kensington Palace. They discussed their work for AIDS-related charities. Diana had become patron of the National AIDS Trust after seeing babies born to HIV-positive mothers in New York, and Adrian helped to run the AIDS Crisis Trust. When his closest friend died of AIDS, Adrian suspected that it was only a matter of time before the virus claimed his own life. Diana's friendship remained constant despite a marked change in his personality when he discovered that he was indeed infected.

His services to the performing arts, most notably Diana's beloved dance, were recognised when he was awarded a CBE in the 1991 New Year's Honours list. Diana made several visits to his home in Great Cumberland Place to comfort him and in August of that year, as he lay dying in the Lindo wing of St Mary's, she broke off her holiday at Balmoral to fly to his bedside. Altogether Diana spent twenty-two hours with the forty-one-year-old art dealer in his final days. She held his hand and recited the Lord's Prayer over his bed with another friend Angela Serota as he drifted in and out of consciousness. He died at one a.m., minutes before she returned to his bedside, but she remained to console his grieving family and did not leave the hospital until eight a.m. Later she sat down and wrote to Angela: 'I reached an inner depth that I would never have thought possible. My view of life has taken another direction and has become more positive and balanced.'

Her private grief overwhelmed her public face at Ward-Jackson's funeral. A gold-and-diamond necklace she wore at his memorial service had been his farewell present to her. He paid £35,000 for the piece and presented it to her on her thirtieth birthday just seven weeks before his death.

WITHIN a few days of Diana's first consultation with Stephen Twigg in December 1988, the therapist was named in a letter sent to the prominent Mayfair-based surveyor Charles Price. The letter purported to link Price's wife, the actress Jean Harrington, with Twigg and furnished details of the latter's address and the car that he drove.

What the informant did not appear to know was that the Prices had split up earlier in the year. Nevertheless, as his divorce proceedings progressed, Charles Price engaged an investigator to make inquiries into the man who was later credited with instigating Diana's voyage of rediscovery. Twigg, or Steve as he liked to be called, was visiting Kensington Palace once a week to massage her near-nude body while he filled her mind with New Age teachings. Unknown to him, he was being followed everywhere he went by a private eye who carried a camera to snap him. The pictures were handed over to Price.

According to the investigator's report, Twigg hailed from Hampshire, had started his working life as a trainee technician in a government food research laboratory and had worked with a motor spares company before becoming a junior tax inspector. He had been married and divorced. What the investigator had not included was that Twigg was fully trained in Swedish and deep-tissue massage, skills he applied to Diana and other eminent clients including Baroness Falkender, former political secretary to the Labour Prime Minister Harold Wilson, along with a coherent philosophy towards health which links the mind and body in the pursuit of well-being.

Diana's therapist shared his philosophical interests with the former Mrs Charles Price along with an ex-directory telephone number which was traced to a block of flats in Castelain Road, Maida Vale. While she was looking for acting roles in Los Angeles, she had allowed Twigg to use her apartment.

The counsellor who was helping the Princess to achieve a new lease of life was truly a man of the world.

7

THE MAXWELL CONNECTION

'I have told the Prince that I will fire you'
Robert Maxwell

THE revolving door had been a fixture in Fleet Street ever since Caxton fired the first printer's devil. When Wendy Henry spun out of the turnstile at Rupert Murdoch's Wapping HQ, she re-emerged through the revolving front door of his great rival, Robert Maxwell. Ms Henry's editorship at the *News of the World,* making her the first woman to edit a national newspaper in modern times, had been brought to an abrupt halt on 12 December, 1988. Although the paper's weekly circulation had risen to 5.3 million, Murdoch sacked her the day after she ran a story about homosexuals which had an embarrassing royal link. Ever an opportunist, Maxwell stepped in and appointed her the editor of his less successful Sunday tabloid, the *People,* hoping some of Murdoch's readers would follow her to his base at Holborn Circus.

In November 1989, four weeks before he talked about knickers and lavatories in his late-night call to Camilla, an indignant Charles was on the phone to Robert Maxwell. It was not, initially, one of their chummier exchanges. The Prince was very annoyed about a picture of Prince William which Ms Henry had published in the *People* under the headline *The Royal Wee.* The picture showed William, back turned discreetly to the camera, answering a call of nature in Kensington Palace Gardens. It had been taken by Jason Fraser and Maxwell the newspaper publisher had chortled when Ms Henry showed it to him. He had personally approved publication.

'He was very positive about it,' she recalled from her new home in Florida. 'It was a charming picture taken in a public place. Then Maxwell rang me on the Monday to complain and I said, "I think I'd better come and see you". I went up to the ninth floor and saw him in the living room of his suite of offices. He was really nice but he said, "I've had a call from the Prince. I have told the Prince that I will fire you." So he didn't have much alternative did he?' As she disappeared through the revolving door, Maxwell the arbiter of good taste declared that the picture was 'an intrusion into privacy not acceptable to me'.

Neither Maxwell nor Charles knew that, at the time they had spoken, their own privacy was also the subject of intrusion. The newspaper proprietor was the target of a telephone bugging operation by British Intelligence officers, who were taking a keen interest in his subversive activities behind the Iron Curtain.

Treachery was second nature to Maxwell. 'He couldn't shake hands with someone without getting his fingers in their pocket,' said one of his former directors. He trusted no one, sometimes not even himself. With equal impunity, he bugged members of his own family at Headington Hill Hall, his rented mansion near Oxford, and senior executives at Mirror Group headquarters.

'He is a business brigand,' Rupert Murdoch at the time said. 'He almost physically loves the feel of power.'

CHARLES had nothing in common with Maxwell but he was drawn to him just the same. He admired tough men who made millions and got things done through the sheer force of their personalities. One of his heroes was the oil billionaire Dr Armand Hammer, who Diana disliked, and Maxwell, who she detested, was another.

'My aim is to make the world a little better than if I had never lived,' declared Maxwell. It sounded very much like something that Charles had said: 'I would like to leave behind, if I can, in my own small way, a world which is better than I found it.' Maxwell, however, said it first.

'What's he really like to work for?' Charles asked one of Maxwell's editors soon after he took over Mirror Group Newspapers in July 1984. He had consulted Maxwell a year or so earlier about the running of the Prince's Trust. Maxwell nodded sagely and sent Ian, his darkly handsome second son, to work full-time for the Prince. Ian Maxwell described advising young, unemployed applicants on how to start up a business of their own as an 'enriching experience'. In 1992, his younger brother Kevin was charged with theft and conspiracy to defraud and Ian with conspiracy to defraud following the collapse of their father's empire. The charges related to sums totalling more than £200 million.

Maxwell, who had served in the British Army in World War II, winning the MC for bravery in Holland, had courted the royals for years. He was an ardent supporter of the National Society for the Prevention of Cruelty to Children largely because the Queen and the Queen Mother were patrons and Princess Margaret was president. Considering the patrician brutality Maxwell meted out to his own seven children, it was a cause worthy of his endeavours. His biggest contribution was to sponsor a royal gala premiere of a revised version of *The Nutcracker,* danced by the Royal Ballet, at the Royal Opera House. Maxwell's grandly named British Printing and Communication Corporation sponsored the glittering occasion in December 1984 along with Gerald Ronson's Heron International. In August 1990, Ronson was sentenced to twelve months' imprisonment for fraud, false accounting and the theft of £3 million, and fined £5 million in the aftermath of the Guinness share-rigging scandal. Maxwell was lucky to escape charges.

At the Opera House, he beamed down from the Grand Tier, scented with the smell of spiced dried oranges, gingerbread and other Christmas confections, on an audience studded with the kind of titled dignitaries he loathed. Maxwell hated the aristocracy and the feeling was mutual. But he adored the Queen, who sat in the Royal Box with her mother and sister, the royal women in tiaras and evening gowns and accompanied by Prince Philip and Prince Andrew. After the performance, the guests adjourned to the Crush Bar, where Princess Margaret announced that the evening had netted no less than £610,000 for the NSPCC, a record amount for the charity. Maxwell beamed even more broadly as he drank his Moet et Chandon, surrounded by royalty. His ambition was to make himself indispensable to the Queen and, through her son, he was making some headway.

'When William was a toddler, Charles allowed Maxwell to put on a Red Devils air display over Kensington Palace Gardens,' said Margaret Holder, Britain's leading royal researcher. 'He was pictured alongside Maxwell with little William watching the jets fly past. Charles would not allow anyone to be photographed with William at that time. They used to trot him out for photocalls on his birthday and at Christmas and the pictures would go to all the newspapers simultaneously. Charles wanted William's life to be kept private. Yet he allowed Maxwell to use himself, the Prince of Wales, and his son William for this publicity stunt. It indicates that Charles knew Maxwell quite well and there had to be something in it for Charles because he always makes use of people.'

Having established contact, Charles had no hesitation in exploiting the Maxwell connection. 'In 1987, I gave a story to the *Sunday Mirror* saying that some recipients of money from the Prince's Trust were running off with it,' said Ms Holder. 'This infuriated Charles so much that he sent an emissary to see Maxwell who complained that the Prince was very angry and unhappy. Maxwell immediately ordered nice stories about the Trust to be run the following Sunday.'

Charles's obsession with men like Maxwell, a war hero born into poverty in what was then Czechoslovakia, stemmed from his relationship with his father. Prince Philip, Action Man personified long before the term was applied to Charles, had tried to toughen up his son, who tended to be passive and anxious as a child. One reason for this was that Philip frightened him, according to Cecil Beaton, the royal photographer. Beaton noted during a visit to Buckingham Palace that Charles, eleven at the time, behaved 'as if awaiting a clout from behind, or for his father to tweak his ear or pull the tuft of hair at the crown of his head'. Philip took Charles sailing in rough weather and taught him other manly skills. His schooling at Gordonstoun and Timbertop had been as ruggedly inhumane as the public school system would permit. But something was amiss.

An intriguing insight into what the young Charles thought about his father occurred at the London home of the royal author, Elizabeth, Countess of Longford, in the early Seventies. 'He came to a little drinks party I held when I had written a book on Wellington which he was very interested in,' said Her Ladyship. 'He saw a letter which Wellington had written on the eve of the Battle of Waterloo. It was, in a sense, unflappable in that Wellington said he thought it would be all right, but in another sense, you could see he was in a very excitable state. There were various crossings-out in the letter and little mistakes he didn't usually make. With great enthusiasm, Prince Charles said his father was just the same: on the surface he was unflappable, but underneath he had very strong feelings. Prince Charles said it in a way I recognised as a son who admired his father. There was no need for him to have said anything. You could say that in twenty years' time everything changed but I don't believe that.'

What Charles really lacked was a killer instinct like the Iron Duke or Robert Maxwell, and it was Mountbatten who was recruited to find it. 'I remember Mountbatten taking Charles shooting,' said an aristocrat's daughter. 'The beaters sent up wave after wave of pheasants and he had Charles blasting away. It wasn't sport, it was slaughter.' Mountbatten's bloodlust had nothing to do with 'land management', the usual excuse among the upper classes to justify fox hunting and shooting. When he toured India with the Prince of Wales in the Twenties, the two sportsmen went out hunting panthers. The animals they shot had been taken drugged from a local zoo. Lord Louis duly recorded the kill in his diary, along with other prey they had hunted in Australia — kangaroos 'worried to death as they turn up great pathetic eyes at one and never utter a sound', and an emu bludgeoned to death with branches torn from a tree. 'After this, they plucked feathers out and stuck them in their hats,' he wrote.

Charles came to regard Broadlands as his second home and, according to Mountbatten's secretary, John Barratt, Uncle Dickie 'particularly enjoyed having the boy who would one day be King turning to him for counsel'. When an informant came to Fleet Street to sell a story alleging deviant behaviour by Mountbatten, 'Maxwell bought the story and suppressed it', said a Mirror source. It was a small but important favour.

As a working royal, Charles usually bore adverse headlines and the drudgery of his official chores with stoical good humour. He tried to shrug off personal criticism in the Press, once likening himself to a pheasant, there to be shot at. But once details of his married life, his most private of lives, turned up in print, he became more than annoyed, he became angry. This was his Achilles' heel. Charles knew that many of the stories were true, and the leaks only sharpened his sense of outrage. The Press got so close to the truth so often that he clearly feared the newspapers would report his guiltiest secret: the on-going affair with Camilla. In fact, James Whitaker claimed that Stephen Barry had told him that Charles shared his bed with Camilla after the pre-wedding ball at Buckingham Palace on 27 July, 1981. As Barry died of AIDS in 1986, Whitaker had respected the confidence for some considerable time. This was understandable. Aroused, Prince Charles could be a formidable opponent. Those who caught the sharp edge of his tongue were unlikely to forget it.

The chance to express his feelings came when a dozen or so Fleet Street editors were corralled one evening in an upstairs Stateroom at Buckingham Palace. The Palace had decided to do something about invasion of privacy, although a previous appeal to the editing fraternity had met with little success.

The object this time, explained Michael Shea, Press Secretary to the Queen, was to remove Prince William from the firing line of the tabloid circulation war. Whenever Prince William was taken to the park, accompanied by nanny 'Baba' Barnes and a detective, the paparazzi would swoop. A curious crowd would gather around the Prince's pushchair and it was at these times that Charles and Diana felt their first-born was at risk from a possible kidnap attempt, even a terrorist attack. If newspapers, particularly the tabloids, stopped buying pictures of William's visits to the park, the paparazzi would move on to other royal pastures. Logical though this sounded to Shea and his royal clients, it was like asking a fox to walk past the open door of a chicken coop. Even if Fleet Street agreed, the paparazzi could still sell every picture to magazines in Europe and the United States.

After a briefing from Shea, the guests were split up into small groups and offered drinks while Charles and Diana 'worked the room' under the vigilant eye of Palace officials. 'If it doesn't stop, we'll have to cancel my son's trips to the park,' Diana told one group. 'This would be a pity because I want him to mix with ordinary people. I don't want him to be brought up behind the Palace walls.'

Her voice was soft and well-modulated, not at all strident like most Sloane Rangers, who could easily compete against a combine harvester. Some sentences were punctuated by a nervous giggle. It was evident that she was ill at ease and painfully conscious of her height which, at six-foot-plus in shoes, made her very nearly the tallest person in the room. Much of her body language made her seem smaller; she hunched her shoulders, hung her head and looked up, eyelashes flashing, in the familiar coquettish way that made men swoon. Turning, she said in an aside to Peter Thompson, then editor of the *Sunday Mirror:* 'Oh my goodness, they're all so SHORT.'

Diana's habit of looking up from beneath her eyelashes with that famous tilt of her head had intrigued Harry Arnold ever since he first noticed it in 1980. 'Diana collects scalps,' he said. 'Many of my friends have experienced it, Andrew Morton has experienced it, and so have I. You will be in a room full of people and her eyes will lock on you and you will have this sudden panic when you think she is looking at you. You will suddenly look behind you, thinking there is somebody there but there is no one. Then you get the euphoric feeling that she is giving you the eye because that is just how it looks. She holds this gaze for a fixed amount of time and you think, "My God, does she fancy me?" That is what many men have thought. She seems to be thinking, "I know what you are thinking – you are thinking wouldn't it be great if you could sleep with me and you cannot, and I am telling you that you cannot. But I know that is what you would like to do." It's a subtle mind game that I have seen pop stars like the Beatles do with fans. It's a tease.'

On the other side of the room, Charles had seized the chance to give his views on intrusion. He became locked in conversation with one guest and it was apparent to those within earshot that he was becoming angry. Immaculately turned out, his hair neatly clipped and his cheeks glowing pink with the health of the super-fit and very rich, Charles kept his voice, and his composure, under control. But his cheeks turned a brighter shade of pink as he made some strongly held points about the reporting of his marriage.

It was the trivia he found most offensive. What he ate for breakfast or what his wife bought when she went shopping could be of no conceivable interest to anyone. Much to his annoyance, the guest listened politely, but remained unrepentant. 'People are interested in everything you do,' he told Charles in a soft Ulster monotone. 'We give people what they want to read.'

Throughout the evening, Diana raised her eyes to the ceiling, hugged herself with thin arms and twiddled with her sapphire engagement ring. Every few minutes, she glanced over her shoulder to locate Charles in another part of the room and fix him with The Look. Each time, their eyes met for a second and that seemed to reassure her. The distinct impression was that she not only needed her husband, she was very much in love with him.

This was apparently confirmed when she presented him with the winner's trophy after polo at Smith's Lawn a few weeks later. Diana kissed him passionately on the lips in full view of the Press. Cameras clicked furiously; onlookers applauded wildly. This was one royal picture the Princess of Wales wanted to see on the front pages. It was also the last of its kind.

DIANA wasn't the only one living dangerously in the latter part of the Eighties. Charles had never been closer to death than he was at two forty-five p.m. on 10 March, 1988.

'Go, Sir, go,' shouted Bruno Sprecher, the royal ski guide, and Charles took off. Skiing for his life, he outdistanced an avalanche roaring down a mountainside above Klosters. 'The heir to the British Crown, Prince Charles, was able to ski out of the danger area to a place of safety in time,' a Swiss official reported unemotionally. According to those who were present, there was only a matter of feet in it.

Charles's friend, Major Hugh Lindsay, a former equerry to the Queen, was swept away and killed instantly, his skull fractured by a huge lump of ice. 'Major Hugh Lindsay, born 30.04.53, was taken by the avalanche, carried some 450 metres and fell over a small cliff along with the snow of the avalanche,' said the official report. Lindsay, the target of Diana and Fergie's brolly-prodding exploits at Ascot the previous year, had been among the royal party staying at a chalet at Wolfgang, near Klosters.

The official report on the tragedy by the Director of Public Prosecutions for the Graubunden district noted Charles's persistent habit of skiing outside slopes designated as safe. 'Prince Charles, as he has done frequently over the last few years, was on winter holiday in the area of Davos-Klosters and was skiing with his retinue primarily off the prepared pistes,' said the prosecutor. 'The intention was that Prince Charles would ski with his friends, Mr and Mrs Charles Palmer-Tomkinson and other members of his party while the Duchess of York had engaged mountain guide Bruno Sprecher as her personal guide. On the morning of 10 March, 1988, the group met on the Gotschna ridge and subsequently skied down the Drostobel run which had been opened. At this point, two groups were formed, one around Prince Charles, whose group skied on rapidly, and the other group around the Duchess of York who was skiing more slowly.'

Fergie, who was pregnant with Beatrice, suffered a fall into a stream and, after a medical check-up, she returned to the group's chalet to spend the afternoon with Diana. The Princess, not the bravest of skiers, had pleaded a touch of flu and stayed behind.

'Sprecher was left with no work to undertake,' said the prosecutor. 'He was therefore invited by Prince Charles's group to join them in further descents. After lunch the group consisted of Prince Charles, Charlie Palmer-Tomkinson, his wife Patty, Major Hugh Lindsay, Bruno Sprecher and Police Corporal Domenic Caviezel, who had been assigned responsibility for the personal safety of Prince Charles. They skied a route variation which took them in the direction of Hagglamad and which would then lead through the steep Rosslerkeller run. Prince Charles and Charlie Palmer-Tomkinson led the way on to the steep slope and waited for the others at what was regarded as a safe location. After the complete group had stopped on the steep slope, large masses of snow above them suddenly detached themselves.

'Four people were able to ski out of the way in time. However, Major Hugh Lindsay and Patty Palmer-Tomkinson, who were standing higher up and further back, were caught by the falling snow. While PC Caviezel was using the radio which he carried to notify the emergency and mountain rescue post and to summon aid, Sprecher was first to ski down the steep Rosslerkeller run, skiing round the sharp fall, to arrive at the mouth of the avalanche. There he was able to locate Patty Palmer-Tomkinson by means of the Barryvox avalanche locating device which he carried with him. Mrs Palmer-Tomkinson was buried under some fifty centimetres of snow.'

Charles relived the horror in a statement to the authorities. 'It was all over in a terrifying matter of seconds,' he said. 'Herr Sprecher reacted with incredible speed and total professionalism. He skied down to the bottom of the avalanche as fast as he could, having called to the Swiss policeman to radio for a helicopter. Having reached the foot of the avalanche, he located Mrs Palmer-Tomkinson and dug down to her. Mr Palmer-Tomkinson and I skied down and arrived just as Herr Sprecher had reached Mrs Palmer-Tomkinson's head. He had given her mouth-to-mouth resuscitation and revived her. He gave me the shovel to dig her out but I tried using my hands as well. At this point I stayed with Mrs Palmer-Tomkinson while he quickly went to try and locate Major Lindsay with Mr Palmer-Tomkinson. They found him fifteen yards above Mrs Palmer-Tomkinson, but tragically he had been killed outright during the fall, despite Herr Sprecher's valiant attempts to revive him by mouth-to-mouth resuscitation.'

'In his case, all the lady doctor of the REGA Service who had arrived with the rescue team could do was to declare him dead,' said the prosecutor, adding that Charles's skiing party had 'disturbed the snow cover by their presence and triggered the slab avalanche themselves. Other causes for the triggering of the avalanche may be excluded.'

However no individual could be held responsible because the party were 'a common risk group, indulging in skiing outside the secured pistes while taking a certain element of risk into account. Through his own personal decision to ski over the fatal slope, each individual consciously took upon himself the risks thus arising.

'Heads of state, the members of their family and their retinue enjoy diplomatic immunity in Switzerland,' the prosecutor explained. 'Prince Charles at no time invoked his immunity. It was much more the case that he made himself available to the investigating authorities from the very beginning. The criminal investigation has been discontinued.'

When news of the avalanche reached London, Maxwell immediately ordered his Gulfstream jet into the air to fly a *Mirror* team of reporters and photographers to the scene. In the confusion, it had been feared that Charles might have been killed. Maxwell was overjoyed when he learned that his life had been spared.

Although shocked, it was claimed that Charles was anxious to continue the holiday but he listened to Diana's advice to return to Britain. They flew home from Switzerland with Major Lindsay's body in a British Aerospace 146 jet of the Queen's Flight. His widow Sarah, who was expecting their first child, watched as the flag-draped coffin was received at RAF Northolt, Middlesex.

Prince Charles wrote to a friend: it's nice to know I would have been missed. I only wish everyone could have survived. But that's fate, I suppose.' Fergie was more sentimental. 'God takes the good first,' she said. As a personal tribute to the young major, Diana promised Sarah Lindsay that she would never ski at Klosters again.

IF anyone doubted that Maxwell's joy over Charles's deliverance was genuine, the question mark was removed on the heir's fortieth birthday later that year. The publisher donated £500,000 to the

Prince's Youth Business Trust, a gift he described as 'his own special birthday present to Prince Charles'.

Charles did not discover that the security services had bugged his friend until after the crooked tycoon had died. Maxwell plunged from his yacht *Lady Ghislaine* and drowned off Gran Canaria in November 1991 only days before a Swiss bank exposed his criminality. Considering his connections with the Communist Bloc, including a personal relationship with the murderous regime of the Bulgarian thug Todor Zhivkov, it was understandable that Maxwell attracted the scrutiny of British Intelligence. The bugging, however, failed to stop him from secretly plundering £800 million in company assets and in shares belonging to the pension funds of his employees.

It emerged that the top-secret Government Communications Headquarters (GCHQ) at Cheltenham had been monitoring Maxwell's private calls for some time, certainly during the period of Wendy Henry's dismissal. The Joint Intelligence Committee, which co-ordinated and assessed information from MI5 and MI6, passed 'raw intelligence' from these calls to the Prime Minister's office and Cabinet Ministers. 'The sigint (signals intelligence) I saw in the autumn of 1989 included intelligence data on Robert Maxwell taken from telephone conversations and faxes intercepted in Israel and the Mediterranean, probably from his yacht the *Lady Ghislaine*,' Robin Robison, a former JIC officer, told the *Financial Times*. It was later learned that GCHQ could also monitor any phone line in Britain, including Maxwell's Ericcson system at the *Daily Mirror*.

Only thirty-five miles from GCHQ, Cyril Reenan twiddled the dial of his scanner along the wavebands allocated to radio telephones. He overheard a trainer talking to a jockey about a horse running at Newbury. 'I heard him say the horse was sure to win and it was a rank outsider,' he said. 'My wife was out shopping. As soon as she came back, I told her, "We're going to Newbury races". I took £100 with me but I lost my nerve and just put £20 on the horse to win. I was shaking like a leaf. It was in a photo finish and then it was announced as the winner at twenty-five to one. I won £500 plus my £20 back.'

His hobby had become so profitable that he invested £1,012 in an IC-R700 scanner which could monitor one hundred calls. He also installed a twenty-year-old tape recorder and dangled a microphone down in front of the scanner.

One day, he thought, he might hear something worth recording.

8

SEX, LIVES AND AUDIOTAPE

'You're awfully good at feeling your way along'
Camilla Parker Bowles

THE Squidgy episode in Diana's nightmare began to the sounds of revelry. One night in the summer of 1989 she partied with a couple of pedigree chums from the Gilbey and Guinness dynasties. The Princess arrived alone at the party, hosted by one of her friends, the former Julia Guinness, daughter of the brewing family.

Julia, who was married to Old Etonian banker the Honourable Michael Samuel, was the sister of one of Diana's *betes noires,* Sabrina Guinness, who had preceded her in Charles's affections. They had a passionate fling in 1979 but it was a passing fancy that soon ran its course. Diana, however, showed traces of jealousy when she bumped into Sabrina at the hairdressers after her marriage. 'Diana walked in and caught sight of her straight away,' said Kevin Shanley. 'Somewhat indignantly she enquired, "Is that who I think it is?" Before I could reply, she added, "I wish you had told me one of his exes would be here."'

But Julia had been a good friend to Diana and they sometimes lunched together, once at a Kensington restaurant where they sat and chatted for two hours over two green salads. The bill for £14 was the smallest the management could recall. Charles's relationship with her sister wasn't Julia's only connection with the Windsor boys. She had dated Prince Andrew several times when they were teenagers. She was in his company when he was turned away from Annabel's one night for not wearing a tie.

One of the other guests at Julia's party was James Gilbey, a relation of the Gilbey's Gin empire whose family motto was Honour and Virtue. His father Ralph was a retired wine merchant who lived with his wife Barbara in a Somerset farmhouse. He shared at least one thing in common with Charles: at school, he had been called 'Fatty'. Over a few drinks, Diana shared her troubles with the young motor trade executive, or used car salesman as he modestly called himself. She was helpless and angry, desperately in need of a soulmate. Gilbey listened attentively. 'James attracts women who want to sob and pour out their troubles,' said a friend. 'He makes a woman feel special – like she is the only person in the world who matters to him.'

Gilbey, a darkly handsome Libran, had known Diana during her bachelor-girl days at Coleherne Court. He had attended Ampleforth, the alma mater of Andrew Parker Bowles. Gilbey was shocked by what Diana told him about her husband and the officer's wife. She gave him her telephone number at Kensington Palace and, genuinely moved by her plight, he kept in touch.

It would be disingenuous to suggest that he didn't find her immensely attractive and at six-foot-three-inches tall, Gilbey was one of the few men Diana could look up to. He was also an optimist. Several false starts not only in the used car business but also in love, had taught him the power of positive thinking. Diana was drawn to his New Age philosophy. She saw Gilbey several times before her brother's wedding to the model Victoria Lockwood in September. Listening to the couple make their wedding vows in a church near Althorp, Diana reflected on the husband sitting beside her. He was, in her words, 'stuffy, old and boring before his time'. She also knew that he had been unfaithful to her.

'Diana had never slept with anybody except Charles,' said a friend. 'Charles went to the altar and made a vow before not just God and her but the rest of the world that he knew he wasn't going to keep. It's nearly two hundred years since a royal who was to be king did that, and that was Prinny. He is blacker than a great many of his ancestors.'

'Prinny, the Prince Regent, had gone through a marriage ceremony with his widowed mistress Mrs Fitzherbert in his twenties even though she was a Catholic,' said the royal historian. 'But he dumped her and married Caroline of Brunswick to pay off debts of £500,000. He had a string of mistresses before, during and after the wedding. Caroline was an exceedingly ugly woman who refused to wash below the waist. When George met her, he ordered a large brandy. He stayed drunk and, on his wedding night, he collapsed in the fireplace. His bride left him there. Somehow, they had a daughter, Princess Charlotte. Caroline travelled around Europe with an entourage of lovers and her affairs were so notorious that George charged her with adultery. She was put on trial at the House of Lords where she claimed she had only committed adultery once – with Mrs Fitzherbert's husband.

'When he succeeded to the throne as George IV, Caroline was Princess of Wales but although she became Queen Consort she wasn't crowned. She tried to break into Westminster Abbey during his coronation but he had prizefighters stationed at the doors to keep her out. She continued to make trouble for him and, soon afterwards, she was taken ill at the theatre and died of inflammation of the bowel. The suspicion was that she was poisoned.'

Diana had at least one chance to step back from her entanglement with Gilbey, but ignored it. He invited her to dinner at his flat in Lennox Gardens, South Kensington, and she was photographed by Jason Fraser leaving the one-bedroom premises at one fifteen a.m. i suppose it wasn't that wise for Diana and me to meet in those circumstances,' said Gilbey, even more unwisely, it's hard for the Princess to keep up old friendships.'

It was a measure of Diana's desperation that she continued to take Gilbey's calls. She might like to say, 'I treat the Press as though they were children,' but she knew that once the tabloids scented a big royal story with her name on it they would pursue it to the end. Around this time, Andrew Morton decided to write a book called *Diana's Diary.* When he read about Diana's late-night visit to James Gilbey's flat, he recognised a potential entry. Morton started to make some tentative inquiries. At this stage, he had no inkling that Gilbey was already calling the Princess of Wales 'Squidgy'.

ONE old friend who really needed Diana's help was the Duchess of York. The Yorks were living at Castlewood House, a mansion loaned to them by King Hussein of Jordan, while work proceeded on Sunninghill. Although Andrew was frequently away, Sarah had unexpectedly fallen pregnant with their second child. 'Fergie's life was in a mess and she was very unhappy,' said a friend. 'Andrew wasn't coming home on some of his shore leave – he was going to his old quarters at Buckingham Palace or Windsor Castle to see his mother – and he was spending time with Liz Nocon.' Elizabeth Nocon, wife of Andrew's photographic guru Gene Nocon, had been the Prince's confidante before his marriage. Fergie felt excluded from the friendship and there were arguments when Andrew did go home to Castlewood.

When Fergie told Diana about the new baby, the Princess decided it would be a boy, and she suggested he should be called Elvis. Fergie laughed good-naturedly at the dig. Her exploits with the movers and shakers of the Showbiz Set were something of a family joke.

If Andrew was unavailable, Fergie had grown-up things to do on her own. Her first two Budgie books had just gone on sale in the United States and she was going to promote them in New York. She had also accepted an invitation from Lynn Wyatt to visit Houston for a festival of British opera. As an added inducement, Lynn had recalled her son Steve for the occasion. Fergie wanted to meet Steve, whom she had heard about from one of his former American girlfriends. He sounded divine.

It had, however, taken all of Steve Wyatt's dimpled smiles, Southern drawl and saccharine charm to make his mark in London society. He came to the capital to work in the oil broking business for his stepfather Oscar at Delaney Petroleum, based in St James's. 'I met him when he was being touted around Europe as a sort of eligible bachelor,' said the young Chelsea deb. 'He was just hanging out, going to parties, stuff like that. I met him at a drinks party in Kensington because someone thought he was the man for me, but he wasn't my type. He has bad acne scars on his face and his lips are so big he looks like Bette Midler dressed as a man.'

Wyatt's 'fun' personality and spiritual approach to life, however, were immensely attractive to the Duchess of York. She began a less than clandestine affair with him soon after Lynn introduced them at Allington, the Wyatt's French-style chateau in opulent River Oaks Boulevard. Lynn knew so many royals, the house was known as the Wyatt Regency.

Fergie met up with Wyatt again on 8 December at Constable Burton Hall in Yorkshire, where he was shooting with friends including the actor Nigel 'The Charmer' Havers, Patrick, the Earl of Lichfield and the Royal Ballet dancer Wayne Eagling. 'It was the first time anybody knew they were seeing each other,' said Maggie Wyvill, the *chatelaine* of Constable Burton. 'But at that stage she was very much pregnant, and at that point there was nothing going on between them.'

Before long, however, Fergie was so smitten with the Texas playboy that she was often sighted with him at the trendy Cosa Nosheries around Knightsbridge while Andrew was away. When other commitments stopped her from going to a party he was attending, she rang friends the next morning to check who else had been there and to whom Wyatt had spoken. 'She rang him constantly at his office,' said a friend in the oil business. 'She kept after him.' Staff at Sunninghill were instructed to count the rings if line five, her private number, rang while she was away from the house. 'Nobody, but nobody was permitted to answer the calls on line five,' said an insider. 'But we knew she had a code for Wyatt's calls.'

The Duchess had flown south from Yorkshire on Sunday, 10 December, to join Andrew, who had been shooting at Sandringham. Fergie liked to say, 'You can always tell the way I feel by looking at me'. If Andrew was perceptive, he would have noted that his wife was deeply enamoured – and it was not with him.

ONE week before Christmas, a group of drinkers adjourned to a house in Merseyside after closing time at their local pub. For entertainment, the host, a man known to the outside world as Ordinary Joe, switched on his radio scanner and, as the revellers drank from cans of beer, they listened in to intercepted calls.

Suddenly, they heard a voice that one of them recognised. It was the Prince of Wales, not speaking in a recorded broadcast but talking live on the telephone. He was reading out the text of a speech he had prepared to an attentive listener.

Charles had been to Wales that day to visit a youth enterprise centre at Greenfield, Clwyd. After that, he presented awards at the township of Mold, visited an Abbeyfield Society old people's home and finished his official engagements at Wrexham Technology Park. Fairly tired, he drove to Eaton Hall in Cheshire, home of his close friend, Anne, the Duchess of Westminster, to spend the night. After a late dinner, he went up to his room and lay down on the bed. It had not been a particularly tough or demanding day on the royal circuit, but Charles was needy. He picked up his portable phone and dialled Camilla at Middlewick House.

They had been speaking for quite a while – fifty minutes, according to one source – and it was after one a.m. before the Merseyside partygoers switched on a tape recorder. Ordinary Joe recorded the date – 18 December, 1989 – as a voiceover in the process. Camillagate was born.

At first, the secret listeners tittered at the suggestive nature of the conversation:

Camilla: Mmmmm ... you're awfully good at feeling your way along.

Charles: Oh stop! I want to feel my way along you, all over you and up and down you and in and out. . .

Camilla: Oh!

Charles: Particularly in and out.

Camilla: It's like that programme Start the Week. I can't start the week without you.

Charles: I fill up your tank.

Camilla: Yes, you do.

The eavesdroppers soon realised, however, that the heir to the throne was involved in a deeply satisfying sexual relationship with a woman other than his wife. 'You have to hear the longing in his voice when he says "Ooooh daaarling" to realise that she knew just how to turn this guy on,' said one who listened to the whole tape. 'She certainly sounds earthy.'

It was obvious that the lovers met on a regular basis, and that they were planning another meeting.

Camilla: Darling, listen. I talked to David tonight again. It might not be any good.

Charles: Oh, no!

Camilla: I'll tell you why. He's got these children of one of those Crawley girls and their nanny staying. He's going, I'm going, to ring him again tomorrow. He's going to try to put them off till Friday. But I thought as an alternative perhaps I might ring up Charlie.

Charles: Yes.

Camilla: And see if we could do it there. I know he's back on Thursday.

Quite a few other people, it seemed, were privy to the deceiving of Diana and although the eavesdroppers had no way of identifying any of them, it reinforced the notion that this was not a fleeting romance but a long-term relationship. The woman referred to her husband, who was absent in London, as 'A' – and it seemed that he, like Diana, was also being deceived. The lovers expressed their longing to meet before Christmas because the prospect of spending the festive season apart was painful for both of them.

Camilla: It would be so wonderful to have just one night to set us on our way, wouldn't it?

Charles: Wouldn't it! To wish you Happy Christmas.

Camilla: Happy, oh don't let's think about Christmas. I can't bear it.

His mistress clearly provided the Prince with loving security and, when his confidence deserted him, assured him that he was attractive to other people and clever, 'I got the impression that he felt very lucky to have someone as wonderful as her to love him,' said the listener.

Charles: 'Night, darling. God bless.

Camilla: I do love you and I'm so proud of you.

Charles: Oh, I'm so proud of you.

Camilla: Don't be silly. I've never achieved anything.

Charles: Yes, you have.

Camilla: No, I haven't.

Charles: Your greatest achievement is to love me.

Camilla: Oh darling, easier than falling off a chair.

Charles: You suffer all these indignities and tortures and calumnies.

Camilla: Oh darling, don't be silly. I'd suffer anything for you. That's love. It's the strength of love. 'Night-night.

When Charles rang off with a final 'I love you', the drinkers rewound the tape and played it again to make sure they hadn't been dreaming. Analysed in more detail, the conversation showed that Charles was a man who felt no guilt or shame in expressing his sexual needs to the woman he desired. He was dependent on her and the manner in which she freely encouraged him showed that she not only understood his need but reciprocated it. The tape was so explicit that a frisson of excitement ran around the room. The only problem was: what could they do with it?

NEW YEAR'S EVE. Diana hadn't spoken to James Gilbey for twenty-eight hours when she switched on the TV set in a private sitting room at Sandringham House. She was dressed casually in black jodhpurs, a pink polo neck sweater and black pumps. Downstairs, the other royals were gathering to see in the New Year. It had been a difficult day in the bosom of the Family. She turned up the sound on the TV and dialled Gilbey's carphone number: 0860 354661.

She and Charles had lunched with the Queen, Prince Philip and the Queen Mother, but Diana hadn't felt much like even keeping up pretences. She had felt so wretched that she wanted to burst into tears. But she had managed to control herself, helped by the remembrance of Gilbey's frequent pep talks.

After lunch, she and Charles had gone out to tea with William and Harry, but the atmosphere between them was strained. Although they travelled back in the same car, with the princes behind in another, they talked very little. Charles told his wife that he wanted to spend the evening at Sandringham. Living with him, Diana decided, was real, real torture. She wanted 'to go out and conquer the world' or, less grandiosely, 'do my bit in the way I know how'. Charles would be left behind.

Gilbey, wearing a day-old pair of jeans, a pink striped shirt, apple-green pullover, green socks and brown suede Gucci shoes, was driving to spend the night with friends near Abingdon. He planned to go shooting the next day. When his car phone rang, he pulled into a lay-by on the downs outside Newbury to speak to the woman he called Squidgy.

Not far away in Oxford, Jane Norgrove, a twenty-five-year-old typist, tuned in a £95 second-hand scanner in her bedroom and switched on her tape recorder.

James: And so darling, what other lows today?

Diana: So that was it ... I was very bad at lunch. And I nearly started blubbing. I just felt really sad and empty, and I thought, 'Bloody hell, after all I've done for this f**king family.'

James: You don't need to. Cos there are people out there – and I've said this before – who will replace the emptiness with all sorts of things.

Diana: I needn't ask horoscopes, but it is just so desperate. Always being innuendo, the fact that I'm going to do something dramatic because I can't stand the confines of this marriage.

Gilbey slipped into his New Man role of confidant and comforter, reassuring Diana but urging her not to suppress her feelings. Her self-esteem was at stake, he pointed out, and she needed to take direct action in facing up to at least one of the problems. This is what the therapists call 'tough love'. Stop pitying yourself and fight back.

James: OK then, Squidgy. I am sorry you have had low times. Try, darling, when you get these urges – you just try to replace them with anger, like you did on Friday night, you know.

Diana: I know. But do you know what's really quite, umm ...whatever the word is? His grandmother is always looking at me with a strange look in her eyes. It's not hatred, it's sort of interest and pity mixed into one. I am not quite sure. I don't understand it. Every time I look up, she's looking at me and then looks away and smiles.

James: Does she?

Diana: Yes. I don't know what's going on.

James: I should say to her one day, 'I can't help but ask you. You are always looking at me. What is it? What are you thinking?' You must, darling. And interestingly enough, one of the things said to me today is that you are going to start standing up for yourself.

Diana: Yes.

James: Mmmm. We all know that you are very capable of that, old Bossy Boots.

In another part of the house, the Duchess of York was preparing her children for bed. Although she had problems of her own, she was fully conversant with Diana's agony. At another time, she would say: 'No matter what hell I'm going through, it's nothing compared with my sister-in-law.'

Diana: The Redhead is being actually quite supportive.

James: Is she?

Diana: Yes, she had. I don't know why.

James: Don't let the (garbled) down.

Diana: No, I won't. I just talk to her about that side of things.

James: Do you? That's all I worry about. I just worry that you know she's sort of... she's desperately trying to get back in.

Diana: She keeps telling me.

Gilbey's own love life had been anything but smooth and, he told Diana, he and a friend had discussed the 'Transfer List'.

139

James: Mark Davis kept saying to me yesterday, 'Of course you haven't had a girlfriend for ages.' 'What's the Transfer List looking like?' He said, 'What about that woman in Berkshire?'

Diana: Oh God.

James: And I said, 'No, Mark, I haven't been there for three months.' He said, 'Have you got any other transferees in mind?' I said, 'No.'

Diana knew all about the Transfer List. There was a wine bar in Belgravia where the list was rarely off the menu. The progeny of earls and dukes, brokers and bankers from the City, rich builders and anyone who qualified for the title of playboy worked it like a singles bar. They discussed the young lovelies, some married, who had become available for one reason or another. Smooth transfers of affection from one partner to another was what the list was all about. But Gilbey wasn't really interested. His need for Diana came across time and again. He felt no guilt or remorse at expressing his desires to a married woman. He was, she told him, 'the nicest person in the whole wide world'.

James: (sighing) Squidgy . . . kiss me (sounds of kissing by him and her). Oh God, it's wonderful isn't it? This sort of feeling. Don't you like it?

Diana: I love it.

James: Ummm.

Diana: I love it.

James: Isn't it absolutely wonderful? I haven't had it for years. I feel about twenty-one again.

Diana: Well you're not, you're thirty-three.

It was obvious that Gilbey neither liked nor trusted the Duchess of York and, once again, he warned Diana about her motives.

Diana: Fergie said to me today that she had lunch with Nigel Havers the other day and all he could talk about was you. And I said, 'Fergie, oh how awful for you.' And she said, 'Don't worry, it's the Admiration Club.' A lot of people talk to her about me, which she can't help.

James: I tell you, darling, she is desperate to tag on to your coat-tails.

Diana: Well, she can't.

The couple arranged to meet with the help of Ken Wharfe. Diana would say she was going for acupuncture treatment on her bad back. Gilbey cautioned her: 'Squidge, cover them footsteps.' But he was impatient to see her again.

James: Kiss me please (kissing sounds). Do you know what I'm going to be imagining I'm doing tonight about twelve o'clock? Just holding you close to me. It'll have to be delayed action for forty-eight hours.

Diana: (laughs.)

James: Fast forward.

Diana: Fast forward.

When the call ended, Jane Norgrove removed the tape from her recorder and put it away. 'I didn't even listen to it – I just put the tape in a drawer,' she said, i didn't play it until weeks later and then I suddenly realised who was speaking on the tape. I knew it was Princess Diana.'

The secretary wasn't the only eavesdropper to hear Diana and Gilbey talking. Cyril Reenan, the Abingdon radio enthusiast, recorded a similar conversation, but he was quite sure that the date had been 4 January, 1990. If true, this meant that the call had been recorded elsewhere on New Year's Eve and re-broadcast. The conspiracy theory that MI5 or another branch of the secret service were trying to discredit the Princess of Wales stared with this disclosure.

'There were rumours about her (Diana's) marriage and I knew I had some astonishing news and I quite expected it to break in a day or so,' said Reenan. 'After all, if I had managed to pick up the conversation, surely someone else would have too.' When nothing happened, Reenan phoned the *Sun.* 'I've got the biggest royal story since the Abdication of the King,' he claimed. Later, he would call it 'the biggest mistake of my life.'

A FEW days later, an early-morning conversation between Prince Andrew, speaking on a portable phone aboard his ship *Campeltown* just off the Dorset coast, and Sarah, back home at Sunninghill, was picked up on a £300 scanner and recorded.

Andrew: Are you feeling any better?

Sarah: Yah. I'm just sort of disenchanted, really, I just want to run away and stay with Mum in Argentina. Got to get away from everything. I just feel, I just want to run away. Preferably with you, but I can't do that. We're both chained to our stupid duties and ruining our lives together. But if that's what your family want then that's what they want. I've lost my spirit today. If they want to have another unhappy marriage they're going the right way about it.

Andrew: But darling, what have they done to make it unhappy?

Sarah: Well you've done it, haven't you? You've told them that we've had a discussion, a heated discussion.

Andrew: I didn't say we had a heated discussion.

Sarah: Well, you did. You told them that we were in opposition about something. You thought it was a bad idea and just tell me if I'm going mad or not, that's what you probably said to her. Anyway, never mind, forget about it. Speak to you later.

Andrew: All right, darling.

This call was recorded by 'a member of the public' in the Portsmouth area. This tape was also sent to the *Sun*. Reviewing the situation, Kelvin MacKenzie, the editor, noted: 'It is a very curious thing when three tapes of the Royal Family are produced within thirteen days. You must think there is probably a plot.'

Stuart Higgins, the robust young executive who had delivered Squidgy to the *Sun,* spelled out his editor's concern in greater detail, 'I can't believe that all these things are accidents and what amazes me all the more is that nobody among the authorities seems to have any kind of interest in conducting an investigation into it,' he said, 'I know we keep saying that, but they still don't. I would have thought it was a matter of enormous bloody concern, not just a sordid newspaper interest but from a proper investigation interest. I can't understand such adamant failure to investigate it. I've never been questioned by the police, never been asked by any authority where the tapes come from, where I'd kept them or if I'd been doctoring them.'

Another person who believed that a conspiracy was in progress was Lady Tryon. 'What I suggest is that people stop and think deeper about all these so-called revelations,' she said. 'I believe that republican groups are trying to undermine the country and bring the monarchy down. I suggest that the people and the Press are being manoeuvred by somebody to bring about the monarchy's destruction.'

THE faint-hearted turn back when they see the sign: *You Are Now Entering Sun Country.* It stands above the security doors guarding the spacious editorial offices of Britain's biggest-selling daily. This is Kelvin's Kingdom, HQ of the Currant Bun, as the staff fondly call their paper, on the sixth floor of News International's high-tech printing plant at Wapping on the River Thames.

MacKenzie had run the most profitable of Rupert Murdoch's titles for ten years, a feat which owed much to his rapport with the republican-inclined proprietor.

Murdoch's global duties as the head of The News Corporation, based in the United States, meant that he had to delegate some of his responsibilities at Wapping. On 3 January, 1990, the day before Reenan thought he taped his Squidgy call, Murdoch appointed Andrew Knight as chief executive of News International.

Knight had nurtured an aversion to bugging ever since he discovered that his home telephone had been tapped when he was editor of *The Economist* some years earlier. The bug was discovered when his then wife, Sabiha – later Lady Foster, wife of the architect Sir Norman Foster – made a call to discuss a dinner menu with an Italian chef. The line was very bad, punctuated by disconcerting phuts and clicks. Sabiha hung up to re-dial and heard a recording of her previous conversation being played back.

'It seems absurd that anyone should want to tap my telephone,' Knight said at the time.

When Reenan rang the *Sun,* he spoke to Stuart Higgins, who was working on the paper's news desk. 'He said he had something which he thought was potentially dynamite and which he described as very damaging to the monarchy,' Higgins recalled, it took me days to convince him that we should listen to the tape. I had no idea of its enormity until I heard it.'

Higgins, who had met Diana during his time as a reporter in the West Country, fixed up a meeting with Reenan and another *Sun* reporter, John Askill. He was fairly confident that he would be able to recognise the Princess's voice. Unlike most people in Britain, he had actually heard her speak. 'We met him at Didcot railway station in Oxfordshire and sat in his car,' said Higgins. 'He was in the driver's seat and his wife sat in the passenger seat. He played the tape on a rather battered cassette recorder but it was very bad quality. We had a cassette recorder with us and it was a bit clearer on that.

'We took the tape back to the office and it took a long time to transcribe it.

'I was astonished – I just couldn't believe it. We went through all sorts of emotions -whether it was an elaborate fake or whether it was soundalikes trying to cause some damage. We got the tape analysed and went through it, line by line, to corroborate all the evidence that was available at the time. There were lots of pointers to it being the Princess of Wales because of various comments she made, but there was no clue as to who the man was. Indeed, the only time we'd heard Gilbey mentioned before was when Jason Fraser took the picture of Diana visiting his flat. Within a week of actually receiving it from Cyril Reenan, though, it was obvious that it was genuine. It was really decided very quickly after that that it would never be published. For a long time, the tape was in the bureau of my home at Teddington.

'The Norgrove tape of the same conversation came in some time later and that was down to Phil Dampier (the paper's royal reporter at the time). I was flabbergasted, absolutely flabbergasted when I heard it. I mean, the tapes almost molded together and they provided enormous evidence of the association. It was easy to prove it was Gilbey because of the various pointers there.' Still the *Sun* held back and both Squidgy tapes were deposited at the Midland Bank in Fleet Street for safekeeping.

'I realised the significance of the tapes two and a half years ago and I never envisaged the day when they would be published,' said Higgins. 'Although it was written all the time that the marriage was in trouble, there was never any clear evidence. So we didn't publish. I think it is on the record as being said that this was a decision taken by Mr Murdoch.'

The Australian-born media magnate was given a ringside seat from which to evaluate the marriage for himself a few months later. He and his wife Anna were invited to the fiftieth birthday party of King Constantine, the exiled Greek monarch. Charles and Diana were among the guests.

The party was held at Spencer House, previously Diana's London home, which had been sold to the Rothschild family for £9 million a year earlier. The mansion, bordering Green Park, was a few doors away from the Murdochs' penthouse in St James's Place. Lord Rothschild had spent £15 million restoring its Georgian grandeur. The guest list included the Queen, Prince Philip, Prince Andrew, but not the Duchess of York who was in America, and the crowned heads of Spain, Denmark, Sweden, Holland and Belgium. 'Tino', as Prince Philip called his Greek cousin, arrived in a green Porsche convertible from his home in a cul-de-sac at Hampstead Garden suburb. The Murdochs and Prince Andrew arrived on foot.

Most of the 650 guests consumed smoked fish, poussin with fresh vegetables, strawberries and vintage Bollinger in a marquee draped with pink chiffon and lit by crystal chandeliers. The top forty, which included the Royal Family and Rupert and Anna Murdoch, dined inside the house with Constantine and his wife Queen Anne Marie. After dinner, the guests mingled in the gardens or danced to the music of Lester Lanin's orchestra. A green canopy surrounded the house to foil even the sharpest paparazzi. Tino's family and friends picked up the bill for £250,000.

When Murdoch returned home, his butler Philip Townsend asked him if he had enjoyed the evening. 'Oh yes,' replied Murdoch. 'There were nine royal queens and about forty of the other sort.'

'Whatever do you mean, darling?' asked Anna Murdoch.

'I mean nine real queens and forty poofters.'

'You are not allowed to say that, darling.'

'I'm allowed to say it,' her husband replied, it's the *Sun* that's not.'

The abundance of tiaras and titles failed to impress Murdoch who had been seated next to the Queen. 'Even with all those queens, it was no big deal', he told his butler. He was quite dismissive about Prince Charles: 'He sat there like a zombie. No one seemed particularly interested in him.' Murdoch would have had his undivided attention had he mentioned the two tapes sitting in a bank vault in Fleet Street.

Three weeks later Charles broke his right arm in two places when he fell from his pony Echo while playing polo at Cirencester. Until then, he had been cautious whenever Camilla visited Highgrove. After his accident, he became positively careless, it was a very bad break, so bad that he nearly fainted when he saw the bone sticking through his elbow,' said a polo source. 'He was in terrible pain.' it was a silly thing to do,' Charles admitted. 'I was a silly fool.'

When he was well enough to leave hospital, his damaged arm in a sling, he posed for pictures with Diana before she drove him to Highgrove. But minutes after she dropped him off, she left the estate to drive back to Kensington Palace. Charles sent his detective to collect Camilla from Middlewick House. According to PC Andrew Jacques, one of the police guards assigned to Highgrove, the couple adjourned to Diana's private sitting room. Noticing a light in the room, Jacques peered through a chink in the curtains and saw Charles and Camilla 'dancing cheek to cheek'.

'Though the Prince had his arm in a sling, they were smooching to the very romantic music,' claimed Jacques after he had left the police force and become an insurance salesman. 'Eventually, they disappeared down on to the sofa out of my sight. I moved away, but when I returned fifteen minutes later, the light was still on. I saw Camilla emerge from behind the sofa and shake her dress. Then Charles stood up. He looked down and intimated that because one arm was in a sling, he couldn't readjust his clothes.'

Camilla became Charles's nurse as well as his lover and helped him to cope with his duties as best he could. The couple spent hours inside the seven foot high walls of the private vegetable garden, where not even his children were permitted to roam. Charles was suffering from delayed shock and depression. 'I think they put it on backwards,' he said after an operation. 'I had to encourage him to go through the pain barrier and force himself to do some pretty nasty things,' said Sarah Key, his Australian physiotherapist. 'The arm had stiffened up. We could straighten his elbow but the problem was getting it to bend. Because of who he is I think he feels the need to prove himself and drive himself that much harder.'

To help Charles keep in touch with his friends, Camilla drove him to social events and encouraged him to rise above the pain. 'They were going around to dinner parties together in the Gloucestershire hunting circle,' said a Highgrove insider. 'They were more and more accepted as a couple among their friends.' As travelling to his office at St James's Palace was excruciating, Charles asked people to visit him. He received them in his study. 'Charles started to invite people he would normally only have seen in London down to Highgrove while he was recuperating,' said a Palace insider. 'They were allowed to see, among other things, that Camilla Parker Bowles was acting as his hostess in Diana's place. Slowly, some of these people talked and the circle widened.'

If Charles had ever learned anything from his father, it should have been that he needed to maintain the utmost discretion about his private life. Prince Philip knew that loose talk could be dangerous.

TO his utter dismay, James Gilbey learned that the Squidgy call had been taped. When he told Diana, she was devastated. Unable to read the signs at all clearly from that distance, she suspected that her husband and the Highgrove Set had something to do with it. This unfounded fear motivated many of her future actions.

'The *Sun* approached Gilbey in early 1990 to say that they had the tape and they'd identified him,' said a Fleet Street insider. 'He'd learned by this time to say nothing, but he turned white with shock.' At that time, Andrew Morton was toiling away on his first Diana book, *Diana's Diary*. Soon after the *Sun* confronted Gilbey, Morton approached him through an intermediary to inquire about the dinner date at Lennox Gardens. Gilbey responded: 'I'm sorry, I can't help you.' Morton's name meant nothing to him at that stage.

A few weeks later, as the time approached for Morton to deliver his manuscript to the publisher, the writer announced to a friend: 'I've got to the bottom of the Gilbey thing. Diana was helping him with an emotional problem – a broken romance.' A mutual friend, he said, had helped him to get the information.

Despite a modest upbringing as the son of a picture framer in Yorkshire and a higher education at the very red-brick Sussex University, Morton was surprisingly well-connected. He played squash with Dr James Colthurst, one of Diana's friends, and he and the Princess attended the same society wedding during 1990. Diana put Morton on her Christmas card list. It was just another piece in the jigsaw.

The Queen had already been alerted to problems in the Yorks' marriage by a miserable Prince Andrew. When Her Majesty asked to see her for a private chat, Diana feared the worst. Her mother-in-law, she decided, must know about Squidgy.

147

9

THE SQUIDGY SYNDROME

*'The marriage was made in hell and they're both well
out of it'*
Stuart Higgins

IF the Queen had heard the name Squidgy at that point, she might have mistaken it for some household product she had seen advertised on TV. One of Her Majesty's endearing qualities was the way she either mixed up words or forgot them completely. 'What's that thing that goes round and round and plays records?' she once asked. 'A gramophone, Ma'am,' replied a helpful aide.

Surrounded by medieval rituals, a few trusted friends and her favourite corgis Spark, Myth and Fable, Elizabeth II acted out a history of which she was justifiably proud in grand homes and castles. By any standards, she led an extraordinary life, but sceptics who questioned whether she had lost touch with reality were wide of the mark. Although one courtier admitted privately that the Queen had become a little eccentric in later life, she still had more political savvy than anyone else in the Palace. She also possessed a modern intelligence-gathering service that was frightening in its scope. At five foot four inches tall, she was small but perfectly informed. 'She sometimes knew things the Prime Minister doesn't know,' said Sir Edward Heath, one of the nine holders of that office during her reign.

The Queen had learned from her sources a great deal about the private lives of members of her family and their friends. Added to her own insight, it amounted to a very comprehensive picture. 'The Queen knows what's going on,' said the Palace insider, it is a mistake to underestimate her. She has a ruthless streak.' Her Majesty could not have been happy with what she saw and heard during the final year of the 'Me' Decade – the egotistical Eighties. There had been, she noted, quite an outbreak of 'Me-ism' among the younger royals.

In the Forties, the Windsors had been a compact unit which George VI referred to in a letter to Elizabeth as 'our family, us four, the "Royal Family" .. . with additions of course at suitable moments!!' There had been many additions since then, but the effect had been to scatter the Family rather than unite it.

Increasingly the Queen has become an isolated figure,' wrote Elizabeth Grimsditch in the *Sunday Express.* 'Her closest friends are elderly, her children she sees rarely. Princess Anne is the only royal who drops in on her mother, and then only when the staff are informed. Touchingly, whenever she does, the Queen insists on making tea for her personally.'

Prince Philip preferred the atmosphere at White's Club in St James's Street to stuffily formal weekends at Windsor Castle. The Palace discounted suggestions that he stayed overnight in a suite of rooms at the club after enjoyable evenings in the company of like-minded friends.

Even if one or more of her three sons were spending time at the castle, they kept to themselves, often dining from trays sent to their rooms. Charles had to make an appointment if he wanted to dine with his mother at Buckingham Palace. When he played polo at Windsor Great Park, he would arrive and depart without seeing his mother at the castle.

The Queen's visits to Sunninghill to see the Duchess of York and her granddaughters were restricted to just forty-five minutes while afternoon tea was served. She then drove straight back to Windsor. She rarely visited Kensington Palace to spend time with Diana and her sons. They had to visit her.

Much of Her Majesty's day was spent working on her red despatch boxes and studying other reports which were regularly handed to senior Palace courtiers by Scotland Yard. These were compiled from at least two dossiers about the royals and the people they met either socially or in their work. Detectives assigned to the Royal Protection Branch, who shadowed the royals whenever they left home, not only kept tabs on their friends and acquaintances, they were obliged to report any incident which might jeopardise their safety. 'Anything to do with personal matters goes through a channel for sensitive information,' said a former royal minder. 'The protection of lives and property, which is a more practical concern, goes through another.'

The Queen also received briefings from the Prime Minister at their meetings every Tuesday at six-thirty p.m. in the Audience Room at Buckingham Palace about specific matters which had been brought to his attention by the heads of British Intelligence. Information concerning the royals was passed to the Prime Minister's office through the Joint Intelligence Committee (JIC). Government eavesdropping was carried out at the GCHQ listening station at Cheltenham, dubbed The Puzzle Palace.

'If you think the staff sit hunched over a radio set wearing earphones and clutching a notebook you'd be wrong,' said investigator Gerry Brown. 'The radio messages are fed through computers which switch on and record conversations automatically when they pick up key words such as Hijack, Kidnap, Cocaine — or even Squidgy.' It was claimed, however, that a twenty-four-hour electronic watch was maintained on members of the Royal Family by a team of six civil servants who monitored the switchboards of Buckingham Palace, Windsor Castle, Kensington Palace and Balmoral Castle.

'Monitoring royal calls is carried out as a matter of routine at GCHQ,' claimed a security source quoted in the *Mail on Sunday*, it is imperative that the intelligence services know the movements or intended movements of the Royal Family at all times. Some of this team's work is designed to screen out nuisance calls getting through to the royal residences. But it is mainly to provide a running service of vital information about the royals.' Through one arm of this network or another, Her Majesty learned about her daughter-in-law's trysts with James Gilbey. More worryingly, she was told they had caused a potentially dangerous breach of security.

Like Diana, the Queen had known about Charles and Camilla for years, but Her Majesty had given her tacit approval to the liaison. 'She was reluctant to intervene so long as they kept it completely secret,' said the Palace insider. 'Charles knew he was flirting with danger, but he needed Camilla. In the Royal Family, having a mistress was far from unusual; in fact, it was normal.'

'There's the most peculiar attitude among the British upper classes towards royal infidelity,' said the titled Chelsea lady. 'An honourable position is definitely to be a royal mistress. It really is strange. If you go back in history, the Dukes of Grafton, Richmond and Gordon, and St Albans were all the offspring of mistresses. It hasn't actually changed. There were an awful lot of people greasing up to Camilla in Gloucestershire.'

Moreover the Queen's relationship with her heir left a lot to be desired. He found her distant, she found him difficult. 'Her Majesty, like her forebear Victoria, is capable of forming deep prejudices,' revealed royal author Douglas Keay. 'She can take a strong dislike to a person, sometimes for what might be considered a trifle by others. One courtier advised me, "Once she get her knife into someone it doesn't matter what that person does, her opinion won't alter." Elizabeth II has never forgotten the advice of her father George VI. He told her, "Whatever you show or say will be remembered by that person for the rest of his or her life. So you must never show displeasure unless you actually want it to be remembered." ' Charles was more familiar than anyone else with his mother's increasing ability to be displeased.

The Queen also knew from Andrew that his marriage was in difficulty. She was aware that her son's long absences from home dismayed the Duchess but she was not aware that his bullying had driven her into the arms of Steve Wyatt. However, when Fergie called on Wyatt at his apartment at 34 Cadogan Square, Chelsea, the meetings were logged in security reports filed to Scotland Yard. 'Do you think he is the sort of person you should be encouraging, dear?' the Queen asked Fergie after she had invited Wyatt to a Buckingham Palace ball.

Diana posed a much more serious problem. 'Fergie was getting away with blue murder but it didn't really matter,' said a tennis-playing friend of the Princess. As the next Queen, Diana had constitutional responsibilities that didn't concern the Duchess of York. The House of Windsor had invested a great deal in her future and there were disturbing signs that the investment was at risk. Her presence at Charles's side was his biggest single asset in 'selling' him as one deserving of the Crown after his mother's death.

By law, Charles had been forbidden from marrying a Catholic and, after the age of twenty-five, he could marry only with the consent of both Houses of Parliament and the parliaments of the Dominions. A Protestant virgin like Diana had been the only choice from a constitutional standpoint. Once she had married Charles and produced an heir, she had not only ancient royal duties to perform but, in the liberated, modern world, great power as well.

The Windsors' legal right to rule depends on the 1701 Act of Settlement, which complements the Bill of Rights of 1689 'for the further limitation of the Crown and better securing the rights and liberties of the subjects'. Its aims were twofold: to ensure a Protestant succession to the throne and a parliamentary system of government. The British monarchy had been Protestant, or more specifically Church of England, ever since James II, a Catholic, had been expelled in 1688 and the throne handed to William and Mary. In taking the Coronation Oath, the Sovereign became Defender of the Faith and Supreme Governor of the Church of England.

The Royal Encyclopaedia, approved by Buckingham Palace, states: 'The Act of Settlement thus reinforced the fundamental principle established in 1688-89, that Parliament had *the right to determine both the succession to the throne, and the conditions under which the Crown could be held.*' In other words, the Windsors rule not by divine right but by the will of Parliament. It was incumbent on Charles and Diana, therefore, to safeguard the Windsor lineage; to put the future of the monarchy, as opposed to the wellbeing of individual members of the Royal Family, above all else.

It had been taken for granted at the time of her wedding that Diana was willing to make this sacrifice. Provided she was discreet, though, it was perfectly all right for her to meet male friends in private. The trouble was that Diana had given her bodyguard the slip in the past, once driving off on her own to the West End and precipitating 'a frightful kerfuffle' at the Palace. When these matters were raised with Charles, he could only shrug and repeat that he was powerless over his wife. Of all people, he was the last one she would take seriously. The Queen decided it was time to take action herself.

Before the Squidgy tapes had been securely locked away in the Midland Bank, Gilbey had blithely romanced Diana using the perfect cover that they had been 'just good friends during her days at Coleherne Court'. If people accepted they weren't lovers then, there was no reason to suspect them now. So that was all right. Yet after the slip at Lennox Gardens, they went to extraordinary lengths to avoid being photographed together. When Diana took Gilbey to San Lorenzo one night, a detective persuaded a paparazzo who was loitering with intent outside not to take their picture as they departed. As payback, he was promised an exclusive photo opportunity with the Princess on another occasion. The cameraman watched Diana and Gilbey leaving the restaurant after a meal — and didn't take their picture.

The meetings became more contentious when Diana began to borrow a flat in Walton Street close to San Lorenzo so that she could talk to Gilbey in complete privacy. 'When they went to the flat, Diana used to leave her bodyguard sitting outside in the car,' said a source close to Gilbey. 'She would switch off some kind of gadget she has with her in case of a terrorist attack. I believe it's an electronic device and she would disable it in some way. This meant the detective completely lost contact with her. He had to report this back to his bosses in the Royal Protection Branch. He needed to cover himself because he was unable to guarantee her safety under such circumstances. The report was passed to the Queen's people and she was informed. I understand that Diana was told off by the Queen in person.' Diana left that meeting with a profound sense of relief. The Queen obviously hadn't heard the ticking of the Squidgy timebomb.

Her Majesty, in fact, had been distracted by other signals which told her that the time had come to protect her birthright. The age of thrusting, intrusive European unity threatened all things of a uniquely British stamp. Among endangered species in the new order was the House of Windsor itself. If Maastricht ever achieved its ultimate goal, Europe would become one super-nation with a brand new constitution ruling the lives of *citizens* rather than *subjects.* Fanciful though this sounded, it could not be ignored.

Privately, the Queen mapped out a secret agenda with the express purpose of defending her sovereign role for future generations no matter what other institutions might be swept away in a new, federalised Europe. The pint and the mile might disappear but the Crown would remain intact. New words like 'the ERM', 'the Single Market', 'the ECU' and 'the Maastricht Treaty' had more significance for Elizabeth II than the curiously banal 'Squidgy'.

'The Prime Minister was informed of the Queen's desire for a moderate, entirely voluntary process of change to modernise the monarchy,' said a reliable Westminster source. 'She had on-going discussions with several key advisers, including the Archbishop of Canterbury and four Privy Counsellors. She knew she would have to bow to calls for her to pay income tax, but she wanted the initiative to come from above, not below. She was also very concerned that, although she had no intention of abdicating, Prince Charles should be seen as a worthy successor.'

Exactly a year after his Christmas call to Camilla, Charles warned against the dangers of trivialising royal life. 'What worries me is this trend to reduce everything to a kind of radio play or a soap opera,' he complained. 'Are we going to reduce everything to an idiot simplicity?' The soap opera in which he was a star performer started auditions soon afterwards in the unlikely venue of a greasy spoon cafe on the outskirts of London. Before the final credits started running, his fitness for kingship had been seriously challenged.

THE success of *Diana's Diary* was gratifying for Andrew Morton in more ways than hard cash. He had built up some high-quality contacts. More important, Diana liked it. His first meeting with Diana had been in Australia during her tour with Charles and William, or Wills as everyone called the infant prince, in 1983. It had provided him with a valuable perspective which he was able to draw upon later.

It was a really successful tour and when people were telling me all these things about suicides and bulimia and, you know, the bitterness and hostility between Charles and Diana, I kept thinking back to what seemed to me a very friendly tour,' he said. 'They seemed to be very loving and together, and I could not believe it. And yet apparently on that tour she would go back to her room and burst into tears. It was the first major tour she had ever done and she just couldn't cope with it at all. I along with everyone else was beguiled by the image – I didn't know what the reality was at that time.

'I also met her in New Zealand, Portugal, Spain, Italy, Canada a couple of times – seven, eight, possibly ten times, I suppose. Even if it's light, bright and trite, you get an impression of somebody and I thought she was dry and quite sharp. She did not seem to take it too seriously and she was very realistic about things. The image at the time was of a demure, pouting, rather willowy Princess whereas she had a far more vigorous and down-to-earth sense of humour.'

Morton's nickname among some of his royal rivals was the Sorcerer's Apprentice. He was given the title after he replaced James Whitaker, deemed to be the Sorcerer, as royal correspondent on the *Daily Star.* It was a deft piece of sleight of hand in this job that caused Morton to be declared *persona non grata* at Buckingham Palace after he published the contents of the Queen's address to the Commonwealth one Christmas. He had picked up the main points of the speech from Michael Cole, whose job as accredited royal correspondent for the BBC made him privy to the annual pre-recorded secret. Cole inadvisedly let down his guard during a pre-Christmas lunch of royal writers which, he assumed, was off the record. He was promptly sacked when his words turned up in print. 'I admit it was a mistake,' Morton told Megan Tresidder. 'I should have cleared it with him first. I regret that mistake. It was a shabby episode from which no one emerged very well.'

Early in 1991, Morton started work on a new royal book on the apparently safe, though infinitely fascinating subject of *Diana's Health & Beauty Secrets.* 'He'd done another book in the meantime called *Inside Buckingham Palace* and it hadn't sold as well,' said the Fleet Street insider. 'He told a friend, "The next one's on Diana – it's the only thing that sells." ' 'I could happily live off the ashes of the House of Windsor for the next twenty years,' Morton was reputed to have once said, a statement he could not recall making.

He did say, however, that writing about the monarchy was, to quote Conrad, like moving into 'the heart of darkness' of the establishment. 'I have always been a great fan of Joseph Conrad and that is my favourite book,' said Morton. 'The monarchy is the heart of darkness of the establishment because all roads ultimately lead to Buckingham Palace. The people who work there are under legal constraints, the people who are associated with members of the Royal Family are under social constraints and people who supply their goods and services are under commercial constraints. So it is a web of secrecy and if you defined Britain as a fairly secretive society, this is the ultimate in the secretive nature of it.'

However Morton knew as well as anyone covering royalty that the royals did, in fact, talk to reporters to put across particular points. When Prince Charles told James Whitaker that he had met Princess Marie Astrid of Luxembourg only twice in his life, he was knocking down a *Daily Express* story saying that the couple were about to announce their engagement. He did not, however, want to be quoted by name. 'Could you just say a close friend told you?' the Prince asked the reporter.

Diana was skilled in similar tactics. 'She is very adept at getting her view across, sometimes subtly and sometimes brutally,' said Harry Arnold. 'One simple but blatant example was when Prince Harry was born and Princess Michael of Kent was saying he had red hair — and, goodness, she was not far out really. But Diana was in Wales and during a walkabout she kept saying, "My baby is fine but, by the way, he has not got ginger hair," knowing that we were all hanging around. It was meant for us. So she does plant information in a fairly unsophisticated way. But I also think she is capable of doing it in a sophisticated way by giving friends certain facts to pass on.'

Penny Thornton, who had become Diana's astrologer on the recommendation of the Duchess of York, found to her cost that her former client possessed a very sharp cutting edge indeed. Ms Thornton was contracted to the *Today* newspaper to write a daily column. When she was quoted in connection with Diana's personal problems, the Princess decided to act. On the flight from Nepal back to London, she sought out the paper's royal correspondent, Charlie Rae, in the business class section of the aircraft. After some small talk, she said: 'By the way, will you tell whoever needs to know that I have only met Penny Thornton once and that was back in the mid-Eighties.'

When executives at the paper sought reassurance, Ms Thornton immediately sat down and wrote to Diana, asking her why would she have written 'so often – letters which I treasure – to someone you have hardly ever met?'

She never received a reply so she mentioned the dilemma to a contact in a county police force, who raised it with Ken Wharfe. The astrologer said that she received a verbal message from Diana, saying: 'I said no such thing. Don't worry about it. I have always valued you as a true friend and confidante.'

As Morton made his first calls, the doughty figure of Lord McGregor of Durris took over as chairman of the new Press Complaints Commission. This was a voluntary body whose membership was drawn from the upper and lower reaches of the Fourth Estate as well as other parts of society. Its objective was to enforce a code of conduct governing the invasion of privacy. If this system of self-regulation worked, it would preclude the need for statutory controls over the media. Nothing less than the freedom of the Press was at stake.

McGregor, a Yorkshireman like Morton, is the son of a farmer. He had been made a life peer in 1978 after serving as chairman of the Royal Commission on the Press. He was, therefore, no stranger to muck-spreading of one kind or another. Top of his agenda was newspaper reporting of the Royal Family or, more particularly because it quickly emerged as the number one priority, the private lives of the Prince and Princess of Wales. He resolved to approach this uncertain terrain not as a pathfinder for the establishment or the Press barons but on behalf of the ordinary citizen. He soon found that he had entered the heart of a very dark forest where deception and intrigue were part of the scenery.

When they deigned to comment at all, Buckingham Palace haughtily denied that there was anything wrong with the royal marriage. One report of a rift was dismissed as 'complete rubbish'. Confessing anxiety over the situation, McGregor invited Sir Robert Fellowes, the Queen's Private Secretary, and Charles Anson, her Press Secretary, to lunch at the commission's headquarters in Salisbury Square, just off Fleet Street. As Sir Robert was also Diana's brother-in-law, it was accepted that the guidance they received was coming from highly privileged sources. Everything was all right at Kensington Palace, according to the Men from the Mall.

Sir Robert responded by inviting Lord McGregor and other members of the commission including Lady Elizabeth Cavendish, an extra lady-in-waiting to Princess Margaret, and Sir Edward Pickering, the *eminence grise* of the Murdoch empire, to a return lunch at the Palace. This cosy luncheon club kept in touch with the avowed aim of exploring 'the possibilities of mutual assistance'.

In other words, how to deal with freelance mavericks like Andrew Morton who were outside the direct control of either editors or Palace officials. 'Morton went alone – and this is his secret,' said the Fleet Street insider. 'He hunted alone.'

Working out of his first-floor office in a yellow brick building opposite Joe's Cafe, Morton built up a picture of Diana and Charles that had never been seen before, it is explaining to the outside world that this is the reality and then trying to get them to believe it,' he said. 'People actually believe the image of dashing, charming princes and beautiful, alluring princesses because it is deeply enmeshed in their psychology from childhood. I was intrigued as an individual about Diana's own childhood because her brother John had died after ten hours. I wanted to know how she felt about that – that's what I was interested in.'

In May, McGregor suddenly realised that someone was deliberately laying a false trail when he spoke to Lord Rothermere, last of the hereditary Press barons and proprietor of the *Daily Mail.* 'Lord Rothermere told me at a private dinner in Luxembourg that the Prince and Princess of Wales had each recruited national newspapers to carry their own accounts of their marital rifts,' he wrote in a letter to Sir David Calcutt, QC, head of a Government enquiry into Press controls.

If McGregor sensed that he was losing his way, the calls Andrew Morton was making would have confirmed his worst fears. 'He went to Diana's friends and he asked about the diets she used,' said the Fleet Street insider. 'Some time that summer, she gave the go-ahead for Carolyn Bartholomew to talk about bulimia. The food issue came first – before Camilla and all that stuff about suicide attempts. But he was still doing *Diana's Health & Beauty Secrets* into the summer of 1991.'

As it had been suspected for years that Diana suffered from an eating disorder, probably *anorexia nervosa,* this would have been an important revelation. But it would have been nowhere near as damaging to Charles as an expose of his relationship with Camilla. A deeply entrenched fear about her own position influenced Diana's decision to go for the conjugal jugular. 'She knew from her pals in the Press that Charles had approached several top people in the media to put across his point of view,' said the source. 'She believed that Charles used people in the media when it suited him.'

The most blatant example of this was a story leaked to the *Daily Mail* by the Prince's friends that Diana had vetoed plans for a party to celebrate her thirtieth birthday in July. 'She didn't want a party because Charles was so busy with Camilla Parker Bowles, but two of his friends went to Nigel Dempster and told him that Diana had refused Charles's offer of a party,' said the Fleet Street insider.

It was indicative of the Princess's state of mind that the story infuriated her: 'She knew that the Sun had at least one Squidgy tape because they had told James Gilbey. Diana's greatest fear was that the Charles camp would use the tape against her. No one is saying that they would have done it, just that her fears grew. So Di had a meeting with her brother Charles, James Gilbey, Carolyn Bartholomew and a couple of other pals – a council of war, if you like. They decided she had to strike first.'

Morton was chosen as the messenger for Diana's side of the story 'because he was already researching his book on health and beauty, and she trusted him'. This scenario baffled Morton, who said: 'Why single out some guy you don't know and, more importantly, you don't know whether you can trust?'

Was he chosen?

'No.'

Had he been fed with information?

'I wish they had done!'

Morton claimed that Diana had never discussed her marital problems or anything else with him personally. She had simply told the friends he had approached to 'make up your own mind'. Harry Arnold put it succinctly: 'Diana went along with what was happening. Charles had no say. She had engulfed him.'

James Gilbey had been 'serving his time' as a prisoner of Squidgy for exactly a year when the authors questioned him about his role in the Morton book. Asked in August 1993 if Diana had told him 'to make up his own mind', he said: i must say my recollection of events, as you can imagine, becomes more and more distorted as more and more things are apparently quoted back which I said many years ago. But I'm sure if that's what Andrew said, that's what Andrew said. I don't know. I haven't got a tape recording of the conversation that took place between us. If that's what I did say, I'm very surprised that he said that to you knowing full well that you're likely to publish it. I'm very sort of amenable about these things. I don't want to be awkward about it.'

Morton's quest had begun in earnest when one of his contacts arranged to meet him in a cafe at North Ruislip outside London soon after Diana's tenth wedding anniversary on 29 July. He revealed what Morton called 'the flip side of the fairytale'. Diana had seriously considered calling off the wedding, the contact told Morton, because of the Prince's continuing friendship with Camilla Parker Bowles.

'I had a long interview with a guy in this working man's cafe where many things were hinted at but nothing was confirmed,' he said, clarifying the position, it was basically, "This is what you should be thinking about." There were bits and pieces coming in from different sources over a period of time. I read a clutch of books about Diana that came out for the thirtieth birthday and the tenth anniversary and I thought, "They're not taking the story any further". I realised that I could just have a go.

'The idea was to concentrate on Diana from the start and see what it was like through her eyes. Ultimately, you mesh it all together – and Hey Presto!'

Morton called his publisher, Michael O'Mara, an American from Philadelphia, with the news that he was on to a really mega royal story.

'Camilla was an evolving thing because it was building up the evidence and just trying to work it out from the dates,' said Morton, it is just detective work really, isn't it? You have an idea of what is going on and, having a thesis, you develop it and try to explore certain avenues. The bulimia had been half hinted at a long time before, but I interviewed Carolyn Bartholomew (about that). I confirmed the suicides by a separate source other than Gilbey.

'So much that has been said about this whole affair has been done with the benefit of hindsight. The key is that in March 1992 you would not have said, "Is it a conspiracy?" The fact is that all of these things have happened independently of me. The Andy and Fergie separation was first, Anne's divorce second, then Diana did the Egypt trip on her own and the India trip where there was that misguided kiss (between her and Charles). A pattern of events was building up to a climax – symbolically, the fire at Windsor Castle. Fortunately, I did not have a box of matches.'

Not since Prinny and Caroline had the Royal Family faced such a brutal stand-off between two of its married members. If a measure of sanity had prevailed, some kind of moratorium could have been agreed between the warring partners. Morton would have published Diana's bulimia secret and Squidgy might have remained on deposit at the Midland Bank.

This could well have averted two of the most crushing blows of *annus horribilis,* but it wouldn't have stopped the Fergie Follies.

AS ever the team player, Fergie wanted Diana's connivance to confirm to the world that royal life was unbearable and the Queen's sons inadequate. But the Princess had rejected the idea out of hand during Christmas at Sandringham. She decided to let Fergie make her 'mad break' alone, believing she could manipulate events to her advantage from inside her marriage, in her own way, Diana's obsessional behaviour is obviously very sick,' said the titled Chelsea lady. 'But she's got a much stronger sense of self-preservation than Fergie.'

Even at the eleventh hour, Lord McGregor tried to clear a path through the undergrowth. 'I told the then Secretary of State for Home Affairs, Kenneth Baker, of my anxieties in December 1991,' he said, 'and suggested that he might wish to consider how the Palace Press Office could act to limit the damage.' Just to make sure no base remained uncovered, McGregor also tipped off John Major's Press Secretary, Gus O'Donnell, thus ensuring that the Prime Minister was alerted to the dangers of the internecine warfare going on inside the House of Windsor.

The heavy duty artillery was all lined up. When Diana returned to the safety of Kensington Palace from the unfriendly shooting country of Norfolk, she put her own plan into action. One of the phone calls she made was to Penny Thornton at her home, Branshott Court, Hampshire. 'My marriage isn't the only one in disarray,' she said. 'Sarah and Andrew have also got problems.' Ms Thornton said she recorded that call in her diary under the date: Thursday, 2 January, 1992.

Diana knew from her friends that Morton had made considerable progress on several aspects of his new work, secretly renamed *DIANA: Her True Story*. A major breakthrough had been securing the co-operation of her masseur/therapist, Stephen Twigg, who had helped to restore Diana's confidence after the Year of Living Dangerously. Morton said that Twigg decided 'on his own volition to speak to me'. 'I have subsequently found out that he spoke to the Princess of Wales who said, "Don't do it," ' said the writer. 'Now I would hardly call that co-operation.'

Twigg's dilemma was that although he wished to respect the confidence of his client, he saw that here was a chance for a wider audience to be told about his work. 'Basically, the situation was that people close to the Princess were telling Andrew about me and my influence in her situation,' Twigg recalled. 'As a result, he came to me and my immediate inclination was not to have anything to do with him, but subsequently common sense prevailed and I decided I'd better know what he was going to say even if it meant contributing.'

Matthew Freud, a public relations consultant who was later hired by Twigg, said it was his understanding that up to a matter of weeks before publication of the book, 'Stephen still hadn't told Diana that he had talked to Morton.' She was well aware, however, that her brother Charles had personally guided him through her childhood and that her father had provided the publisher with pictures from the family album and a selection from the portfolio of Patrick Demarchelier, one of which had appeared on the *Vogue* cover. The photographer was as surprised as anyone when he was told they would turn up in *DIANA: Her True Story.* 'Patrick didn't know any of that,' said his agent, Brian Bantrey. 'They were all pictures that her father had.'

But still Diana raised the ante. 'She suddenly released permission for all the Camilla stuff to go in,' said the Fleet Street insider. Terrified of the Squidgy threat, Diana had decided to bring her husband's mistress out into the open.

'I remember very distinctly it was 12 January, 1992, that I had a call from Andrew (Morton) asking me to do a tiny piece of research on Camilla Parker Bowles for his new book,' said Margaret Holder, the royal researcher, immediately he said it, I knew it wasn't a health and beauty book at all. He said it wasn't urgent but his voice betrayed that it was. I knew he worked to deadlines at the end of March so I got on with it fairly quickly. In fact, he asked for two names, Camilla Parker Bowles and Emilie van Custem (one of the Highgrove Set). It was very simple, basic research and he was happy with it.'

Word of Morton's enterprise reached Sir David English, the highly experienced editor of the *Daily Mail,* 'I knew months before it was written that Andrew Morton and his agent were claiming to be producing a book about the problems of the royal marriage – with the full co-operation of the Princess's side,' he said, i found it difficult to believe that Morton would be given such information and made my own inquiries. At a reception in early March, I actually asked the Princess of Wales about the book. I told her that if it was not true it would be a most damaging and dangerous book. In that conversation, I was left in no doubt that she not only knew about the book, and what its contents were, but also did not feel it would be a danger to her.'

He added: 'I think it was perfectly obvious to any editor at that time that the two rival camps in that marriage did have access to various newspapers. I can say that certain friends of the Prince spoke to senior people at the *Daily Mail* about his point of view.'

Diana's next call to Penny Thornton was made the day after the Queen had visited Sunninghill on Sunday, 8 March, 1992, to try to mediate once more in the Yorks' troubles. She had driven across from Windsor Castle to join them for afternoon tea, but only Beatrice and Eugenie enjoyed the Victoria Sandwich sponge cake served with fresh strawberries and cream. 'Sarah is very unhappy with Andrew,' Diana told the astrologer. 'She is going to do something very dramatic.' Ms Thornton logged this call on Monday, 9 March.

Right on cue, the lawyers were called to Sunninghill the following weekend. The Queen's solicitor, Sir Matthew Farrer, and another lawyer discussed the legal implications over a late dinner with Fergie and Andrew. The meeting broke up and the lawyers departed around midnight. News of it reached the *Daily Mail*. The story of the Yorks' break-up carried Andrew Morton's byline. Other reporters believed his information came either from one of Fergie's friends or from legal circles.

'At the end of that week, I was told by Arthur Edwards, "Watch your phones," and somebody else rang and said, "Be very careful because they want to find out who your mole is",' said Morton. 'Then two weeks later, my office was broken into. They just kicked down the door, opened a load of files and things. The only thing stolen was a camera.' The book was on hard disc in Morton's Epson computer, 'but it was in such a jumble at that point and you would have to spend a lot of time looking for it. I wrote it in January and February, edited it in March and added a bit more in April,' he said, it was a very tight schedule. I was due to interview Lord Spencer in the week that he was taken ill. Now the next question is, "Would he have approved the contents of the book?" I don't know.'

Believing he had attracted the attention of the Special Branch or a similar agency, Morton stopped using his office telephone to avoid bugging. 'I used payphones and spent a fortune on phone cards,' he said, it was not advisable to use the office phone because you never knew who was listening. Mike [his publisher] would ring me from his office in North Clapham and I'd ring him back from a payphone. We would see each other most days. It was a classic symbiotic relationship between publisher and author.'

As a further security precaution, O'Mara wisely decided to move the printing of the first edition outside the British Isles. 'The first print was in northern Finland because we assumed, rightly, that people would try to get hold of the book beforehand and to try to stop anybody from either injuncting it or from stealing it. This kind of journalism is a bit like a chess game where you have got to identify the opposition and work out their moves a few down the line. As it was, I got a call from a news agency pal of mine saying, "We've been given a few hundred quid from a newspaper to get hold of a copy of your book." They thought we were using our usual printers out in East Anglia. So those precautions were necessary. That was the nerve-racking period, giving birth.'

Rumours about the book started to cause alarm at Buckingham Palace, where Morton was regarded with some suspicion. 'By late April, I had been told by a very good source that the Queen herself had been informed about the book and was very worried about it,' said Margaret Holder. 'She was concerned that the Princess of Wales might be giving out information. I found out that a number of the Princess's friends had spoken on the record for this book and it was clear to me that this could not have happened without Diana's consent. A definite message was being put across as part of a strategy to impart to the world the story of her misery.'

Extracts of *DIANA: Her True Story* were due to be published on 7 June, 1992, in the *Sunday Times,* which had paid £250,000 for the serial rights. The alchemy of the Sorcerer's Apprentice was about to produce a sizable chunk of gold. For Lord McGregor and other notables on the Press Complaints Commission, however, it was a prelude to disaster. 'A frenzy of reporting by most sections of the media followed and details of the split between the Prince and Princess of Wales were publicised widely for the first time,' McGregor recounted. 'The impression that the Princess of Wales and her friends had co-operated with Andrew Morton in the writing of this book was denied by Charles Anson and Sir Robert Fellowes.'

On the evening the *Sunday Times* went to press, there was only one story. 'ITN (the television news service) phoned me and said the Palace were flatly denying that the Princess of Wales had anything to do with the book,' said Margaret Holder. 'They wanted someone who was reliable to put the opposite point of view. I wanted to speak to Andrew so I rang his wife Lynne and she said he was away somewhere, which I later found out was the Lake District. He rang me back and I told him, "From my long knowledge of the Royal Family, you could not have done what you have done without Diana's express approval." He replied, "Exactly." '

Prince Charles was devastated when he read in the opening instalment that his cold and hostile attitude towards his pregnant wife had driven her into throwing herself down a flight of stairs at Sandringham. 'I can never forgive her,' he said. 'I cannot comprehend how she could have done these things.'

For Diana, the tension had been even more nerve-racking than for Andrew Morton as what amounted to an act of revenge reached its moment of execution. The world now knew her shameful secrets. Her father had died in March and she was still grieving his death. She felt unloved and unprotected. Visiting a hospice in Merseyside, the crowd greeted her with cheers and people called out: 'We love you.' Diana suddenly burst into tears and, sobbing uncontrollably, fled from the scene. The cameras, normally so flattering, captured her distress.

So effective was the Palace camouflage that Lord McGregor was still unable to see the wood for the trees. He issued the most damning indictment ever levelled against journalists, accusing them of 'dabbling their fingers in the stuff of other people's souls'. 'I arranged a meeting with three commissioners, Lady Elizabeth Cavendish, Sir Edward Pickering and Mr David Chipp, at which we drafted the attached statement criticising severely Press reporting of the state of the marriage,' wrote McGregor. 'Before it was issued to PA (the Press Association), I read it over the telephone to Sir Robert Fellowes, in the presence of my colleagues, and asked him for an assurance that the rumours linking the Princess of Wales and her friends with involvement in leaking information to the Press were baseless. Sir Robert Fellowes gave that assurance ...'

Andrew Knight, now executive chairman of News International, decided it was time to tear down some of the foliage that obscured

McGregor's view. 'The following morning I was told by Mr Andrew Knight that the Princess of Wales was participating in the provision of information for tabloid editors about the state of her marriage and was going to make herself available to be photographed with a friend who was known as one of Andrew Morton's sources,' wrote McGregor. 'I took further soundings and was satisfied that what Mr Knight had told me was true.'

Knight confirmed that McGregor had been shocked to learn that cameramen had photographed Diana visiting one of the book's chief sources, Carolyn Bartholomew. Newspapers had been alerted by an anonymous caller that Diana would visit Carolyn's flat in Fulham on the evening of 10 June. The informant had phoned a *Sun* executive at his home at eight o'clock in the morning with news of the rendezvous. When Diana arrived in her Mercedes convertible twelve hours later, several photographers had taken up position in the suburban street. Some of them had been hanging around for hours. The visit was irrefutable evidence that Diana openly approved of the role Carolyn had played in the book.

Sir Robert apologised to Lord McGregor, stressing that his assurance had been given in good faith. 'Whitehall sources said Sir Robert asked the Princess about the allegations and she denied them,' reported George Jones, Political Editor of the *Daily Telegraph*. 'The Princess had, in practice, been invading her own privacy,' concluded Lord McGregor, who accepted that Sir Robert had not misled him intentionally. 'I feel like I was used.'

It was the biggest establishment cover-up since King Edward VIII's affair with Mrs Simpson in the 1930s,' thundered the *Daily Mirror* when the truth finally came out. 'Before he was revealed to have had an adulterous affair, David Mellor (the disgraced National Heritage Minister) warned newspapers about their conduct. He said the Press was drinking in the Last Chance Saloon. But the Last Chance Saloon is crowded by a bunch of hypocrites from Buckingham Palace and the Palace of Westminster. And they are serving the drinks.'

One of the few stores to ban the Morton book was Harrods, owned by Mohammed Al Fayed, a friend of Charles and his father. 'Our customers would not expect us to stock such a scurrilous book,' said Michael Cole, who had gone to work for the Knightsbridge store after leaving the BBC.

'It was like lancing a boil,' said the clinical Andrew Morton.

The Queen called Charles to a meeting with Prince Philip at Buckingham Palace and, enraged as he was, he had to listen to his mother's advice. Her Majesty suggested a cooling-off period of six months before any final decision was taken on the question of separation or divorce. Diana was informed of the Queen's wishes and agreed to go on a cruise with Charles and the princes as well as turning up at Balmoral for the annual summer holiday. 'She wasn't happy, but she agreed,' said a friend.

Andrew Knight seemed to confirm her worst fears when he wrote in the *Spectator* magazine that 'documented stories of regal infidelities' were locked away in a safe. His organisation had deliberately refrained from publishing them, even paying money to prevent them falling into the hands of tabloid competitors. He was, surely, referring to the existence of the Squidgy tapes.

Not surprisingly, the House of Windsor had passed the seventy-fifth anniversary of its creation on 17 July without a single hurrah. No one at the Palace wanted to draw attention to its origins. The House had come into being when King George V changed the family name from the Germanic Saxe-Coburg and Gotha to the very English sounding Windsor in 1917 during the Great War against his cousin the Kaiser. The choice had been forced upon him by strong anti-German feelings among his subjects.

In his meticulous way, George's grandfather, Prince Albert of Saxe-Coburg, had chosen Balmoral as the site for a royal retreat after studying weather reports for Upper Deeside. It had, he concluded, purer, fresher air than anywhere else in Scotland. But for Charles and Diana, the outlook was extremely bleak that summer, and for Andrew and Fergie even worse. Whatever their expectations, however, nothing could have prepared the young royals for the apocalypse that lay ahead.

ON a typical rainy midsummer day, a character straight out of Central Casting kept an appointment he had agonised over for three weeks. Nervously, he glanced at his watch as he entered the building in London's East End. He was late and he knew it.

'He came in wearing the proverbial raincoat, an awkward, bulky grey-haired man of about fifty and I thought he was either shy or embarrassed,' said Constance Regnier, London boss of the giant

German publishing group, Burda. in any event, he was not a go-getter; he was not a huckster. There had been some warm-up on the telephone when he first contacted me. He had, he said, this deep, dark secret about the Royal Family and would I be interested? It was so unbelievably enticing that to ask me afterwards if I would be interested was almost an insult. Then he phoned back a week later to make an appointment.

'I was amused and curious. He sat down, not facing me but keeping the chair at right angles to me so that his body language was talking away from me. But I could tell that he was awkward, he *felt* awkward, about what he was doing. When I questioned him, he said he was just a middleman. The people he was working with were extremely concerned and nervous. He was so nervous himself I didn't push him for his name. He produced an abbreviated transcript of the Squidgy tape. I was interested but I was cautious. I said I needed some evidence that this was genuine and he replied that he was working on that, but it would take a while.

'We chatted about the Royal Family and what all of this meant and he thought that someone was out to get Diana. I asked him who his employers were but he wouldn't say. I didn't press him because he was so secretive and awkward and *unpunctual* about the whole thing that I felt sorry for him. He said there was a tape of the conversation and when I asked him who the man was in the transcript he said: "We think it is Hewitt."

'He left my office promising to produce the tape, but even though he phoned several times promising to bike it over to me the messenger never arrived. There was a mysterious delay of a couple of weeks. I was quite annoyed but, lo and behold, it did arrive by bike one day in a Jiffy bag with no return address. This was a sample tape of edited highlights but he later sent the full tape, about twenty minutes, and a full transcript of the conversation. He phoned the next day to get my reaction and I said, "It sounds like dynamite but is it the Princess's voice? And if it is, how much do you want?" He said the tape was being tested for authenticity in America and he sent me a fax the next day asking for £50,000. It was absurd – he was reaching for the moon. Then silence again. It was another two weeks before he phoned me, this time saying he was in Australia.'

By that time, the circus had moved on and the big top was pitched in the grounds of Balmoral Castle.

IN planning Balmoral, Prince Albert envisaged a baronial-style castle equipped with the very latest mod cons. Beneath the Gothic turrets and inside the smooth white granite walls, he wanted every comfort that money could buy. A watercolour painted by James Roberts in 1857 showed the beautiful drawing room, furnished with gilt mirrors, tartan-covered sofas and a white marble fireplace with alabaster lamps. It was a showpiece of elegant highland living. The builder whom Albert had hand-picked to install modern plumbing and central heating, even though his wife's obsession with fresh air meant she kept windows wide open in the middle of winter, was Camilla's illustrious forebear Thomas Cubitt. This was just one of her connections with the stately pile.

High above the square tower on the south-east side of the castle, the Royal Standard testified to the Queen's arrival on Sunday, 16 August, 1992. She had sailed to Scotland in *Britannia* with the Duke of Edinburgh and Prince Andrew in the hope of gaining some respite from the rancour that was tearing the Family apart. The Queen was particularly fond of Balmoral because, like Sandringham, it remained her personal property. She loved to ride through the heather and take walks in its gardens with her grandchildren. It was at Balmoral that Philip had proposed to her and where he cooked his famous barbecues for all the Family.

The other performers in this dynastic melodrama dutifully turned up, not knowing that the script was already being written in two unlikely centres: Paris, France, and Lantana, Florida. Diana arrived with William and Harry to join Charles, who had flown in to Aberdeen airport with Fergie, Beatrice and Eugenie. The Duchess had just returned from holiday in the South of France, where a fresh suntan had helped her to cope with the angst in her life.

Diana and the princes took up residence at Craigowan House, a large hunting lodge set amid pine trees on a hill inside the Balmoral perimeter. Fergie moved into a suite with the princesses in the castle proper – as did Charles and Andrew. Although Andrew reverted to the rooms he had used as a bachelor, Fergie wasn't comfortable with the arrangement. 'Andrew knew that Johnny Bryan was with her at St Tropez and he questioned her about it,' said a friend. 'He wasn't happy – not because he feared Bryan was getting too close to the Duchess, but because he felt the other man was taking his role as a father.' Andrew had heard that, while on holiday, Eugenie had started calling Bryan 'Daddy'.

Fergie thought it might be wiser to put some distance between herself and the problem. The American's hold on her was stronger than ever, not only in matters financial, and she wasn't prepared to undergo a third degree from the husband she was hellbent on leaving. She asked the Queen if she could move into Craigowan House with Diana. Her Majesty agreed. Anything for a quiet life.

But the Queen's hopes of finding peace in the most stressful year of her reign were short-lived. Just five days after she arrived, pictures of Fergie's topless frolic with Johnny Bryan at St Tropez were splashed across the front page of the *Daily Mirror* under the headline *FERGIE'S STOLEN KISSES*. Fergie had been forewarned of the disaster because Bryan, hearing about the pictures, made an abortive attempt at the eleventh hour to get a High Court injunction to prevent publication. He also contacted Lord McGregor, who patiently explained that he had no powers to act.

Fergie, in the words of the friend, 'was completely floored' when copies of the *Mirror* and its sister paper the *Daily Record* arrived at Balmoral. The salacious nature of the pictures was far worse than she had envisaged. Many of them had been taken through pine trees between a hill-top vineyard and the pink-painted villa Le Mas de Pignerolle, the House of the Pines. They showed Fergie cavorting beside a kidney-shaped pool with the man she had aways insisted was merely her financial adviser and a close and trusted friend of her husband. In one picture, he was sitting at her feet, sucking her toes; in another he was stretched out on top of her in his pink bathing trunks. The film had been flown secretly to Paris for processing and the prints sold to a hastily despatched emissary from the *Mirror* for £60,000. In Fleet Street terms, it was an unbeatable scoop for the paper's editor, Richard Stott, and the paper instantly sold out.

After breakfast, the Queen summoned Fergie to her private suite and, in a curt three-minute exchange, it was decided that it would be best if she returned to London. Princess Anne, an implacable foe of both Diana and the Duchess, was more outspoken, 'I will not sit at the same table as that woman,' she stormed. 'The Duchess was red-eyed and went about with a hollow look on her face,' admitted a Balmoral source.

The new scandal only confirmed to Diana that, in the game of Unhappy Families, she had been dealt a winning hand. She wasn't entirely sure, though, how to play it. This uncertainty was partly a reflection of her growing sense of isolation inside the Family. She had held Balmoral in contempt ever since her first visit as a married woman. She also suspected that the other royals, particularly the Queen Mother, were *au fait* with what happened every time Charles and Camilla visited the Balmoral Estates. Charles preferred to stay at Birkhall, the Queen Mother's white-walled Queen Anne house a few miles away, often with Camilla and Kanga among the house guests. In Diana's mind, this amounted to a conspiracy and she felt disinclined to spare royal feelings, any more than she had over the Morton book. The Windsors, she decided, were self-centred and spoiled.

Quietly, the Princess made secret arrangements with the help of her staff. At least six airline seats were booked under assumed names. Then she went to see the Duchess of York. The two young women talked late into the night, not always as friends. Sources reported that raised voices could be heard coming from the lodge. Fergie made several long, sometimes tearful phone calls. 'She talked about leaving Britain for good and going into exile abroad,' said the Balmoral insider. 'She wanted to fly to Argentina to be with her mother but she knew she would lose the children if she did that. The strain was terrible.' To make things more complicated, it was Princess Margaret's sixty-second birthday the following morning and a big party had been planned for that night. Fergie dreaded the thought of it; Diana had plenty to fear as well.

Shortly before six a.m., long before Margaret had even woken up, Diana swept through the castle's wrought-iron gates with her lady-in-waiting and a detective. She was wearing her working clothes: a navy-blue jacket with matching blouse and a blue-and-white striped skirt. At six fifty-five she caught Air UK's Flight 601 from Aberdeen, bound for Humberside four hundred miles to the south. She shared the thirty-seater plane with businessmen and oil riggers, but the first few rows of the aircraft had been reserved to ensure privacy for the royal party. At Humberside airport, the plane was met by Special Branch detectives and Diana was driven in a black Granada to her destination, the Dove House Hospice in Hull. While Fergie was still dragging herself out of bed for a picnic with the princesses and Charles was planning a day's shooting, Diana was out and about doing the Work.

She had performed the opening ceremony at the hospice for thirty terminally ill cancer patients in the middle of the Morton expose and no one had expected her to return so soon. But Diana had remembered a promise she made to a dying man on her first visit and she had resolved to keep it. Only a handful of people knew about the trip. The arrangements had been made in utmost secrecy and neither airport staff nor workers at the hospice were expecting her. 'This visit is a lovely surprise for everyone here,' said John Fenwick, the hospice's chief executive. 'We are all thrilled.'

Undeterred by his wife's absence, Charles kept his appointment to shoot grouse with his father at Delnadamph, sixteen miles from the castle. At one p.m., the Queen joined them for lunch, bringing William and Harry with her. She had spent the morning with Margaret and her mother, although it was far from a festive occasion. Prince Andrew and his advisers stayed inside the castle to discuss not only how the St Tropez photographs had been taken but their impact on his separation. The presence of his daughters in some of the pictures seriously challenged his view that Fergie was a perfect mother.

By late afternoon, it was clear that all was not well with the Duchess. After she returned from the picnic, one of her staff called a doctor to the lodge. There were fears that she was on the verge of a nervous breakdown. Further south in Dove House, Diana was undergoing therapy of her own choosing. She visited the wards and heard that a shortage of cash was threatening the running of the newly-opened hospice. 'We had to lay off some staff because money is so tight in the recession,' Diana was told. She spoke to every patient well enough to meet her, holding their hands as she sat on their beds. 'Her visit has really made a difference,' said the wife of a man dying from bone cancer.

In Craigowan House, the visiting medico gave Fergie a sedative to calm her down and recommended that she stay put for the night. This meant she missed Princess Margaret's birthday celebrations, which coincided with a dinner party to honour the Queen Mother's ninety-second birthday. As Fergie slept, Diana left the hospice after eight hours and was driven back to the airport to catch the return flight. She was late for the party, but happy inside herself, it was typical of Diana that she could carry out some good works in the middle of a crisis and then plunge straight back into the problem,' said the Balmoral insider.

It was, in fact, a typical symptom of the Squidgy Syndrome.

EMBOLDENED by Fergie's disgrace, Diana was even more determined in her resolve. Treating the Duchess merely as a preliminary to the main event, she confronted Charles to discuss their own wretched predicament. She had resented the spotlight being turned away from her, no matter how harshly it had fallen on the Redhead who, when they were friends, she had called 'Duch' after her own childhood nickname.

Fergie's problems, she believed, were of her own making and they seemed inconsequential compared with her own. 'Royal marriages are too restrictive for the people who are sucked into them,' said the mother of a former royal girlfriend, 'I was appalled when, shall we say, a certain interest was being pursued in my daughter. But she was far too intelligent to get into such a situation.' Diana might have been 'sucked in', but she was, she felt, smarter than Fergie in finding a way out. She decided it was time to wring some concessions from the war-weary Windsors. Her first demand was that she and Charles should lead separate lives. She would stay at Kensington Palace with unlimited access to the princes While he would be based at Highgrove with unlimited access to Camilla Parker Bowles. It turned out to be a case of extremely bad timing.

Across the Atlantic, the *National Enquirer,* a mass selling tabloid based in Lantana, Florida, revealed the existence of the Squidgy tapes for the first time. The story was written by Noel Botham, a skilled operator from the days when Fleet Street was based at the correct address. He was now owner of The French House, a venerable drinking establishment favoured by writers and artists in the red-light district of Soho.

It was arranged through Lantana and then a stringer (local reporter) up in the North and myself actually got to grips with the story and wrote it,' said Botham. 'We had a transcript, not the tape itself, and we were told that the actual people supplying it thought at that stage the man was probably James Hewitt.' Over in Lantana, the *Enquirer* declined to elaborate. This was only one of many curious links in the Squidgy chain.

The Palace Press Office immediately branded the tape a hoax, 'an absolute fake', and an amateurish one at that. In the absence of any proof, reporters who listened to pirate copies and read censored versions of the transcript had to agree its provenance did seem suspect. 'A contact played some of it down the phone to me,' said one journalist. 'My reaction was like John McEnroe, "You cannot be serious!" It was such childish drivel. For one thing, who in their right mind could possibly think of the Princess of Wales as someone called "Squidgy"? But I can see now that it was too rambling and unscripted to be a fake. Clearly, it was part of a dialogue that had been going on between these two for some considerable time.'

On 15 August, a Squidgy transcript marked Strictly Confidential was passed to the authors by one of our sources. This version contained the following passage:

Diana: Well, he's sort of heterosexual and everything else, I think.

James: Heterosexual, is he?

Diana: Mmmmm.

James: What do you mean heterosexual?

Diana: Everything.

James: Oh, he's everything. That's not heterosexual. Oh, Squidge. (Laughs.) You're so ... (Laughs.) Do you know what heterosexual is?

Diana: No.

James: You and me. That's hetero. The other's sort of alternating current. I never know. What is it? Uhhh, bi. Is he bi?

This transcript ended at the point where Gilbey told Diana he was wearing brown suede Gucci shoes. It did not include references to Diana spending money on clothes for James Hewitt nor a swimming excursion Diana had planned with Fergie. As both of these exchanges were on the Reenan tape, the transcript was almost certainly taken from a pirate copy of the Norgrove tape, which Phil Dampier had secured. 'When I left the *Sun*, I had to leave the tape with them, obviously,' said Dampier. 'I didn't have a copy and that was the end of my involvement.'

At Balmoral, Fergie packed her bags and prepared to return to London with her daughters on Sunday, 23 August. The other royals turned up in force at Crathie Kirk, just outside the castle gates. Determined that the Family should at least appear united, the Queen greeted the enthralled crowd with a delighted smile and a regal wave. 'There was forty years' experience in that smile,' one newsman said admiringly.

Diana and Charles arrived in the same limousine but she averted her gaze away from him as well as the crowd. Andrew looked pale and grim, his jaw set firmly, but he managed a smile after the service.

Down in *Sun* Country beside the Thames, Stuart Higgins, promoted to deputy editor, was standing in for the editor. The *Mirror's* St Tropez coup had forced the Sun's hand in a circulation war which now centred almost entirely on royal sensations. 'We did well considering we didn't have one single Fergie picture,' said Stuart Higgins. But we used our cunning to get our hands on some and we published the only one that was topless because the *Mirror* thought it was in bad taste.'

Higgins knew that Squidgy, the story he had sat on for two-and-a-half years, was easily the biggest gun in the armoury. 'The fever was so hot that we struck back with the tapes because other people had started running them,' he said. 'We had gathered that the *National Enquirer* was running excerpts from one tape. I still have no idea how they got it. What we must remember is that the tape they published was the Norgrove tape; it wasn't the Reenan tape. The Norgrove tape could have gone anywhere and obviously people have pointed the finger at Phil Dampier, who had left the paper. He assures me personally that he hasn't sold it. I'm also sure that no one from the *Sun* ever passed on any material whatsoever. As far as I know, John Askill and I were the only ones who ever held transcripts and copies of those tapes. The *Sunday Express* and the *News of the World* also ran sections that day, but not the full transcript. So we decided to run the whole lot because, from that moment, the conversation was in the public domain, although we only published a self-censored version of it. We left out the parts that we thought didn't reflect too well on the Princess of Wales.'

Higgins scribbled a banner headline across the layout pad on his desk, *MY LIFE IS TORTURE,* based on Diana's miserable disclosure to Gilbey: 'It's just so difficult, so complicated. He makes my life real, real torture, I've decided.' As five pages of the paper were being filled with the Squidgy transcript, omitting references to self-gratification and pregnancy, Diana took her children swimming at the Craigendarroch Hotel near the village of Ballater. As she tucked the princes into bed that night, the first of the TNT Newsfast juggernauts thundered down the covered van way from the Wapping press halls and out on to the highway. Unleashed from behind the razor wire, Squidgy was finally off and running.

'Do I like the Princess of Wales?' reflected Stuart Higgins. 'Yeah. During their courting, I thought she was absolutely beautiful and I still think so. I feel quite sorry for her now, although I think there is another side to her. The Prince of Wales's friends have got more interest in portraying her as perhaps being a bit more manipulating and scheming, but that's part of the process of growing up. The marriage was made in hell and they're both best out of it.'

At Balmoral, Diana would have completely agreed.

WITH mounting trepidation, the Princess faced the Queen, Prince Philip and Prince Charles at a private meeting inside the castle. The tables had been neatly turned but instead of backing down, Diana decided that attack was the best form of defence. Her suspicion was that her husband's allies were behind the Squidgy disclosures. She threatened to walk out on the Royal Family unless her demands were met. Upping the ante once again, she demanded 'a legal separation, a private income and her own court with a palace and staff', according to a Balmoral source. 'She tried to hold the Queen to ransom,' said the source. 'She said she would walk out when Harry started boarding school in September.'

But the Queen, summoning all her reserves of prudence, managed to instigate a shaky truce. She pleaded with Diana to think of the consequences to her children if she split up the marital home. Diana wavered. Faced with an openly hostile Prince Philip and an indecisive Prince Charles, she realised that the Queen was offering a sensible compromise. Reluctantly, she agreed to wait until Christmas and, in a major concession to her mother-in-law, she agreed to make a state visit to Korea with her Husband for the sake of appearances.

The Princess of Wales flew back to London satisfied that although she had given in, she had left no one in the Family in any doubt about her feelings towards her husband. 'She was so close to going but she stepped back out of respect for the Queen,' said a friend. Her Majesty breathed a sigh of relief and prepared to attend an event that she never failed to enjoy, the Braemar Games. After the marital arts she had been demonstrating at Balmoral, caber-tossing, hammer-throwing and stone-putting were child's play.

ONE of the two sections that Stuart Higgins had excised from the Squidgy transcript showed a hidden side of Diana's character which was considered too shocking even for intrepid readers of the *Sun*.

James: I know. Darling. Um! More. It's just like sort of ... um ...

Diana: (Interrupting.) Playing with yourself...

James: What?

Diana: (Giggling.) Nothing.

James: No, I'm not actually.

Diana: (Giggling.) I said, it's just LIKE ...

James: Playing with yourself.

Diana: Yes.

James: Not quite as nice. Not quite as nice. I haven't played with myself actually. Not for a full forty-eight hours.

Diana: (Giggling.)

James: Not for a full forty-eight hours.

'People thought that this could not be Diana talking about masturbation on the phone,' said Harry Arnold. 'But it struck me as very like Diana because when you speak to her at Press receptions, which are unreportable, she often turns the conversation in a sexual way. I launched a trivia quiz called Royal Trivia which contained 1,400 questions about the Royal Family. I told the Princess of Wales about it at a reception in Australia. I said, "I have just launched a trivia quiz," and she said, "Sex Trivia I suppose. Is it?" And she laughed. I had to say, "No, Royal Trivia." But here is a woman who is quite aware of her sexual power.'

The Squidgy episode was fresh in Arnold's mind when he made a trip to Merseyside a few weeks later to check out the sexual power of another woman. He codenamed the assignment 'Secret Squirrel' after the tabloid epithet bestowed on Cyril Reenan. Arnold, who had joined the *Daily Mirror* as chief reporter, had received a call from a man he would identify only as 'Ordinary Joe'. The caller said he had a taped telephone conversation between the Prince of Wales and a mystery woman. Would the reporter like to hear it?

Fear of legal reprisals had kept the tape under wraps for nearly three years. 'He was frightened,' related Arnold after Camillagate had more than settled Diana's score with her husband. 'You have to understand that we are dealing with an Ordinary Joe who stumbled upon a conversation with Prince Charles. And, understandably, he was pretty nervous. It was only after the Squidgy tapes broke that he thought, "Well, they got away with that one". So he made the call. I think he felt that it was too big to keep to himself. I tend to understand that it was pretty frightening.'

Ordinary Joe met Arnold close to his home and, once a rapport had been established, showed him the scanner and the cassette recorder that had monitored the call. Then he played the tape.

'When I heard it, I was never in doubt for one second that it was the Prince of Wales,' said Arnold over a gin and tonic in Ye Olde Cheshire Cheese, a favoured watering hole off Fleet Street. 'I have been covering the Royal Family for many years and have stood talking to Charles face to face on many occasions. But I did not know who the female voice was at the time.'

Arnold took the 'Secret Squirrel' tape back to Holborn Circus with him and Ordinary Joe came down to do a deal on his earth-shattering piece of merchandise. He returned to Merseyside £30,000 richer. 'Strangely enough, money was never paramount in his mind,' said Arnold as the roast beef arrived in a panelled enclave of the pub. 'Yes, it was a financial arrangement but his main concern was that he never wanted to be found out.

'The editor, Richard Stott, gave me the task of authenticating the tape and we certainly did not rush it. We had to establish that it had not been tampered with or spliced in some way, and that the people were not actors. We gave it to one of the top experts in electronics in this country who put it through every test he knew. Then we had an expert in phonetics, a professor, check the man's voice against known recordings of Prince Charles. He verified that it was one and the same man. The harder one was to get Camilla's voice because she had rarely if ever given interviews on tape. I carefully rehearsed what I was going to say and rang her number. By an extraordinary piece of luck, she was out but there was a recorded message of her voice on the answer-phone. I taped her voice three times and sent the tape off to the professor. He confirmed that the woman was Camilla Parker Bowles.

'I then researched every reference on that tape to names and places, sometimes one word. It was like a detective investigation. It took me three days to crack Northmoor because there is no village or town called that and there is a reference to "Nancy" – how do you check that? So I went back to square one and got cuttings out of the library of all his known friends and sorted through them one by one. I was going through stories about Hugh van Custem and found one that said he had sold his Northmoor stud farm.

'Nancy was much harder because her real name is Anne, Duchess of Westminster. She is an elderly lady and Charles says she might be jealous if he brought Camilla to her home. But I could see that she might be offended if she had taken a shine to Charles and he was to bring another woman into the house to sleep with, which is what was being proposed or considered. Then, when Camilla says, "The little green-eyed monster might be lurking" it took quite a few replays to catch those words. When she says "A's coming home" I had to listen several times to realise that she is saying the letter A for Andrew Parker Bowles. It was not easy.

'Richard had made a decision early on not to run the transcript, ever. I went home for the weekend and thought about it. By then, I was 1,001 per cent certain who they were. I'm a hard news reporter and when I came in on Monday I wrote a splash (page one lead story) which said, "The heir to the throne has been conducting an adulterous affair with the wife of one of his closest friends before and during his marriage to the Princess of Wales". Richard's hair stood on end and it was the fifth draft that they used after the lawyers saw it. I was never in any doubt from day one that we had got the goods on the Prince of Wales. It ended the marriage. But I wasn't at all gleeful about it.'

The story appeared in the *Mirror* on 13 November — the Queen's unlucky number. Although it held back references to Tampaxes and 'pressing the tit' on the portable phone, the public were told that, in response to 'Bye, my darling', from Camilla, the Prince had replied, 'Love you'. It was abundantly clear from this story that Charles was having an affair.

The next day was his forty-fourth birthday. He spent it alone. He was about to fly to Strasbourg on his first visit to the European Parliament, fulfilling a long-term ambition. Asked what he wanted to be, a much younger Charles had replied, 'I want to be King of

Europe'. But he was only joking. After Camillagate, his primary concern was to ensure that he followed his mother on to the British throne.

The Way We Were: The Queen, happy and glorious, waves delightedly from the balcony of Buckingham Palace after Trooping the Colour in 1985. Diana, still the brightest star in the Family, watches Prince William's antics beside his grandmother. (*Alpha*)

Gone with the Windsors: Eight years later, Diana has disappeared from the Family line-up as a far less regal Queen presents Lord Linley's fiancee, the Hon. Serena Stanhope, to the crowd in June 1993. (*Daily Mirror*)

Flirt Skirt: Diana poses for cameramen at her kindergarten in the seethrough skirt that shocked Prince Charles before their engagement. This picture seriously challenged his girlfriend's 'Shy Di' image at the Palace. (*Rex Features*)

Puppy Love: Diana was noticeably chubby at the time of the royal engagement in 1981. As she posed with Charles at Buckingham Palace, it was also apparent that she was taller than her husband-to-be and that the hem of her blue Harrods dress had been hastily lowered. (*Alpha*)

Slenderella: Painfully thin and tense, Diana nevertheless attended the Birthright Ball in 1989 as her marriage to Prince Charles disintegrated.

(*Dave Chancellor/Alpha*)

The Kiss-Off: Two pictures capture the love that turned to scorn in the marriage of the Prince and Princess of Wales. Diana fondly embraces Charles after a polo match at Windsor Great Park in 1987 but she deliberately avoids his lips during their State visit to India in 1992. (*Rex Features*)

(*above left*)Robber Baron: Prince Charles allows his son William to be photographed with Robert Maxwell, the crooked Daily Mirror publisher, at an air display by the Red Devils in June 1985. The picture shows how close Charles had grown to the robber Press baron. (*Daily Mirror*)

(*above right*) Shopafrolic: Diana enjoys nothing more than taking her sons William and Harry into the High Street for a casual day's shopping under the watchful eye of Inspector Ken Wharfe, the royal bodyguard. (*Dave Chancellor/Alpha*)

(*above left*) Trunk Call: Charles keeps some distance between himself and Camilla Parker Bowles during a polo meeting before their affair was exposed in a late-night phone call. (*Rex Features*)

(*above right*) Deb's Delight: The Hon. Mrs Rosalind Shand and her eldest daughter Camilla pose in front of a family portrait at her coming out party in March 1965 before her first meeting with Prince Charles led to romance. (*Desmond O'Neill*)

(*above left*) Fond Blonde: Charles embraces Lady Tryon, the Australian friend he calls Kanga, after a polo match. He confided his feelings for Camilla to her during his troubled marriage. (*Alpha*)

(*above right*) Battle Front: Looking terribly strained, Camilla bites her lip as she faces the camera before the El Alamein service at Westminster Abbey prior to the break-up of the Prince and Princess of Wales in 1992. (*Daily Mirror*)

The Work: Princess Diana comforts William Drake, a patient at the London Lighthouse AIDS Centre in July 1992 after the publication of Andrew Morton's book revealed the heartache of her private life. (*Reuter*)

(*above left*) Galloping Major: Princess Diana coyly rests against an armoured vehicle while Major James Hewitt enjoys a private joke during the time he was giving her riding lessons. (Les Chudzicki)

(*above right*) Pedal Power: A worried James Gilbey arrives by bicycle at the British Grand Prix in April 1993 after the notorious Squidgy phone call had attracted interest in his friendship with Diana. (*Daily Mirror*)

The Presence: Resplendent in a diamond-encircled sapphire set in a seven-strand pearl choker, Diana follows her friend the Hon. Rosa Monckton into the midsummer cocktail party at Tiffany's in Mayfair on 30 June 1993 – the eve of the Princess's thirty-second birthday. (*Alan Davidson*)

(*above left*) Turning Point: Diana called the Queen 'the best mother-in-law in the world' and just before the birth of Prince William in 1982 they presented a united front on the balcony of the royal pavilion at Smith's Lawn – even if they were looking in opposite directions. (*Alpha*)

(*above right*) Joint Favourites: Diana and the Queen Mother enjoy Derby Day at Epsom racecourse before Charles's grandmother began to unsettle the Princess with her 'strange looks'. (*Sporting Pictures* [UK])

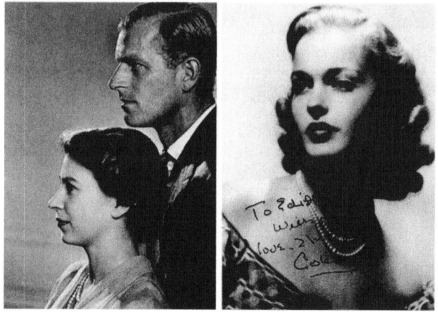

(*above left*) Devoted Couple: Princess Elizabeth and the Duke of Edinburgh provided this charming profile for Karsh of Ottawa in 1951. Elizabeth succeeded the throne a year later and she made her husband The Prince Philip in 1956. (*Camera Press*)

(*above right*) Prince's Pin-up: Cobina Wright Jnr, an American film star, enchanted Prince Philip of Greece when they met before his romance with the King's daughter. They have remained close friends for more than fifty years.

189

(*left*) Royal Star: Sir Cecil Beaton posed Princess Margaret in front of her Annigoni portrait to achieve this striking double-headed effect in February 1958 – two years before her engagement to Antony Armstrong-Jones. (*Camera Press*)

(*right*) Theatre Lover: Scotch and Malvern water in hand and an ever-present cigarette in its holder, Margaret relaxes after a night at the Richmond Theatre in November 1991. Her health suffered badly from drinking and smoking. (*Today*)

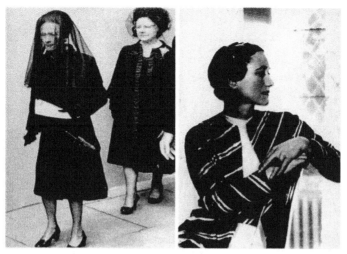

(*above left*) Mortal Enemies: Fighting back the tears, the Duchess of Windsor leaves St George's Chapel after the funeral service for the Duke of Windsor in June 1972. The Queen Mother, who never forgave the then Wallis Simpson for marrying her brother-in-law, keeps a few respectful paces behind. The Royal Family refused all of the Duke's entreaties to have his wife recognised as Her Royal Highness. (*Press Association*)

(*above right*) Femme Fatale: As Wallis Simpson said herself no one ever called her beautiful, but her haughty, angular appearance and the sexual experience she gained in Chinese brothels made her so captivating to Edward VIII that he surrendered his throne to marry her. (*Press Association*)

Brolly Follies: Diana and the Duchess of York upset the Family by poking friends' bottoms with rolled-up umbrellas at Royal Ascot in June 1987. But this escapade signalled the beginning of the end of their friendship. (*Rex Features*)

(above left) Crying Shame: Diana sobs uncontrollably during a public engagement just after Andrew Morton revealed the true state of her loveless marriage in June 1992.

(above right) Sob Sister: Fergie breaks down and weeps during a visit to the Motor Neurone Disease Association's conference in Birmingham – her first public duty following the Daily Mirror's publication of the St Tropez pictures in August 1992. (*Press Association*)

Hey Dude: Steve Wyatt, Fergie's former Texan buddy, shelters from the rain with a friend at the Pavarotti concert in Hyde Park three months before holiday snaps of him and the Duchess of York were discovered at his former Chelsea apartment. (*Alan Davidson*)

Johnny Be Good: John Bryan, who replaced Wyatt in Fergie's affections, smiles through the drama of August 1992 when the St Tropez pictures revealed the true nature of his friendship with the Duchess of York. (*Nunn Syndication*)

Strained Relations: The Spencer family were briefly reunited when Diana received the Freedom of the City at a ceremony in London in July 1987. Watching proudly (from the left) are Raine, Countess Spencer (Diana's stepmother), Johnnie, Earl Spencer (her father), Charles, Viscount Althorp (her brother), Mrs Frances Shand Kydd (her mother) and Ruth, Lady Fermoy (her grandmother). (*Jim Bennett/Alpha*)

PART TWO

THE FAMILY

10

CROWN OF THORNS

'I never served an apprenticeship'
Queen Elizabeth II

DIANA positively blossomed when she left Prince Charles three months after Squidgy. Contrary to popular belief, she accepted her new status outside the Family with more grace than many thought possible. This was partly because, in the words of John Major, 'there is no reason why the Princess of Wales should not be crowned Queen in due course'. In other words, she hadn't been sacked from the job – there was still a slim chance so long as she and Charles remained married. Although most people ridiculed the idea, queenship only ceased to be an option if she divorced Charles.

As the Prime Minister repeated his assertion in the New Year, he seemed to believe it. Relations between Diana and 10 Downing Street were, in fact, excellent. Far from being crushed and feeling rejected, the Princess shrewdly seized the opportunity to build some powerful new alliances. One of the people she courted was Baroness Chalker, the Foreign Office's Minister for Overseas Aid, who was only too willing to help promote the Work.

'I think she's quite happy not to be Queen – who needs to be Queen when you're Princess Diana and you've got the adulation and all the rest of it?' asked the titled Chelsea lady. 'You actually don't need to be Queen when you're the most famous woman in the world and Mother Teresa as well.'

Few people knew better than Diana that the Queen was saddened and resentful. With characteristic restraint, Her Majesty politely called her critics 'those whose task it is in life to offer instant opinions'. But privately she felt betrayed from within by those whose solemn duty it was to serve her. Only now, as the facade cracked around her, could she survey the full extent of the damage of which a burned-out Windsor Castle was but a symbol. Among the tiaras was a crown of thorns.

'Her Majesty could not look at the failed marriages of three of her children without looking at herself,' said the Palace insider, it made her realise she was as much a victim of the System as anyone else.'

The Queen also had to face the bleak prospect that her place in the world outside her immediate sovereign circle was threatened as never before. Victoria, her great-great-grandmother, had been Queen of Great Britain and Ireland, Empress of India and titular head of an empire so vast that the sun never set upon it. The decline that followed her death had been comparatively swift and, pressured by European federalism and Commonwealth nationalism, it had gathered a new momentum in the Nineties.

To calls for a cheaper, republican Britain, Palace strategists asserted frostily that Her Majesty was the Head of State of seventeen countries, the Commonwealth and a lot more besides. She was, they said, a true internationalist. An American-style Presidency would cost far more than the monarchy and, judging by the lack-lustre performance of Bill Clinton in the White House, the presidential alternative was hardly an attractive option.

The Palace refused to entertain the possibility that other Commonwealth countries, namely New Zealand and Canada, might follow Australia's lead along the road to a republic. Paul Keating, the Labour Prime Minister, had been re-elected after promising that his Government would hold a referendum on the question of establishing an Australian republic by 1 January, 2001. The Queen's profile would disappear from currency, all reference to her would be eliminated from the country's oath of allegiance and the Union Jack would vanish from the Australian flag.

Keating, fiercely proud of his Irish roots, stressed that none of this was personal. He was so fond of Her Majesty that he had once placed a guiding arm around her waist, a gesture he shared with Francois Mitterand and Robert Maxwell. His next move was to brief the Queen on the findings of the Republic Advisory Committee, which had been appointed to draft various options for amending the constitution.

'It would be fair to say that of the dwindling band of Australians who still support the monarchy, most of them are, in fact, Elizabethans rather than monarchists,' said Malcolm Turnbull, an avowed republican and the committee's chairman. 'If, Heaven forbid, the Queen tripped over one of her corgis and perished or simply abdicated, Australia would become a republic within twelve months.

'I don't think there is much confidence among Australians in the next generation. The Camillagate thing arguably did Charles an irreparable amount of damage. It's one of the great jokes of all time, someone aspiring to be a tampon. I think Diana is an attractive, well-meaning person but fits of suicidal depression and the bulimia problem do not inspire a great deal of confidence.

'There is, however, enormous affection for the Queen among republicans and I'm a great admirer of the way she has fulfilled her role,' said the advocate who had successfully defended *Spycatcher* in the celebrated case of Regina v Peter Wright. 'Nonetheless, I don't think she should be Head of State of Australia. The republican movement in Australia is unrelated to the marital problems of the Royal Family, Fergie's toe-sucking activities and so forth. It is really no more than an affirmation of the unique national identity of Australia. The original symbol, the Crown, had substance when Australia was a subordinate dominion of the British Empire and when Australians saw themselves, and were seen by others, as being Britons.

'But time and tide have drained the substance away from the symbol. So you have a symbol without substance.

'We are seeking to replace that symbol with one that is appropriate to Australia's needs and aspirations – an Australian Head of State in the form of a non-executive, largely ceremonial President.'

The model was Ireland's Mary Robinson rather than the expensively coiffed incumbent of the White House.

CONSIDERING the drama surrounding her, it was little wonder that nothing amused Her Majesty so much as playing a role other than her own. She had played The Monarch so often that she was not just synonymous with the role, she *was* the role. This could be tedious.

Her alternative repertoire dated from Christmas pantomimes at Windsor Castle. At seventeen, the Princess, dressed in kimono and white silk pantaloons, had played Aladdin. She burst out of a laundry basket in front of her special guest, an admiring Prince Philip. As she tap-danced and sang, Philip applauded wildly. Margaret might be the Family's most enduring actress, but she did not have the stage to herself. Christmas games of charades at Sandringham could be fiercely competitive if the sisters were on opposing sides.

One impromptu performance, however, caused some consternation among officers of the Royal Yacht *Britannia*. As the 'royal-palace-at-sea' cruised at twenty knots, the Queen turned up unexpectedly on the bridge. Among her various titles was Lord High Admiral of the United Kingdom, a position she treated with the utmost respect. But inexplicably she affected the mannerisms of a West Country yokel. A rolling gait and a suitably bucolic expression made the performance even more realistic. The only missing prop was a piece of straw between her teeth. Mystified though the officers of the watch were, Her Majesty kept up the pretence for some minutes, 'I'm told she was very convincing,' said a naval source. 'The captain, Rear Admiral Paul Greening, played it absolutely straight. He called her Ma'am and ignored the fact that she was addressing him in this peculiar voice.'

Her Majesty can also be quite idiosyncratic in her choice of the people she asks to meet outside the scope of her official duties. Sometimes the most unlikely players in show business attract her interest. The pop duo Wham!, who rated as the sexiest male performers of the Eighties, were astonished when they received a royal summons. 'I got a message saying simply that the Queen wanted to meet George Michael and Andrew Ridgely,' said Bryan Morrison, the pop music magnate who later founded the Royal County of Berkshire Polo Club. 'So I immediately drove them to meet her. She was at the Guards Polo Club in Windsor Great Park. I introduced them and they chatted to the Queen for quite a while – it was all very informal.'

Another quirk is that, when she dines at the homes of friends, she insists on eating from her own plates and with her own knives and forks. Prior to her arrival at the Chelsea home of Lord and Lady Westbury on St Patrick's night in 1993, crockery and cutlery were delivered from the Buckingham Palace kitchens. A servant carrying the boxes into the apartment in Ropers Orchard off Danvers Street explained that the Queen 'liked her own things'. The mild-mannered hosts took no offence. David Westbury's mother had grown up with the Queen Mother and it was his father who had discovered Tutankhamen's tomb with the archaeologist Howard Carter and the then Earl of Carnarvon, grandfather of the Queen's friend, Lord

Porchester. The Queen was particularly fond of Ursula Westbury, whose coming-out dance she had attended. Lord Scarborough, a member of the Westburys' Yorkshire racing set, and the former deputy prime minister Lord Whitelaw, were among the ten guests but neither would discuss the outing afterwards, beyond Willie Whitelaw's curt observation that it was 'a wholly private affair'.

Her Majesty's prospective hosts also had to be made aware of what she would and would not eat and drink. They were informed by the Palace that, unlike her husband, the Queen never touched oysters and usually avoided red meat. Furthermore, no one was permitted to serve her veal after the television writer Carla Lane wrote to her about the cruelty involved in its production. She preferred simple dishes to gourmet meals and liked her chicken and fish gently spiced with ginger, lime and lemongrass. 'The Queen is no fan of garlic,' said her former cook, the Swedish-born Mrs Alma McKee who also volunteered that Prince Charles enjoyed banana and jam sandwiches and often asked for meat balls.

Another royal cook, the Buckingham Palace chef Colin Alderson, made it known that the Queen liked a poached egg for breakfast served in a hollowed-out slice of fried bread and that Prince Philip always took with him to Ascot a box fitted with twelve tiny drawers which had to be filled with bite-sized sandwiches. On special days, the Queen ordered rabbit to be prepared for the royal corgis and on one of those occasions, when *Watership Down* was the movie of the moment, a houseman was scolded by the Queen for jesting as he fed them the morsels: 'You've seen the film, you've read the book, now eat the cast.'

Aboard the Royal Train, she invariably asked for fish and the fishmonger was required to produce sole, salmon, lobster and smoked Scotch haddock for long journeys. When travelling the Queen carried ample quantities of Earl Grey, Chinese and Indian teas along with her favourite chunky-cut marmalade. Foreign servants noted that at tea time she would serve Prince Philip personally, cutting the bread and even stirring his tea for him.

Eating in Third World countries, the Queen developed the ploy of pushing heavily-spiced items to one side and pecking with such apparent appreciation at the rest that no host could take offence, although on a 1986 visit to China she was unable to avoid one delicacy served at a banquet: sea slugs. 'They're quite delicious,' she told her host, President Li Xiannian.

Like her eldest son, she never liked champagne but hosts would be advised in advance that she did enjoy a glass of white wine (preferably German) with her food.

All of these traits more or less ran in the Family. Queen Victoria, for instance, insisted that her breakfast egg was served in a gold egg-cup and she ate it with a gold spoon. Eccentricity wasn't at all unusual. Her Majesty's great-grandmother, Queen Alexandra, gave away priceless heirlooms like these on a whim to friends. Lord Esher, the most tactful courtier of his time, was entrusted with the delicate task of getting them back. Not unnaturally, the Windsors liked to hang on to their treasures.

ELIZABETH was born to the Duchess of York at two forty a.m. on 21 April, 1926, exactly six months after Alexandra's death at Sandringham. To honour her memory, the little princess was christened Elizabeth Alexandra Mary, but she called herself Lilibet. The birth took place at the home of her mother's parents, the Earl and Countess of Strathmore, at 17 Bruton Street, Mayfair, later the headquarters of a property company. Margaret Rose arrived four years later at Glamis Castle and the two sisters were raised in a twenty-five-bedroom house at 145 Piccadilly, later the Inter-Continental Hotel.

As a child, Elizabeth kept a stable of wooden horses in the upstairs nursery. Each morning, they would be wheeled about for exercise after first being groomed and saddled. When Margaret was old enough, she was enlisted as a stable hand and Elizabeth taught her the routine. As there were thirty horses in the collection, each with its own name, there was a lot to take in. Moreover, the horses had to be unsaddled and stabled every evening before bedtime. Elizabeth would not go to sleep until the ritual had been carried out to her satisfaction. It wasn't so much a game, Elizabeth explained seriously, more an education for later life. She never forgot she was a princess of the royal blood.

She was just as fussy about her clothes. Unless she had checked several times that her shoes were placed side by side in the right order and her dresses neatly arranged, she was unable to go to sleep. Diana was said to have adopted a similar compulsive habit during stressful times in her marriage. Sweets were also given fastidious treatment. 'The two little girls had their own way of dealing with their barley sugar,' recalled Marion Crawford, their governess, in her bestselling royal book, *The Little Princesses.* 'Margaret kept the whole lot in her small, hot hand and pushed them into her mouth. Lilibet, however, carefully sorted hers out on the table, large and small pieces together, and then ate them very daintily and methodically.'

Elizabeth grew up a happy, confident child who was the apple of King George V's eye. Her grandfather doted on her, but she was never spoiled, although she had toys, clothes, jewels and luxuries beyond even the richest child's dreams. She was only nine when the King died and Uncle David, who read stories to the little girls, ascended the throne.

Her parents spent weekends at Royal Lodge, a large pink house with flat white battlements in Windsor Great Park, where Elizabeth loved to saddle up real ponies. She and Margaret chased their pet corgis through the grounds and played games on the crazy paving in a sunken rose garden.

It was in April 1936 that Uncle David, or Edward VIII as she tried to remember, turned up unexpectedly one afternoon, steering an American station wagon into the circular driveway. Out stepped four strangers, one of them a striking woman.

'Crawfie, who *is* she?' Elizabeth asked her governess, puzzled by the American accent, lacquered mahogany hair and tailored clothes. Inside the drawing room the woman strode over to a window and summoned the King to her side. 'David, don't you think those trees could be cut down and part of that hill removed?' she asked. 'There'd be a much better view then.' There was a stunned silence from the Duke and Duchess of York, who were being reminded that the King was their landlord.

After tea the princesses watched from an upstairs window as the visitors departed in the big American car. Elizabeth, Wallis Simpson recalled, was 'a long, slender, beautifully made child', and Margaret 'an enchanting doll-like child with a small, fat face'. Long before they met again, Mrs Simpson's sway would have scarred the House of Windsor forever.

ELIZABETH fell madly in love with Prince Philip when she was a thirteen-year-old schoolgirl and, if she ever loved another man, it was love of a different kind.

Prince Philip of Greece had seen the Princess at the wedding of his cousin, Princess Marina, to the Duke of Kent and, after the Abdication, at the coronation of George VI. But they first met in July 1939, just before the outbreak of war, at the Royal Naval College at Dartmouth in Devon. The eighteen-year-old cadet turned up at the home of his commanding officer to pay his respects to King George VI and his daughters. He was, said Crawfie, 'a fair-haired boy, rather like a Viking, with a sharp face and piercing blue eyes'.

He suggested that the young sisters should accompany him to the tennis courts for 'some real fun jumping the nets'. 'She (Elizabeth) never took her eyes off him the whole time,' Crawfie recalled. 'Lilibet said, "How good he is, Crawfie! How high he can jump!"'

As Elizabeth and her family sailed away in the old Royal Yacht, *Victoria & Albert,* Philip and some other cadets gave chase in small boats. Long after the others had given up, Philip kept going, waving and shouting. 'The young fool,' stormed the King, fearing for his safety. 'He must go back.' It was only the first time that Philip would raise the royal blood pressure. But the effect on Princess Elizabeth was mesmeric. She 'watched him fondly through an enormous pair of binoculars' until he disappeared from sight.

The hand of Lord Louis Mountbatten had been instrumental in arranging that auspicious first meeting. Elizabeth's tender age failed to cause Philip's uncle the slightest discomfort. He had been in Dartmouth to make sure things went smoothly. Philip's performance, he noted, had been 'a great success'.

A marriage between the House of Windsor and a member of his family, between Elizabeth and Philip to be precise, fitted into his plan for a Mountbatten Lineage among Britain's royal dynasties. His next step was to arrange a posting for Philip on HMS *Ramillies.* When Philip went on board on 24 February, 1940, in Colombo, Ceylon, he introduced himself to the ship's captain, Harold Baillie-Grohman. 'My uncle has ideas for me,' he told his commanding officer. 'He thinks I should marry Princess Elizabeth.'

'Are you fond of her?' asked the captain, startled by such impudence.

'Oh yes,' Philip replied cheerily, 'I write to her every week.'

Apart from brief encounters during Philip's home leave, the courtship was conducted largely through the Royal Mail. Mountbatten was ecstatic when Philip informed him that Elizabeth had accepted him at Balmoral on 11 August, 1946. She made her decision without telling her parents. The King was furious.

To overcome one of the monarch's objections, Philip volunteered to drop his Greek title and call himself Lieutenant Philip Mountbatten RN. He would also apply for British citizenship. When Elizabeth agreed to wait until she had turned twenty-one, the King realised that he was fighting a losing battle. 'I was rather afraid that you had thought I was being hardhearted about it,' the King wrote to Elizabeth when she was wearing Philip's wedding ring. 'I was so anxious for you to come to South Africa as you knew. I can see you are sublimely happy with Philip which is right but don't forget us.'

On the evening of her birthday, Elizabeth made a broadcast during the South African tour, binding herself to the monarchy, 'I declare before you all that my whole life, whether it be long or short, shall be devoted to your service and the service of our great imperial Commonwealth to which we all belong. But I shall not have the strength to carry out this resolution unless you join in with me, as I now invite you to do; I know that your support will be unfailingly given. God bless all of you who are willing to share it.'

Her sincerity touched Philip deeply, knowing as he did that she intended him to be her Prince Consort in this lifelong commitment. Pushed by his wife, King George finally gave his official blessing to the betrothal on 9 July, 1947. For the couple's marital home, the King acquired a twenty-five-roomed house called Sunninghill Park. Set in 668 pleasant acres in the Royal County of Berkshire close to Windsor Castle, the residence had been used as an air force base during the war but had been extensively damaged by fire. Just two weeks after workmen started rebuilding it, another fire destroyed the south wing. A new house would not rise from the ruins until Elizabeth's favourite son, Prince Andrew, had written a new chapter in royal romance.

'ELIZABETH and Philip were an absolute godsend,' enthused the titled Chelsea lady. 'I remember going to see the film of the Royal Wedding and it was absolutely wonderful. Life had been so austerely drab and suddenly we had Norman Hartnell poncing around and all these wonderful frocks. It was a real opiate for the masses – I mean, after the war the Royal Family could do absolutely no wrong. All the rumours about Prince Philip were totally quashed and one's elders said, "Don't be so wicked as to even talk about it". Obviously the gossip was going on in London but Elizabeth was so popular it was unthinkable. Everybody copied her clothes and, when Prince Charles was born, women's magazines ran articles on how to knit his baby jumper with little feathers on it.

'When the Duke got his first ship, HMS *Magpie*, Elizabeth followed him to Malta where she was more or less an ordinary naval wife and the mother of two young children. She watched polo with the other wives and went on family picnics. It was the only taste of freedom she ever had. Everything happened in 1952. She stopped being a young girl and a young mother.'

King George VI died of lung cancer on 6 February, 1952, when Elizabeth was still only twenty-five. She and Philip were visiting a game reserve in Kenya and she dashed back to London in a blaze of publicity. Like Victoria before her, 'she took things as they came, as she knew they must be'.

Although a heavily addicted smoker, the King had put his illness down to 'the incessant worries and crises through which we have to live'. 'He smoked 150 cigarettes a day for years,' said a royal medical source. 'Even after his last operation, he couldn't give it up.' Much to her father's dismay, Margaret had started smoking and when he complained, she simply increased the length of her ivory cigarette holders. 'She is so addicted to nicotine I once saw her light up after lunch at the Royal Lancaster Hotel without waiting for the loyal toast,' said a reporter on the royal beat. The Queen was also a smoker, but only in secret. 'The staff knew because they emptied the ashtrays in her private rooms,' said one raised in the Royal Mews.

Queen Elizabeth II threw herself into the New Elizabethan Era with great courage. Resolved to fulfil the pledge she had made on her twenty-first birthday, and renewed at the Coronation in 1953, she realised that there would be a high price to pay. Her personal liberty would have to go, but she had always known that. While she was touring Britain's overseas possessions with Philip, she would have to leave Charles and Anne at home in the care of her mother, who was still grieving the loss of her husband. There would also be long, testing times when she would be separated from her husband, now the proud holder of UK Passport Number One.

Not once did Elizabeth flinch. 'From the moment the King died, the Queen didn't have a moment to spare,' said Godfrey Talbot, the distinguished BBC Court Correspondent. 'She reluctantly had to abandon her children and they virtually didn't see their parents for months on end. It was very unsettling and bewildering for a little boy and he turned to granny for a shoulder to cry on. During the first five years of the Queen's reign, the Queen Mother was both mother and father to Charles and Anne.'

This wasn't the only sacrifice the Queen had to make. The Crown started to take over her personality. 'Monarchy is a very difficult thing – for the monarch,' said a leading psychiatrist. 'When does he or she cease being the title and assume what you might call their real identity?'

So committed was Elizabeth to the sovereign's traditional role that she turned a deaf ear to suggestions that it might be wise to open up a little and become more democratic. 'I never served an apprenticeship,' she reflected ruefully when the mistakes had been made.

This wasn't strictly true. She had been trained from an early age in the rites of royalty. She had also been tutored in constitutional history by a former teacher at Eton, who had the disconcerting habit of addressing her as 'Gentlemen'. Yet her mentors, the diehard Queen Mary and the Old Guard at Buckingham Palace, had singularly failed to anticipate the changing nature of life in the kingdom over which Elizabeth now ruled. Moreover, the advent of television meant that there was an instantaneous feedback on history as it happened. The BBC's live outside broadcast of the Coronation had been an unqualified success. But once the camera started to pry into less salubrious areas, many people did not like what they saw. 'Reality television', as it became known, created a potent political force by revealing the two-nations concept of the kingdom – the haves and the have-nots.

As a symbol of a glorious imperial past, Elizabeth was the youthful embodiment of an almost sacred ideal. But after Britain's catastrophic involvement in the Suez invasion, the ideal itself had been called into question and found to be wanting. The days of gunboat diplomacy were well and truly over. Eden was exposed as a deeply flawed Prime Minister and Macmillan's rise to power over Rab Butler, the Queen's favourite politician after Winston Churchill, owed more to the byzantine intrigues within Westminster than to any electoral mandate. This left the monarchy exposed in a particularly vulnerable way. The existence of a dynastic head of state and the lavishly expensive ceremonial that had come to be associated with it were still plaited together. But the fabric of society itself was being woven into exciting new patterns. No one was asking the Palace for permission.

'Who would have guessed the Queen would have grown into her job the way she has?' countered the informed peer. 'Philip protected her in those early decades marvellously well. He was a very good consort.' The truth, however, was that the Queen lost touch with her people. For the first time, the monarchy was openly criticised. Malcolm Muggeridge's article in the *Saturday Evening Post,* 'Does England Really Need a Queen?', and Lord Altrincham's portrayal of her tweedy, elitist court in the *National and English Review* caused a furore. His Lordship called the Queen 'a priggish schoolgirl, captain of the hockey team, a prefect and a recent candidate for confirmation.' Both men were ostracised and Altrincham (John Grigg) had his face slapped by an angry royalist.

A decade passed before the monarchy could shake off the malaise of the late Fifties and re-establish contact with the masses. Neither the birth of Prince Andrew nor the wedding of Princess Margaret to Antony Armstrong-Jones in 1960 achieved the desired effect. 'The Sixties were exciting but they were different because people stopped copying the Royal Family,' said the titled Chelsea lady. 'You stopped looking at the royals and started looking at Carnaby Street and pop stars. All the fashion, everything, came from the bottom, not the top.'

The notion of due deference to one's betters started to crumble. Royalty became an irrelevance in an age of populism. Michael Caine's antihero *Alfie* and Julie Christie's cover girl *Darling* became typical role models for a generation. Cockney, Scouse, Geordie and other regional dialects hitherto confined to the football terraces joined BBC English on the airwaves. Pirate radio stations located offshore, the most famous called *Caroline,* bombarded the kingdom with irreverent new sounds. There was a high-spirited, bloodless revolution going on and the royals were excluded from it. Uniforms and medals were sold in Carnaby Street boutiques not as symbols of imperial gallantry but as psychedelic fashions and accessories.

When John Lennon announced at the height of the Swinging Sixties that the Beatles were more popular than Jesus he could have added, 'And the Royal Family as well'. When the Beatles went to Buckingham Palace in 1965 to receive MBEs, they showed no particular reverence for the surroundings. According to John Lennon, they smoked dope in the Palace loo. 'I think the Beatles think MBE stands for Mr Brian Epstein,' said the trendy Princess Margaret, referring to the group's manager. She, for one, had the time of her life as a fully-fledged member of the permissive society.

EVERYONE remembered the most quotable part of the Guildhall speech in which the Queen said: '1992 is not a year on which I shall look back with undiluted pleasure. In the words of one of my more sympathetic correspondents, it has turned out to be an *annus horribilis*. I suspect I am not alone in thinking it so.' Significantly, Her Majesty went on to say:

'No institution – City, monarchy, whatever – should expect to be free from the scrutiny of those who give it their loyalty and support, not to mention those who don't. But we are all part of the same fabric of our national society and that scrutiny, by one part of another, can be just as effective if it is made with a touch of gentleness, good humour and understanding. This sort of questioning can also act, and it should do so, as an effective engine of change.'

By royal standards, this appeared to be radical stuff indeed. Her Majesty had publicly acknowledged not only a need for reform but a willingness to be reformed. After Macmillan's Winds of Change came the Windsor Change. The Queen, however, was working to a timetable she had drafted after consultations with her closest advisers. In truth, she was still in the driving seat of the engine and she had no intention of handing over the controls.

The first key date in the new agenda was her declaration on Christmas Day 1991 that she intended to serve her people 'for years to come'. Charles already knew that his mother hadn't shown the slightest inclination of stepping down, but this brief reference let the rest of the world know that it could stop speculating. Abdication was still the dirtiest word in the royal vocabulary.

Having established security of tenure, she moved on to tackle the next, and most problematical, area of the monarchy – royal finances. For forty-one years, she had steadfastly refused calls from Socialist and Conservative quarters alike that she should pay income tax. But she now sensed a backlash from economic forces outside her control as the worst recession since the Wall Street Crash started to bite deeply.

'In the latter part of the twentieth century, the Royal Family had stripped away their financial responsibilities and had more financial privileges that at any time in their history,' said Andrew Morton. 'There was a turning point when the Queen was exempted from paying the Poll Tax and she was probably the most privileged she had ever been. In an historical sense, that is when a dynasty has to beware because in 1913 the Russian Royal Family celebrated their tercentenary with elaborate celebrations in Moscow and St Petersburg and four years later it was over. Similarly, the House of Windsor in the latter part of the Eighties and the early Nineties were celebrated as no other family. They were lauded on television, the Press were largely uncritical and they seemingly enjoyed the respect of Parliament. The hegemony seemed to be complete and yet a year later – BANG! 1992 was a fulcrum year.'

Everything that had been preached during the Thatcher era about a 'value for money' society in which everything had to earn its keep turned against the monarchy. High expectations instilled by the optimism of the previous ten years were suddenly dashed aside. People living outside London, which suffered from what Morton called 'the metropolitan mindset', were adamant that it was time for Her Majesty to join the real world and pay taxes like everyone else.

At Buckingham Palace, there was also the added complication of the Family. 'The Queen had known since the beginning of 1992 that the Charles and Diana story was going to break,' said the Palace insider. 'She decided then to pay tax and chop the Civil List without further ado. It was intended as a tactical move to defuse the situation.' The Queen did not believe that the crisis in the marriage was so great that the couple would officially separate as a possible prelude to divorce. An unofficial, unannounced 'separate lives' agreement, her advisers believed, would be sufficient to paper over the cracks. 'The one thing she wasn't prepared for was the problem in the Yorks' marriage,' said the Palace source. 'Andrew came as a complete shock — it came from nowhere.' Instead of having to deal with the ramifications of one failed marriage, she had been faced with what the Conservatives like to call 'a double whammy'.

Her feelings towards Diana were summed up in a remark she made to a friend: 'Life is more difficult now that we've got this tiresome girl.' Ironically, she had always got along with Sarah in a quaint sort of way. She firmly believed that once Steve Wyatt had been chilled out of her life, she would start to mend her ways. She couldn't accept that the Duchess would walk away from the wealth and privilege of her position. When the St Tropez pictures surfaced, Her Majesty insisted on some extremely tough terms for the financial side of the separation. Fergie, who had behaved like a pools winner ever since joining the Royal Family, got only £600,000 – with strings attached. If she and Andrew divorced and she remarried, she would have to repay half that amount.

In September 1992, in the middle of those prolonged and often fraught negotiations, Her Majesty revealed her tax strategy to John Major during his visit to Balmoral. In view of the family difficulties, it was agreed that an announcement should be delayed, but Major nevertheless leaked her intention to cut £1.4 million from the Civil List. 'This made it seem as though it was his idea,' said a Labour opponent. 'John Major will emerge as the unsung hero of 1992,' countered Morton. 'Unlike Mrs Thatcher, he has a very cordial relationship with the Queen and, unlike Mrs Thatcher again, he was able to suggest certain things, or to implement certain ideas from the Queen's side which have helped to bring the monarchy forward a little. But, unfortunately, she was negotiating from a defensive position as opposed to a position of authority. If the Queen had agreed to pay tax five years ago, she would have been praised to the heavens.'

A large part of the problem was that nobody, including the Queen, knew the full extent of her wealth. It had been calculated variously at £50 million, £250 million, £2.5 billion and £7.5 billion. Even the lowest figure made her one of the mega-rich. Parsimonious by nature, she held back until fate itself intervened. On Black Wednesday, 16 September, the economy faced its gravest crisis in living memory. Interest rates blipped up and down on the economic cardiograph, rising and falling four times in a single day. The Bank of England poured £10 billion from the national reserves into the money markets in a vain attempt to stem a concerted run on the pound. Finally, the Chancellor, Norman Lamont, pulled Britain out of the exchange rate mechanism, effectively devaluing sterling by twenty per cent. It was a chaotic piece of mismanagement typical of the Chancellor's unreliable grip on the economy. Britain had become the sick man of Europe. Compared with the billions made by speculators who gambled against the pound, the Queen's pledge of a £1.4 million saving seemed trifling. She would have to think again.

SEVEN days after the initial Camillagate revelations in the *Daily Mirror,* a largely unexplained fire swept through Windsor Castle, damaging seven State apartments. It was the Queen's forty-fifth wedding anniversary, and she was alone as usual. Prince Philip was attending a World Wide Fund for Nature conference in Buenos Aires.

The fire generated a great deal of sympathy for Her Majesty until, while the embers were still warm, the National Heritage Minister, Peter Brooke, jumped to his feet in the House of Commons and promised that the taxpayer would meet the full cost of repairs estimated at £60 million. The Government, however, had seriously misread the mood in the country. To quell universal indignation, Major immediately declared that the Queen and Prince Charles had agreed in principle to pay tax. Details would be announced in the New Year. Everyone apart from the Queen, the Queen Mother and Prince Philip would also be dropped from the Civil List. For a Prime Minister pledged to a 'classless society', the trapeze artist's son from Brixton seemed to spend an inordinate amount of time walking the royal tightrope.

The details duly appeared in the form of the grandly titled Memorandum of Understanding on Royal Taxation, signed by officials representing the Queen, Prince Charles, the Treasury and the Inland Revenue. It was made public just as a Gallup Poll showed that all sections of society wanted a reformed monarchy and four out of five people thought that 'too many members of the Family lead an idle, jet-set kind of existence'.

As usual, the Queen was thinking a couple of moves ahead. She agreed to open up Buckingham Palace to the public, the proceeds going towards the cost of repairing Windsor Castle.

The *Wall Street Journal* estimated that the monarchy cost Britain's taxpayers 'almost double the combined cost of the monarchies of the Netherlands, Sweden, Spain, Belgium, Denmark and Norway'. This uncomfortable disclosure was reinforced by a careful reading of the Memorandum on Taxation. It stated that while the Queen would be taxed on her private income, her prodigious inherited wealth, which included the deeds to Sandringham and Balmoral, and royal perks, such as *Britannia,* would remain untouched. She and Charles, who was a party to the arrangements on behalf of the Duchy of Cornwall, could also opt out of the scheme from 6 April, 1994, 'or any later date'.

Apart from a Civil List payment of £7.9 million to meet expenses the Queen incurred in carrying out her official duties, it cost a total of £50 million to maintain her royal residences, to keep *Britannia* afloat, the Queen's Flight airborne and the Royal Train on the rails. A further £20 million went on providing twenty-four-hour security for the Queen and her family. *Britannia,* decked out with a full complement of 249 Royal Navy crew, cost £35,000 a day to run. When in use, the ship had a twenty-six-strong Royal Marine band to provide music and the flowers on all six decks were hand-picked in the Windsor Castle gardens. If costs were calculated on the basis of the twenty-seven days the Royal Family actually used the yacht in 1992, the figure was £463,000 per working day. This included a two-week holiday in the Caribbean for Prince Philip to get some remedial winter sun.

As for the Civil List, the memo showed that the state would no longer pay for Prince Andrew (£249,000), Princess Anne (£228,000), Princess Margaret (£219,000), Prince Edward (£96,000) and Princess Alice of Gloucester (£87,000). The total of £879,000 would be paid out of the profits available to the Queen from the Duchy of Lancaster, her ancient landed estate. Every penny would be tax deductible in assessing her tax and capital gains liability. So would many other items of Royal Household expenditure, right down to the buttons on a footman's jacket.

The old arrangements involving the Crown Estate, which owned property valued at £1.8 billion, and the Duchy of Lancaster, with assets valued at £55 million, would remain in place. The Crown Estate, which owned 250,000 acres of agricultural land in England and Scotland and prime residential and commercial sites mainly in the heart of London, was the holding of the sovereign in the right of the Crown — in other words, it wasn't considered a private possession. The sovereign had continued to surrender most of its revenue of around £70 million a year to the Exchequer in exchange for the Civil List.

The Duchy of Lancaster, however, provided a tax-free revenue of more than £3 million a year, which was paid to the Keeper of the Privy Purse for Her Majesty's use. As well as land holdings, the Duchy had diversified into stocks and shares and amassed liquid assets valued at £22 million. In 1992, the Queen withdrew £3.75 million from the Duchy's profits, mainly for her private expenditure and her relatives.

The bottom line of the whole deal was that the Queen would pay between £1 million and £2 million a year in tax on the income from her personal wealth. The Duchy of Cornwall, which had £35 million in assets apart from land holdings as diverse as Dartmoor Prison and The Oval cricket ground, was similarly blessed. Charles could claim the cost of running Highgrove and the money he paid to support Diana and the princes as tax deductions.

The tax deal completely ignored the extra costs involved when the Royal Family travelled abroad on official visits. The bill to the taxpayer for clothes, including Prince Philip's suits and the Queen's outfits, food, accommodation, the salaries of additional staff and presents for their hosts averaged £4,158 a day, the Foreign Office disclosed in answer to unrelenting parliamentary probing. In the financial year 1992-93, the Queen and the Duke received £157,000, the Prince and Princess of Wales £133,000 and other royals £163,000 – a total of £453,000 in extra funding. The Waleses' valedictory trip to Korea, it was revealed, had cost taxpayers £57,000 and they hadn't even got a happy, smiling picture for their money.

ALTHOUGH opinion polls showed a decline in the monarchy's popularity, the memo proved that the Queen still maintained a great deal of clout. 'The strength of monarchy does not lie in the power that it has but the power that it denies others,' Sir Antony Jay explained in the TV documentary *Royal Family* as long ago as 1969. Applied to her tax situation, this meant she had done exactly as she wished.

Prince Charles updated that view when he told royal writer Douglas Keay: 'I don't think people realise just how much influence the monarch does and can have. And its influence is very often more effective than direct power.' During the worst moments of the *annus horribilis,* some of this influence seemed to have been exercised by a process of osmosis.

'The Queen doesn't need to issue commands asking for action to be taken,' said a Whitehall insider. 'Her closest advisers sense that a particular thing needs to be done and they know a man who'll take care of it. The Good Chap style of government ensures that things are done on a nod-and-a-wink basis.'

This placed the blame for much of the mishandling of the Diana and Fergie problems fairly and squarely on the Palace secretariat, headed by Sir Robert Fellowes, a tall, bespectacled Old Etonian married to Diana's sister Jane and the cousin of Major Ron Ferguson. His problems started when photographs of the Duchess of York sharing a holiday in Morocco with Steve Wyatt turned up in the Texan's Chelsea apartment months after he had moved out. The Andrew Morton book, the St Tropez pictures, Squidgy and the first rumblings of Camillagate placed Sir Robert in a no-win situation. But he was unquestionably loyal to Her Majesty, even at the risk of incurring the wrath of his relatives.

'The Duchess of York bitterly recalls his treatment of her before the breakdown of her marriage,' said writer Christopher Wilson. 'He would barge into her room at Buckingham Palace, without knocking, with a handful of Press clippings flapping in his hand. "Not done very well today, have we, Ma'am?" he would bark as the Duchess was forced to leaf through a hotchpotch of reports of her previous day's doings. It was inevitable Fergie would get things wrong – but instead of help from the one courtier who could guide her, she was met with a wall of indifference.'

When the Yorks' separation was announced, Charles Anson, the Queen's Press Secretary, delivered a critique on the Duchess of such devastating invective to Paul Reynolds that the BBC court correspondent reported: 'The knives are out for Fergie at the Palace.' Anson apologised to the Duchess for his remarks and to the Queen for his blunder. Inexplicably, he kept his job. if I were running a mighty enterprise, my first-line managers would not have been the present courtiers,' said the informed peer. 'I think they are men fundamentally decoupled from reality.'

'They are prats – they aren't streetwise and there is no one who can handle the Press,' said Harry Arnold, who has dealt with the Palace Press Office for years. 'We have the situation of the Queen's second son, whom we accept she loves and some say she favours, being made to look an idiot by trying to conduct a marriage with a woman from whom he is separated – a woman who was humiliated by a civil servant, Charles Anson. It seems extraordinary to me, but the Queen allowed him to stay in office. I think her judgement has been appalling.'

More important than her Palace executives were members of the Privy Council, the Queen's powerful constitutional advisers over whom she presided. 'When Henry VIII was on the throne, the idea of the Privy Counsellor grew because you had access to the King's privy – you were able to sit with him while he was on the loo in the water closet,' said Andrew Morton. 'The idea of the King or Queen having a private life was inconceivable.' This concept had changed somewhat during the intervening five hundred years. 'Becoming a Privy Councillor is much more significant than gaining a peerage or being a courtier,' said a Whitehall source. 'The Queen feeds some extremely personal opinions into the Privy Council using the mechanisms at her disposal. They have a great reverence for this particular monarch.'

'If there is a hidden agenda relating to the monarchy, the Privy Council will want to see as little change as possible,' said the informed peer. 'They recognise social pressures but will not scramble into change just because there's a feeding frenzy in the tabloids. These are thoughtful men who feel extremely privileged to be where they are.

'But there will be good quality concessions to tidal shifts in opinion. Paying income tax, cutting the Civil List and opening up Buckingham Palace to the public are practical steps. But they won't change the monarchy. What happens, though, if you abolish the hereditary component in the House of Lords? How would that affect the monarchy? If the monarchy had the only remaining line of succession, it would seem an absurd anomaly.'

MANY of the Queen's friends over the years have owed their position entirely to the hereditary system, but some are self-made.

So personally enthralled with his sovereign was the life peer Lord Rab Butler that, as a director of Courtaulds, he arranged for her to acquire one of the world's largest cotton plantations at Scott, Mississippi, a community situated on the banks of the Mississippi River on the border of Arkansas. Worth more than £15 million, it consisted of 38,000 acres of rich soil and a factory as well as a mill employing hundreds of black labourers. She even received American government subsidies for not planting cotton, according to Senator Thomas McIntyre of New Hampshire.

Her Majesty's old friends have long included the Duke of Grafton, who was once tipped as the bachelor most likely to marry her. His estate, Euston Hall in Norfolk, is conveniently close to Sandringham to allow him to be summoned in times of trouble. Her Master of the Horse, Lord Somerleyton, of Somerleyton Hall in Suffolk, officiates at all important equestrian ceremonial events and once amused her by gracing the great hall of his home with a huge stuffed polar bear. The Marquess of Abergavenny, Her Majesty's representative at Ascot, and his younger brother, Lord Rupert Nevill, are always on hand to chat about racing matters. One she can call on for advice in more formal matters is the Duke of Norfolk, the Premier Duke and Earl Marshal of England and father-in-law of the television personality Sir David Frost.

Foreign royals with a place in her heart include her husband's cousin, the exiled King Constantine of Greece, who has been known to dash to her side from his home in Hampstead at the first inkling of a family crisis. She also cares greatly for Prince Georg of Denmark, who married Prince Philip's favourite sister, Sophie. King Juan Carlos of Spain grew closer to Her Majesty when he proved an able link to Charles, taking the opportunity during their shared family holidays on the island of Majorca to counsel him on how his marital difficulties added to his mother's burden of worries.

The only colonial in this privileged pack had been the Australian Sir William Heseltine who worked hard during his terms as Press Secretary to try to present the Royal Family as real people living in the modern world. She rewarded him for his efforts by making him her Private Secretary before Sir Robert Fellowes.

But it was the Earl of Airlie who was appointed as her Lord Chamberlain, titular head of the Royal Household. A man whose forebears had been royal courtiers for generations, his connections with court go even further: his brother, the Hon Sir Angus Ogilvy, is married to the Queen's cousin Princess Alexandra, and his American heiress wife became a lady of the bedchamber.

Douglas Keay observed that the Queen's friends need to be 'keen on racing, shooting, dogging and stalking. Broadly, they could be described as dull but good'.

Among the less grand women she is known to trust is Nancy Fenwick, wife of a former Head Keeper at Windsor Castle, Bill Fenwick. Known as the Queen's Dog Lady, Nancy is responsible for breeding the royal corgis and would summon HM to her home to witness the puppies' arrivals whenever she was in the vicinity, regardless of the hour. 'You have to be pretty close to get the Sovereign out of her bed for the birth of a dog, but that's just what Nancy does,' said a courtier familiar with the Queen's favourite people.

During her lifetime, Princess Grace was among those whose company the Queen especially enjoyed. Once, at a party at Claridge's, the Queen watched Andrew, fuelled only by orange juice, careering round the dance floor and asked Grace: 'What would you do with a son like that?' The former film star replied: 'I wouldn't worry. I always tell my son Albert that if he could stick to orange juice his future would be assured.'

One who can always be relied upon to make her laugh is the American Du Pont heiress, Sarah Farish, the wife of oil tycoon William Stamps Farish III. The Queen stays at the Farishs' ranch during her trips to attend bloodstock sales in Kentucky. Sarah is reputed to be one of the few people outside the Family permitted to kiss the Queen.

Her Majesty's closest female friend, however, is Myra, Lady Butter, a member of the dynasty who own the famous Luton Hoo estate in Bedfordshire. It was at a winter ball at Luton Hoo in 1891 that Prince Albert, Duke of Clarence, the eldest son of Edward VII, proposed to Princess Mary of Teck. When he died unexpectedly, she married his brother who became George V. The Queen loved the stately home so much that she returned to it each year with Prince Philip to celebrate their wedding anniversary. Prince Charles had once shown an interest in Myra's daughter Sandra, and her son Charlie – nicknamed Balmoral Butter after one of the products from the royal estate's dairy – is a close friend of Prince Andrew.

One year older than the Queen, Myra is a great-niece of Russia's last Tsar, Nicholas II, and her great-great-grandfather was Alexander Pushkin. Behind closed doors she and the Queen are 'Myra' and 'Elizabeth'. In London, the Butters live in Rutland Gate, Knightsbridge, a short distance from Buckingham Palace, and their grand Scottish home, Cluniemore at Pitlochry, is only thirty miles from Balmoral.

'Myra is one of the Queen's dearest friends,' confirmed a titled lady of their mutual acquaintance, it is a very, very, very close connection. Myra is partly Russian and has this sort of slanty-eye look like Tally Westminster, the Duchess of Abercorn and Georgina Phillips, the present owner of Luton Hoo. It comes from her mother Zia, the Countess Anastasia Mikhailovna de Torby. She was the daughter of the Grand Duke Michael of Russia and as such was a Romanov, but she lost all her titles as a result of coming here. She married Harold Wernher, heir to the Electrolux and South African gold and diamond mining fortunes as well as Luton Hoo.

'Myra Butter didn't have a title until her husband, Major David Butter, was knighted but she had even dukes eating out of the palm of her hand. She has been a key player for a long time and what she doesn't know ain't worth knowing. When the Queen is at Balmoral, Myra is never far away. She is a very key figure in the Queen's life.'

'WE may change the monarchy but we are not going to lose it,' said the royal historian. 'They are there to de-focus the political scene. Look at the Edinburgh Conference on Maastricht – everyone in the country was talking about Squidgy. Look at the General Election – the main topic of conversation was Fergie's split with Andrew.

'The House of Stuart were the last monarchs who had any real power and they were a very good line as monarchs went. The reason Charles II was allowed to behave so badly was that his excesses were de-focusing. The Fire of London and the Great Plague took place during his reign. The Protestant puritans had built up a powerbase but did little to deal with poverty or bubonic plague.'

After her grandfather, George V, the Queen most admired Victoria among her ancestors. Queen Mary noticed a distinct similarity between Elizabeth as a child and the young Victoria, particularly in their regal bearing. During 1992, Elizabeth was reminded of one of Victoria's most famous utterances. 'Please understand that there is no one depressed in this house,' she had said calmly on being told about reverses in the Boer War. 'We are not interested in the possibilities of defeat; they do not exist.' Stubborn and blinkered to the end, Victoria had a fatal seizure when she was told some more bad news from the front.

The old Queen was far from the paragon of popular myth. 'She was in her old age a dignified but rather commonplace good soul, narrow-minded in her view of things, without taste in art or literature, fond of money, having a certain industry and business capacity in politics, but easily flattered and expecting to be flattered, quite convinced of her own providential position in the world and always ready to do anything to extend and augment it,' wrote Wilfrid Scawen Blunt, a distinguished diarist of the period. 'She has been so long accustomed to success that she seems to have imagined that everything she did was wise and right.' This included 'a craze for painting the map Imperial red'.

The nationalist Blunt (no relation) was scathing about the true nature of Victoria's legacy. 'The Queen has left an unknown number of millions, it is said, to her family, but the heir to the Crown (Edward VII) is to have his debts paid by the nation at a time when not a single million has been spared for the famine in India – truly we deserve to follow Spain and Rome and the other empires into the gulf.'

Heart of Darkness, which Conrad wrote in 1899, two years after the breast-beating of Victoria's Diamond Jubilee, was scathingly critical of 'the dreams of men, the seeds of commonwealth, the germs of empire' that had plundered Africa and Asia in the name of colonialism, it was just robbery with violence, aggravated murder on a great scale, and men going at it blind – as is very proper for those who tackle a darkness,' said Conrad's seafaring hero, Charlie Marlow. 'The conquest of the earth, which mostly means the taking it away from those who have a different complexion or slightly flatter noses than ourselves, is not a pretty thing when you look into it too much.' The decline of the British Empire started with the death of its longest-serving monarch in 1901.

'Victoria was always presented as a virtuous prude in widow's weeds, but long before that she was a strong-willed and emotional woman,' said the royal historian. 'Her appetite for sex was such that she wore out Albert, who was prone to bouts of depression and self-doubt. Her diaries were so sexually explicit that her daughter Beatrice censored them for public consumption after her death. Victoria was anything but the strait-laced lady she was made out to be. She was the first member of the Royal Family to dance the waltz in public. The waltz was considered very undignified because the partners hold each other close.

'Before her succession, Victoria was kept away from the Court because of its immorality. She stayed at Kensington Palace, which was also a hotbed of plots and intrigue. Albert was appalled at the immorality he found in Buckingham Palace. He drove the nobility and their mistresses out to provide a decent atmosphere in which to raise his children. Unfortunately, his own brother Ernest, Duke of Saxe-Coburg and Gotha, suffered an attack of venereal disease during a visit. The Queen's physician was called to treat him and the word was quickly passed around the Palace. One reason Victoria is reputed to have said lesbianism didn't exist is because of her own experiences with Florence Nightingale. When she retreated to Osborne House, her servant John Brown became very powerful. The Queen is reputed to have become pregnant by him.

'Victoria was only a great queen because of Albert and the Prime Ministers who served during her reign, Melbourne, Gladstone, Peel, Palmerston and Disraeli. Once again, the monarchy was used to de-focus attention from the Industrial Revolution, child prostitution and the slums. The newly emergent middle class styled itself on the home life of our own dear queen as a buffer against Victorian misery.'

'Nothing will happen quickly to change the present monarchy,' said the informed peer. 'One hundred years is quite an acceptable pace of change in this country. One of the qualities that Britain has that other countries find enviable is its extremely leisurely pace of change.' 'Not too fast, not too slow,' was the way Lord Airlie put it. It was precisely this snail's pace that used to infuriate the Prince Albert of his generation, Philip Mountbatten RN.

11

THE PRINCE & THE SHOWGIRL

'Philip was really smitten with Cobina'
Lady Edith Foxwell

ONE of the things, and there were several, that annoyed Diana about Fergie was her good relations with their in-laws. Before her fall from grace, the Duchess of York had been the more favoured daughter-in-law. After August 1992, the competition ceased to matter.

During a long honeymoon period before that, Fergie made strenuous efforts to amuse the Queen and charm Prince Philip. She went riding with Her Majesty at Sandringham and Balmoral, gave her unexpected little gifts and made sure everything was to her liking when she came to afternoon tea at Sunninghill. Her earthy humour strongly appealed to Prince Philip, who had been known to pat a well-rounded bottom in his time. Both grandparents adored the little princesses, Beatrice and Eugenie, who called Philip 'Gramps'. Beatrice shouted it so loudly during a carriage race that he almost lost control of the horses. What annoyed Diana more than anything was that she knew Fergie was ingratiating herself to cover up a massive inferiority complex. Behind their backs, the Duchess referred to Elizabeth and Philip as 'Brenda and Stavros'.

Philip, for one, was less than amused when he found out. Not that the Duke of Edinburgh was a spoilsport. His buddy Frank Sinatra said of him: 'He has what I consider to be the most important attribute in a man – a great sense of humour.' Famed for his ferocious temper and withering scorn, Philip, in fact, has the gift of being able to laugh at a joke at his own expense. When a bust of himself was unveiled, he tweaked its prominent nose and quipped: 'That's me to the life – Schnozzle Mountbatten.' He liked to tell people that, among the fiercely loyal tribesmen of New Guinea, he was known as 'Number One Fella Belong Missus Kween' and when a friend observed that young Prince Charles was 'the image of his father', he replied: 'I know, but perhaps he'll improve with age.'

The one thing that he would not tolerate was any slighting reference to his ancestry. Coming from Fergie, the Stavros jibe hit a very raw nerve. 'I am not a Greek, but I was born in Greece,' he once declared, creating a furore in Athens. He was born at Mon Repos, the family villa on Corfu, the fifth child and only son of Prince Andrew of Greece and Princess Alice of Battenburg. His correct surname before he adopted the anglicised Mountbatten was Schleswig-Holstein-Sonderburg-Glucksburg. He was descended from Danes and Germans. To marry the Queen, he renounced his Greek title and became a British citizen. 'Dig Philip in that particular rib and you get a reaction,' said a friend.

Philip was acutely aware that his father had died as an exile in Monte Carlo, where he drank heavily, lost his money at the tables and took a mistress called Doris. Nor was he any happier about Fergie's nickname for the Queen, Brenda. He knew that Fergie delighted in doing an impersonation of the Queen. But as mimicry was an accepted party piece among the Windsors, this was a less heinous offence.

Diana's personal experience was that her father-in-law could be extremely tetchy if he felt the behaviour of any member of the Firm reflected badly on Her Majesty. She had felt the sharp edge of his tongue after she attended the State Opening of Parliament in November 1984.

For months, Diana had been urging her hairdresser, Kevin Shanley, to change the Diana Cut which had become her trademark.

'I think it's time my hair went up,' she told him.

'I don't think so,' cautioned Shanley. it would make you look old before your time.'

Diana persisted. 'Well, my husband would love to see it up,' she said, 'I really want my hair up for the State Opening of Parliament.'

Shanley refused to carry out her wishes and, to avoid trouble, passed his most famous client over to his colleague, Richard Dalton. The result was a classic chignon, the startling, upswept hairstyle known as the Royal Roll. It caused a sensation, but not the one Diana had anticipated.

As was the custom, the Queen travelled to the Palace of Westminster in the Irish State Coach pulled by four Windsor Greys, a Household Cavalry escort leading the way. The Imperial State Crown, removed from its place among the Crown Jewels at the

Tower of London, travelled ahead of her in another coach. There was, however, only one focal point. The TV cameras fixed on Diana's Royal Roll. Inside Westminster, the Queen and Prince Philip moved through the Royal Gallery to the House of Lords. Philip smiled, but he was seething inside.

Invited by Black Rod into the Sovereign's presence, Members of Parliament proceeded two by two to the House of Lords. Since the Gunpowder Plot of 1605, the Parliamentary vaults had always been thoroughly searched by the Yeoman of the Guard (and, in more recent times, members of the Anti-Terrorist Squad) before this event. Seated on her throne in the Lords, the Queen read the Gracious Speech, which outlined Government policies for the next session of Parliament. None of this pageantry rated headlines the following morning. Nearly every newspaper featured pictures of Diana's new hairstyle while none showed the Queen carrying out her most important constitutional duty. The only explosion was inside the Palace. 'This isn't done,' Philip told his daughter-in-law as soon as he got a chance. 'You don't put on a new hairstyle when we go to these important dos. It's the Queen's day, not yours.'

To make matters worse, the new style was greeted with wails of dismay. No one liked Mr Richard's handiwork. It was called a 'Disaster' and 'Diabolical'. The next time she saw Shanley, Diana told him: 'I won't be doing that again for a number of years.'

If a mere hairstyle could provoke such an outburst from Philip, the Squidgy tapes signalled the final parting of the ways. The Duke's rage towards his daughter-in-law made Diana's position in the Royal Household untenable long before the separation. Philip, according to Andrew Morton, wrote Diana 'an angry letter' to which she replied only after consulting a lawyer. At Royal Ascot, the Duke pointedly ignored his daughter-in-law when she passed him in the royal box. To make the snub more hurtful, Andrew Parker Bowles was invited for afternoon tea on the Queen's instructions.

As the rift between Diana and Philip had turned into a central theme in the overall drama, she took the unprecedented step of issuing a statement through Buckingham Palace more or less exonerating him. The Princess had returned ahead of Charles from the disastrous tour of South Korea, where the Waleses' demeanour was so grim that they were called 'The Glums'. The statement read:

'The Princess of Wales would like to single out from the recent wave of misleading reports about the Royal Family assertions in some newspapers this week directed specifically against the Queen and the Duke of Edinburgh. The suggestion that they have been anything other than sympathetic and supportive is untrue and particularly hurtful.'

The careful wording was a classic piece of avoidance because it completely ignored the reason why her royal inlaws needed to be 'sympathetic and supportive'. Besides, at least in Philip's case, it was patently untrue.

IF she compared Prince Philip with her father, Diana could see why she felt uncomfortable in his presence. The eighth Earl Spencer came from a dynasty that had produced 'no eccentrics, no villains, no lunatics, but a long line of worthy, sincere Englishmen'. Diana had forgiven Johnnie Spencer for his cruelty towards her mother. He might lack Philip's larger-than-life aura, but she could talk to him safe in the knowledge that he loved her deeply.

The Duke of Edinburgh was the exact opposite: abrasive, impatient, controversial, superior, almost unlovable. Early in her marriage, she developed the technique of teasing her father-in-law, or pretending to listen to his advice, or flattering his vanity. It took all of her acting skills to pull off a role for which she felt completely inadequate.

The forty-year age gap between them was inescapable. When Diana turned ten, Philip was already fifty, and he celebrated his sixtieth birthday just seven weeks before her wedding. In the intervening years, she had known him as Aunt Lilibet's husband at neighbouring Sandringham and followed him around the estate with the other guns. As she grew older, she realised that he was a figure of towering importance in public life. It was difficult to reconcile the two personae. The more Diana became acquainted with the Philip Legend, the more he became an enigma to her. His four children presented conflicting profiles of the same father.

Charles, from the daunting standpoint of eldest son, felt threatened on two counts. Not only was he the successor to his mother's crown, he was heir to his father's estate in the conventional sense as well. In either role, he was keenly aware that Philip found him wanting. This hurt Charles's pride a great deal, and he was not averse to fighting back. Addressing a prize-giving ceremony to promote 'solidarity between generations' in 1992, Charles pointedly ignored his father's influence on his life, warmly recalling instead chats he had enjoyed with the Queen Mother and Earl Mountbatten. 'Sadly, so often nowadays there is less and less contact between generations,' Charles said. 'I have found it an enormous benefit to be able to talk to my grandmother and to my late uncle.'

According to Stephen Barry, Charles kept a photograph of him with his father on his desk. He had written on it: 'I was not made to follow in my father's footsteps.' This amounted to a declaration of independence by the Prince of Wales, hitherto Charles Mountbatten-Windsor. 'Not to put too fine a point on it, Charles fears his father,' said the Palace insider. 'So much of his early life was spent in his shadow.'

After Charles broke his arm at polo, Diana suggested he retire from what the informed peer called 'his drive to perform upper-class, dangerous things'. She knew that, if he was trying to win reassurance, it certainly wasn't from her. 'I have always been intrigued by the kind of activities which offer danger and excitement,' explained Charles, it's a great challenge to overcome a certain element of natural fear.' it would seem that he is trying to impress his father, not realising he never will,' said the informed peer. 'But I detect in Charles the American concept of the encapsulated mother. He has carried it inside him through life and he checks his actions against what his mother would think. But I no longer think that Charles agonises over his mistakes. I read in his face that he has psychologically quarantined himself from the hurt.'

To Princess Anne, her father was the fount of wisdom, inspiration and strength. She used him as the touchstone in measuring other men. She had always been his little girl, an adventurous tomboy with angelic blonde curls and grey-blue eyes: the perfect daughter. When Philip returned from a four-month absence from home, six-year-old Anne had beaten her older brother up the stairs into his aircraft and jumped into his arms. Charles hung back. Sensing that he was a shy mother's boy, Anne had delighted in bullying him. Like many possessive daughters, only she felt justified in criticising her idol. If anyone else did, she leapt to his defence. Diana had to take care that she did not arouse the Mountbatten streak in her sister-in-law. 'I just don't like her,' she is known to have said.

The age gap between the Queen's children did not save Andrew and Edward. But whereas Andrew sought to win approval by outdoing his elder brother, Edward found it was far wiser to steer clear of trouble. He later tackled the problem by making himself really useful to Philip by organising the Duke of Edinburgh Awards. 'They have grown very close,' said a friend.

As old age set in and his family's troubles multiplied, Philip became more detached. He has withdrawn into a small circle of friends such as the Duke and Duchess of Abercorn who joined his annual cruise on the *Britannia* (undertaken at vast public expense). Sasha, the Duchess, greatly admires Philip, whom she has known since she was a child at Luton Hoo.

Another is Jane, Countess of Westmorland, a keen horsewoman who shares many of Philip's interests, even giving him riding whips to add to his carriage-driving collection. They often sit together at the Royal Windsor Horse Show and other equine events. 'Philip takes gentlemanly care of Jane,' said a titled lady of their acquaintance. 'I've seen him share his rug with her on a cold day at Windsor.' Lady Westmorland's husband, the fifteenth Earl, was regarded as the greatest charmer at court. He was Master of the Horse and his faultless, good-humoured manners won him an abiding place in the Queen's affections. When he died in 1993 after a paralysing stroke, Philip ensured that his widow continued to receive royal invitations. Although in her sixties, Lady Westmorland retains her striking good looks.

Carriage driving also brings Philip into the company of Patricia Kluge, a forty-four-year-old divorcee and owner of Mar Lodge next to the Balmoral estate. Patricia, a former belly dancer from Liverpool, was previously married to John Kluge, the American billionaire who sold his TV interests to Rupert Murdoch. Philip is not the least embarrassed that the exotic Pat once starred in the soft porn movie *The Nine Ages of Nakedness*.

The Prince still keeps in touch with one of his earliest loves, Cobina Beaudette, who was a lovely young American actress/showgirl called Cobina Wright Jnr when they met just before the war. 'Her mother was Cobina Wright Snr, who was one of the most well-known gossip writers in Hollywood,' said Lady Edith Foxwell, her British-based cousin. 'She was on a par with Louella Parsons and Hedda Hopper. They did the films and Cobina did the social side of it for the Hearst Press. She was an enormous friend of William Randolph Hearst.' One story the gossip writer never penned was about her daughter's romance with the young Prince Philip of Greece. As a result, she was invited to the royal wedding.

'Cobina Jnr is exactly the same age as me,' said Lady Edith, who was born granddaughter of the ninth Earl of Cavan in 1918. 'She made a few movies when she was about eighteen, including several with Betty Grable, and she was in *Flying Down to Rio* with Carmen Miranda. She was really gorgeous and such fun. I remember going to see her sing at the Pierre Hotel in New York – and she was only fourteen! Then she met Prince Philip long before he married the Queen. Beatrice Lillie introduced them.' Ms Lillie, one of the greatest comediennes of the century and the widow of Sir Robert Peel, Bt, had taken a friendly interest in the young American star.

'Philip actually had a job at the Travellers Club in Paris and he was very smitten with Cobina,' continued Lady Edith. 'She saw a lot of him then and she always remained friends with him afterwards. Nobody left anybody – the war came and she had to go back to America and he rejoined the Navy. She was married to Palmer Beaudette during the war and she had four children, three sons and then a daughter called Cobina Caroline, C.C. they call her: C.C. Beaudette.'

'I have never discussed our relationship with the Press or anybody,' said Cobina Beaudette from her home in California. 'Obviously it was before he was married but we have been very good friends for fifty-some years and I value our friendship so I won't discuss it. We write occasionally and he sends me Christmas cards.'

Philip suffers terribly from arthritis but he can still sign his own cards, although he prefers a lap-top computer for writing personal letters. Forced to give up polo at fifty when even equine painkillers ceased to work, he turned to carriage racing as a substitute. The Queen watches from the sidelines whenever he competes. When he won first place driving her Fell ponies at the Royal Windsor Horse Show, she cheered as though he was Ben Hur.

RIGHT from the start, no one summed up the spirit of the New Elizabethan Age more than the Duke of Edinburgh. When he moved into the big house at the end of the Mall, he brought with him a fierce determination to follow in the footsteps of Prince Albert. He regarded what he called 'the quirk of circumstance' that had placed his wife on the throne so young as a personal challenge. Queen Victoria had been younger, but so had Albert, who was only twenty when he married. This made Philip's sense of vocation even keener. Drilled in the modern British Navy, he became a loose cannon crashing against the bulwark that separated the old order and the brave new world of the Fifties. Nothing and no one were spared. He told industry to 'pull its finger out', questioned hidebound attitudes towards youth, education and the environment, argued famously with Press barons and challenged the status quo. Philip had always despised 'swank and swagger' and he gave Britain the benefit of his opinions in the salty language of the sea. 'It wasn't easy for him in the early days of her reign because he was so anxious not to let the Queen down,' said an old friend, in those days, he did have stage fright and nervous tension, but he gradually got over that. Nevertheless, the job was a fearful strain.'

Philip spoke his mind on the most explosive of topics, regardless of the consequences, if the monarchy has no part to play, let's end it on amicable grounds and not have a row about it,' he suggested. 'I get a little annoyed when people suggest we are clinging on for our own benefit. We are not. The monarchy exists for the benefit of the people and, of course, if they don't like it, they should get rid of it.' No one in Britain had heard a royal speak so plainly before. The courtiers were aghast. 'Deep down inside him there's a core of honesty and it's this that makes him seem rather blunt to people,' said the old friend. 'Basically, he's a humble person. This may not seem apparent to those who think he's arrogant, but what looks like arrogance is really only the bluntness and honesty coming out.'

Quite a few people found Philip not only arrogant, but selfish and manipulative as well. 'He knows exactly what he's doing and he's a pretty neat judge of what's going to happen,' said the informed peer. 'He's the walking embodiment of a number of very old-fashioned masculine virtues: courage, resolve and bloody-mindedness. His purpose, which is often directed at nice things happening to himself, means that he hasn't heard more generally received signals. If he had thought for one micro-second, he would have realised that his bluff, off-the-cuff sailorman comments would have resonated; that they would have rebounded. But he enjoys being identified as not very diplomatic. It contributes to his self-image of a shire-plus-Monte Carlo international tough guy.' 'Much of Philip's criticisms are him playing devil's advocate – it's a tactic to knock down some of the Aunt Sallys in society,' said a more kindly disposed member of the aristocracy.

Yet Philip's zest for life would have defeated less energetic mortals. One summery Sunday, the Duke was with the Queen on Holy Island off the Scottish coast. At eleven o'clock, they attended morning service and he read the second lesson. At twelve ten, he planted a tree in the market square. At one o'clock, he skipped lunch and walked to the lifeboat station. The royal barge of the *Britannia* took him eight miles down the coast where a car was waiting to rush him to Acklington air force base. Aboard a Heron of the Queen's Flight he ate sandwiches and touched down in Berkshire at three thirty-five. He ran from the plane, jumped into his waiting Lagonda and drove at breakneck speed to his destination. Later that day, he flew back to Scotland and chased *Britannia* in a motorboat to rejoin his wife.

Philip took his polo seriously.

The sudden dash had been to Smith's Lawn for an important match. To him, a round trip of 1,000 miles to play his favourite sport was a minor inconvenience. To others, it was a reckless extravagance.

In his most active years, no one was closer to Philip, nor understood him better, than his right-hand man, Lieutenant Commander Michael Parker. A debonair naval officer with a mischievous streak, Mike Parker would have fitted easily into the court of Elizabeth I alongside Drake and Raleigh. He was sharp and he had style. He was also the keeper of his master's secrets. When Parker departed the Palace, the whiff of scandal tarnished the Queen's marriage as no other episode in her reign.

The Duke had met Parker in 1941 when they were first lieutenants in sister warships on the east coast of England. Philip was twenty and Parker, an Australian-born Catholic, twenty-one. They formed an uninhibited friendship, partly because the Duke was then an unknown foreign royal going by the name of Prince Philip of Greece. What's more, he was penniless, which made it easier for the two young men to fraternise on equal terms. They later served in the

Pacific and, when Philip's royal connections became public, Parker helped him to avoid harassment during their shore leave.

When newsmen finally caught up with Philip at an Australian racecourse, he told them: 'You've got the wrong man – that's Mountbatten over there.' He pointed out Mike Parker, bearded like himself and dressed in identical naval uniform. Adopting a phoney English accent, Parker kept up the deception while his friend enjoyed his day at the races.

Their affinity was so strong that, having shared the dangers of war, they eagerly fell upon the spoils. Blond-haired Philip, his figure tall and slim, his eyes a piercing shade of blue, was an instant hit at parties in Sydney and Parker's home town, Melbourne. 'There were always armfuls of girls,' the Australian admitted. When Parker was romancing his first wife, an auburn-haired Wren called Eileen Allan, he teased the still-unattached Philip: 'Don't worry, old boy, some nice girl will come along for you one of these days.' Philip, in fact, was at the time deeply involved in private correspondence with Princess Elizabeth.

After the war, Parker drifted into civvy street and worked as a rope salesman for his father-in-law at an office in Bond Street. While Philip's engagement to his princess was still a secret, he wrote to Parker: 'What are you doing these days? Do you like it? If not, I need an equerry.' Parker entered royal service as an aide to Princess Elizabeth and the Duke.

From the start, he upset the Old Guard of courtiers, who were opposed to outsiders joining their ranks. He didn't have the necessary background; he wasn't 'Old Boy Net'; he didn't know the form. Their suspicions were confirmed during the Duke's stag party at the Dorchester Hotel. Traditionalists among the guests were appalled to see Parker wrestling on the floor, trying to take the trousers off a resisting young naval officer. The Duke, laughing helplessly, enjoyed the prank along with his best man, David, Marquess of Milford Haven, and his uncle Lord Louis.

When Parker reported to Buckingham Palace, it was no coincidence that he found he had been assigned the pokiest office in the whole place. It overlooked a gloomy courtyard and, through a threadbare screen, he could plainly see an old hand basin in one corner. A practical man used to thinking on his feet, Parker accepted the challenge. Within days, he had transformed the room into snug, cabin-like quarters, decked out with comfortable furniture and pictures of his favourite ships and other momentos from his travels around the world. On his desk, next to a photograph of his wife and children, was one of Philip's innovations, a newfangled intercom system. Passing courtiers were startled to hear a loud disembodied voice booming: 'Go and boil your head, Mike Parker. Go and boil your head.' It was Philip, speaking from his own office, to test the squawk-box.

To jog Philip's memory, Parker introduced a card index system which recorded personal details about the people his boss met on official engagements. Their cars had mobile phones. They used helicopters, much to Churchill's dismay until Parker persuaded the Prime Minister to try one himself. The new technology raised eyebrows, but it worked. In the spirt of the space age, Philip was more Prince Cosmonaut than Prince Consort.

Their jokes, however, were more suited to the wardroom than the sovereign's seat of power. The occasional thunderflash, a firework used in military operations, was let off, much to the consternation of Palace staff. King George VI sent for the culprits and ordered them to stop. They aimed a model electric cannon which Parker kept in his office at a particularly stuffy member of the Royal Household who was located across the corridor. When they opened his door and pressed the button, the cannon fired, spraying the target with white soot, leaving him looking 'like a snowman'. He stormed into Parker's office to find that Princess Elizabeth, laughing merrily, had been one of the conspirators. There were now two loose cannons inside the Palace.

The high jinks stopped after the Duke and his equerry, given to jumping on rugs and skidding down the highly polished corridors, crashed into the door of the King's study. They were said to have been sternly rebuked. But the King was fond of Parker who, like himself, had suffered terribly from stomach ulcers in the Navy. When the King was struggling over the blueprints of a new Royal Yacht, it was Parker, a supremely efficient organiser, who helped simplify the designs to His Majesty's satisfaction. The King never saw the results of their endeavours; he died before even the keel of *Britannia* was laid down. Parker, who was accompanying Princess Elizabeth and the Duke on their tour of Kenya, broke the news of his death to his friend.

'He looked as if the whole world had dropped on him,' Parker said. 'I never felt so sorry for anyone in all my life.' Philip admitted that the King's death changed his life with the Queen. 'Within the house, and whatever we did, it was together,' he said. 'I suppose I naturally filled the principal position. People used to come to me and ask me what to do. In 1952 the whole thing changed, very, very considerably.'

When the Queen came to the throne, Parker volunteered to leave the Royal Household to avoid conflict with hardcore courtiers who wanted the monarchy to maintain a discreet distance from the masses. He was keenly aware of the forces ranged against him. But the Queen refused to accept his resignation. 'Nonsense! You're one of the family,' she replied. 'We could not do without you.'

He stayed on as private secretary to the Duke, who wanted to modernise the Palace, which he called a rumbling old juggernaut. One of the first things they did was to count the number of rooms. The tally reached 600 and included nineteen state rooms, fifty-two royal and guest bedrooms, 188 staff bedrooms, ninety-two offices and seventy-eight bathrooms. Philip wanted to know why, when he ordered a sandwich, it took four flunkeys to deliver it from the kitchen, but he was told bluntly to mind his own business. The hierarchical structure of the Palace had been in place for generations, a son often inheriting the job of his father. They regarded Philip in much the same way as Prince Albert had been viewed: 'A German princeling, *not* whom she should have married.' With barely concealed irritation, he tried to suppress his anger.

In the final stage of the coronation ceremony, the homage, Philip kneeled at the Queen's feet before kissing her left cheek and this symbolised his new position. He had to stand beside her as she sat on the throne during the State Opening of Parliament, and he learned to walk a respectful three paces behind her on official visits. He had no keys to the royal boxes, so he was unable to guide her in the way Albert helped Victoria. 'I'm just an amoeba, here to procreate members of the Royal Family,' he stormed. But he refused to give up.

Philip had introduced Mike Parker to the circle of friends he maintained well away from the Palace. He made him a member of the Thursday Club, an exclusive luncheon party which met, among other venues in later years, at Wheeler's Oyster Bar in Charlotte

Street. The language was ripe, the jokes navy blue and the pranks sometimes more than a little foolhardy. Philip loved the boyish bawdiness; it was his escape from the straitjacket of Palace protocol. One lunchtime, three thunderflashes were let off, one of them exploding in a fireplace and covering Philip in soot. Police who rushed in to the private room on the fourth floor fearing a bomb attack were not amused.

Although most of the guests such as the actors David Niven, Peter Ustinov and James Robertson Justice, the royal photographer Baron, the harmonica player Larry Adler and Arthur Christiansen, editor of the *Daily Express,* were above reproach, others proved that royalty had to be constantly vigilant. Among them was Stephen Ward, the society osteopath, 'a silly little drug-ridden queer', in the words of one who met him. Ward, a gifted artist who had sketched members of the Royal Family including Prince Philip, achieved notoriety as the procurer of Christine Keeler and Mandy Rice Davies in the Profumo Scandal of 1963. The sketch linked Philip's name to persistent, though false, rumours that he was the unidentified 'Man in the Mask' at one of Ward's orgies. Another guest was Kim Philby, the Soviet master spy who fled to Moscow. One of his agents, Sir Anthony Blunt, was strategically installed at the Palace as Keeper of the Royal Pictures. The KGB were thus perfectly placed to know exactly what was happening inside British royalty.

When his own Palace Revolution achieved only limited success, Philip shared the frustration with Mike Parker. Sometimes at night, they would slip out of the Palace for less than formal meetings with other acquaintances. Mayfair was across Green Park one way and St James's the other. The royal staff soon got used to these unscheduled expeditions. 'Murgatroyd and Winterbottom have popped out for a stroll' became a catch-phrase.

According to Parker's wife Eileen, Philip sometimes returned so late that he was locked out. Rather than alert the guard, Parker would give the Queen's husband a leg-up to climb over the Palace walls. 'Philip had a chauffeur who wasn't on the normal rota,' said a resident of the Royal Mews. 'The other drivers said he would tell one of them to park an unmarked car at a designated location somewhere in London. The driver would return to the Palace by bus. Then Philip would sweep out of the gates in an official limousine with his standard flying, attend a function, switch cars and disappear into the night.'

Philip had acquired a taste for nightlife as a bachelor after the war when one of his companions was Helene Foufounis, a playmate from childhood. She had two children, Max and Louise, by her second husband, French flying hero Marcel Boisot. Philip was their godfather. Philip and Helene, a toothsome blonde, met up in London during the war and, when it ended and her marriage broke up, they spent some hilarious times together in Paris. She was the 'mystery blonde' who barged into the men-only club, the Traveller's, scandalising its old-fashioned and chauvinist members. When they met for tea at the Ritz on one memorable occasion, Philip arrived less than stylishly on a borrowed woman's bicycle. 'After tea, we raced each other from the Place de la Concorde to the other end of the Champs-Elysees, me on the Metro, he on his two-wheeler,' said Helene. 'I was excited to get there first and see him pedalling furiously, his knees almost under his chin. He didn't care a bit about looking so funny.'

Helene returned to London to appear as a cabaret singer at the Pigalle, where she adopted the stage name Helene Cordet. She took her children to see their newly-married godfather at Clarence House and, after the Coronation, at Buckingham Palace. Their names were linked romantically many times and it was falsely rumoured that Philip was Max's father.

Even after his marriage, Philip loved the lively banter of the cocktail circuit. Inevitably, beautiful women found themselves in his company. Just as inevitably, there was trouble. Patricia Kirkwood, a blonde musical comedy actress, recalled meeting the Duke when she was appearing at the Hippodrome only a year after the royal wedding. He arrived in her dressing room from a late, late Thursday Club lunch with their mutual friend, the lordly Baron, and another naval officer. Pat slipped into a dazzling gown from Saks Fifth Avenue, split skirt rolled on to one hip to show the legs Kenneth Tynan had described as 'the Eighth Wonder of the World'. Well after midnight, the quartet headed for Les Ambassadeurs next door to 145 Piccadilly but found their entrance barred. 'We've already played God Save the King,' said the maitre d'. 'We're closing.' Philip stepped forward. 'Tell them to play it again,' he suggested. He was recognised and a table was quickly found.

After dinner, Philip wanted the party to adjourn to the Milroy Club, a fashionable nightspot upstairs. 'We'd all been drinking champagne and Philip – he told me not to call him Sir or Your Highness – asked me to dance,' said Ms Kirkwood. 'I must have created a bit of an impression because he said, "Hubba, hubba". He wouldn't let me sit down and we were on the floor for nearly two hours, dancing everything from waltzes to sambas. It was very embarrassing because his wife was very close to the birth of Prince Charles.'

Among the patrons at 'Les A' and the Milroy that night were a number with Palace connections. The story of The Duke and the Showgirl reached King George at Buckingham Palace even quicker than it hit Fleet Street. He was appalled at his son-in-law's unbecoming conduct and a royal storm cloud settled over Philip, Baron and the Thursday Club. 'The King told Philip that this really is not on,' said the Duke's unofficial biographer John Parker. 'He gave him a right old dressing down.'

Miss Kirkwood went on to marry four times and, at seventy-two, remains slim and astonishingly youthful. When she decided to make her stage comeback in April, 1993, her Press agent contacted the newspapers. 'Pat Kirkwood, one of the living legends from the golden age of stage and screen musicals, and the star whose name has been persistently linked by royal biographers with that of Prince Philip, is returning to the British stage after a long absence,' the Press bulletin gushed. 'We did not have an affair,' Ms Kirkwood said emphatically. 'I never saw Prince Philip socially again. I only ever saw him again at a Royal Variety Performance or in the stalls with his family.'

The Queen cannot have been happy. She adored her husband and the gossip must have hurt her deeply. The rumours of a royal rift gained momentum when Philip embarked on a four-month solo cruise in *Britannia* which meant he would miss Christmas and New Year with the Queen and their two young children. It was, in fact, a far-sighted venture encompassing not only the 1956 Olympic Games in Australia but New Zealand and other far-flung British possessions such as the Falkland Islands and Antarctica. But scandal trailed in *Britannia's* wake.

When Philip sailed away from Australian shores, he left behind the impression that he was a man who lived life to the full. There was also the unmistakable feeling that he was up to something. As he and Mike Parker had made many friends in Sydney during the war, it was only natural that they should include private outings on the itinerary. This led to the unfounded belief that Philip, aided and abetted by Parker, was secretly meeting a string of women. Sudden departures from the official schedule, two of them on the same day, fuelled the potentially damaging speculation.

At five fifteen one evening, Philip left Government House after a busy day on the red carpet circuit. He boarded a naval crashboat at Man o'War Steps near Circular Quay and travelled swiftly across Sydney Harbour towards the mansions of Vaucluse. Several small craft tried to follow the crashboat but were quickly outdistanced. Philip returned to Man o'War Steps at seven p.m. and, after jumping jauntily ashore in front of a small crowd, he was surrounded by no fewer than ten plain-clothed and uniformed policemen. Something was in the wind. When a photographer tried to take his picture, a detective blocked his view. He seized the photographer by the shoulders and disconnected the flashgun. 'The Duke has been for a swim,' he said. 'No pictures can be taken.' At eleven ten the same night, Philip swept out of Government House for another private visit. This time, his limousine was escorted by two squad cars and a third unmarked vehicle. The secrecy, and heavy-handed security, created a mystery which some Australians found highly suspicious.

It was ironic that the scandal which would destroy Mike Parker's royal career caught up with him on the voyage home. *Britannia,* the yacht he had helped the King to design, was steaming up the coast of Africa in February 1957, when his Scots-born wife Eileen suddenly announced that they had parted. Her lawyers said that she would be suing her husband for a legal separation under which she would retain custody of their two children. This should not normally have created more than passing interest. But it closely followed the end of Princess Margaret's love affair with the divorced Group Captain Peter Townsend, whom Philip and Parker both happened to dislike intensely. Marital problems at the Palace, even among the lower orders, was big news. The events that followed removed Parker from public life and cast a long shadow over the marriage of the Queen and Prince Philip.

Using the ship's radio-telephone, Parker was able to ascertain that his wife had arranged a meeting with Commander Richard Colville, the Queen's Press Secretary, at the Palace. She told him that they were estranged and that she intended to take legal action. Colville, alert to the dangers not so much to Parker, whom he disliked, but to his royal employer, persuaded her to wait until he returned to England before making any announcement. But the story that a court case was imminent leaked to the newspapers.

Eileen insisted that her decision had nothing to do with her husband's Palace job or the royal tour. Ah-ha, exclaimed the scandal-mongers, there must be something else. Parker, according to gossip, had developed 'an extravagant liking for parties and high living'. 'Seafood, Continental cooking and champagne are all very much to his taste,' one writer noted disapprovingly. Worse, he had been seen in London 'in company with an attractive brunette with dark, wavy hair, grey-green eyes and an aquiline nose'. The obvious conclusion was that Parker was a reckless *bon vivant* who was flaunting his infidelity in front of the public.

Instead of toughing it out, Parker consulted his solicitor by phone and then went into a huddle with Prince Philip. The outcome was that he quit his job and Philip accepted his resignation. His motive was to save the Duke from any further embarrassment; the effect was the exact opposite. His sudden departure was interpreted as confirmation of his guilt. Some sections of the Press, particularly in the United States and on the Continent, reasoned that Philip must be guilty as well, even if only by association. The two men were inseparable. They played cricket together, swam together in the Palace pool, and parried together outside its walls. They were even playing squash when the Queen had given birth to Prince Charles, and Philip had to be summoned from the court. Surely at least some of the rumours about Her Majesty's husband had to be true.

When *Britannia* docked in Gibraltar, Philip drove Parker to the airfield and boarded the London-bound plane for a farewell chat before take-off. On landing in London, Parker was besieged by newsmen. Colville turned up to tell him: 'You're on your own.' But Parker, fiercely loyal to Philip and the Queen, refused point-blank to give his side of the story. His silence only caused further damaging speculation. It was claimed he had been meeting his mystery woman at Baron's flat, scene of Philip's own supposed assignations.

The truth was far less sensational. 'The marriage was collapsing before Mike ever set foot in the Palace,' said a friend. 'He had wanted to go back to Australia and his wife wanted to stay in Britain. They had two young children to educate. The main reason Mike took the job as equerry was to resolve this dilemma. It gave him a perfectly valid reason to stay in England, but it meant that he saw less and less of his wife. In the end, he moved out of the marital home in Kensington long before the journey with Philip.' Parker's mother confirmed this version: 'Michael's was a wartime marriage and it was breaking up long before he joined the Royal Household.'

The Queen, who had been kept largely in the dark, flew to a reunion with her husband at the start of a State visit to Portugal. She was in high spirits, donning a false beard to surprise Philip as he entered her aircraft. Unfortunately, Philip had shaved off the growth he had been sporting during his travels. Still, they laughed about it and tried to rise above the scenes of near frenzy that the 'royal rift' had precipitated in the crowds waiting to greet them.

Parker cleared out his desk and, in the Queen's absence, became *persona non grata* at the Palace. Immediately she returned to London, however, Her Majesty summoned him into her presence and made him a Commander of the Royal Victorian Order, a personal award for services to the Royal Family. On 22 February, 1957, she had an even bigger surprise for her husband:

'The Queen has been pleased to give and grant unto HRH the Duke of Edinburgh the style and titular dignity of a Prince of the United Kingdom. The Queen has been pleased to declare her will and pleasure that the Duke of Edinburgh shall henceforth be known as His Royal Highness The Prince Philip, Duke of Edinburgh.'

This put a stop to some of the gossip, although others pointed out that she had still not officially named her husband Prince Consort.

Prince Philip continued to see his old friend, portlier and balding slightly, outside the Palace. He invited him to meetings of the Thursday Club, which now convened on Mondays in Kensington. At the Cowes regatta, Philip greeted him warmly, even allowing him to take Prince Charles for a picnic. When courtiers questioned the wisdom of this, he turned on them in a blistering rage and told them he would choose his own friends no matter what they thought. Mike Parker might have lost his royal job but not his links with royalty. He would turn up again in highly intriguing circumstances.

IT was in the summer of Parker's official departure that the film star Merle Oberon came to pay her respects. She arrived in London to show off her new fiance, a Mexican-Italian steel magnate called Bruno Pagliai. Philip and the actress had been close friends. Merle wanted to reassure Bruno on that score and to introduce him to her royal circle, which included the then Duchess of Kent and Lord Mountbatten.

At forty-six, Ms Oberon had lost none of the exotic beauty which had made her a box office star ever since she played Anne Boleyn in *The Private Life of Henry VIII* with Charles Laughton, and Cathy in *Wuthering Heights* with Laurence Olivier. Her first husband, the film-maker Sir Alexander Korda, had cast the unknown extra in her first major role after spotting her in a studio canteen.

She had been born, she claimed, Estelle O'Brien Merle Thompson in Tasmania, the Australian island state that numbered Errol Flynn among its native sons. Korda, a Hungarian, knew that she had been working as a dance hostess at the Cafe de Paris. He changed her name to Merle Oberon, selecting the surname from the King of the Fairies in *A Midsummer Night's Dream,* and married her. In truth, Merle was an Anglo-Indian who had been born Queenie Thompson into crippling poverty. She escaped to England, disguising her Indian mother as a maid. The elaborate fantasy she concocted to hide her real identity lasted long after her six-year marriage to Alexander Korda. 'I knew she was really Queenie Thompson from Calcutta and I always thought how stupid it was to pretend,' said Lady Edith Foxwell. 'She was no more from Tasmania than I was.'

With Korda's help, Merle had become a friend of Noel Coward, Churchill and Lord Beaverbrook. She had partied with Edward and Mrs Simpson in the Thirties and was appalled when, at dinner one night, the next King of England extolled the virtues of Nazi Germany.

But it was Mountbatten who sang her praises to Philip once the war was over. 'Mountbatten urged Philip to get involved with charity work and he did a lot as President of the National Playing Fields Association,' said John Parker. 'There was a link with show business to raise funds and Frank Sinatra and Ava Gardner came over to Britain to help. It was about that time that Merle Oberon was involved as well. She was introduced to Philip by her old friend Mountbatten.'

The Duke was captivated by Merle's smooth, oval face dominated by almond-shaped eyes of luminous green. Green was his favourite colour. 'Her beauty was exotic – like an ivory mask which was tacked on to her face,' said the actress Claire Bloom. 'What was so sad is that anyone should have to cover up her past and her background as Merle did.'

After traipsing around the high spots of the season, Merle married Bruno at a small chapel near the Colosseum in Rome and flew to Nice for a honeymoon in the South of France. The woman who touched Philip's heart then returned to Mexico to set up house. She gave Philip an open invitation to stay with her any time he liked, but the ubiquitous Mike Parker got there first.

While his divorce was still pending, Parker started to enjoy his freedom. He turned up at a royal film premiere in the company of Baroness Nancy von Hoyningen-Heune, whose German husband Ernst was 'working in New York'.

The Baroness, a stunning redhead, was the former Miss Nancy Oakes, a thirty-two-year-old heiress. Her father, the millionaire gold prospector Sir Harry Oakes, had become rich overnight after discovering the second wealthiest gold mine in the world at Lake Shore in the Canadian wilderness. He went to Australia and married Eunice McIntyre, the woman who had grub-staked him twenty years earlier. They were living in Nassau when the Duke of Windsor arrived to take over at Government House, safely removed, Churchill hoped, from his dangerous Nazi cronies in Europe. Sir Harry had been murdered at his mansion in what had been labelled the Unsolved Crime of the Century. He was found in his bedroom, his head battered and his scorched body covered in feathers. With the assistance of two American detectives he called in from Florida to investigate the crime, Windsor tried to frame Nancy's first husband, Count Freddie de Marigny, for the murder. 'Freddie was a big, attractive man who towered over the Duke and they hated each other,' said the royal historian. 'Windsor knew Freddie was innocent but he was determined to hang him. Fortunately, the defence were able to prove in court that Freddie's fingerprint had been planted at the murder scene and he was acquitted. The Duke promptly deported him. Anyone who believed the Duke was unfairly treated by the Royal Family or the British Government is entirely misguided. He should have been charged with treason for collaborating with the

Nazis, and he should have been exposed for trying to execute an innocent man.'

Nancy joined Freddie in exile in Cuba, but the marriage was annulled and she married Baron Ernst von Hoyningen-Heune. Ironically, one of his family, Baron Oswald Hoyningen-Heune, had been German Minister in Lisbon at the outbreak of World War II. He had specific instructions from Hitler to kidnap the Windsors if they would not stay in Europe of their own free will. This was part of a plan to set up a pro-Nazi regime in Britain with the former King as its quisling. 'The Duke believes with certainty that continued heavy bombing will make England ready for peace,' the baron told Berlin in a secret despatch, which was uncovered after the war. Churchill spirited the Windsors away from Portugal to Nassau before the Duke could cause any more damage.

Now at Christmas, 8,000 foot above sea level in Mexico City, Nancy invited the newlyweds Merle and Bruno to a lavish party. Guests danced to the Latin rhythms of an orchestra playing on a flower-decked launch in the middle of the swimming pool. Among the guests was her frequent escort, Commander Mike Parker.

After they were spotted at the royal film show, she said: 'There is absolutely nothing between us. It's all so hideously embarrassing. He is just a nice guy in a tough spot. This has put him in such an awkward situation, poor dear.'

In the rarefied atmosphere of Mexico City, Nancy, Mike, Merle and Bruno posed happily for photographs of the festive occasion.

Not long after, Parker accompanied Nancy when she went to visit her mother in the Bahamas. He had just been divorced after admitting adultery. In Nassau, he was booked into the Olympia Hotel when the Governor, Sir Raynor Arthur, invited him to move into Government House. Parker extended his stay.

'Nancy Oakes and various other people were trying to get the Oakes murder case re-opened and they would use anyone and everyone who was around – Mike Parker, Mountbatten, anyone. I am sure that was the case,' said John Parker, author of *King of Fools,* the definitive unauthorised biography of the Duke of Windsor. 'Philip hated the Windsors more than anyone else but the Palace were trying to suppress anything of a scandalous nature.

'I am sure the murder involved money and Harry Oakes attempting to get around the laws of currency that applied in the Bahamas at that time. He used the Duke of Windsor to help him and Windsor put a lot of money through the same channels himself.' According to John Parker, one of Sir Harry's business associates, a shyster called Harold Christie, 'was certainly involved in the hiring of a hit man to murder Harry Oakes'.

After much heated wrangling, Nancy pointedly declared: it (the case) should be cleared up once and for all, regardless of who might be affected by the truth.' She was referring to the Duke of Windsor. Scotland Yard detectives were sent to Nassau, but they were hastily recalled on orders from Whitehall before they could question any witnesses. The stalwart Sir Raynor declared the case closed. 'There will be no new inquiry,' he said.

'I met Nancy when she was going around with Mike Parker in London and I stayed with her in Mexico City,' said Lady Edith. 'She talked about the death of her father constantly. It was made to look like a ritual killing to blame it on the blacks. They put out a rumour that he was having lots of affairs with black women which I think was a load of old cobblers. But the whole thing has almost destroyed Nancy.'

Subsequently Mike Parker succeeded in carving a very particular niche in the world of high finance, using contacts from his Palace days. He was on the board of at least seven major British companies and worked as 'sales and general policy consultant' to the Lockheed Aircraft Corporation. He was on the payroll when the giant US planemaker was accused of bribery and corruption on a massive scale. Prince Bernhard of the Netherlands, Prince Philip's friend and president of the then World Wildlife Fund, was alleged to have pocketed $1.1 million for helping Lockheed to clinch big aviation deals. No charges were laid against the protesting Prince, but he was forced to resign from the fund. Throughout the controversy, Parker remained charming but tight-lipped.

When Philip finally made a solo visit to Merle, she was living in an idyllic white marble palace called Villa Ghalal (a local word meaning Love) on a clifftop overlooking the Pacific at Acapulco. Her husband was 'working in Mexico City', so Merle went to meet the Duke's plane on her own. At the airport, she informed the British ambassador that she had come to collect her house guest. His Royal Highness, she was politely told, would make the journey in an official car. 'Then you can find him somewhere else to stay,' Ms

Oberon declared haughtily. Protocol was waved aside and a triumphant Merle swept off with the Prince, leaving the ambassador speechless on the tarmac. 'The Queen knew all about Philip's friendship and she trusted him implicitly,' said a friend. Ms Oberon was quite specific on that point. 'I don't believe in extra-curricular activities in a marriage,' she said. Philip was feted at a dinner under a canopy of trees and he and Merle strolled along the villa's tropical terraces to the sound of a waterfall. He returned on more than one occasion and, in a romantic gesture, once fired a salute from *Britannia* as he was passing along the coast. Queenie Thompson had finally got the recognition she had craved all her life.

DIANA blamed not only his parents but Lord Mountbatten for Charles's inability to relate to her problems. Uncle Dickie was an ardent bridge player, but marriage wasn't his strong suit. Nor were women in general. Diana knew his reputation for seducing young men eager for advancement in the Royal Navy. 'So bright, so bent,' opined the informed peer. This filled her with misgivings. Her circle buzzed with stories about Dickie's marriage to Edwina.

I met Mountbatten on several occasions and he was singularly uninterested in women,' said a lady of letters, in his Navy days, he was a known homosexual. My relative, Dr Douglas Wright, was Surgeon Commander on one of Mountbatten's ships before World War II. He told me he was summoned to Mountbatten's cabin and found him taking a bath. He proceeded to make a pass at the doctor but was turned down.'

'What about your career?' asked Lord Louis.

'You don't understand,' replied Dr Wright. 'I'm planning to make a career outside the Navy.'

When Mountbatten persisted, he was told: 'Just remember, I'm the doctor – the man with the needle.'

'Sure enough,' said his relative, 'Mountbatten got a dose of the clap in the Far East and Dr Wright had to treat him.'

'Edwina had many lovers because Mountbatten was hopeless in bed, although they managed to have two children,' said the royal historian. 'She loved ritzy nightclubs like the Kit-Kat or the Embassy, but she also liked slumming it in the bohemian joints of Fitzrovia. Apart from Pandit Nehru, whom she met much later, she was very keen on Hutch, a black singer and pianist. People who heard the rumour thought she was having an affair with Paul Robeson and it became the subject of a libel case, which Edwina won. It was Hutch they had in mind.'

Mountbatten, the man born with a silver tongue in his mouth, had made powerful enemies during his sorties into the aristocracy. As he grew older and more eccentric, the rumours spread wildly. One of his quirks was to play golf blindfolded to make the game more difficult. This was fun, and harmless, as were many of his idiosyncrasies. But other gossip accused him of indulging in 'sado-masochistic activities'.

'He was said to have been seen furiously riding his horses in black leather, accompanied by similarly garbed women of the nobility, driving spurs into the horses' flanks until they bled, and whipping himself into an orgasmic frenzy as he did so,' wrote royal author Charles Higham. 'He would apparently subject his female partners to picturesque punishments, all of which at least one member of his staff diligently reported.'

Just six weeks before his assassination at the hands of the IRA, Mountbatten sat at the bureau in a small upstairs room of Broadlands and talked about Edwina. After her death, he had inherited the estate, which gave his enemies yet another reason to dislike him. This day, he looked far beyond the manicured lawns which sloped down to the River Test and into the generous chunk of Hampshire which was now his and through which he still rode every day.

'I came first to Broadlands on a glorious June day in 1922,' he told Chris Hutchins. it belonged to Edwina's family and I was calling on her father, Colonel Wilfred Ashley, later Lord Mount Temple, on my return from India where we had become engaged. I'd originally met Edwina in England when she called to see my parents. I had been greatly attracted to her – she was a very pretty and charming girl – but I'd done nothing about it.

'Her grandfather had died and he had turned out to be a multi-millionaire. I didn't feel like marrying a girl who was very much richer than me. I went off to India with my cousin, the Prince of Wales. We were living in a little house in Delhi when Edwina arrived to stay with the Viceroy, the old Marchioness of Reading. At a Viceregal ball on February 14, 1922, between dances four and six, I popped the question and she accepted me.

'There were all kinds of problems to overcome, arrangements to make. The Prince of Wales telegraphed his father George V to get his permission and I wrote to my mother. The Viceroy wrote to Edwina's aunt to this effect: "I'm worried about Edwina; I'm afraid there's nothing that can be done about it: she's very much in love with young Lord Louis. He's a good-looking young chap but I only wish she could marry someone with better career prospects." ' The Viceroy was not to know that the good-looking young chap was himself destined to be (by appointment) the last Viceroy of India and after independence (by invitation) the nation's first Head of State.

Despite his own noble birth – his great-grandmother and godmother was Queen Victoria and his mother's youngest sister was the last Tsarina of Russia – Lord Louis had no home to call his own when he met his wife-to-be.

'My father (Prince Louis of Battenburg) had a castle in Germany which he sold in 1920. I'd told him that I didn't want to live in Germany whatever happened, and I told my mother, who had Kent House on the Isle of Wight, that, being in the Navy, I had no intention of having to catch a boat every time I wanted to go home. When I got engaged to this girl, I discovered to my astonishment that she was heiress to the house called Broadlands and so I thought I'd better go and call on her father. Thankfully, he took a less dim view of me than the Viceroy of India! We got married on 18 July, 1922, and the Prince of Wales was my best man.' This blind spot was astonishing, considering Mountbatten's reputation as one of the most intrepid social mountaineers of his age.

Broadlands already had a history of its own. The Ashleys were descended from the Viscounts Palmerston, the third of whom was Prime Minister in Queen Victoria's time. But it was the second Lord Palmerston who left his mark on the now magnificent Georgian mansion, including the remarkable collection of Greek and Roman sculptures he collected during a grand tour of Europe more than two centuries ago. Strolling across the lawns outside, Lord Louis looked up at the east face with its towering pillars. 'The house was built well over 400 years ago; the first Palmerston got it with all the land – five-and-a-half thousand acres – for £26,500. But the second Palmerston was responsible for giving it this squared Palladian style.' Back in the house, Lord Louis walked through the dining room with its collection of Van Dycks, the Wedgwood room where the family took tea, and the library where a black and white photograph of Princess Anne looked incongruous among grand oil paintings of the three Viscounts Palmerston.

That was Mountbatten, incongruous. The Queen Mother had her own reasons for mistrusting him deeply. He had claimed after her husband's death that, as Elizabeth had married his nephew, the House of Mountbatten now occupied the throne of Great Britain, Northern Ireland and the Dominions. Churchill intervened angrily to reinstate the Windsors. But Tricky Dickie still claimed victory. In *The Mountbatten Lineage*, he wrote: 'The House of Mountbatten reigned for two months but historically it takes its place among the reigning houses of the United Kingdom.'

He had yearned to write those words most of his life.

12

THE BOWES LYONESS

'The more I see of her, the more I like her'
Prince Albert

MORE than anything, the death of Ruth, Lady Fermoy might have been expected to reunite Diana and the Queen Mother. The grand old lady passed away on the morning of Tuesday, 6 July, 1993, the day the nation was due to pay tribute to her royal friend. But Diana was missing from the excited throng that gathered in a garden party setting near the statue of Achilles at the entrance to Hyde Park, unaware of the sadness that clouded the summer sunshine.

Although Kensington Palace was only a mile away along Rotten Row, Diana was understandably in mourning for her grandmother. Besides, she and the Queen Mother had fallen out so long ago that her visits to Clarence House were just a memory.

It had already been a difficult day for the Queen when, a few minutes after midday, she pulled a lever to unveil the commemorative gates that marked the life of her mother, the extraordinary woman born ninety-three years ago as Elizabeth Bowes-Lyon.

To drumbeats and a trumpet fanfare, giant cranes lifted the pink drapes that hid the two pairs of intricately woven metal gates from view. A steel cable, however, caught on a spike on top of one gate, ripped some of the material from its moorings and left it flapping like a tattered flag above Her Majesty's head.

'It's just like the Grand National,' said an American tourist, referring to the starting wire that had fouled the field at Aintree. Nothing, not even a simple unveiling ceremony, seemed to be going smoothly any more. Things had been even more chaotic at Buckingham Palace that bright summer's morning. At ten twenty-five a.m. while the Queen was still inside the Palace, fourteen women demonstrators had cut the wire protecting the outer walls and climbed into the gardens. After the break-in by Michael Fagan, who wandered into the Queen's bedroom unannounced eleven years earlier, every known security device had been installed to guard the Palace at a cost of millions a year. Alerted by jangling alarms, police located the intruders with the help of video cameras hidden in the grounds. Seven were quickly rounded up. But another group, armed with banners and placards protesting against British nuclear tests in the Nevada Desert, headed towards the Palace to see the Queen. They were at large for fifteen minutes before police grabbed them. Her Majesty was furious at yet another bungle in her midst on the very day the nation was honouring the woman she still called 'Mummy'.

Others, including Diana, found her a far more disconcerting character, regal but quite sharp, a Bowes-Lyoness, in fact. More than any other royal, the Queen Mother had the power to disturb her deeply, yet they were similar in two respects. The Queen Mother understood the workings of Diana's mind precisely because she was not only from the same stock, she was just as fiercely protective towards her own interests. Her antennae picked up Diana's distress signals soon after the marriage and she quickly realised that Diana was everything Lady Fermoy had said. Too young, self-centred and prone to exaggeration. 'She is very human, but saint she ain't,' opined the titled Chelsea lady of the Queen Mother.

Diana knew she had made a fatal mistake by discussing the Queen Mother with James Gilbey. 'His grandmother is always looking at me with a strange look in her eyes,' Diana said on the Squidgy tape, it's not hatred, it's sort of interest and pity mixed in one.' When the tape became public, Diana knew she had committed the unpardonable sin of revealing her true feelings not only about the Queen Mother but 'this f***ing family', as she had unwisely called the other royals. It was at this point that the Queen Mother knew Diana had to go.

Her method was to refuse to attend Princess Anne's wedding to Commander Tim Laurence, it was said that she did not approve of second marriage. It was said that she did not want to travel up to Scotland in the cold. Rubbish! She told the Queen and Prince Charles she would not sit in the same church as Diana,' said the Palace insider.

The situation was all the more awkward for Diana because Lady Fermoy had still been a lady-in-waiting at Clarence House. 'Diana is worried that the Queen Mother will pursue a vendetta against her to the end. She knows what happened to the Duchess of Windsor. You have to remember that long before the Queen Mother became the nation's favourite granny, she was a young woman who had to tackle some very serious problems,' said the friend. 'She was only thirty-one when Mrs Simpson first met Edward, the same age as Diana in 1992. There is absolutely nothing anyone can teach her about royals behaving badly.'

'The similarities between the Queen Mother and Princess Diana as young women are quite striking,' said the royal historian. 'The point of departure comes because Lady Elizabeth married Prince Albert, not his brother, the Prince of Wales, whom she would have preferred. To put it bluntly, he looked her over, but she wasn't his type. It was the other way round for Diana. She switched her sights from Prince Andrew to Charles once he became a better prospect. Like Diana, the young Elizabeth was extremely ambitious. All those protestations that she didn't want to marry into the Royal Family are poppycock. She was very keen to marry David and only accepted Bertie after he proposed for the third time. By then, it was obvious that the next king was out of reach.

'When he abdicated, she was appalled that her husband might be passed over for one of his two other brothers, George and Henry. This was a possibility because the Abdication affected the succession. I suspect that Edward's cronies put this about to upset Bertie. George, the Duke of Kent, was a bisexual drug addict and Henry, the Duke of Gloucester, an alcoholic. She was determined that Bertie should get the Crown.'

Many years later, the Queen Mother explained: 'It was my duty to marry Bertie, and I fell in love with him afterwards.' 'Call it duty if you like, but it confirms the belief that he wasn't her first choice,' commented the royal historian. 'Of course she wanted her husband to be King.'

'What the Special Branch had on the Duke of Kent at the time doesn't bear thinking about,' said the titled Chelsea lady. 'Nightmare! And his brother! There was a big party at St James's Palace in aid of the King Edward VII Hospital and the Duke of Gloucester was there ROARING drunk. I mean, it was unbelievable, but he produced two very nice children.'

Diana also knew that the Queen Mother's marriage had not always been as happy as fond memories painted it. 'The image is that they had this idyllic marriage,' said the titled Chelsea lady. 'During the Blitz, she was a very, very good wife. But they often had dinner in separate rooms at the Palace because they were on "non-speak". The King had a terrible temper and would suddenly burst into fits of rage, which his family called his "gnashes". He would quite lose control of himself, but most of the time he was a civilised man who adored his wife and family. If one actually analyses it, she has just been a very good royal. She hasn't got this extra dimension that Diana has suddenly dug up from somewhere, this spiritual thing.'

Like Diana, Elizabeth Bowes-Lyon was born before her father inherited his earldom. 'He celebrated so much that he forgot to register the birth,' said the royal historian. 'To this day, the Queen Mother doesn't know where she was born.' When she was four, her father became Earl of Strathmore and Kinghorne. He took over Glamis Castle, the Scottish ancestral home, complete with ghosts, that went with the title. Ten miles north of Dundee, the red sandstone castle was the scene of King Duncan's murder in *Macbeth*. The third earl retained the last jester in Scotland, unsportingly dispensing with his services after he made the mistake of proposing to his daughter.

Elizabeth Angela Marguerite had been her parents' ninth child, but one daughter had died in childhood and only two girls, Mary and Rose, now survived. Thus the Queen Mother had two elder sisters and, also like Diana, she had a baby brother.

When World War I broke out, Glamis Castle was converted into a Red Cross hospital for wounded soldiers brought in from the trenches. Lady Elizabeth, fourteen at the time but already exhibiting a home-spun star quality, visited the packed wards. Her presence was so uplifting that one patient called her 'a Scottish Florence Nightingale'. 'It's easy to imagine Lady Diana in the same role,' said the royal historian. 'She looked after her sisters and younger brother like a little mother, and was always tending wounded birds and animals.'

But like Diana, the Queen Mother had the protective instincts of a lioness beneath a friendly smile. 'The claws came out the moment she sensed the presence of a dangerous adversary. When she knew she had to fight, it was to the death,' said the titled Chelsea lady. 'In the case of Wallis Simpson, literally to the death.' This was the side of Charles's grandmother that Diana feared most. She recognised exactly the same feelings in herself.

THE woman known to the world as Mrs Simpson was conceived in deception, delivered in deceit and lived all her life surrounded by lies. She was born Bessie Wallis Warfield on 19 June, 1895 (not 1896 as she liked to claim), just 362 days after Edward, or David as he was called, the eldest son of the then Duke and Duchess of York, later King George V and Queen Mary.

Edward's mother, the impoverished Princess Mary of Teck, had previously been engaged to George's brother, Prince Eddy, whose sexual behaviour was so bizarre that he was at one time a suspect in the hunt for Jack the Ripper. When he died suddenly of pneumonia, his fiancee sensibly married his younger brother and became a mainstay of the monarchy for half a century.

Whereas Edward made his appearance at the White Lodge in Richmond, Surrey, Wallis arrived, protesting noisily, at Square Cottage, a rough-hewn cabin at Blue Ridge Summit on the Pennsylvania-Maryland border. Her birth was kept a secret because she was born out of wedlock. Wallis's mother, an obliging blonde called Alice Montague, had conducted a secret affair with Teackle Warfield, the tubercular fourth son of a grandiose but fading Baltimore family. She became pregnant even though Teackle was forbidden to have sex because of the danger of infection.

To keep the birth secret, Bessie Wallis was not even baptised and, when she was confirmed into the Episcopalian faith, her baptism record was falsified. This meant that two of her three marriages, including her union with the Duke of Windsor, would have been invalid in the eyes of the Church if the secret had come out. It was only one of many secrets she tried to hide from the world.

When the Queen Mother was born somewhere in London on 4 August, 1900, five-year-old Wallis was living with her widowed grandmother, Anna Warfield, in a four-storey terraced house in Baltimore. Her father had married Alice a few months after his daughter's birth, but the stigma of illegitimacy remained. An atrocious snob (the family boasted about its connections with British aristocracy), Anna ran her household according to a very strict regime. Wallis learned from an early age that servants could be abused, threatened and, if necessary, deprived of their livelihood.

She developed the arrogance of someone who, although privileged, knew that something wasn't quite right. Conversations stopped abruptly when she entered a room. Servants gave her meaningful, insolent looks. She developed a thick skin, burying the shame deep inside.

Even as a young child, Wallis was obsessed with the fashion and manners of high society, particularly the far-away world of the English royals. She developed a schoolgirl crush on the Prince of Wales, a golden-haired Adonis who stared rakishly from the magazines she collected. Other girls of her generation might have had innocent dreams of marrying a prince. Not Wallis. Her obsession nagged at her mercilessly.

In retaliation, she developed a teasing manner with young male admirers. 'Nobody ever called me beautiful or even pretty,' she said with withering honesty. 'My jaw was clearly too big and too pointed to be classic. My hair was straight when the laws of compensation might at least have provided curls.' But she had entrancing violet eyes (Wallis Blue, as the colour was later called) and she knew how to make the best of herself. Just five feet tall and neither rich nor attractive, she learned to bend men to her will. She threw tantrums to get her own way, then charmed her beau into believing that he was marvellous until a better prospect came along.

When she was nineteen, she had the misfortune to meet a young man who was even more wilful, selfish, arrogant and dangerous than herself, an airman called Earl Spencer (no relation). 'He was laughing but there was a suggestion of inner force and vitality that struck me instantly,' she recalled. He was, in fact, cruel and tough, a pugnacious drunk and a secret bisexual who liked to dress up in women's clothes. Wallis was fatally attracted to him.

Wallis Warfield and 'Win' Spencer Junior, as he was called after his second name Winfield, were married in November 1916 and their turbulent eleven-year union turned Wallis into a scheming, man-hating vamp. Often drunk and abusive, Win Spencer accused his wife of adultery and, to eliminate the risk of secret liaisons, left her sobbing behind locked doors at their home near a naval base in San Diego. She could do nothing right. Even her cooking drove him into a frenzy.

Wallis cheered up when the Prince of Wales, en route to Australia aboard HMS *Renown* with Louis Mountbatten, arrived in the

Californian port on a goodwill visit in April 1920. David, Dickie and Prince George had just set up a male *menage a trois* at York House, a large apartment in St James's Palace. David and Dickie were suspected of being lovers, and George later enjoyed an affair with one of Dickie's close friends, Noel Coward. David's favourite pastime was knitting. 'They were all genuinely bisexual – it's only in the late twentieth century that if you go to bed with a man you're gay,' said the royal historian. 'The norm among upper class English men is that they swing both ways.'

The tour was also intended to separate David from Freda Dudley Ward, one of the married women he preferred over available single girls of his own class. To adoring royalists, however, the Prince of Wales was the world's most eligible bachelor, a brave, attractive, intelligent young soldier who would one day make a fine king.

Like his brothers, he had suffered at the hands of the drunken father he so desperately wanted to impress. George V inspected his sons as if they were midshipmen on the quarterdeck, ordering pockets to be sown up if a young hand strayed from its proper place. One reason Bertie stammered so badly was that he had been forced to switch from writing with his left hand to his right. David, however, did not lack self-confidence. He was progressive and, for a while, seemed blessed with a social conscience.

As he disembarked in San Diego, he knew nothing of Wallis's existence, and her girlish dream of meeting her Prince eluded her in the most hurtful way. She and her husband were deliberately excluded from any of the social events the Prince attended with top brass and local dignitaries. Consigned to the fringes, Wallis blamed Win, and she was probably right. His boorish, drunken behaviour had alienated even the most tolerant of his commanding officers. Wallis could only glimpse Edward, cool and shining in neatly-pressed tropical whites, as he shook hands with distinguished guests at a mayoral ball at the Hotel Coronado. Only a dozen paces separated them but, cordoned off as she was and craning to see over the heads of the excited throng, he was as untouchable and unavailable as ever. The Prince departed early, and Wallis noted the gossip that he spent the rest of the night in the anything-goes nightspots of Tijuana.

A few weeks later, a meeting of great significance to Wallis took place in the heart of London society. It would, ultimately, shape the destiny of Britain's modern monarchy and cause her years of grief. The Season was recovering its momentum after the austerity of war and, during a dance given by Lord and Lady Farquhar at 7 Grosvenor Square, Lady Elizabeth Bowes-Lyon was formally introduced to Prince Albert. Royal sentimentalists claimed that the two had met as children when five-year-old Elizabeth, noticing how shy the King's grandson was, had fed him the crystallised cherries off her sugar cake.

In Mayfair, Bertie was much taken by the exquisite young debutante on his arm and was soon writing to his mother: 'The more I see of her, the more I like her.' But she turned him down twice, only accepting his proposal a year later after he took her for a walk in her favourite woods near her family's country house in Hertfordshire. The Duke and Duchess of York, as they became, were married at Westminster Abbey on 23 April, 1923.

Wallis visited England for the first time soon after the Yorks returned to London from their honeymoon at Glamis Castle. Devouring the Court Circular in *The Times,* she read that Elizabeth had made her first appearance as a member of the Royal Family. Unmissable in pictures of the occasion, an RAF pageant at Hendon airfield, was the young Duchess's smile, the famous bow-lipped beam that would become her trademark. One day Wallis would refer to her, insultingly, as 'Cookie'.

More interesting to Wallis was the latest news about the peripatetic Prince of Wales, who was making a second visit to Canada as part of his global tour of Britain's imperial possessions. None of the newspaper reports mentioned anything about the high jinks the Prince and his companions got up to on this trip or on his previous journey to the Southern Hemisphere. During a dinner party in Australia, for example, the Prince's Chief of Staff, Admiral Sir Lionel Halsey, decided to dress up in a skirt and pinafore. As spirits rose, blankets, mattresses and squeezed oranges were thrown around the house and water drenched the weeping hostess's valuable oriental carpet. At other parties, David stripped the trousers off a Guards officer, rode around the room in a pram at breakneck speed and threw pillows like rugby balls until they split open. His favourite party piece was to entertain the ladies by drawing pigs on a piece of paper while his eyes were shut. All these events were recorded in the

Diaries of Lord Louis Mountbatten 1920-1922. it is very difficult to keep David cheerful,' sighed Lord Louis.

The Prince was still completely out of reach, but Wallis had at least touched base with his world of sombre, grey palaces, archly gothic hotels and quaint customs. She now understood the English a little better. She was unimpressed. She was, however, intrigued by a notable social reform, the Matrimonial Causes Act, under which women could divorce their husbands for adultery. This enlightened piece of legislation, which she would need to draw upon one day, gave her cause to examine her own mockery of a marriage. Win was often unfaithful, sometimes deserting her for other men. Her pride wounded, Wallis developed the severe, angular appearance which, along with her striking violet-blue eyes, became her own trademark. She resolved to use her husband's naval contacts to further herself, certain of only one thing: she wasn't going to end up a loser like him.

When Win was posted to gunboat patrol duty in the South China Seas, Wallis seized her chance. She joined him in Hong Kong, where he took her to one of the Crown Colony's singing houses, a high-class brothel in Repulse Bay. It was there, and later in Shanghai, that the future Duchess of Windsor learned the skills for which she became notorious. Entranced, she observed prostitutes beguiling their rich, over-fed and often drugged clients with the art of oriental love-making. Wallis took part in threesomes and studied the techniques.

It was through this experience that she was later to gain her sexual hold over Edward. For good reason, the Duchess referred to him by the unkind pet name of 'Little Man'. 'The royal surgeon who examined him told me his penis was so small he couldn't have normal sexual relations,' said the royal medical source. 'Wallis Simpson had learned a prostitute's trick when she worked in a Chinese brothel. She placed allum, a mineral used in tanning hides, in her vagina to make it tight. She was the first woman Edward could make love to in the normal way and it gave her enormous power.'

The China Report, which was compiled by the British secret service after King George V exclaimed: 'Who *is* this woman?' in 1935, revealed that Wallis indulged in what were called 'perverse practices' in these luxurious establishments during 1924-25. 'They (the prostitutes) were known as the Fang Yung dispensers, adept in techniques in which the woman induced her male partner into deep relaxation through massage over every part of the body, using the tips of the fingers,' recorded royal author John Parker. 'By this method, prolonged sexual arousement of the male is achieved.'

In Shanghai, Wallis plunged headlong into the war-torn city's corrupt gambling, drug-taking and sexually abandoned nightlife. She was suspected of having had sex with rich men in exchange for 'presents', of winning at fixed roulette tables, of selling drugs to the debauched clientele and of pedalling the secrets she coaxed from British naval officers to a foreign power. Many of these accusations were well informed, others conjecture. Doubts were even raised about the existence of the China Report, but it has been not only seen but read by reliable sources.

'I have spoken to three highly placed people who confirmed its existence and one of them had read it,' said John Parker. 'China was a hotbed of spies and intrigue, and she was in the thick of it. She was actually running a house of ill repute that attracted all kinds of diplomats and naval personnel so it was natural that she was kept under constant observation.' The evidence painted the unmistakable picture of a ruthless woman prepared to sell herself, and betray others, to get what she wanted.

After dumping Win Spencer in the divorce courts, Wallis moved to London where she married her second husband, Ernest Simpson, at Chelsea register office. Simpson, who she stole from his wife, was a half-English, half-American businessman involved in shipping.

A former Guards officer, he was unaware that his bride's finishing school had been an Asian whorehouse. The marriage suited both of them. Simpson encouraged Wallis to meld into her new surroundings while he stood back, drank a little, smoked a lot, and made a few useful contacts. In 1930, they were living at 5 Bryanston Court in George Street, W2, and mixing with expatriate Americans who, either through marriage or money, were linked to influential figures in society. One of them, Viscountess Thelma Furness, was the twin sister of the millionairess Gloria Vanderbilt. She was also Edward's current mistress; a married woman like many of his other conquests. He called her 'Toodles'.

Thelma, a darkly simmering beauty of Spanish blood, invited the Simpsons to her country home, Burrough Court at Melton Mowbray, for a house party. Never dreaming that Wallis might pose a threat, she introduced her to the Prince of Wales. Edward met Mrs Simpson. The date was Saturday, 10 January, 1931. The first eye contact established that he was weak and submissive, she tailor-made to dominate. It was far from love at first sight. Wallis, however, had achieved her purpose and the prospect of the chase excited her enormously. Edward had unwittingly set himself up for the kill.

Needing a country residence to entertain friends and lovers away from the more confining atmosphere of York House, the Prince of Wales had moved into Fort Belvedere. He had spent the summer renovating the eighteenth-century castellated house near Sunninghill and clearing away overgrown shrubs to plant a proper garden. Edward described it as 'a peaceful enchanted anchorage where I found refuge from the cares and turmoil of my life'. He had, in fact, moved into a prison where he could easily be separated from his family and old friends. It was to be the last peaceful summer of his life.

By the time Elizabeth encountered Wallis Simpson in person, it was too late to save him. Wallis had executed the coup she planned so cleverly with breathtaking audacity. All of Edward's paramours, including 'Toodles' Furness and Freda Dudley Ward, the long time favourite who George V called 'the lacemaker's daughter', had been vanquished from his life. 'You can see what a so-and-so he was from his treatment of Freda,' said the titled Chelsea lady. 'Just overnight – BANG! No letter, no nothing. Just silence.' He even stopped having what one royal private secretary called 'street-corner affairs'.

Wallis was virtually running The Fort and treating everyone there in a very hjgh-handed fashion. The staff hated her; she fired the most recalcitrant. Cut-off, Edward had been at her mercy. In private, the soft, lilting Southern drawl she had cultivated in polite society gave way to harsher tones. Her handwriting revealed 'a woman with a strong male inclination ... she *must* dominate, she *must* have authority... (she is) sadistic, cold, overbearing, vain.' (This was written *before* the extent of her hold over Edward, or the reason for it, was known.)

The role-playing that Edward found sexually exciting made him a slave. Wallis punished his every misdeed like a martinet, rapping his knuckles or belittling him with sharp rebukes. He was soon buckling her shoes (among other perversions, he had a foot fetish), painting her toenails and begging for cigarettes like a trained poodle – and that was in front of the servants.

Bewitched, Edward began paying her in money and jewels for her services, if she were what I call a respectable whore, I wouldn't mind,' complained the Prime Minister, Stanley Baldwin. Wallis frankly admitted that she did not love Edward, but he couldn't live without her. Moustache bristling ineptly, Ernest Simpson fell in with the arrangement. His wife terrified him, too.

Elizabeth heard the scandal that followed the Prince and 'his American floozie' wherever they went. At a Buckingham Palace reception two days before the wedding of George, Duke of Kent, to Princess Marina of Greece, they came face to face. Edward had smuggled Wallis, stunning in a violet *lame* gown with bright green sash, into the party. The King was furious at the deception and Queen Mary fixed her with a look that came straight from the North Pole. Elizabeth's famous smile disguised her real thoughts. 'The Duchess was never discourteous, but you could always tell when she did not care for someone,' said one who was present, it was very apparent to me she did not care for Mrs Simpson at all.'

When George V died at Sandringham, he expressed his hatred of Edward and Mrs Simpson in the most practical way. He cut his eldest son off without a penny. The grand old King Emperor was thoughtfully killed off with an injection of morphine and cocaine by his doctor, Lord Dawson of Penn, to catch the last edition of *The Times.* This unlawful act of euthanasia went unpunished because the Family had been consulted in advance, but it gave a new meaning to the term 'deadline'. 'Dawson later admitted that the moment of the King's death was timed for its announcement to be made in the respectable morning papers, and *The Times* in particular, rather than "the less appropriate evening journals",' wrote Sarah Bradford in her biography of George VI. 'He even telephoned his wife in London to advise *The Times* to hold back the morning's edition as the announcement of the King's death was to be expected.' This kind of news management makes Diana's efforts at playing up to the media half a century later seem harmless by comparison.

Queen Mary even permitted the *Daily Mirror to* photograph the monarch's corpse for the front page, another progressive, if somewhat macabre, royal first. 'Queen Mary was not a well woman, partly because of her uncertain childhood. Her parents were chronic spendthrifts even though the family had no money,' said the royal historian. 'This deeply embarrassed her as a young woman and she became shy and withdrawn. She had always loved collecting things but she became a kleptomaniac, an illness that progressed with age. She used to take things: a sugar bowl would go missing during one of her visits. Sometimes a lady-in-waiting would return an article which had found its way into the royal handbag. She would also admire other people's antiques and expect them to be given to her.'

Queen Mary passed away just before Elizabeth's coronation in 1953, having ignored Edward's often frenzied entreaties to have his wife recognised as Her Royal Highness. She remained as emotionally aloof as ever towards her eldest son, denying him the love which he had craved since childhood and which she was incapable of giving. All of his bizarre behaviour, including his infatuation with Wallis Simpson, could be traced to the treatment he received in the nursery.

As Mary had lacked any maternal instincts and her. husband had wanted his children to be rarely seen and never heard, Edward had been abandoned into the care of a sadistic nanny who alternately adored and abused him. One of her practices was to pinch him severely on the arm just before delivering him into his parents' presence. Bawling loudly, the young Edward would be swiftly handed back into the clutches of his tormentor. He was at Wallis's mercy because she fulfilled the roles of mother, lover and nanny. She indulged his bisexual flings with other men, then tortured him with her own infidelities.

Chris Hutchins was staying at the Waldorf Towers, Manhattan in June 1971 in a suite just below the penthouse. At six o'clock one evening, he got into the lift to go downstairs to the lobby. There was one other occupant, a lone figure draped in a grey herringbone overcoat, its collar turned up protectively against an imagined chill.

'Almost immediately, I was aware of two things: This man had a presence which was not of normal men; I could *feel* something special about him. Then, rather than recognise him, I *realised* who he was: the Duke of Windsor,' recounted Hutchins. 'I turned to face him and, sure enough, it was the famous exile whose face I had seen a thousand times in newspapers. He didn't turn away; he seemed accustomed to people looking at him. His hands were thrust deep in the pockets of the overcoat, which seemed several sizes too big.

'I didn't know then, but he was suffering from cancer of the larynx and he had only a year to live. It was his face that mesmerised me: not so much the Windsor bags under the eyes or the familiar twist of his mouth. The overwhelming impression was one of deep and inconsolable sadness. The pain of it was etched into every line of his face. The lift doors opened and I watched him move slowly across the lobby, a tragic figure in an overcoat tailored for another, much bigger, man.'

Edward, disillusioned and disappointed to the end, died on 28 May, 1972, at a house which once belonged to Charles de Gaulle in the Bois de Boulogne. His Duchess, the royal who never was, flew to England for his burial at Frogmore. She was permitted to stay at Buckingham Palace. The Queen Mother greeted her as distantly as good manners would allow. The Queen, however, consoled her aunt during the funeral service by touching her gently on the arm and offering her some kind words.

The Duchess lingered for another fourteen years in her Paris home, which she converted into a shrine to Edward's love. She died on 24 April, 1986, and was buried beside him at Frogmore. She had called her memoirs *The Heart Has Its Reasons,* a title that another in the Family, HRH Princess Margaret Rose, could identify with very strongly indeed.

13

THE AGONY AUNT

'We're very glad to get rid of Diana'
Princess Margaret

THE showdown Princess Margaret knew was inevitable between Diana and herself could wait no longer. Not always the most tactful royal, Margaret had nevertheless allowed the feud to simmer away in deference to her nephew's wishes. As his personal agony aunt, she often gave Charles the benefit of her advice whether he had sought it or not. But she accepted that the last thing he wanted was a confrontation between her and Diana which would prove damaging to him and his sons. So Auntie Margo, the only royal with a real past, held her tongue.

Despite her troubled life, Margaret had never flinched in one important role. Bonded like twins in childhood, she had been, and always would remain, the Queen's most steadfast defender. When the Abdication had become final on 11 December, 1936, the young Elizabeth had dashed upstairs at 145 Piccadilly to tell her sister.

'Does that mean you will have to be the next Queen?' asked Margaret.

'Yes, one day,' replied Lilibet.

'Poor you,' said Margaret.

She had never really envied her sister this awesome destiny even if the actress in her might occasionally compete for the limelight. Like Prince Charles, however, she had difficulty in coming to terms with her lack of a clear-cut royal role. By her very position, the Queen had given them something in common.

As a child, Margaret had been small, dark and chubby while Elizabeth was taller, blonde and slim. Describing the sisters in their swimming costumes, Marion Crawford wrote: 'Lilibet looked so pretty in hers. She was a long, slender child with beautiful legs. Margaret looked like a plump navy-blue fish.'

When her father ascended the throne in 1936, Margaret was reputed to have said petulantly: 'Now that Papa is King, I am nobody.' But six-year-old Margaret was simply reacting to the news that she was no longer Margaret of York. As she had just learned to spell 'York', her confusion was understandable. In fact, she immediately became second in the line of succession, a position she held until Prince Charles was born twelve years later. By 1993, she had slipped to eleventh place after the Queen's four children and her six grandchildren.

Sometimes the little sisters had argued over trivial things and there were occasional fights. 'Lilibet was quick with her left hook,' according to Crawfie, but 'Margaret was more of a close-in fighter, known to bite on occasions.' Although Lilibet complained loudly that 'Margaret always wants what I want', her sister, in fact, resented her mother's practice of saving hand-me-down dresses for her to wear. Outbursts of childish jealousy had been little more than the normal rivalry between siblings. Whatever disagreements they may have had, nothing was stronger than her loyalty to her sovereign sister.

Painful though it was, Margaret even understood the Queen's position in opposing her marriage to Peter Townsend, a man twice her age whom she had loved since she was sixteen. Rumours that she had refused to speak to her sister for a year after the enforced break-up were untrue. 'Margaret was very upset, naturally,' said a friend. 'But she didn't blame the Queen, she blamed the System.' She did, however, have reasonable grounds for disliking Prince Philip, who saw her as haughty, spoiled and, in her affair with a married man, deceitful.

Margaret's power lay in her ability to twist her father around her little finger. 'I know I should not spoil her, but I cannot help it,' he confessed. His pet name for her was 'Meg'. When he sensed that she had grown fond of his equerry, he tried to keep them apart. Not once did he suspect that the affair was anything more serious than a schoolgirl crush on a handsome older man. One source suggested that the sweethearts had been caught making love at the Palace, but if that were true the news was certainly kept from the King.

Nevertheless, something seems to have disturbed him. Five days before Charles was born he issued a decree which affected Margaret for the rest of her life. He ruled that the children of Elizabeth and

Philip should be born princes and princesses, but that Margaret's children should not receive the same royal titles. This anomaly seemed to suggest that the King doubted his younger daughter's ability to make a suitable royal marriage.

Peter Townsend had been married to Rosemary Pawle, the daughter of a brigadier, since July 1941 and the couple had two small sons. When she became aware of her husband's romance, the cheated wife reacted with bitterness. Her unhappiness was apparent to Eileen Parker, who met her soon after her husband, Mike, started working for Prince Philip.

'Rosemary Townsend and I were married to men being seduced away from us by the lustre of glittering prizes,' recalled Eileen. 'She was a wife and mother who had to stand by while Princess Margaret (hardly out of ankle socks) led her husband around the Palace by his nose. She could sound bitter sometimes. One night we found ourselves next to each other at a reception. I was a comparatively new Household wife and she asked me how I was enjoying life. "It has its moments," I said. Rosemary gave me a pitying look. "You wait," she said. "There's lots more in store for you – and not all of it good." '

The Townsends separated discreetly and Rosemary started seeing another man, John de Laszlo. On 20 December, 1952, she was divorced on the grounds of her adultery with de Laszlo, whom she later married. To her friends, it seemed that Rosemary, the guilty party in the divorce, had taken the blame for her husband's illicit affair. This, in theory, left Townsend legally free to marry Margaret.

Summoning all the courage of the Battle of Britain fighter pilot he had been, Townsend told Sir Alan 'Tommy' Lascelles, Elizabeth's Private Secretary, that he was in love with Margaret and that she returned his feelings. 'You are either mad or bad,' barked Lascelles.

Townsend reported this unpromising reaction to Margaret. 'I shall curse him to the grave,' she said later. As the Queen's reign was just a year old, Margaret was persuaded, albeit reluctantly, to wait two years before making her plans known to the world.

There was a further disappointment for her at Elizabeth's coronation on 2 June, 1953. The Duke of Edinburgh replaced her as Regent in the event of the Queen's death before Charles reached the age of eighteen. The comeback was immediate. After the vows had been made and Elizabeth had worn the crown for the first time,

Margaret and Townsend were sheltering with others on the porch of Westminster Abbey until a downpour had subsided. Nonchalantly, Margaret brushed a piece of fluff off Peter Townsend's RAF uniform in full view of reporters. This one small gesture told newsmen who had come to cover a joyous State occasion that they had also witnessed an intimate moment in a very dangerous love affair. When the Townsend issue boiled to the surface soon afterwards, Margaret found that Philip, for once, sided with the old guard at the Palace. He spoke out uncharitably against Townsend, whom he had grown to loathe during his service as equerry at the Palace. The Duke's hostility was entirely due to his belief that Townsend had tried to influence the King on the subject of his own royal union. He made his feelings known while Margaret, torn between love and duty, was at her most vulnerable.

It was left to the new Prime Minister, Sir Anthony Eden, a divorcee who had happily remarried without wrecking his political prospects, to explain the impossibility of her position to the Princess. The Cabinet, he said, would not condone her marriage to a divorced man. Her thoughts on this piece of hypocrisy were unrecorded.

Townsend encouraged her to take the excruciating step of breaking off their relationship permanently. He even helped her to write the epitaph. It was published on 31 October, 1955, two months after Margaret turned twenty-five.

'I would like it to be known that I have decided not to marry Group Captain Peter Townsend,' the statement said. 'I have been aware that, subject to my renouncing my rights of succession, it might have been possible for me to contract a civil marriage. But, mindful of the Church's teaching that Christian marriage is indissoluble, and conscious of the Commonwealth, I have resolved to put these considerations before any other.'

The dry, formal language gave no inkling of the heartache Margaret was suffering after those two painful years of separation. The lovers had corresponded almost every day. She had mistakenly believed that if she waited, her wishes would be granted. The thought that she had been unjustly punished for falling in love with a married man stayed with her. It is doubtful if she ever forgave.

To console herself, Margaret bought a tiara which, by custom, only married women wore. The Duke openly ridiculed her. But Margaret never allowed Philip's antagonism to come between her and her sister. 'Anyone who offends the Queen makes two enemies,' said the friend. It came across in little ways. If someone mentioned 'your sister' to her, she immediately put them in their place. 'You mean Her Majesty,' she would say witheringly.

After Townsend, Margaret's lifestyle would have scandalised the country had it ever been made public. The Press kept dutifully silent, though, and there was a collective sigh of relief when she announced her engagement to Antony Armstrong-Jones, the photographer she met at the wedding of her friends, the Honourable Colin Tennant and Lady Anne Coke. The Snowdons' marriage ended unedifyingly after both partners took lovers during the course of a very libertarian 'separate lives' agreement.

At sixty-two, Margaret entered the fray of 1992 with more campaign medals won in lost causes of the heart than anyone else in the whole scenario.

MARGARET had spent part of the summer cruising off the Turkish coast with friends, including her irrepressible Irish court jester Ned Ryan. By chance, they had met up with Charles and Diana, who were going through the motions of a second honeymoon with their sons on board the *Alexander,* owned by the Greek shipping tycoon John Latsis, who also owned expensive chunks of Mayfair. As the two groups of royalty and their entourages spent a day together exploring the coast, Diana's distant behaviour towards her husband confirmed to Margaret that the marriage was going through its death throes. Her moody silences, it was claimed, were the result of a radio phone call she had intercepted between Charles and Camilla. Diana supposedly picked up the phone in her cabin and overheard some of the love talk. Whatever the reason, Diana stayed close to her sons, pointedly ignoring invitations to join the others.

At Balmoral, Diana's efforts to promote her own cause soon after Fergie had fled Balmoral infuriated Margaret so much that she felt compelled to speak. Diana listened as the words came tumbling out. Auntie Margo accused her of being 'insensitive and utterly selfish'. Bitterly, she added: 'You just don't realise – and probably don't care – how much you have hurt the Queen. She deserved better.' To Diana, the outburst merely confirmed that the Family had united against her and she would be better out of it.

Margaret was so incensed that, even four months later, she described the scene when she was among friends at Bowood House, the Earl of Shelburne's mansion in Wiltshire. She had just returned from a holiday on Mustique with Viscount Linley and Serena Stanhope. 'She still felt strongly about Diana's behaviour,' said an insider. 'The conversation turned to another aristocrat who was having problems with his girlfriend and Margaret said, "They don't know how to get rid of each other." Then she added, "We're very glad to have got rid of Diana." '

Auntie Margo couldn't resist having the last word.

AT Kensington Palace, Diana realised that her travails in getting out of a marriage were not unlike Margaret's difficulties had been in getting into one. The royal system had defeated both of them. Short on laughs, she relished a tasty vignette which reached her circle from the Caribbean. The Queen's sister, it transpired, had taken a leaf out of Imelda Marcos's book during her annual holiday and was holding roving dinner parties at the homes of absent owners.

Margaret had flown to Mustique to recuperate at Les Jolies Eaux after being treated in hospital for pneumonia, another of the illnesses contracted from her sixty-a-day smoking habit. She had spent five days at the King Edward VII Military Hospital in London, ill-health and unhappiness are things she can do without,' said a charity executive who works closely with her. 'She has had enough problems in life.' Still frail, Margaret made it plain to her son David, Serena and the other house guests that she would prefer it if they stayed away from Basil's Bar, the island's seafront watering hole.

'Everyone goes to Basil's to watch the sun go down at five thirty in the evening,' said a holidaymaker privy to the secrets of Margaret's circle. 'So there was some grumpiness about the ban. To make life interesting, the Princess decided to dine in some of the empty villas. She would ring up Mick Jagger's people if the tenants were away and say, "We would like to use Stargroves for dinner this evening. I trust that will be in order." She sends her cook on ahead with all the food and then turns up with her guests to spend the evening.' Only one owner, pop idol David Bowie, had objected to Margaret's movable feasts, saying: 'I built this house and I don't see why I should let a load of strangers wander around snooping in my bedrooms.'

'I was at school with one of Imelda Marcos's goddaughters and she said Imelda did exactly the same thing, only she went much further,' said the holidaymaker. 'She would admire a painting on the wall and expect the owner to give it to her. Her hosts began to lock up everything before she arrived.' Margaret, of course, did not go that far. But to the other residents it showed that she viewed herself as the undisputed queen of the tropical isle.

Few complained because she was a popular figure and they looked forward to her arrival in time for the St Valentine's fancy dress party on 14 February. Her presence in their midst also guaranteed that rental prices remained among the highest in the Caribbean. No fewer than forty villas were available for rent at up to $15,000 a week to well-heeled holidaymakers who liked to swim, sunbathe and siesta in luxurious surroundings.

Diana had never visited the island which, though it shone like a piece of jade in the Caribbean blue, was rightly named after the French word for mosquito, <i>moustique</i>. The afternoon arrival of free-biting mosquitoes signals an early curfew to outdoor activities. There is little else to do at night except chat over drinks. 'Hollywood doesn't go to Mustique because of its drawbacks, the mosquitoes being the worst,' said one suntanned survivor. 'None of the food is fresh, the fruit juices are all canned and the meat and vegetables are brought in frozen. Yachties drop in to moor their boats because they think they are going to see Mick Jagger and Jerry Hall having a rum punch at Basil's Bar, but it doesn't happen. David Bowie goes there specifically to be alone with Iman. He doesn't see anybody; he carves things out of stone and plays chess. At Basil's Bar, people just sit there in the evening passing the spray cans. You get all dollied up in something cool and silky, put on your expensive perfume and then sit there covering your scent with mosquito repellent.'

Colin Tennant, later Lord Glenconner, had paid £45,000 in 1958 for this swampy piece of real estate just three miles long and a mile and a half wide. As a wedding present, he had given Margaret ten acres on a headland where the waters of the Caribbean meet the Atlantic. Lord Snowdon hadn't shared Margaret's enthusiasm for the tropical speck, even though his uncle Oliver Messel had designed Les Jolies Eaux and many of the other homes on the island.

Guests paid $8,000 a week plus five per cent government tax and a three per cent administrative charge to stay there. The Mustique Company also suggested that a gratuity of one and a half to three per cent of the total rental should be paid to staff. The U-shaped villa was built around a courtyard with its sitting room pointing towards the waters of Gelliceaux Bay. Opening up the doors, guests could convert the living area into a spacious, open-air veranda. Outside, they walked across a paved sun deck and through Roddy's Garden to the swimming pool and gazebo. The young Roderic Llewellyn had planned the garden, ablaze with oleander and hibiscus, when he was Margaret's toy-boy lover. But it was years since he had visited Mustique and dutifully carried buckets of water from the beach to wash the sand off her feet as she left it.

'The people who are renting Mick Jagger's house at the moment are the Kauzovs, Sergei and Ally,' recounted one who had stayed there in March, 1993. 'They are paying $8,000 a week because they bought The Great House from Lord Glenconner and they are having the whole place landscaped. It's costing a fortune. A botanist has been flown in from England to do all the plants. Sergei was the third husband of Christina Onassis and he was given a huge settlement when the marriage ended. He put it into shipping in Russia and now he's a freighter tycoon. Christina was Jamie Blandford's step-sister and, of course, his father Sunny was one of the Margaret Set. Ally commutes from the Kausovs' house in Knightsbridge with their daughter Maria, a two-year-old. They have a Norland nanny who is permanently in uniform and looks immaculate. Everyone else just wears a swimsuit and a sarong during the day and it's really funny to see the Norland nanny pushing her pram as though she's in Kensington Gardens.'

Guests recalled the fate of another nanny, Barbara Barnes, who had departed Kensington Palace soon after partying in Mustique. 'Barbara had looked after the Glenconners' children and she was invited to Lord Glenconner's sixtieth birthday party as a friend,' said one. 'By all accounts, it was an excellent do and everyone was photographed in fancy dress. Diana already thought Nanny Barnes was too close to her sons and the pictures only made things worse. She more or less froze her out after that and she left in the New Year.' Diana's petulance annoyed Princess Margaret, who was extremely fond of Baba.

At one party, guests conferred over an item of gossip which had reached them from Los Angeles concerning Prince Andrew and his friendship with the actress Catherine Oxenberg. 'He likes her because she's very shy and quiet and very feminine,' said one guest. 'I think men are intimidated by me,' Catherine was quoted as saying. 'They assume that if you are pretty and comfortably off then you must have someone in your life.'

British-born but LA-based, Catherine is the daughter of Princess Elizabeth of Yugoslavia and fashion millionaire Howard Oxenberg. As a teenager, she had been named as a possible bride for Prince Charles. After her long-playing role as Joan Collins' daughter, Amanda Carrington, in *Dynasty,* she played the Princess of Wales in American TV's *The Royal Romance of Charles and Diana.* 'I feel a tremendous amount of compassion for Diana, for her sense of becoming a woman through motherhood,' said Catherine, who has a young daughter called India. 'Ten years ago she was naive and struck with fantasy – you would never have guessed what lay beneath the surface.'

The actress was also the cousin of another Mustique holidaymaker, the Duke of Kent. 'I remember queuing up for food at one of those incredible parties Colin Tennant gave and standing right next to me were the Duke and Duchess of Kent,' said a former visitor. 'The man who stood next to me said, "Look at that!" and I remember staring down and seeing that the Duke of Kent has only got four toes.'

Despite the island's general air of informality, Margaret insisted on royal protocol being observed unless she was in a playful mood. This grated on some visitors who believed a more egalitarian style was appropriate to the holiday setting.

'I was staying at Patrick Lichfield's house in the mid-Eighties and Princess Margaret was next door,' recalled Marcelle d'Argy Smith, editor of *Cosmopolitan* magazine, I mean, that Ma'am thing is a bit much on holiday; it really is. Everybody does it all the time and it is pathetic. I just cannot curtsy or bow. The very first time I met her I remember saying, "Hello, Ma'am, you are still not smoking after all that?" It had been all over the newspapers that she had been in hospital. But she was quite pleasant to talk to. Every single night she insisted on coming in and watching *Fawlty Towers* re-runs and this dominated the entire household of eight or ten people. I remember Patrick at that time was married to Leonora (Lady Leonora

Grosvenor) who said, "Patrick, you have got to stop this. If she comes in one more time, I will go mad."

'Margaret is probably quite good fun and I don't think she is malicious in any way, but they (the royals) have no conception about how selfish they are. You cannot blame them entirely, watching the antics of the people around them. They live in an unreal world because everybody does what they want them to do. Nobody will say, "Come on, we are completely bored with this, Margaret, let's do something else."

MARGARET had tried just about everything else. It was no wonder she identified with Basil Fawlty, the argumentative, accident-prone hero of the comedy series. Conflict of one kind or another had been her talisman long before Princess Michael and the Duchess of York started to interest followers of royal scandal. As her neighbour at Kensington Palace, Diana had seen at first hand the lifestyle that had turned the royal lodger in Apartment 1A into a sick woman.

The drawing room of Margaret's home, which occupied four storeys in the north wing of the Aunt Heap, had long been the scene of some of the raunchiest parties in the Royal Borough, 'I used to dread being invited back to Kensington Palace after the theatre,' said a leading West End designer. 'One of Margaret's friends would issue the invitations and you were expected to attend. These parties went on until the early hours. You couldn't leave until she went to bed.'

Margaret played down her reputation as a hard-drinking night owl. 'When my sister and I were growing up, she was made out to be the goody-goody one,' she said. 'That was boring, so the Press tried to make out that I was wicked as hell.'

During the Sixties, the Partytime Princess had frolicked with some of the greatest ravers of the age, including Mick Jagger. She and the young, androgynous Rolling Stone attended a rave-up held in the grounds of Prince Rupert Loewenstein's Kensington mansion. All the guests were requested to dress in white, so Jagger turned up in a white party dress. 'Nothing created more of a stir than the couple of the evening – Mick Jagger and Princess Margaret – who compared hem lengths, then shook it up on the dance floor,' recorded Christopher Andersen in his unauthorised Jagger biography.

She grew very attached to Brian Epstein, manager of the Beatles, who often squired her to the unisexual parties that pleased them both. 'Brian had exquisite taste in clothes, the arts and the presents he gave,' said a friend. 'The night he met Margaret he was living at the Grosvenor House Hotel and I picked him up to take him to the Dockland Settlements Ball. He was meeting royalty for the first time and he was so nervous about impressing Margaret that he borrowed my cuff links for good luck. They were the same pair I had lent John Lennon for the Beatles' first Ed Sullivan TV appearance in America.' Margaret was devastated when Epstein died from a drug overdose at his new home in Chapel Street, Belgravia, just one month before his thirty-third birthday.

At one West End premiere, Margaret astonished everyone by turning up in a low-cut, tight, green dress, the bosoms of which had two large white hands sewn on to them. 'She was sharp and witty,' said the designer, 'and full of frustrated energy. I told her I went to SLADE art college and she quipped, "Oh, you're a slave, are you?" '

In some ways it is not surprising that many of her high hopes are now broken, that though she still inspires the loyalty of her friends, she is spending her sixties broken in health and sometimes in spirit,' remarked Richard Davenport-Hines in *Tatler*. 'Yet she might have coped with her difficulties if she had been born half a generation later. All the inherent difficulties of being second-best princess have been hugely aggravated by being the princess who grew up in the stultification of the Forties and Fifties and had to cope with the social revolution of the Sixties and Seventies.'

Certainly no one could accuse Margaret of not trying to have a good time, no matter what the prevailing social climate. Barely out of adolescence, she turned to fast company who used drink and drugs to add spice to the post-war years of austerity. She had inherited two of her father's vices: a weakness for nicotine and a fondness for alcohol.

One of her friends was Robin Douglas-Home, a tall, blond Army officer of impeccable aristocratic birth. He was the grandson of the sixth Earl Spencer on his mother's side and the nephew of the fourteenth Earl of Home, later the Prime Minister Sir Alec Douglas-Home, on his father's. After Ludgrove prep school, he had gone to Eton and taken a commission in the Seaforth Highlanders. Quitting the Army to write novels and advertising copy, he also worked as what *The Times* grandly called 'a Mayfair cocktail-time pianist'. Whenever the Margaret Set went on the town, the winsomely handsome Robin was invariably at the keyboard playing his signature tune, *I'm in the Mood for Love.*

Margaret made sure he was among guests invited to the smart house parties she attended, sometimes sending her car to pick him up at his flat off Hill Street, Mayfair. Her favourite party piece was to sing Cole Porter songs to his accompaniment. When the Queen and Prince Philip danced to his romantic music at Buckingham Palace, his place among the gilded youth of his day seemed assured.

'Close friends believe that if Robin had cared – or played his cards right – he could have married Princess Margaret long before Antony Armstrong-Jones came on the scene,' wrote royal author Unity Hall. 'The fact he had no money would hardly have stood in his way. Prince Philip was penniless when he married the young Princess Elizabeth.' But Robin passed up his chance and pursued another princess, the very blonde and beautiful Princess Margaretha of Sweden. It was fifteen years before he fatally tried to correct his mistake.

In her twenty-eighth year, Margaret sat for Cecil Beaton at Clarence House, one of six solo sittings she favoured him with between 1949 and 1960. The Beaton collection clearly showed her evolution from a 'five foot two, eyes of blue' teenager into an experienced young sophisticate. The 1958 post-Townsend portrait could easily have made the cover of *Vogue,* but it was far more than a mannequin shot of the period. There was a movie-star quality about it that made Margaret, ebony hair cut short and fringed, the eyes knowing, the lips closed upon a secret smile, a rival for Elizabeth Taylor and other screen goddesses. This was royalty goes to Hollywood.

'Margaret was an extremely attractive young woman and being seen with the Margaret Set was considered very, very glamorous,' said the titled Chelsea lady. 'They frequented the Cafe de Paris, the 400 Club and the Stork Room. I remember going to the Cafe de Paris when Marlene Dietrich was singing there and seeing Margaret with a party of friends. She was smoking out of a long, black cigarette holder and she was beautifully made up for those days. She had the tiniest little waist and, like Elizabeth Taylor, these cornflower blue eyes. She was such fun. You got a shock when you realised who it was because she was literally like a Dresden doll. Whereas you are stunned by Diana and how tall she is when you meet her, Margaret was just absolutely, ravishingly beautiful.'

One of the trends she inspired was to go out minus her stockings. Bare legs were considered very fast, but other bright young things copied her instantly. 'I cannot imagine anything more wonderful than being who I am,' she proclaimed during the good times. Others spotted danger ahead. 'There is already a Marie Antoinette aroma about her,' noted the mischievous diarist Sir Henry 'Chips' Channon, father of one of Margaret's neighbours on Mustique, the Honourable Paul Channon, MP.

The footlights always sparkled for Margaret and she was attracted not only to the glamour of the performance but to the performers themselves. As a nineteen-year-old, she went to see Danny Kaye at the Palladium and insisted on going backstage to meet the American entertainer after the show. 'All of us in the royal party trooped down to his dressing room and Princess Margaret bounced up and down saying, "Do *Balling the Jack,* Danny. Oh, please do *Balling the Jack,"* ' recalled Eileen Parker in her memoirs. This was the start of a friendship for Margaret which was very much outside the aristocratic circle.

'Wherever she went, Margaret was accompanied by a string of prancing Scottish lairds,' recounted Eileen. 'But all the time the Margaret Set were chasing themselves, she was in love with Townsend.' She started coming home well after midnight, but the King raised no objections. He knew that life for his younger daughter was difficult in the shadow of her famous sister.

Danny Kaye, who could sing, dance and act, encouraged Margaret's talent for mimicry. For one special event, he taught her to do the can-can. A close friend was Sharman Douglas, daughter of the American Ambassador, who was invited to join Margaret's carriage for the ride down the straight one Derby Day. When the Douglases held a fancy dress ball at the US Embassy, the cabaret came direct from Buckingham Palace.

'Mike (Parker), Prince Philip and Princess Elizabeth went as the three characters in Bing Crosby's hit *The Waiter, the Porter and the Upstairs Maid,'* recalled Eileen Parker. 'They came on and sang the song to a mimed tableau of their own invention. This won first prize, but Margaret upstaged everybody. She appeared in a can-can routine as Madame Fifi. She wore lace panties, black stockings and suspenders and finished by hoisting her petticoats and wiggling her bottom in a finale that brought wolf-whistles.'

Less than six months after she had broken up with Townsend, Antony Armstrong-Jones entered Margaret's life, though it was to be another four years before she agreed to marry him. He had been Baron's assistant and, although making his mark as a society photographer, he was regarded as a bohemian.

An Old Etonian who walked with a limp caused by infantile paralysis, Tony's raffish charm and intriguing sexuality attracted Margaret far more than the aristocrats who were anxiously trying to woo her. They were soon passionate lovers. She secretly visited his home, a single white room in an end-of-terrace house at Rotherhithe with a view across the Thames to Tower Bridge. 'Tony gave her a life she'd never known before – the freedom to be herself away from the prying eyes of servants,' said a friend. She called him 'Tone' and he called her 'Pet', *infra dig* nicknames suited to the working-class location of their lovenest.

When Peter Townsend wrote to her just before Christmas in 1959 saying he was marrying a Belgian heiress, Marie-Luce Jamagne, twenty-six years his junior, Margaret reacted as though still on the rebound. 'I received a letter from Peter in the morning and that evening I decided to marry Tony,' she told another friend. She also had to tell the Queen that she intended to wed a commoner.

'Anyone who thinks that the turmoil at Sandringham over the Waleses and the Yorks is something new is quite mistaken,' said the royal historian. 'Sandringham has a history of royal crises. As in any other family, emotional issues come to the fore at Christmas and New Year.'

The Prime Minister, Harold Macmillan, arrived at Sandringham to find the Queen's uncle, Henry, Duke of Gloucester, beside himself with anxiety. 'Thank heavens you have come, Prime Minister,' said the Duke. 'The Queen's in a terrible state – there's a fellow called Jones in the billiard room who wants to marry her sister, and Prince Philip is in the library wanting to change the family name to Mountbatten.'

This time there was no denying Margaret's wishes. She and Tony were engaged in February 1960 and the wedding date was set for 6 May at Westminster Abbey. The fellow called Jones became the Earl of Snowdon and he moved into Kensington Palace with his royal wife. Their first child, David Albert Charles Armstrong-Jones, Viscount Linley, was born on 3 November, 1961. Lady Sarah Frances Elizabeth followed on 1 May, 1964.

The family was now complete but instead of settling down into a happy, stable married life, the Snowdons began to indulge their instinct for self-destruction and there was a surfeit of like-minded co-stars.

One of Margaret's closest friends was Peter Sellers, the comedy actor of *Pink Panther* fame, who told friends they had been lovers. Certainly Margaret was close to him and helped him through one bout of ill health after another. Four days after he married Britt Ekland, the young Swedish actress, he flew to America to make *Kiss Me Stupid* and suffered the first of several massive heart attacks. To coax him back to work, Margaret persuaded him to direct a spoof film in which she starred as Queen Victoria. She gave it to her sister as a birthday present, in one sense, he was a male version of Margaret,' said a friend. 'At one level, they were both great mimics who loved to act the fool but, underneath it all, the sexual thing made them terribly unhappy.'

The Snowdons' marriage hit serious trouble when the outrageous flirting and well-lubricated carousing gave way to adultery. While Lord Snowdon was carrying out a photographic assignment in India for the *Sunday Times,* Margaret had a brief fling with a mutual friend. Stricken with remorse, she made the mistake of ringing the man's wife to say how sorry she was that it had happened. Although both marriages stayed more or less intact, there were frequent arguments in Apartment 1A.

Tony wasn't always the nonconformist he had once been. When an old friend blew his horn to attract Tony's attention as he was turning into Kensington Palace one day, he got a curt note telling him that such familiarities were no longer welcome.

Other affairs followed for both of them. Margaret sought the company of less critical men and encouraged one of them, Robin Douglas-Home, to such an extent that he urged her to leave her husband. Robin fell madly in love with Margaret the second time around after his own private world had crashed in ruins. Rejected by Princess Margaretha, or more accurately, snubbed by her family, he had married the leading fashion model Sandra Paul in July 1959. But he found it impossible to give up some old habits. His unpredictable libido, which led to him being caught in the act with a titled lady in the back of a car, and a cruel streak, which he blamed on the public school system, landed him in the divorce court.

'When I received a petition for cruelty I can only describe one's feelings as though a small bomb had gone off inside your head,' he said. 'Five years of one's life, say seventy per cent of which were happy, reduced to a great wad of foolscap typed out by leering little clerks in solicitors' offices.'

He drank heavily in the clubs where he had been a respected performer and gambled well beyond his means in the casinos. He was going down for the third time when Margaret came to the rescue. She invited him to her home and allowed him to escort her to first nights and cocktail parties. Realising that his declarations of love were serious, she tried to let him down gently, but her ardent suitor persisted with his attentions. So persuasive was he that Margaret gradually began to respond in a way that she would live to regret. According to Robin's friend and drinking buddy, the ubiquitous Noel Botham of Squidgy fame, Margaret began to reciprocate his feelings. She started an adulterous affair with Robin on 10 February, 1967, and wrote passionate love letters to him, which he kept for reasons that later became less than sentimental.

Once the Press noted the Margaret and Robin were keeping company and started to report their nocturnal escapades, she took a diplomatic holiday in the Bahamas on her own. When Robin badgered her to divorce her husband and marry him, she went to Balmoral and wrote him a letter which dismissed him from her life. Her rejected lover, however, did not go quietly. He threatened to sell Margaret's love letters unless he was given cash to pay off his debts. When Margaret refused to submit to blackmail, he offered the letters to New York publishing houses. For years, they were locked in a Manhattan safe where, like the Squidgy tapes, they remained a timebomb on deposit.

Broken by drink, drugs and self-pity, Robin committed suicide eighteen months after his royal affair ended. He was only thirty-six. His body was found at his home, Meadow Brook, Sunset Lane, West Chiltington. As a suicide note, he left a tape-recorded message which said: 'There comes a time when one comes to the conclusion that continuing to live is pointless.'

Shaken, the Snowdons reviewed their behaviour and worked out an agreement under which they would remain a married couple but lead separate lives. Tony would turn up in public with attractive younger women, driving Margaret into fits of jealousy. She would not agree to a divorce, however, because of the embarrassment it would cause her sister.

There were also the children to consider.

ONE evening in the early Seventies, Princess Margaret, dressed in a mink coat, stood impatiently in a school cloakroom and addressed her daughter. 'For goodness sake, Sarah, where are your gym shoes?' she asked the young schoolgirl. If she had come to parenthood later than her sister, Margaret had turned out to be a good mother. 'My children are not royal,' she declared firmly and she and Tony raised them accordingly.

'Sarah was a sweet little girl, completely natural and totally unspoiled,' said a parent at the Francis Holland School. 'She was passionately fond of ballet, drawing and dancing and she really worked very hard. I can still see Margaret standing in the cloakroom in this fabulous coat; otherwise, she was just like any other mother. The complete addict had produced two stable children; both kids got on and did something with their lives. Tony was a good father, too. He always came to the school and sat on the benches to look at the gym displays, very often with his mother, Lady Rosse. She'd be wearing wonderful clothes and be virtually sitting on the floor with Tony. Other children were often invited to Kensington Palace.'

In September 1973, Margaret went on holiday alone to the Tennants' home in Scotland. Once again, her old friends were instrumental in introducing her to a young man to whom she was enormously drawn.

Roderic Llewellyn, second son of the show-jumping baronet Sir Harry 'Foxhunter' Llewellyn, was only twenty-six and drifting through life when he was unexpectedly invited to join the house party. His name had come up on a list of eligible young men. Somewhat bemused as he had never met his hosts, Roddy turned up as instructed at the Cafe Royal, just off Princes Street in Edinburgh, for lunch. For a blind date the casting turned out to be inspired. The sexual chemistry between the highly-strung and delicately handsome Welshman and the Queen's sister was immediate and reciprocal.

They held hands, looked lovingly into each other's eyes and shared a bedroom.

Six months later, Roddy was introduced to the delights of Mustique. Much as he adored his royal lover, however, the pressure of keeping their liaison secret proved too much for him. Roddy had tried to commit suicide twice before they met and, fearing the onset of another breakdown, he phoned Margaret to say he was leaving the country indefinitely. On a flight to Turkey after travelling to Guernsey on the first available plane, he confided to a stranger that he was having an affair with a married woman and the sexual side of the relationship was getting him down. Margaret, distraught at what he might do to himself rather than at the prospect of losing him, took several Mogodon sleeping tables, but recovered two days later. Roddy travelled around Turkey by bus, then slipped quietly back into Britain and, having resolved his inner conflict for the time being, resumed the affair.

Liz Brewer, the Belgravia public relations consultant, remembers the rapport between the Princess and her lover, 'I met my ex-husband John Rendall through Roddy Llewellyn, who was a very good friend,' she said, 'I didn't think John was interested in me, but it turned out that he was, anyway. One day the pair of them said, "You've got to come and meet Princess Margaret." They picked me up in the famous blue van and drove me to Kensington Palace. They were outrageously dressed in sort of boots and sweatshirts and I was in hot pants and boots.

'Roddy warned me before we went in, "She likes a very deep curtsy." I said, "I cannot do a deep curtsey in hot pants." He said, "You must." When we got to the door, Margaret answered it herself with a cigarette in one hand and a drink in the other. Roddy ran round to the back of her and signalled me to deep curtsy. I was trying but he kept signalling, "Not deep enough, not deep enough." At that point, she noticed I was looking at something over her shoulder and turned around. "Oh Roddy, you are naughty," she scolded him. "How outrageous!" '

Not long afterwards, however, the same self-destructive feelings overwhelmed Roddy again. This time he took Valium and ended up in hospital for three weeks. It was evident that the union was potentially lethal to both partners. In 1976, they were back at Mustique and, as they relaxed on the beach with friends, Ross Waby, a New Zealand journalist working out of Murdoch's New York bureau, photographed them together for the first time in their two-and-a-half-year relationship. When the snatched picture appeared on the front page of the *News of the World,* Lord Snowdon seized his chance and pressed for a legal separation. He already had a new partner in his life, Lucy Lindsay-Hogg, whom he married after his divorce in 1978.

Thoroughly dispirited over the end of her marriage and the inevitable break-up with Roddy, Margaret drank so heavily that she developed alcoholic hepatitis. She also underwent exploratory surgery on one of her lungs after smoking caused her further health problems.

But Margaret lost none of her well-honed social instincts. She was amazingly accurate in her reading of the state of play in the Yorks' marriage a few months before it broke up. During a visit to Sunninghill, she spotted Fergie pulling faces and making jokey gestures behind Andrew's back. When he realised what she was doing, he became very upset and his aunt noticed that he was angry as well. Turning to a companion, Margaret said: 'I give that marriage six months.'

She was right – with time to spare.

14

FERGIE'S REVENGE

'She was too much herself and I think that's the problem'

C.C. Beaudette

PRINCE Andrew knew he was tempting fate. His mother had asked him to write down a list of suitable brides and he had put C.C. Beaudette right at the top. The Queen's reaction was predictable. 'Like hell,' said Her Majesty, according to C.C.'s relative, Lady Edith Foxwell. Before Koo Stark and Sarah Ferguson, Andrew had given his heart to Cobina Caroline Beaudette, known to all and sundry in her native California as C.C.

Ironically, C.C. was the beautiful daughter of his father's old actress flame, Cobina Beaudette. As Lady Edith explained, Prince Philip had been smitten by the stunning Cobina when Beatrice Lillie introduced them as teenagers. The Queen had always been jealous of her and the thought of the screen *femme fatale's* daughter marrying her favourite son did not appeal at all, no matter how nice she was.

At Philip's invitation, both mother and daughter had joined the royal party on board *Britannia* in 1976. 'I remember it was at Cowes for a beautiful festival,' said C.C. Beaudette, speaking at her home near Solvang, north of Santa Barbara. 'There were many beautiful boats and *Britannia* was one of them.' The following year, C.C. stayed with her cousin Edith at her splendid country residence, Home Farm at Sherston in Wiltshire. She loved country life and Prince Andrew joined her there for more than one romantic weekend.

'How does one know how serious it was?' said Lady Edith. 'But when the Queen asked Andrew for his list, I understand C.C. was the first name he wrote down. C.C., who was born within a year of my own daughter Atalanta in 1956, remained single until some time after Andrew and Fergie were married. The Queen does make decisions about her children, but all the bloody wrong ones.'

'We have been friends for a long time,' confirmed C.C. Beaudette. 'He is a good friend and his father is a good friend – there is a history of generations of friendship in our families. I have very few friends and I certainly wouldn't do anything to encourage any more attention than is presently being given.' Referring to the Windsors' problems, she added: 'No family has ever been that much in the public eye. I think it is very difficult for everyone. And they are good people. I don't know anyone who could live such an open life and not be ridiculed for something – whether it be the tie you are wearing or the colour of your underwear. People are always trying to find fault and it's just ridiculous.' Not the sort of married life she would have enjoyed, then? 'Well . . . it's very difficult for anyone not in a situation like that to live in a situation like that,' she replied tactfully.

When Sarah Margaret Ferguson and not C.C. Beaudette became Her Royal Highness, Duchess of York, people in high places started to worry. Fergie's problems might be her own affair, to put it politely, but her actions could threaten the future of the monarchy. One who expressed his misgivings was a Conservative peer in the House of Lords. 'That girl will single-handedly bring down the House of Windsor,' he told a relative. 'He was right because she set everything in motion – it was like a domino effect,' said the relative. 'With her background, it was inevitable that she would be indiscreet and stupid. The very fact that Fergie could have an affair made everybody think that Princess Diana could have an affair. It rolled on from there.'

Not all aristocrats, however, shared this pessimistic view. Some enjoyed Fergie's bizarre behaviour, which showed little sign of abating after the separation. On one occasion, she lunched with the Duke of Marlborough in a private room at Green's restaurant, run by Simon Parker Bowles, brother of Andrew, in St James's. 'I was lunching with Simon,' said Sarah Kennedy. 'He said, "You'll never guess what those two are eating downstairs – smoked salmon covered with tomato sauce and Coca-Cola." Isn't that unbelievable? I recoiled from that. Smoked salmon with tomato sauce *and* Coca-Cola. With all that money! Thank God we're all different.'

Fergie's downhill run had started in Verbier long before she was ever considered as a potential royal. She socialised with a blue-blooded set which loved to mix excitement with pleasure at Paddy

McNally's chalet. One of the high-living aristocrats she partied with was Marlborough's heir Jamie, the Marquess of Blandford, who graduated from softer drugs to heroin and cocaine until he was hopelessly addicted.

'Verbier is where Jamie Blandford started his drug-taking,' said the Chelsea socialite Viviane Ventura. 'Jamie was gorgeous. I mean, he was such a wonderful young man. You know the problem with drugs; some people are weak and some are strong. He was such a good-looking guy and so together and charming.' 'He had tracks right up his arm,' said a recovering addict who met him in a detox centre a few years later.

When his marriage to Becky Few Brown fell apart after the birth of their son, he started smoking crack, the most powerful derivative of cocaine. Jamie was eventually admitted to a treatment centre in North London after a run-in with the police.

Knowing the dangers of drug abuse, McNally had made his position quite clear during his years as king of the mountain in Verbier. 'I have a strict house rule that no one who has anything to do with drugs is allowed to stay with me,' he said. One young aristocrat, a woman, who admitted she had snorted cocaine at the chalet, nicknamed Cocaine Castle, confirmed that McNally didn't use narcotics himself.

But drug-users among the Verbier Set circumvented McNally's house rule. They were ruthless in the methods they employed to smuggle Category A drugs into the Swiss resort. One of the unsuspecting carriers was Ms Ventura, who had been invited to stay at the chalet one Christmas.

'I'd had a call two days before my departure saying that they couldn't get a turkey big enough for Christmas Day, which is actually quite believable because turkey isn't the thing in Switzerland. One of the Verbier Set delivered a turkey to me at my house all wrapped up in a Harrods box and ready to go in the oven. It was standing on top of my luggage in full view and I drove it with three kids, two of mine and one of a friend of mine, across three borders. The turkey was full of drugs, as it turned out, and I had been the perfect pigeon. I didn't know what was in it till the next day, although I was aware of girls in the house digging into it in the early hours of the morning. They were all in the kitchen doing something to the turkey.

'The next day we were having lunch at the top of the mountain and a friend of mine said, "I think you should know who your friends are." She had a violent row with her husband because he didn't want her to tell me. I didn't know what they were rowing about and then he stood up and threw his napkin on the table and walked away and said something like, "If you tell her, you can take the consequences." So I said, "What's all this about?" and she said, "Well, you just brought a turkey full of cocaine."

'I gathered the kids and came back to the chalet. I was absolutely distraught. I abhor drugs. It was the day before Christmas and I couldn't get hold of my solicitor. I didn't know whether I had become a criminal. I was being physically sick. I moved out of the house that evening and into a hotel. I confronted one of them later and told him how awful it was that I had been used as a drug courier and he said: "Well, you didn't get caught, did you?" Then he used an expression I remember very vividly because I'd never heard it before. He said, "Why are you getting your knickers in a twist?" I have confirmation from another of the men there that it was cocaine, cocaine for the season. Jail? Forget me. It would have destroyed the lives of my children.'

McNally was forty-five when he started his affair with Fergie, twenty-two years her senior. After stints as a journalist and as racing manager to Niki Lauda, the Austrian world motor-racing champion, McNally started to exploit an obvious source of revenue. Allsport, his Geneva-based company, sold advertising space on hoardings at Grand Prix tracks around the world. The global televising of motor-racing meant that corporate sponsors paid highly for the best sites.

When she moved into the chalet, Fergie cooked their favourite meals for the McNallys, steak and kidney for Paddy, sausage and mash for his two sons. McNally's protestations that he had no intention of marrying her did nothing to deter her. 'She was totally besotted and in love with Paddy McNally,' said a visitor to Verbier. McNally teased her about her weight but he also coached her on the slopes until, the tail of her home-made Davy Crockett hat flying behind, she was more than a match for many of the men on the most demanding black runs.

McNally's favourite watering hole was the Farm Club, the nearest thing Verbier could offer to Annabel's. He held court in a reserved alcove at a wooden table laden with bottles of Russian vodka.

Acceptance into the inner circle was by invitation only. The social cachet it carried in this alpine enclave of Sloanedom was enormous. Young chalet girls eager for some of the magic to rub off on them gravitated towards his table.

Whenever he flirted with an attractive newcomer, Sarah would initially storm out in a rage and burst into tears. She once unceremoniously dumped a bucket of iced water over his head to cool his ardour. Gradually, she became adept at shutting out aspiring rivals. 'I'm Sarah,' she would tell the interloper, drawing herself up to her full five foot eight inches, 'I'm Paddy's girlfriend.'

Looking more vampish than sophisticated in skin-tight black leather trousers and high heels, she made sure the message hit home. She drank vodka, smoked Marlboro cigarettes and joined in the often waspish conversation. 'Sarah became used to a bit of heavy, sharp banter across the table,' said Dai Llewellyn, the convivial brother of Roddy, it was fast teasing and she was no slouch at it.'

In the spring of 1985, Diana put Sarah's name forward to the Queen as a guest at Windsor Castle during Royal Ascot. When the coveted invitation duly arrived at Fergie's home in Lavender Gardens, Clapham, she told McNally, who offered to drive her to Windsor. 'Sarah was still very keen to marry Paddy at that stage and she thought he might be jealous,' said a friend. 'But he just took it in his stride. Even when Fergie let him know that Andrew was taking an interest, he wished her well. She finally realised that he was never going to marry her so she accepted Andrew on the rebound.'

McNally attended the royal wedding at Westminster Abbey on 23 July, 1986, but showed no inclination to follow his erstwhile girlfriend down the aisle. He remained dedicatedly single. It was to McNally that Fergie turned when her marriage started to go disastrously awry. They met privately at a terraced house in Radnor Walk, Chelsea.

'She's a frightened little girl beneath that exhibitionist front,' said a friend. 'Once she got into the Royal Family, she tried to please everyone – Andrew, his parents, the courtiers, the public and the Press. She never really had a chance. It's only natural that she turned to Paddy for some good advice.'

Recognising the symptoms, Diana was one of the first to realise that Fergie should never have been there in the first place and even started to deny that she played any part in their romance. 'Diana initially welcomed Sarah's presence because of the interaction between them,' said a highly placed royal source. 'She is very competitive, but she was aware of the power of the courtiers and she warned Sarah about some of the things that had happened to her. Sarah thought she could handle it even if Diana was cracking under the strain. It worked well for a while, but Diana's own marriage was under increasing pressure. Arguments with Prince Charles, mainly over his friendship with Camilla, were followed by long, brooding silences. Diana had plenty of worries of her own.'

Once Fergie started to excite the attention of the media, the Princess put some distance between herself and her best friend. She wasn't interested in competing for the headlines she had dominated for so long. Moreover, most of the coverage was highly critical of Fergie's disastrous fashion sense, her penchant for accepting freebies and her perennial weight problems. Diana stepped back, became involved with charity work, notably among AIDS sufferers, and let Fergie get on with it.

'One reason Diana cut her off was that she suspected she was spying on her to ingratiate herself with Charles,' said a friend in whom the Princess confided. 'She believed Fergie was checking out the handwritten codes on her mail at the Buckingham Palace sorting office and telling Charles the names of people writing to her.' Diana had many similar fears, most of them unfounded.

When Fergie was pregnant with Beatrice in 1988, her father's sexual behaviour at the Wigmore Club created a scandal that affected her deeply. She tried to shrug it off but, although the Queen stood by her and Charles gave his polo manager his total support, it still hurt. She began bingeing from the refrigerator and her weight shot up. 'I really blimped out,' she said.

Diana was appalled by Major Ron's behaviour and she was deliberately cold towards him ever afterwards. She warned Fergie that her father was bringing her down. The Squidgy tapes revealed that Prince Charles, probably acting after a plea from Andrew, had co-opted Sir Jimmy Savile to try to help Fergie.

Diana: Jimmy Savile rang me up yesterday and he said, 'I'm just ringing up, my girl, to tell you that His Nibs has asked me to come and help out the Redhead, and I'm just letting you know so that you don't find out through her or him. And I hope it's all right by you.' And I said, 'Jimmy, you do what you like.'

Gilbey: What do you mean 'Help out the Redhead,' darling?

Diana: With her publicity.

Gilbey: Oh, has he?

Diana: Sort her out. He said, 'You can't change a lame duck, but I've got to talk to her 'cos that's the boss's orders and I've got to carry them out. But I want you to know that you're my number one girl.'

As the conversation had taken place on New Year's Eve 1989, Fergie's problems had been causing concern in the Family for at least two-and-a-half years.

The house-warming at Sunninghill on Friday, 5 October, 1990, should have been the start of a fulfilling life for the Yorks. Instead, it sharpened the decline of their marriage. Steve Wyatt turned up with his buddy, Johnny Bryan, according to an American friend, and the die was cast. For the first and only time, all the players were under the same roof together. Fergie and her mother had said a tearful farewell that day to Hector Barrantes at a memorial service arranged by Lord Vestey. The Duchess missed her stepfather, who had lost a long and painful battle against cancer of the lymph gland. However, she changed into a stunning emerald green dress, put a matching bow in her hair and greeted the guests to her extraordinary new home.

'About seventy people, including Prince Edward, Billy Connolly, Pamela Stephenson, Viscount Linley, Susannah Constantine, Elton John and Michael and Shakira Caine sat down to a lobster dinner,' said one who was there. 'The party had a jungle theme and the staff were all dressed up as Tarzan and Jane. Then about two hundred more people arrived and things really took off. Fergie cheered up and it was so much fun that no one wanted to leave.'

When he returned to his home in Cheyne Place, Chelsea, Johnny Bryan phoned Witney Tower Jnr, an old friend in New York. 'He said he had just been to this fabulous party at the Duke and Duchess of York's house,' said Tower. 'He said Elton John had played the piano and they stayed up very late. He said the Duchess was very nice and he had a good time.'

But Fergie couldn't settle down at Sunninghill despite its overstated luxury and an abundance of home help. She felt trapped and claustrophobic despite the wide open spaces of Windsor Great Park. 'It is very difficult to get any privacy – in fact, I don't have any,' she told Georgina Howell. 'Oh, there are times when I don't have anybody in the house and we can just be a family together. I sometimes give everyone the night off and go into the kitchen and make a cheese sandwich. But you have staff, you have security, you always have to be aware. You're always on show, twenty-four hours a day.'

Anyone familiar with Fergie's passion for champagne-style entertaining found this difficult to assimilate. Right to the end, she invited friends to no-expense-spared dinners and many stayed overnight, including Johnny Bryan. The refrigerator was stocked with such extravagant items as caviare, out-of-season strawberries and every conceivable flavour of exotic ice-cream. When Buckingham Palace sent her warnings about overspending, she would retort that she bought so much because she was not able to predict what Her Majesty's son would most enjoy on his weekends at home.

In reality, her relationship with Andrew was a sham. Their home life quickly became a nightmare because marriage was torture for her. She lacked confidence and no matter how well things might seem to be going, she felt threatened and anxious. She was incapable of being a slave to another person or a system. An inflated sense of her own identity did not allow her to hold anything back. If Andrew ventured an opinion, Fergie snapped back at him. 'Screw your neck in, Andrew,' she said impatiently in front of an interior decorator. The Duke walked away. An argument usually followed such an outburst. Andrew, however, had started to realise that something was wrong with his wife.

'The fact is that this young lady owes her status in life to that one memorable day (when she married Prince Andrew) and that's all that has changed her from being any other girl on the streets of London to the person she is,' said Gene Nocon, the Prince's photographic guru, from his home in San Diego. 'I've seen her character change and not for the better. You know she was such a nice person when we first met her, we are beginning to wonder if that niceness was just an interesting ploy. The real person is Prince Andrew. He's the person I met and still love. They don't come any better.'

There was one simple explanation for the extraordinary change in the Duchess. To deal with her weight problem, she had started taking courses of amphetamine-based slimming pills which were originally prescribed for her in Paris and later in Harley Street. Mixed with alcohol, they had disturbing, mood-altering side-effects. She not only lost weight but her self-control as well. 'I've tried everything, believe me, all the fad diets, the pills, the lot,' she said later. 'But all that is very bad for you.'

In Fergie's eyes, Andrew simply couldn't do anything right. When he played with his daughters, she told him to stop upsetting them even if they were just splashing about in the bath. At Eugenie's second birthday party, Andrew was asked to judge a face-painting competition among the excited young guests. He declined, saying ruefully: 'I'm only allowed to judge police horses and things like that.' Fed up with arguments, the Prince sought refuge in his study, where he watched videos, or he left the house altogether and spent hours playing golf.

Andrew had been the Family's prankster, the whoopee cushion king of the practical joke. This was a trait he inherited from his grandfather, George VI. Beneath the worried frown and despite his painful shyness, George had loved to enliven dull Family occasions with the howls of a victim who had fallen for one of his tricks. But when Andrew discovered that Fergie was laughing at him instead of with him, another of the King's characteristics began to surface – a bad temper, known in the Family as 'Hanoverian spleen'. The Prince had not been raised to deal with emotional problems, certainly not in a wife, and he took it badly. Some of their arguments bordered on domestic violence.

When he was entitled to leave from the Navy, he went home less often, preferring one of the boltholes at Buckingham Palace or Windsor Castle. Once, he arrived at Sunninghill to find that Fergie had taken Beatrice away for the weekend without telling him. They were barely on speaking terms.

C.C. Beaudette, who Andrew had kept in touch with, said: 'He has had a very, very difficult time. It might even be a curse being born into a family that is so much in the public eye.' It was at polo a year before the break-up that the Duchess finally came face to face with Andrew's former sweetheart.

'She was very nice, very warm and sweet and wonderful,' said C.C. 'She is a very nice girl and she means well. She was too much herself and I think that that's the problem. It's pretty obvious she just wanted to be herself.'

FERGIE'S sexual adventures with Americans, first with Steve Wyatt and later with Johnny Bryan, were not careless flings to enliven a boring life. Rather, they were her revenge on her husband. She blamed him for everything: her inability to fit in as a royal, her unfulfilled sexual needs, her shortage of money for the Gold Card shopping binges she loved to undertake in Paris, New York and Los Angeles, and even her weight.

By punishing Andrew, Fergie believed she was also exacting retribution on the Family. But her manner changed abruptly whenever her mother-in-law arrived for afternoon tea. The Queen saw only a doting wife and a loving mother; an enthusiastic and devoted member of the clan. Fergie's relief once the Queen had departed, however, was palpable. 'Her attitude was, "Phew, I got away with it again," ' said a former friend of the Duchess. 'It was so hypocritical.'

The kamikaze manner in which she conducted herself with both American lovers made disclosure inevitable. 'She was throwing down a challenge to Andrew,' said a still loyal friend. 'I believe she wanted to be found out – it has to be seen in hindsight as a cry for help. Andrew eventually recognised that, but he was slow off the mark.'

The more Fergie felt alienated in Britain, the more she gravitated towards America where her title was priceless and she could behave exactly as she chose, once knighting a pet dog with a table knife. 'I do love Americans, actually, because they are free in themselves, aren't they?' she told Barbara Walters on American TV. 'They have a very much more relaxed attitude than the British people. I certainly can relate to it because I'm a little wild.'

In seeking a remedy for her matrimonial and emotional ills in America, Fergie was following the footsteps of Edwina Mountbatten. Whereas Edwina had been feted in Hollywood by Charlie Chaplin and Douglas Fairbanks, Fergie made friends with Sylvester Stallone, the Rambo actor, and Marvin Davis, the oil billionaire turned movie mogul who threw a star-studded dinner party for her at his Beverly Hills home. Both women adored the nightlife in New York.

'Edwina was much tougher than Fergie, rather ill-mannered and bored with her marriage to Mountbatten,' said the royal historian. 'She and Fergie both gave America a whirl for the same reason: to see if they felt any better over there and they probably did. Royalty does very well in America. Edwina was running away from Dickie and, by all accounts, Fergie couldn't stand Andrew or his family.

'It's interesting that one of Edwina's lovers, Hugh Molyneux, was replaced by Laddie Sanford, whom she had met at a party on Long Island. Like Johnny Bryan, he was a polo-playing American with two sisters. She invited him back to the family home in England for her third wedding anniversary, not unlike Bryan turning up at Sunninghill. She really gave Dickie hell. He realised too late that she was openly unfaithful to him and that neither his dignity nor his social standing mattered a damn to her. Andrew's situation wasn't much different. After Dickie found out, he and Edwina agreed to stay together but sleep in separate beds and lead separate lives. Divorce was a nasty word in the Twenties. At least Andrew has his career and his freedom.'

At the height of the emotional trauma, Edwina was struck down by a mystery illness, partly caused by the violent purging she induced to lose weight. Like Fergie she also worried incessantly about her emotional and physical well-being. 'She got better when she devoted herself to good works for the St John's Ambulance Brigade and other charities,' said the royal historian. 'But her affair with Pandit Nehru shows that it didn't make her celibate.'

It was only after Fergie admitted herself to therapy that she was able to accept that her problems were buried deep inside her psyche. By then, the consequences of her actions had affected everyone whose name followed the Queen on the Civil List. 'If you think about the Windsors, they've behaved in the most incredibly tacky way compared with other European royals,' said a disillusioned Sloane Ranger. 'To be quite honest, I think it serves them right. I don't have any sympathies with them at all and I think very few people do.'

Fergie's behaviour had even had damaging repercussions in matters of national interest. Just before the Iraq invasion of Kuwait, Fergie arranged a small dinner party at Buckingham Palace for Steve Wyatt and one of his most influential contacts in the Middle East, Dr Ramzi Salman, head of Iraqi state oil marketing. When news of the *soiree* leaked out, it created an international incident. Members of the Royal Family and the Palace secretariat were appalled that Fergie could have been so indiscreet. The Kuwaiti Royal Family, living in exile in Kensington, were on excellent terms with the House of Windsor.

The matter did not go unnoticed at the headquarters of British Intelligence in Curzon Street, Mayfair. 'You can imagine what happened when they fed Steve Wyatt's name into the computer,' said an expert on Middle Eastern affairs. 'All the bells would have gone off. His stepfather Oscar was a buddy of Saddam Hussein and he was importing vast quantities of oil from Iraq into America. No wonder the Queen was worried.' When a friend in the oil business raised his association with one of Saddam's right hand men with Steve Wyatt, the usually amenable Texan was unforthcoming. 'That,' Steve Wyatt told Dyer O'Connor firmly, 'is a no-go area.'

As fighting broke out in the Gulf War, the *Sunday Times* took the royals to task for their failure to give a lead to the nation. Fergie, in particular, was still pursuing pleasurable activities at this crucial time, jetting off to Switzerland on a skiing holiday and, according to the paper, 'playing with her gang, very publicly, at a high-spirited dinner in a London restaurant'.

Soon afterwards, an executive told the editor, Andrew Neil, that Fergie had approached his wife at a party. 'Can you get News International off my back?' the Duchess enquired. Neil mentioned the incident to Rupert Murdoch, who was unperturbed. According to his butler Philip Townsend, he thought the Queen's daughter-in-law was a 'nice, jolly girl'. 'A few years ago she would have been propping up the bar in a pub,' Murdoch added, 'and you wouldn't have looked twice at her.'

Just about everyone in Britain was looking at her now, thanks to the efforts of her financial adviser.

JOHNNY Bryan was like a man playing Russian Roulette with all the chambers loaded. But after St Tropez, it was discovered that he was mainly firing very noisy blanks. His language, though, could be ballistic. 'She's not some dead common f***ing trashy little model,' he stormed at the height of the *Harpers & Queen* fiasco. 'She's a member of the Royal Family.' Every time he made an utterance on Fergie's behalf, she moved perceptibly closer to the outer darkness. His actions baffled his friends, delighted his enemies and alienated anyone in the middle.

Anthony John Adrian Bryan was born at Wilmington, Delaware, on 30 June, 1955. His father Tony was English by birth but after graduating from the Harvard Business School he started work in America. His mother Lyda, now Mrs Gerry Redmond, was from St Louis, Missouri. Johnny was brought up on Long Island, New York, until his parents divorced in 1964 and he moved to Texas.

Tony's second wife was Josephine Abercrombie, a Houston heiress. This marriage ended in a headline-making divorce when Tony had an affair with Pamela Sakowitz, wife of the apartment store tycoon, Robert Sakowitz. Robert grew suspicious and consulted Oscar Wyatt Junior, his brother-in-law and neighbour in River Oaks Boulevard.

Oscar, whose sons Steve and Douglas were later involved in a long-running legal feud with their uncle over the family fortune, advised him to consult a private eye.

'Robert Sakowitz hired an investigator who had a very sophisticated message interceptor,' said Tom Alexander, Pamela's attorney. 'He put this on the home phone at River Oaks with a relay in the garage. It was plugged into the telephone line and it was voice-activated, which was very unusual at the time.

'Pamela discovered it when she caught him in the garage listening to the tapes. Robert admitted that he was referred to this particular operative by Oscar Wyatt. They were not always such enemies.' Inadvertently, phone-snooping thus made its first appearance in the royal story through the Wyatt-Bryan connection.

Tony married Pamela in 1978, but this marriage was no more successful than the others, it is perhaps no coincidence that his father seemed to single out wealthy, influential and sometimes married women for conquests, me included,' said Pamela from her new home at Squirrel Hill, Pittsburgh, 'I think John has the same approach. I think he is head over heels for her, but I have to say, with regret, that the fact that she is married to the Queen's son and has access to future millions will have helped.'

When Tony got married for the fourth time in May, 1992, one of the guests turned to his daughter Pamela at the reception and said: 'Why isn't Johnny here?'

'Oh, he's helping the Duchess move house into Romenda Lodge,' Pamela replied.

'Hang on, this is his father's wedding,' said the guest, it's not as if she is having to do it with a roof-rack across Fulham. I mean, she has staff to help her do things like that.'

This was precisely why Bryan needed to be on hand. He wanted to be indispensable.

Wyatt had always retained his freedom. 'He was like Paddy McNally,' said a friend. 'She could not get him.' But Bryan had developed a completely different strategy: he was always available, always taking charge. Bald head glistening, he was at the centre of the maelstrom, even if it were largely of his own making. He was the honest broker trying to sort things out as a friend of both Andrew and Fergie or, alternately, the Duchess's financial adviser winning a fair deal for her from the 'arrogant assholes' at Buckingham Palace. 'We all knew what Johnny Bryan was up to ages ago,' said his friend, the *Spectator* columnist Taki. 'All that "financial adviser" stuff had me laughing my socks off.'

Those who were baffled by his hold over the Duchess did not understand her very well. Their relationship had cost Fergie more than one friendship but she seemed oblivious to the dangers. 'She likes being controlled and he would say no where Andrew would never say no,' said a former friend. 'They had a common bond through their family backgrounds. She can twist her father around her little finger – he has no control over her at all – and her mother is more like an old friend. Fergie has never had the security of a proper family life so she looked to other people for it. John Bryan came from a broken home – three, in fact – and he understood her needs. He watched her every move and told her off like a little girl.'

At Balmoral, Diana had warned Fergie that Johnny Bryan was an even worse influence than her father. 'Diana did not spare her feelings,' said a friend. 'She warned her that he was trouble. When Fergie defended him, saying he was fixing up her debts, Diana offered to help in that direction.' Fergie listened reluctantly. 'She feared they would take the children away from her,' said the friend. ' "They're not getting my children," she said – and repeated it over and over again every time Diana suggested she get some professional help.'

Custody was a particularly sensitive issue in Fergie's family. Her father had been granted custody of Fergie and her sister Jane as teenagers after Susie had run off with Hector Barrantes. Jane had lost her children Seamus and Ayesha in a very public divorce in Australia a year earlier. The power of the Palace frightened Fergie once it was explained to her that 'the princesses belong to England'.

'Sarah York is not as tough as Diana,' said one who knows them both. 'Her action was that of a desperate woman trying to save herself. She wanted to be free. It would never have occurred to her that she would be condemned far more viciously than the Princess of Wales.

In the months leading up to the separation, Fergie had taken an active dislike to Diana's squeaky-clean image. She called her Miss Perfect or Miss Goody Two Shoes. 'Fergie was insanely jealous of the Princess of Wales,' said a reliable Sunninghill source. 'She used to watch videos of Diana's news footage and throw things at the television screen. She would scream and shout about her all the time.'

Three days before the St Tropez pictures were published, Diana had addressed a conference on alcohol and drug dependence. 'Addiction is a fast-growing malignancy which destroys almost everything in its path,' she said. 'Addicts can only be successfully helped if they are prepared to tackle reality. They will only try to do that if they believe that there is a chance of succeeding. Sadly, many people still regard addiction as a moral weakness.'

The distressed Duchess could not have had a better counsellor. Diana was speaking with a great deal of practical experience through her role as patron of the Turning Point charity. Diana knew that Fergie's life was out of control and that her mood swings were symptoms of an emotional disturbance. With the Princess's encouragement, she finally took the initiative and began sessions of therapy at the Group Analytic Practice at Paddington in West London.

Her father's problems, however, continued to multiply. He was finally dropped as Prince Charles's polo manager after twenty-one years of unpaid service when the Prince decided to forsake high-goal polo in favour of less competitive matches. By coincidence, Major Ron's affair with the social-climbing brunette Lesley Player had just been revealed in her book *MY STORY: The Duchess of York, Her Father and Me.*

A week after Buckingham Palace announced the Prince's decision, he also quit as sponsorship manager of the Royal County of

Berkshire Polo Club, his only paid job at £36,000 a year. 'I assure you that neither of those situations caused me to make the decision, though I doubt whether anyone will believe me,' he said ruefully. 'I didn't sack him,' said Bryan Morrison, boss of the Royal Berkshire. 'He told me he was going for personal reasons. I wouldn't say he didn't need the money – he probably needs it badly. After Ronnie Ferguson, I just want some peace.'

Matters financial seemed to dog the Ferguson family in every venture they undertook. 'Sarah's image is all she has – we consider it absolutely one hundred per cent her biggest asset,' Johnny Bryan told Vicki Woods, editor of *Harpers & Queen,* reverting to his role as financial adviser. Fergie, he explained, was 'the sole and exclusive owner' of a private company called ASB Publishing, it's a company with only one share and the sole shareholder is the Duchess of York,' he said. 'You want to know why it's called ASB Publishing? A! S! B! Andrew! Sarah! Beatrice! That's what it stands for.' When Ms Woods asked if Prince Andrew was a shareholder, Bryan replied: 'I don't think he's actually a shareholder now. I don't really know, frankly. I don't think that's really relevant. Frankly.' Records at Companies House showed that ASB Publishing, which operated from Bryan's rented apartment, had two directors, Johnny Bryan and James Hughes, one of his American associates.

For a while, Johnny Bryan stopped representing the Duchess and it was believed that their relationship might have reached the end. i prefer to maintain a very low profile for the time being,' he said. As in other areas, his idea of what that constituted was something else. 'I went into Annabel's one night during Ascot Week and saw Fergie and Johnny sitting with four others at a big round table,' said Liz Brewer, it was just inside the door and I noticed them because it was supposed to be my table.' Only days before, the Duchess had been holding hands with Andrew, kissing him fondly and telling everyone that he was the most wonderful man in the world.

To enquiries from friends, Fergie insisted: 'Oh no, John is not around any more.' 'She said this to one girlfriend as she was leaving Romenda Lodge,' said a mutual acquaintance, it was reasonably late at night and once outside the door she realised she had left something behind. She went back and slipped in through a side entrance. When she looked through an open door into the drawing room, there was Fergie kissing Johnny Bryan on the sofa. He had been there all the time.'

As with so many things in her life, the image seemed to matter more than the reality. The apparent signs of a reconciliation with Andrew were no more substantial than that.

Fergie's chance to follow Diana into the Work arrived when she was invited to become a goodwill ambassador to the United Nations' High Commission for Refugees, 'I am honoured and delighted to offer not only my support to the cause of refugees but also my help to raise public awareness about their needs,' she said.

'We have been very impressed by the work of Her Royal Highness and her interest in refugees,' said Madame Sylvana Foa, speaking for the High Commission in Geneva. 'We want someone who has a high profile to help the cause and she was an ideal choice. The Duchess has kept her head up despite all her problems and you have to admire her for that.'

'I'm not just going to be a letterhead,' said Fergie, eagerly grasping the chance. 'I am very, very serious about it. But I won't do anything until I have learned the ropes.'

'There's a warmth about Sarah that is unmistakable,' said Christina Dumond, one of her oldest friends, it's such a shame the public has never known it.'

But even before Fergie could fly to Geneva to collect a UN diplomatic passport, flak jacket and sky-blue beret, her enemies intervened to snatch the prize away. Aware that the Queen was anxious to promote Prince Charles and Princess Anne's trips to the Third World, Sir Robert Fellowes made contact with the Foreign Office. Buckingham Palace's most senior official apparently had little difficulty in convincing Douglas Hurd, the Foreign Secretary, that the appointment was not in the Royal Family's best interests.

So much discreet pressure was brought to bear on the UN agency that it did a swift about-turn and promptly dropped the Duchess from its life-saving endeavours. The UN issued a statement making it clear that it had no further plans to involve her in its work. Fergie was busily working on her suntan in the South of France when she heard about the tactical withdrawal. This was the Good Chap style of government in action and once again she was the victim. 'They wanted to ensure that the Duchess did not embarrass the Royal Family either by her unpredictable behaviour or, Heaven forbid, by upstaging them,' said a Whitehall source. 'The attitude is that if she wants to leave Prince Andrew so badly then she should let go of the royal coat-tails as well.'

Fergie's friend and fellow director of the charity Children In Crisis, Theo Ellert, who meets regularly with her at Romenda Lodge, denied that she was 'looking for personal publicity'. Nor was she lazy. 'The Duchess is one of the busiest people in the world,' she said stoutly. 'Most of her holidays are two days squeezed into the middle of a hectic tour. If a nurse is on night duty, the fact that she puts her feet up on a beach afterwards is not criticised. The fact that the Duchess might do the same is called a holiday. She is a very sensitive person and she has been desperately hurt by the insults and nastiness which are continually thrown at her.'

Fergie's natural generosity always seems to rebound unfavourably. When she bought two hundred teddy bears from Harrods for child victims of the war in Bosnia, she found herself on the receiving end yet again. 'They were paid for by the Duchess out of her own money,' said Ms Ellert. 'They went down wonderfully well.' it's a war-torn, war-damaged country,' remarked Dr John Walmsley of Children In Distress, another charity active in the former Yugoslavia. 'A tin of Spam would have been more appropriate.'

Criticism like this infuriates Fergie. 'I'm a serious person,' she maintained, although she knew in her heart that the public had lost its patience. When she labelled herself 'the scapegoat of the Waleses', she couldn't forget that people treated her royal rival with respect and sympathy. Diana had forged such a strong bond with Douglas Hurd that he overruled his own department whenever they misguidedly tried to give Charles preferential treatment over her.

'Every attempt to starve Diana of the oxygen of publicity has failed,' said the Whitehall source, 'and yet the Duchess has been humiliated at every turn. It seems there isn't room on the world stage for two estranged royal wives.'

Not unnaturally, this upset Fergie and she began to resent the way Diana was being idolised even more. She knew that Diana was far from perfect and that her family were just as mixed up as her own. Why, her own father had even courted Diana's mother before they both entered into calamitous marriages.

15

RELATIVE DESTINY

'You'll cope, I know you can do it'
The Eighth Earl Spencer

THE speed at which Diana drove her red Mercedes northbound on the Ml was indicative of her mood on the morning of 1 April, 1992, the day of her father's funeral. Passing other cars at more than 100 mph in places, the Princess had no need to tell those whose job it was to ensure her safety that she was not merely mournful, but angry. Furthermore, it was not just the 'why my loved one?' variety of anger that went with early grief which was enraging her so. She had left Kensington Palace barely on speaking terms with her husband. Charles had opted for shifting rather than cancelling engagements for the day, clearing a three-hour window in his busy schedule to attend her father's funeral.

It was a bright but bitterly cold morning on which the Spencers gathered in the Northamptonshire village of Great Brington to bid farewell to Johnnie, the illustrious eighth Earl. Television crews, photographers and reporters who had descended the previous day easily outnumbered the local populace lining the route along which the funeral cortege would pass. Their number spilled over into the graveyard of the parish church, St Mary the Virgin. Every available space was filled with the high-tech gadgetry which has become the tools of their trade.

Even above the banter of the newsmen the constant buzzing of mobile telephones could be heard. A group gathered around one familiar Fleet Street royal watcher, kitted out for the job as he considered appropriate in anorak, green field boots and binoculars, and listened intently as he relayed the words being conveyed over his mobile. At the other end of the line was royal spokesman Dickie Arbiter, speaking from his Palace office. The red-faced journalist had attracted the attention of his colleagues by noisily asking Arbiter why Diana had had to drive alone the eighty miles to Althorp House, just a few hundred yards from where this bizarre and impromptu Press conference was being conducted by radio telephone.

He held the instrument away from his ear so that those closest could hear Arbiter explain that it was a very busy day for Prince Charles. In order to attend the funeral at all, His Royal Highness had had to bring forward an eleven a.m. meeting with four or five people and, moreover, he must return to London by mid-afternoon to have tea with the Crown Prince of Bahrain, Sheik Hamad bin Isa al-Khalifa.

At the precise moment the oak coffin containing the body of Earl Spencer was being carried into the church where nineteen generations of his family were commemorated, a rumble in the sky distracted the listeners. Cutting short his phone call, the red-faced one peered through his binoculars and reported to his envious and less well-equipped colleagues that the helicopter hovering over Althorp was a bright red aircraft of the Queen's Flight. He was right. The machine, with Charles at the controls, duly landed close to the matching (though not by choice) sports car in which the mourning Diana had driven herself at such high speed from the same London palace.

Within minutes, a procession of limousines bearing the funeral party had left the great house, travelling across meadows on a private single-track road leading to Great Brington and the South door of St Mary's. The cortege was led by Raine, now the dowager countess, riding in the blue Bentley her husband had presented to her. She was accompanied by the new Earl and his Countess, the former Charles Althorp and Victoria Lockwood. Next came a black Rolls-Royce carrying a sombre Prince Charles and a downcast Diana, who now appeared to be fighting back the tears. A third splendid motor bore her sisters, Lady Jane Fellowes and Lady Sarah McCorquodale.

A cold wind whipped around the northern end of the church and the principal mourners did not pause to acknowledge the crowd being held back by uniformed policemen. It was there that Diana – hauntingly beautiful in a black suit and wide-brimmed hat — finally allowed the first tear to fall just as the organist sounded the opening strains of 'The Lord is My Shepherd'. It was not until a lone trumpeter from Johnnie Spencer's old regiment, the Scots Dragoon Guards, played a lament that she allowed herself to return the glances of her assembled relatives. The family of the man at her side cared little for these people. This was, in many respects, a family at war and her in-laws knew it.

When, as a much younger child, Prince William had shown signs of being hyperactive, the Queen had worried that the problem might be more serious and deep-rooted. His grandmother's fears were ungrounded.

Relieved that she had spared her young sons the ordeal of attending the funeral, Diana looked around from her seat in the choir stalls at the faces in the nave of the church. This was indeed a troubled family, particularly on her mother's side. Her favourite uncle Edmund, the Lord Fermoy, had shot himself at his 700-acre estate, Eddington House, close to the Berkshire town of Hungerford. The forty-five-year-old former steeplechase rider, who had taken it upon himself to vouch for Diana's virginity at the time of her engagement, had suffered a long period of depression prior to his tragic death in August, 1984 – the month before she gave birth to Harry.

Despite an apparently happy marriage to the former Lavinia Pitman (of the shorthand family), His Lordship had taken to seeking affection at the Wigmore Club.

A few days before Fermoy's suicide, friends were invited to shoot pheasant at his home. 'When we arrived, his two boys, both prep school age, were playing Space Invaders but they came out to do the beating,' said one of the party, it was only a rough shoot and quite relaxed until we went inside to lunch. It became very sticky because I noticed that Lord Fermoy wasn't joining in the conversation. He just wouldn't speak and you could tell something was wrong.' Whatever it was that troubled him, Lord Fermoy ended his own life on a bed of straw in the stables, a servant finding his pyjama-clad body.

The same year tragedy struck the family again when Anthony Berry, the Conservative MP married to Diana's Aunt Mary, was killed in the IRA bombing of the Grand Hotel at Brighton which was intended to assassinate the Prime Minister, Margaret Thatcher. No one had needed to tell Diana that the hapless marriage of her mother's sister was all but over when the tragedy occurred. It came as no surprise to her when Rheinhold Bartz, married to the Berrys' eldest daughter Alexandra, later declared: 'Mary had already given him his marching orders. He never forgave her for making a fool of him – perhaps that's why he started drinking too much. Just a month before his death he was disqualified for drink driving.'

Aunt Mary's marital fortunes fared no better when she tried again — and again. Her second husband Denis Gulgan joined a silent monastic order soon after she instructed him to leave her house four years after he had made her his bride. Groom number three, Michael Gunningham, was given his marching orders as he shaved on the morning after they had dined with the Queen of Denmark. Gunningham subsequently tried to kill himself with a drugs overdose at Broadfield Hall Farm, their home in Hertfordshire, but as a *cri de coeur,* his bid was unsuccessful in all respects, for he neither ended his misery nor won back his wife's affections.

Beneath the vaulted ceiling of St Mary's, Lord St John of Fawsley, the former Minister of Arts Norman St John Stevas, stepped up to the lectern to deliver his address. The family had ensured the presence of key reporters and Lord Fawsley, the nation's leading Roman Catholic layman, knew a headline-making opportunity when he saw one. 'Of course there is bickering in every family,' he told his mainly Anglican congregation. 'Birds twitter and peck in their nests, be they large or small. And if the nest is gilded it is sometimes bathed in the glare of media light. . .'

The light which Diana had brought to bear on her troubled family was brilliant indeed and would, she knew, grow even brighter in the weeks ahead. The one man whose counsel she might have sought was now dead before her. She could not turn to her husband: to dance with the man who had brought her to the dance was no longer an option.

As the Nineties dawned, talk in the smarter drawing rooms of England had been divided between the problems in the Spencer family and wicked speculation concerning the Princess's amorous adventures.

Never far from their lips was the eccentricity of Diana's late great-aunt who, according to Rheinhold Bartz, was prone to appearing nude in front of eminent visitors to Broadfield Hall including, on one notable occasion, the Queen's friend Prince Georg of Denmark.

Such behaviour particularly embarrassed Ruth, Lady Fermoy. It was Ruth who had given shattering evidence during Johnnie Spencer's divorce that her daughter, who had gone off with a man who made wallpaper, was not a suitable mother. The testimony ensured that Frances lost custody of Diana, Sarah, Jane and Charles. Frances never forgave her mother and the two women did not speak to each other for the next ten years. They were seen to exchange a few brief words at the memorial service for Lord Fermoy, but had no more than kept up appearances at Diana's wedding to Charles. No wonder Ruth expressed neither surprise nor sympathy when Frances's second marriage to Peter Shand Kydd also ended unhappily.

Memories of such old wounds hung heavily in the air as Charles, the new Earl Spencer, paid respects to his predecessor beneath the roof of St Mary on that early spring day. Not once did those in immediate view see him exchange a glance with his royal namesake and brother-in-law. Spencer was painfully aware that he had become a figure of ridicule within the Royal Family since owning up to an extra-marital affair while his wife was expecting their first child.

Just six months after he had taken Victoria only unto him at a splendid service in this very church on 16 September, 1989, he had whisked an old flame, the gangly journalist Sally Ann Lasson, to Paris for an adulterous weekend. He had first met her four years earlier when Ms Lasson – then married to the songwriter Dominic King – interviewed him at her home for the *Sunday Times.* Ms Lasson, daughter of the noted art dealer Hans Kryvovias-Lasson, said they became lovers two years later and, by her own admission, was somewhat put out when the most eligible bachelor in the land chose to marry Victoria Lockwood whose father worked for the Civil Aviation Authority as personnel director. One month after Victoria gave birth to their first daughter Kitty in January 1991, Sally Ann sold to the *News of the World* her story of a romantic reunion with Charles the previous year. The revelation sent shock waves through the Spencer family, particularly, said a female member of their set, in view of Victoria's pregnancy at the time of his infidelity.

'Having a man's child,' said the friend, 'is the biggest compliment a woman can pay him. It's got to be the biggest ego boost going for a woman to love a man so much that she wants to take an essence of him and reproduce it.'

According to the published account, the thirty-two-year-old divorcee was at her flat in Egerton Gardens, Knightsbridge, when she received a telephone call from Althorp. He told her he was miserable and asked her if she would run away with him. They flew to Paris that same evening, 28 March, 1990. Detailing even the journey, Lasson recalled: 'Charles knew how frightened I was to fly so he kissed me constantly from Heathrow to Charles de Gaulle airport. Except, that is, when I was drinking champagne which was terribly romantic.' That night they dined by candlelight in a suitably romantic restaurant and Lasson said she was 'so crazy with excitement to have my boy back, I could hardly eat'. Having managed some nourishment, however, the pair went back to the Hotel Balzac and made love.

According to more than one of Diana's friends, it was only after consulting her 'in a state of some distress', that Althorp decided to make a clean breast of the matter. In a statement he maintained that he had a 'one-night stand' with Sally Ann in September 1986, and during the following eighteen months she telephoned him with 'obsessive messages'. His barbed statement continued: 'Ms Lasson was extremely jealous when I got engaged and married to Victoria in a whirlwind romance and she made it clear that she had always wanted to be my wife — a thought that had never occurred to me. In February and March 1990, my wife and I went through an extremely messy patch in our marriage and a separation seemed possible. I talked to Ms Lasson about my marital problems – a foolish move in retrospect but, with a failed marriage behind her, I thought she might be in a positive position to give advice.'

The heir to one of Britain's most distinguished titles went on to admit to the Paris episode, 'after a particularly unpleasant series of quarrels with my wife,' and to describe it ungallantly as an experience that 'so sickened me, I did not stay a second night in Paris but returned to London, eager to patch up my marriage'.

If the ninth Earl Spencer was turning the matter over in his mind as he faced the first major family gathering since his ordeal by newsprint, then he may well have recalled his last words on the subject to his unwanted lover after she informed him that she had sold her story: 'You'll be the loser – you're stuffed!'

EDWARD John Spencer was the son of parents who had long served as courtiers. Educated at Eton and Sandhurst, he managed a mention in dispatches during World War II despite the brevity of his military career. He had been *aide-de-camp* to the Governor of South

Australia from 1947 to 1950 when he became equerry to King George VI. He continued in that post under the Queen for another two years, also acting as Master of the Household on a Commonwealth tour.

On the surface he was a man born into greatness who shouldered his own responsibilities so well that monarchs could depend on him to help run their show. Underneath it was a very different story. Johnnie's father Jack, the seventh Earl, was a difficult man who found it hard to relate to others. In the case of his son and heir, this shortcoming transformed itself into bullying. The man who was to father the girl who would marry England's next king became so confused about his role in life that his fellow officers in the Royal Scots Greys regarded him as the stupidest soldier in their midst. He was a powerfully placed man who did not know how to assert himself in the simplest of tasks. Nevertheless, his credentials were exemplary even if many of the seeds of wisdom sewn into him during his schooldays had come from his multi-faulted godfather, the Prince of Wales, briefly King Edward VIII. Although shortage of money forced him to give up his unpaid court duties in 1954, Johnnie's distinguished career of service to the Crown had by then placed him in a position of power and influence over many who served the Sovereign in more humble capacities.

As Charles Spencer stepped forward to deliver a reading from Corinthians over his father's remains, he surveyed those members of the congregation who were now *his* employees, a number of the Althorp estate workers. He was aware that many of them regarded him as an impetuous young man and were worried about how drastically he would reverse changes which his father and stepmother had instituted. It was common knowledge that Charles objected to many of the money-making schemes Raine had talked Johnnie into setting up at Althorp, and in view of the way he had voiced his objections, particularly over disposal of some of the family treasures, it was expected that he would assert all his rights under the English law of primogeniture.

The gilded nest had certainly been rich in treasures. Many of the fine contents of Althorp House had been inherited, bought and set in order by Jack, a notable collector and connoisseur. Even after the erosions of the previous seventeen years, many still remained. Although paintings by Van Dyck and Gainsborough, silver ornaments and even solid gold ice pails had gone, immense prizes of wealth and privilege remained, not least among them Reynolds' portraits of three generations of Spencers and Van Dyck's masterpiece, *War and Peace.*

Although his father had left him an estate worth £89 million, young Spencer still faced the prospect of selling off more family treasures to raise death duties of around £4 million. The paradox of being rich in treasures but badly off in cash terms was one the English aristocracy had had to come to terms with, particularly in lines such as the Spencers where the forebears had bought land in preference to property. Never one to enjoy cavorting with the common herd, however, the new lord was already considering plans to restore his family's privacy by closing Althorp to the public, putting an end to the £2.95 tours which allowed any Tom, Dick or Hank to peer inside the Spencers' cosseted world.

Nicknamed Champagne Charlie by his friends, he had become a career journalist, working as a British-based TV reporter for the American network, NBC. Colleagues could not remember him being noted for his compassionate views and expressed no surprise when he later marvelled at Diana's generosity of spirit. In an observation that said more about himself than it did about his sister, he noted: 'I think it must be very difficult each day to give so much of yourself, of your soul to so many people and not feel in a way that as you've given a great deal, therefore you deserve love and warmth when you go home.' Such remarks sounded alarm bells in the head of Prince Charles. Diana's campaign manager was warming up.

Spencer went on to say: 'I certainly try, when I speak to her on the telephone, to reassure her about how much she is loved, too.' He did not mention that the telephone consolation was a two-way technique but a friend of her husband's later imparted that Diana was forever making bedtime calls to her brother to talk him through some new emotional crisis. Notwithstanding the Sally Ann Lasson escapade, events in his marriage had not been all smoothness and light and Victoria enjoyed town life as much as he loved the country.

Since *Tatler* had chosen her as its Girl of the Year when she was just seventeen, Victoria had been thrown into a jet-set lifestyle she greatly enjoyed. They toasted her arrival in New York, and in Paris she was welcomed with a contract from the premier modelling agency FAN. Dawn Rothstein, a partner in the agency, sang her praises thus: 'She quite simply had the most beautiful face in the world. She was a little short for the catwalk but she worked with most of the top photographers and appeared on countless magazine covers.'

So adapting to life at the Falconry, the Althorps' cottage set amid the peaceful 13,000 acres of his father's estate, proved a testing experience for the high-spirited young bride, and she frequently engineered ways for the pair of them to escape back to London. On one notable occasion, Charles took her to Annabel's where new money rubs shoulders with old tradition. According to a report at the time, the Marlboro-smoking model tugged her somewhat reluctant marquess on to the dance floor, but after a few blasts of nondescript toe-dancing he returned to their table. Left to her own devices, Victoria marched up to a party of estate agents and their friends and asked them: 'Do you know who I am?' The answer from one of the younger members of the group was affirmative and she and he then danced enthusiastically, enjoying a late evening of companionship during which she acquired the appellation 'My Little Ballerina'.

Commenting on how much closer she had seemed to her brother than to her husband, one Spencer friend added that Diana understood him far better than his own wife did. It would take an understanding woman indeed to tolerate his affection for Darius Guppy, the fraudster who had been best man at Charles and Victoria's wedding when Prince Charles and Diana were among the guests and Prince Harry was a pageboy. Even tolerant Diana saw the warning signs when she heard that, following the *News of the World's* publication of Sally Ann Lasson's story, Guppy had vowed to have the paper's owner, Rupert Murdoch, assassinated. The media tycoon was not on record as saying that he slept easier in his bed after Guppy was sentenced to five years in prison for conspiracy to defraud, conspiracy to steal and false accounting, but it was a safe assumption. Murdoch was promised a further three years freedom from concern about Guppy unless the convicted man located £533,000 from his ill-gotten gains and paid it over in fines within six months of his sentencing in March 1993.

With the Spencers promising to look after his pregnant wife Patricia, Guppy was led from the dock to begin a jail term that would allow him ample time to reflect on his life as the closest friend of the man whose sister had married the heir to the throne. His own father, whose grandfather gave the family name to the fish and whose great-grandfather was a confidant of Dickens, had lost large amounts through a Lloyd's syndicate. Determined not to go through life in impoverished circumstances, Darius always had a money-making scheme or two up his sleeve.

It might have been a financial struggle for his parents, Nicholas and Shusha Guppy, to send Darius to Eton but a less sensitive couple might have considered their investment worthwhile when he befriended Charles Althorp. The two went on to Oxford together and buoyed by his friendship with the future earl, Guppy set about becoming a student celebrity with an almost unheard of sense of vengeance. By promising the incumbent editor introductions to pretty girls (a promise like others he failed to deliver), Guppy manoeuvred a takeover of the university's satirical magazine *Tributary* and shared its editorship with Althorp. The move was the foundation of Althorp's journalistic career and he grew to be as impressed with Guppy as the latter was obsessed with English aristocracy. To please his titled friend, Guppy learned to shoot and Althorp would take him round his father's estate at night in a Land Rover killing rabbits. Darius, by one account, would 'fire away like Rambo'.

Althorp's love of outrageous people in spite of his father's warnings drew him closer and closer to Guppy. He even saved Guppy from being beaten up during an excursion into the town of Oxford – just one of the actions for which Guppy intended to thank His Lordship during his best man's speech at Althorp's wedding breakfast. Unfortunately, an attack of nerves at the prospect of addressing an assembly which included the future king and queen of England ultimately prevented the best man from saying anything at all.

After his university days it had been downhill all the way for the doe-eyed graduate who was certainly clever enough to have earned a good living, but could not bear the ignominy of working his way up in the world like ordinary people had to do. It was in the autumn of 1989, so fateful to the Royal Family's fortunes, that Guppy put the final touch to a fantastic plan for what he called the perfect crime. It involved staging a fake armed robbery of sapphires, rubies and emeralds in the heart of New York, claiming back £1.8 million insurance from Lloyd's and salting the proceeds into Swiss bank accounts. The crime was executed in room 1207 of the Halloran Hotel in mid-town Manhattan and when police from the city's Seventeenth Precinct arrived they found Guppy weeping alongside his accomplice, Ben Marsh.

Within three weeks of the insurance payout, in a classic double sting, Guppy and Marsh plundered their own gemstone company of two-thirds of the money, siphoning off at least £500,000 to a bank account in Geneva. Wanting still more, they clumsily circulated the 'stolen' jewels back on the market, making a further £400,000. Another accomplice betrayed the pair, turning Queen's evidence after serving eighteen months for his part in the crime.

In choosing such an unstable character as Guppy to be his close friend and best man, Charles had unwittingly allowed his family to be sullied by association with a wretched criminal.

ONCE the Bishop of Stockwood had delivered his blessing and released Johnnie Spencer's remains to rest among his ancestors, Diana took his widow's arm and helped her to the door where photographers recorded the touching reunion in grief. Raine looked down at the bouquet of white lilies and sweet peas at her feet and smiled as she read the handwritten card: 'I miss you dreadfully Darling Daddy, but will love you forever. . . Diana'. It was recorded as the moment that ended fifteen years of feuding between the two most important women in Johnnie Spencer's life. But not everyone was fooled.

Back at Althorp House, Diana's mood changed dramatically. Knowing that her stepmother had repaired to her boudoir, the Princess sat talking with her brother and sisters in the Tapestry Room. When Raine came downstairs and entered the room, the stepdaughter who had shown her such touching affection in front of the cameras just an hour earlier turned on her heels and walked out of the house to stand beside the ornamental lake. Raine went back to her room and wept. Little wonder Prince Charles had removed himself from the midst of the feuding Spencers by climbing into his scarlet flying machine and returning to London to keep his tea date with Sheik Hamad bin Isa al-Khalifa.

The animosity which Diana, her sisters and brother had shown towards Raine boiled over on the very day of Lord Spencer's death, Sunday, 30 March. Staff at Althorp House, summoned to a meeting to be informed of their master's passing, were also told in no uncertain terms that his widow was no longer welcome in the house. Soon after the funeral, Diana personally inspected Raine's luggage before it was taken out through a side door. Despite holding riches few in the world could match, she could not bear to think of Raine possessing anything of her father's that now belonged to her, her sisters and brother. She ordered a maid to open the four Louis Vuitton suitcases Johnnie had bought for their world tour the previous year so that she could examine the contents. Then, noticing that two pieces of the luggage bore the initial 'S', Diana took a view that they must have been her father's share of the luggage set and told the distressed servant to transfer their contents to black plastic bin liners and return the cases to the master's quarters. Diana even insisted that Raine mark those items of furniture and effects which were hers, so that they could be inspected before the removal men transferred them to her house in Mayfair. Staff at the ancestral home had become unused to seeing (let alone receiving orders from) the Princess. So much did she dislike Raine's company that she had stayed at Althorp on only a handful of occasions in the preceding five years and even then such visits usually ended in strife.

When she did stay on the weekend of her brother's wedding, Diana fell out with Raine over the sleeping arrangements for William and Harry. The Countess had put them in the nursery but Diana wanted them closer to her own quarters. When an argument broke out, servants heard the Countess loudly insist: 'This is my house and those are the rooms I have given you.' Declaring 'Right, that's it. I've had enough, I'm off,' Diana dashed down into the courtyard and told her detective to fetch her car. Another vehicle blocking the way gave her a few moments to defuse her anger and return to the house, but the noisy sequence of events was witnessed by several members of the household who were by now convinced that Diana's serene public image was something of a sham. As on so many occasions, she got her way and her room was changed although the atmosphere was loaded with prickly hate for the remainder of her stay.

No wonder few had seen the slightest nod of assent from Diana when Lord St John had told the funeral congregation that Johnnie might have died fourteen years earlier had it not been for the 'devotion, care and commonsense of his wife Raine who was leading them in their mourning and rejoicing'.

The good lord chose to ignore whatever he had heard about Raine being Diana's *bete noire* in much the same manner as Diana paid no heed to his subsequent call that the dowager countess should be canonised. That was no way to talk of a woman who Diana had once pushed down a short flight of Althorp stairs then neatly side-stepped her as she lay on the floor, frightened and shocked, to march off without so much as a backward glance. 'What has happened to Diana?' Raine later asked her personal assistant and trusted confidante, Sue Ingram. 'I just do not understand that girl.'

What had happened to Diana was that Raine had had the temerity to marry her father. The Spencer children had all been disturbed in varying degrees by the noisy rows between their mother and father. Diana was just six when Frances walked out on Johnnie and only seven when the whole sad business of their bitter parting was publicly aired in a messy and painful divorce.

If not perhaps a marriage wholly made in heaven, the nuptials which united Johnnie and Frances had certainly been most grandly sealed in society terms. The Queen, Prince Philip and the Queen Mother were among 1,700 guests who attended the wedding at Westminster Abbey and a reception at St James's Palace for 900. The death of Frances's father, the fourth Baron Fermoy, allowed his widow to turn Park House on the Sandringham estate over to them. Frances gave birth to her first child, Sarah, almost nine months to the day after their wedding, and Jane followed soon after. It was the loss of a third child, a male, just ten hours after birth that sparked a change in Johnnie's attitude to Frances. Nevertheless, the need to breed prevailed and Diana Frances followed on 1 July, 1961, and finally Charles, the much wanted heir, three years later.

Her friends needed no especially keen sense to detect that ten years into the marriage, Frances had lost her respect for Johnnie and there was plenty of gossip about his sudden rages. During expeditions to enjoy some social life in London she met Peter Shand Kydd at a dinner party. He was everything that Johnnie was not: a rough diamond and a natural extrovert. Shand Kydd had inherited his family's wallpaper business – a trade that did not sit well with Lady Fermoy's grandiose ideas for her daughter – and was married to the artist Janet Monro Kerr by whom he had three children.

During a skiing holiday on which they had persuaded both their spouses to join them, Frances and Peter discovered that they were hopelessly in love and at the age of forty-two (Frances was thirty-one) he left his wife. They arranged clandestine meetings at an address in West London not far from the apartment block in Earl's Court where Diana was living when Prince Charles courted her.

When Frances finally walked out of Althorp saying she wanted a trial separation, Sarah and Jane were away at boarding school and she took Diana and Charles with her.

By the time they returned for a sham celebration of the Christmas festivities, however, Spencer had summoned some inner strength and refused to allow his wife to take the two youngest children away again. They fought, and she lost, a bitter custody battle behind closed doors in the Family Division of the High Court.

She went back into battle in a scandalous divorce action in the spring of 1969 and was devastated when she lost again. In those times it was rare for custody of the children to be given to a father but her allegation of cruelty in the marriage was unproven whereas his of her adultery was indefensible since she had been named as the other woman in the successful case brought by Mrs Peter Shand Kydd the first.

The domestic strife in these times of battle played heavily on Diana's mind and brought on her life-threatening illness, *bulimia nervosa*. A series of nannies – more than one of whom bullied her and Charles – and medical advisers were unable to repair the damage and the Earl had to accept the fact that the failure of his marriage had seriously disturbed his daughter. The seeds of her nightmare had been sewn.

Brought up in the traditional unhealthy way of the British aristocracy, he had been taught to conceal his own emotions and was totally ill-equipped to guide Diana through puberty. Whenever a crisis arose he took the easy way out. 'You'll cope, I know you can do it,' was one of his favourite remarks, flattering but unhelpful. Then, just at the time when she most needed her father, the chocolate box figure of Raine arrived on the scene to take him away. Diana's fury was matched only by her spite for what she saw as the grandiosity of a woman who could not abide traffic jams and would have had her chauffeur drive on the pavement if he could.

BORN on 9 September, 1929, the daughter of Barbara and Alexander McCorquodale (of the wealthy printing family), Raine knew full well what it was to come from a broken home. But whatever the imbalance in her own psyche it was the very reverse of Diana's. She had been brought up by her imperious and socially ambitious mother who as Barbara Cartland was the creator of slushy romantic fiction which was to form a central part of Diana's literary diet. Her parents were divorced when she was just four with Barbara declaring that Alexander was 'a drinker and not a good lover. He left when Raine was very small. She loved him very much but hardly saw him.'

No shrinking violet, Raine's strong will, combined with an ingrained need to feel important, served her in good stead during her formative years. She paid a great deal of attention to her appearance, especially her hair. Wartime rationing being what it had been, she was used to wearing other people's clothes, but the garments, she had been known to point out, always belonged to the *right* other people.

The lessons in elocution and deportment she had received at Mrs Fyffe's School in London, later relocated to Cambridgeshire, served her well in her quest for a life of grandeur to which the compelling Ms Cartland clearly believed they were entitled. Harry Hull, the taxi driver paid four pounds to drive Raine the twenty-four miles to school and back each day, remembered her as 'a bit of a haughty thing' who said she would have preferred him to wear a uniform. The finer points of her education for life were taken care of at lightning speed at a finishing school in the Bernese Oberland town of Murren.

As the debutante Miss Raine McCorquodale, she had been noticed by the mothers of several prominent young men since her coming-out on the lawn of Buckingham Palace on the afternoon of 28 May, 1947. Wearing a second-hand dress bought for five pounds ('Well, it was by Molyneux,' she later protested), Raine underwent the Monarch's inspection ceremony, as was required by young ladies of her day whose parents expected them to marry into fashionable society. So striking a young lady was she perceived at the King's review of the '47 crop and at the forty dances she attended, that Raine was named Debutante of the Year – a title Diana never allowed her to forget.

Raine had known what it was to be pursued by men since the age of sixteen when she received her first marriage proposal from the

Italian doctor treating her adolescent boils. She explained to the foreign medic that the painful memory of her parents' split had made her frightened of marriage. Fearful or not, within a year of rejecting him, she had captured her first husband, Mr Gerald Legge, on the ski slopes of Switzerland.

In a masterpiece of planning, though hardly a subtle manoeuvre, her mother gave a dinner party for twenty-four before Raine's coming-out dance and apart from Raine, her mother and grandmother, all the guests were men. The audition was unnecessary, the cast had already been decided: Raine had fallen for Gerald Legge in what she described as their 'incredibly romantic' mountain-top meeting, and he became a regular visitor to River Cottage, the 400-year-old thatched house at Great Barford in Bedfordshire where she lived with her mother, nursemaid, lady's maid, nanny and Barbara's female secretary.

As the future Earl of Dartmouth and a member of a wealthy family, Gerald was considered eminently suitable for a place in her heart and at the tender age of eighteen she was allowed to marry him. Although not every man found her as bewitching – more than one cad complained aloud of her 'awful teeth and bad breath' – Legge had not been without competition and had she paid more attention to the overtures of Oliver (Viscount) Lymington, she might well have gone on to become the Duchess of Portsmouth. His inadequate health put paid to the prospect.

Attended by no less than sixteen bridesmaids, Raine became Mrs Gerald Legge in a service at St Margaret's, Westminster. She wore a grand tiara loaned by family friend Lady Patricia Lennox-Boyd for the grandest of receptions which was staged at Londonderry House. Lord Mountbatten was among the guests and the wedding presents on display included a set of graduated bows of diamonds from the bridegroom's uncle and aunt, the Earl and Countess of Dartmouth, and a five-strand pearl bracelet with aquamarine clasp and a white fox cape from her mother.

Dividing her time between her husband's penthouse suite atop the Metropole Hotel in Brighton, the country manor in Chipperfield, Hertfordshire, and a Mayfair town house, she progressed, as her husband's relatives died, from being Mrs Legge through Lady Lewisham to the Countess of Dartmouth.

One who remembers her through those heady days, recalled: it was as if she always wanted to create a lasting impression which was all part of her curious charm. Raine appears to be a very vain woman. She likes to show herself and her things off. I remember going round to her home in Mayfair when she was married to Lord Dartmouth. She had a child late in life and made a big point of the pram sailing through the drawing room so everyone could admire her and the child. The house was very stylishly furnished with great attention to detail. Everything was perfect – a very gracious London home. Everyone seemed to take to her simply because she was so likable, although I imagine if you crossed her she would put her foot down and blow you up.'

In recognition of her charitable works William Douglas-Home (brother of Sir Alec who became Prime Minister) wrote a poem for her called *Lovely Lady Lewisham* and, unhindered by an unfortunate singing voice, Raine recorded a lyric written by her mother called *I'm In Love.*

Ms Cartland remained a power to be reckoned with in her life. The Marquess of Bath (then the thirty-four-year-old Viscount Weymouth) recalled: 'I remember being summoned by Barbara to take tea at her house and sitting next to her very nervous daughter, Raine Legge as she then was. I made what was probably a sexist remark and Barbara admonished me by insisting that the woman was the truly dominant member of any family. When I dared to argue the point she rolled up a copy of *The Times* and beat me over the head with it. Poor Raine sat there and said nothing. I was glad to get home to Longleat.'

She bore Dartmouth four children, William, Rupert, Henry and Charlotte, before their seemingly blissful union came to a sudden end. No one but the parties themselves knew what really went wrong inside the marriage. Through Gerald, she had met Johnnie Spencer, who was available following the unseemly defection of Frances. Not only did Earl Spencer need a wife, but his awesome Althorp needed a mistress. The house was dirty and badly run and the finances were in such an awful state that there was never enough money to pay the wages on a Friday. Raine decided to arrange her own fee-less transfer from one earl to the next. Used to speedy processes, she sensed this had to be yet another one, lest his daughters try to dissuade him from the match.

Whatever pressures Diana, Jane and Sarah did bring to bear, her marriage to Johnnie Spencer was largely a happy one, and when it ended in his death she tried to fill the vacuum by experimenting with a number of new liaisons, assuring friends that she would marry again within the year.

There was a flicker of romance with the mega-rich cereals millionaire Francis Kellogg who was besotted by her, according to his friends. Dame Barbara said: 'I think she needs to marry. She is not a person who would ever choose to live alone. But I am sure it will not be Francis Kellogg. He is far too old for her.' What's more, said the Dame choosing to disregard the Duchess of Windsor's view that 'one can never be too rich', Raine didn't need Kellogg's money: 'She has plenty of her own.'

Travelling widely through Europe and the United States, she arrived at one point on her journey in the principality of Monaco to visit friends. It was there, within the set year of Johnnie Spencer's demise, that Raine found a husband to succeed him. At sixty-two, the chocolate box widow had arrived at the door of marital experience yet again thanks to a dinner party encounter in Monte Carlo with Jean-Francois, the Count de Chambrun. The one dinner progressed to another in Antibes and the old electricity began to crackle. 'You know that lovely thing when you look across a room,' she later remarked like a starry-eyed teenager in a suite at the Connaught Hotel in London.

After the second dinner, they had sat up talking well into the small hours, and then the telephone calls started. He rang twice the next day and three times the day after that. When she returned to England, he continued his siege by fax, telling her that he could not wait for her return to France in the company of the woman she describes as 'my totally best friend', Therese Lawson, wife of the former Chancellor, Lord Lawson. The pushy suitor duly arrived in England and Raine took him to stay at the house Lord Spencer had bought her by the sea at Bognor and to visit various friends who, she said, were all entranced by him.

When word reached Diana of the match, she appeared disinterested. As a child she had prayed 'Raine, Raine, go away' so many times that she might have been relieved her prayers had finally been answered. This, after all, was the woman who had even made her father sell his surplus suits alongside tacky souvenirs in the

Althorp gift shop. Nevertheless, the Princess told a lady-in-waiting that she had been 'amused' to discover her stepmother's suitor was not all he might have been. His water filtration company, CHF International, had made just forty pounds profit in the year prior to his meeting the wealthy widow Spencer, the family seat had been sold off and the cost of maintaining his chateau in the south of France was barely met by the cost of letting the place to paying guests. To raise further funds, 4,000 square metres of the grounds surrounding his Chateau Garibondy, near Cannes, had been sold off for the building of low cost houses and flats.

Times had indeed been hard for de Chambrun since French divorce laws had forced him to buy out his former wife's fifty per cent share of the chateau when they separated. The house had belonged to her family, but he wanted to keep it more than she did. When Josaleen, the ex-wife, went to live in Paris, the Count was left with a renovation bill in excess of £1 million and in the three years prior to meeting Raine his charges for letting it out had been £15,950 a week in the high season and £11,500 at other times. The family seat at Marvejols, Nimes, was sold at public auction after his brother Charles, then a National Front mayor, ran into debt and the bank had taken the furniture away.

Unperturbed by any financial clouds on the Count's horizon, Raine enjoyed the new courtship and accompanied him back to the Chateau Garibondy where she weighed up its possibilities for improvement once he had put a stop to his bed-and-breakfast venture. Then, travelling the scenic route home, they drove to Paris ignoring the torrential rain that marred their view of the Massif Central where they stayed overnight at the Hotel Panoramique. Even being compelled to dine in a downmarket cafe wreathed in Galloises fumes, when every better restaurant was closed, failed to daunt the spirits of the woman Diana once pronounced as 'too grand for us'.

In Paris they stayed at her old friend Mohammed Al-Fayed's Ritz Hotel, lunched with Liliane de Rothschild (who found Jean-Francois 'divine') and visited Place des Vosges where the Count de Chambrun proposed marriage and the Princess of Wales's stepmother accepted. Mindful of the pain she had suffered at the hands of her stepchildren, she told her suitor, before accepting his proposal: if there is the slightest *frisson* of disapproval from your children, I take to the hills. I tried so hard with those Spencers and I cannot go through that again.'

Back in London she warned her fiancé how intrusive the Press could be but after the paparazzi's most alert member, Jason Fraser, found them browsing in a village antique shop, he entered into the spirit of the publicity circus and told reporters that they had already enjoyed the honeymoon. It was the sort of confession that fifty years earlier would have required Raine to send a written apology to her mother, but the dowager countess merely nodded in agreement and said, 'Well at our advanced age, no one would think we'd just held hands'.

Her plans for her new home were already advanced: it's so funny, I had said never an old house again,' she told the writer Valerie Grove, I don't want to know about leaking roofs and guttering. But I have started rearranging his house – I can't help it, I always do it – and don't you think it's a scream, I said, "Where's the library?" And there isn't one! So we are making one upstairs and this sounds terribly bossyboots but he says he'll do the outside and I'll do the inside which is so divine because that's what Johnnie used to say. I am not into gardening – or dogs since I was bitten by Mummy's horrible Cairn in the nursery.'

Jean-Francois had met the essential qualifications required by Raine. He did not smoke, he was not ill-tempered and he was full of compliments. She had sorely missed Johnnie's courtesies: 'You know what one misses most? When you're dressing to go out and say, "Shall I wear the red or the blue? And how do I look?" And Johnnie would murmur, "You're always the best." '

The published remark did not sit well with Diana who had always believed her father when he told her that *she* was 'the best'. So Raine, Raine had not gone away after all. The woman who had blocked her from her father just when she needed his loving counsel over her failing marriage was still around. For Diana, there could never be a man to replace Johnnie Spencer and when the woman who had taken him from her found another on whom to shower her affections, it did not seem a time to celebrate. Nevertheless, knowing what a fuss the Press would make if she ignored it, Diana instructed a secretary to send flowers. Biting on the bullet, she also invited the newly engaged couple to lunch at Kensington Palace, just the three of them.

'After the coffee HRH took Raine by the hand and said to her, "Raine, thank you so much for the love you gave my father over all those years," ' Jean-Francois was moved to write to *The Times* about the touching reunion he witnessed. 'Raine and HRH fell into each other's arms and they kissed goodbye in the most affectionate way.'

Goodbye was to be the operative word.

16

EDWARD THE CARESSER

'How would you feel if someone said you were gay?'
Prince Edward

PRINCE Edward had a good eye for an actress. Diana, he decided, was one of the best he had ever seen after watching some of her performances with professional detachment. The Princess called her youngest brother-in-law Scooter, which was kinder than the nickname his colleagues at the Palace Theatre gave him. There, he was known as 'Barbara' after the comedienne Barbara Windsor.

Edward Antony Richard Louis is the most enigmatic of the Windsor children. Single in status and single-minded in purpose, he perplexes people who try to categorise him according to his family's known traits. As he wasn't Action Man like Charles at the same age nor Randy Andy like his other philandering brother, he didn't fit easily into an identifiable male slot. *The Sun* decided that at twenty-five he was 'a lonely misfit' and, in the absence of any evidence to the contrary, declared: 'He does not even seem to be sowing his wild oats as both Charles and Andrew did at his age with a succession of beauties. He has lived the life of a monk, more chaste than chased and seldom, if ever, chasing anything but himself.'

The insinuation was that because he wasn't robustly masculine, he must be secretly gay. But anyone who dined with him at Manzi's, the seafood restaurant in Soho, or mixed with him at parties inside Harrods and elsewhere, knew that he was a nice man and a good companion. In truth, the only reason he hadn't married was, according to a friend, that he was wary about asking anyone to join the Family.

Edward is not only the youngest of the Queen's children, he is also the sharpest. As an observer of the royal world, he has seen every single royal marriage, apart from that of his parents, break up untidily and unhappily. Mark Phillips had been the first to explain to him how difficult it was for an outsider to survive among the

Windsors. The experiences of Diana and Fergie had merely confirmed his brother-in-law's view.

Edward had also learned from the highly publicised mistakes that Charles and Andrew had made before marriage that flings with available women tended to end in big headlines. 'Affable, intelligent and thoughtful' in the words of one former girlfriend, he managed to avoid detection until years after he lost his virginity at the age of sixteen.

Once he overcame a natural shyness and a tendency to blush easily, he discovered that he was attractive to girls of his own generation. Quietly, he became Edward the Caresser, previously the title of his namesake, the more openly libidinous Edward VII. One of Edward's endearing tactics was to invite a new girlfriend to guess the colour of his eyes. Invariably, they said blue. Invited to take a closer look, they noted that the corner of his left eye was, in fact, green.

'No way is he gay – I know that for a fact!' said one of his girlfriends, the blonde television presenter Ulrika Jonsson. 'People misunderstand me,' said Edward. 'They don't know anything about me, apart from listening to lies and distortions, yet they are quick to make judgements.'

Romy Adlington was making her name as a model when the nineteen-year-old Prince invited her out to dinner. She claims that she was responsible for introducing Edward to sex one passionate night at Buckingham Palace. Her assertion raised the intriguing possibility that he might have misled her into believing he was still a virgin. Certainly, he was adept at two-timing his partners. As his eighteen-month affair with Romy drew to a close at Balmoral in 1985, a replacement was already in transit.

'The day I left, another girlfriend of Edward's turned up twenty-four hours earlier than originally intended,' she said. 'The Queen, Philip and Charles had waited up and shortly before eleven p.m. the other girl arrived. This girl was obviously new because when she came in she made straight for a chair which *nobody* sits in – I think it was the one used by Queen Victoria. The poor girl didn't know, of course, but just as she went to sit down, Prince Charles grabbed her in mid-air and said, "Sorry, not that one".'

In his thirtieth year, Edward dated the singer and dancer Ruthie Henshall, who starred in the hit musical *Crazy for You.* But his real love interest was a Sloane Ranger unconnected with the theatre who worked in Knightsbridge and saw him privately.

The sexual conundrum had been brought out into the open in April 1990 when a gossip columnist hinted that Edward had a 'touching' friendship with Michael Ball, the leading man in *Aspects of Love.* Edward flew to New York for the show's Broadway premiere and, when a foreign correspondent approached him at the first night party, he decided it was time to speak in his own defence.

'It's just outrageous to suggest that sort of thing,' the Prince said with controlled fury as other partygoers tried to eavesdrop without spilling their champagne, it's so unfair to me and my family. How would you feel if someone said you were gay? The rumours are preposterous. I am not gay but what can I do about it? The Press has to be a lot more responsible. I just wish I could be left to enjoy what I do.'

Wisely side-stepping a career in the Royal Marines, Edward had become the first royal to find a job outside the armed forces when he joined Andrew Lloyd Webber's Really Useful Group as a production assistant in January 1988. The theatre was Edward's real love and he fought a valiant battle to take his place in the wings. After two years learning the craft, he felt he was ready for bigger things.

When Bridget 'Biddy' Hayward, Lloyd Webber's executive director, broke away to form a new theatre production group with a coterie of other defectors, Edward threw himself into the enterprise. Part of his job was to recruit 'angels' who were willing to risk their money in the commercially treacherous quicksands of the West End. His name undoubtedly had something to do with his success in raising capital, although there was never any suggestion that the Royal Family would underwrite the venture.

As its first show, the company, Theatre Division, planned to stage a 1950 comedy called *The Rehearsal* by the French dramatist Jean Anouilh. One of the first people Edward recruited was Michael Winner, the *Death Wish* film-maker who was also sympathetic towards the living theatre. 'Prince Edward wrote to me and asked me to invest in a new play,' remembered Winner. 'He said, "All this is going to be wonderful. We'll make a fortune." Edward, I said, you are going to lose everything. No company can keep offices and all the staff to put plays on in the West End because it's a very rough business.'

Edward, however, had a stubborn streak and he persisted with the hard sell. Starring Nicola Pagett, *The Rehearsal* opened to mixed reviews at the Garrick Theatre in November 1990 and closed without covering its costs. 'Bless him, I was slightly wrong,' said Winner. 'I think we lost eighty per cent of our money.'

Taking *The Rehearsal's* title at face value, Edward the impresario pressed ahead with the fledgling company's next show, a play called *Same Old Moon* by Dublin-born playwright Geraldine Aron, which he had recommended himself. 'We lost the rest of the money and, after that, the company ran out of funds and vanished,' explained Winner. 'Edward is a very nice person, a decent kid, and he took it philosophically.' Theatre Division went down with debts of £600,000 and Edward devoted his extra time to royal duties, particularly promoting and fund raising for the Duke of Edinburgh's Award Scheme.

When Charles and Andrew's marriages failed in 1992, Edward was cast in the role of troubleshooter if not exactly peacemaker. Shrewder than most people credited, he was the only royal who could talk to the estranged couples as individuals. Moreover, his natural inclination to be non-judgemental and non-malicious made it easier for him to avoid taking sides. He found it difficult, however, to trust Diana.

Although his views remained strictly private, a friend of the Prince said: 'Her behaviour is quite conspicuous of what she's about. She is everything you have probably realised: calculating, self-preserving and absolutely the best actress in the world. The best way to illustrate this was her performance at a funeral I attended. In front of the church where the cameras were on her she was tearful and sad and moving-all those things. The moment she was out of the camera's range she was bubbling and cheerful and full of life. I was watching her very closely and when she went back to the family house, she was so up and full of beans that it had to be seen to be believed. I just noticed a spectacular difference in her performance in front of the camera and then off it. Okay, sure – funerals aren't supposed to be particularly morbid, but at the same time I think she went over the top.'

Edward had been present at Balmoral at the end of the royal honeymoon in 1981. His new sister-in-law's behaviour towards Charles had deeply upset him. He had heard the rows coming from their bedroom and seen the furniture which had been broken during one showdown. It was, he told a friend, a rotten advertisement for marriage.

Although he readily became a favourite uncle to William and Harry and often visited Kensington Palace, Edward was saddened by Charles's unhappiness. He noted that the elder brother he admired so much cheered up whenever Camilla or Kanga were on the scene, either at Balmoral or Sandringham. He knew what was going on in Diana's marriage and he didn't try to interfere.

As the youngest, Edward hadn't been spoiled like Andrew, who was four years older, while Charles, fifteen years his senior, was dealing with more grown-up matters at Gordonstoun before he could even crawl. The Queen was thirty-seven when he was born, and had the opportunity to spend more time with the new baby. She had ensured that he enjoyed relative anonymity until he followed his brothers to Gordonstoun. But Edward felt the sibling rivalry all the more keenly because of the targets the others had set for him. Unsure of his position, he was intrigued by brotherly relations in other families.

He never forgot a visit he made to Longleat, the Marquess of Bath's stately home in Wiltshire. 'He came down with the Queen and Prince Philip for the 400th anniversary, but the date was far from precise because my father had missed it and had to invent one,' said Alexander, Viscount Weymouth, who succeeded his father's title in 1992. 'As we took them on a guided tour, Prince Philip looked up at one of the ceilings and asked, "Is that part of the original Elizabethan house?" I said, "Oh no, that's much more recent." Whereupon my younger brother Christopher said in excited tones that it was, in fact, the original. This blazing row flared up between us. Seven years later, Edward came down on a visit and he remembered the occasion vividly. He called it "that awful row you and your brother had in front of my parents". He obviously identified with it in his own family.'

In fact, Edward outshone both Charles and Andrew academically. He passed nine O levels and gained A levels in English, history, and economics and politics. He played Rugby and squash, sailed well and took part in the school's dramatic productions. In his last term, he was made Guardian, or head boy. He earned his glider wings after his first solo flight in 1980 and two years later qualified for a private pilot's licence in a Bulldog two-seater piston-engined trainer.

As he travelled the world in his father's name, he showed that he was dependable and wise beyond his years. The Duke of Edinburgh gave him more responsibility and noted proudly that the 'afterthought' in his family had turned out well. His new nickname was Rock Steady Eddie. When Romy Adlington sold the story of their romance to the *Sunday Mirror*, he was able to shrug it off as nothing more serious than an occupational hazard of being a prince.

IF Edward needed any further confirmation of the perils involved in bringing an outsider into the Family, it came soon after the Palace announced that Viscount Linley had finally chosen a bride from among his many girlfriends. Fifth in line to the throne when he was born, David Linley had wooed a number of leggy blondes before he proposed to Serena Stanhope, daughter of Charles, Viscount Petersham, heir to William the eleventh Earl of Harrington, an extremely wealthy London property owner.

When she first came to public attention as a Linley interest, Serena was described by a one-time escort, the photographer 'Prince' Hannibal, as 'a bubbly girl who loves to laugh and never sulks'. He also expressed surprise about a revealing dress she had worn on a night out with Linley: 'She must have chosen that dress to please him. She was always very conservatively dressed when we went out.'

Unlike many of Linley's previous loves whose pedigrees lay chiefly in their fathers' business acumen, Serena came from a family which could trace its ancestry back to Charles II and, in the sixteenth century, to the Earls of Bedford, Huntingdon and Worcester as well as Ferdinand I, the Holy Roman Emperor. A noble ancestry, however, did not protect her from the slings and arrows of former suitors and one crawled out of the woodwork on Independence Day in 1993 to offer a lurid description of their affair across two pages of the *People*. Selling what the newspaper described as her 'secret sexy past' was one Alexander Slack, who had been introduced to the heiress by her elder brother William in 1989 when she was just nineteen.

Readers of the Sunday newspaper were treated to a detailed account of how the girl who was to marry the Queen's nephew had made love with Slack in a number of public spaces, including the great squares of Kensington and Chelsea. 'Serena obviously felt like making love and we didn't need an excuse. It was a case of just passion and realising that if we went home we could not get any privacy,' claimed the former commodity broker. Serena was spared nothing. Slack said that they had even made love at her home in the bed her father normally shared with her stepmother, Anita Fugeslang, the former wife of the Earl of Suffolk and Berkshire whom Viscount Petersham had married aboard a yacht off the coast of Fiji.

Slack maintained that in an effort to portray Serena as 'a lily-white princess', he had been wiped out of her past as if he had never existed and that he was hurt. In fact, his own life was in a certain amount of disarray. Six months earlier he had married Diana's cousin, the banking heiress Katie Baring, and the marriage had already foundered when he became a kiss-and-telltale. Published four days after she and her fiancé joined Diana at a high society party in Mayfair, the story certainly hurt Serena, but perhaps even more damaging was the photograph of her which covered the *People's* front page. She was pictured lying asleep on a floor in a black mini-dress that exposed gaping holes in her tights. One of the newspaper's executives said that Hannibal had taken the photograph, something he denied. 'No, that is nothing to do with me,' he said. 'The picture was taken in my flat but I didn't give it to anyone. I don't know why it got into the hands of whoever.' In any event, the paper demanded £5,000 from anyone wishing to reprint the photograph elsewhere.

Linley's love for Serena had blossomed the previous summer on an excursion to the home in Monte Carlo of her mother, the former showjumper Virginia Freeman-Jackson. Unsure at that stage of his intentions, he had telephoned another old flame, Stephanie Struthers, an account executive at the J. Walter Thompson advertising agency, to ask her out two days before his departure. 'Stephanie said he sounded hurt when she declined his invitation,' said a chum of Ms Struthers. 'He asked her, "Have you got anyone else on the go?" When she answered, "No, have you?" he replied, "Oh, I've got about four on the go at the moment." '

Coming from a broken home, Serena was well placed to handle such crises of confidence in Princess Margaret's son. When the time came to deal with the likes of Alexander Slack, David Linley was as supportive as a royal groom could be. Besides, he had not flinched when another ex, the stunning Susannah Constantine, had teased him with tales of her flings during their repeatedly on-off affair.

What Serena didn't know about the royals from her family she picked up from one of her friends, Santa Palmer-Tomkinson, daughter of Prince Charles's close pals, Charles and Patty.

Anyone less versed in royal mores might have been shocked by what happened the night she accompanied her fiancé to Tiffany's.

17

SUPPER AT TIFFANY'S

'This woman is just trying to create an image at the expense of her husband — it's wicked'

FREE of the husband one royal had dubbed The Thinker, Diana allowed herself a wry smile as she passed the gilded, near-naked body of a male model posing as a living reproduction of the Rodin sculpture. The eve of her thirty-second birthday, a hot midsummer's night, found the People's Princess at Tiffany's in Bond Street, Mayfair.

The London branch of the New York emporium was packed with rich and titled customers, carefully vetted so that Diana's secret visit might exclude the idly curious. Her appearance, though, still created excitement among the exquisitely dressed women taking supper at Tiffany's from dainty packets of fish and chips. Caught completely off guard, those in her path dropped into unrehearsed curtsies as Diana swept past. Others jostled forward for a better view. To catch the Princess of Wales, the most famous woman in the world, in person at the height of the Season was better than attending Oscar night in Hollywood.

Seemingly oblivious to the chaos her unexpected arrival had caused, Diana ignored the sound of breaking champagne flutes and the well meant greetings of complete strangers. As though anticipating her reception, she was dressed to kill, her make-up applied so heavily it looked like war paint.

When she passed The Thinker on a staircase on her way to inspect Jean Schlumberger's newest designs on the upper sales floor, it was impossible to tell whether she blushed. She probably didn't. The misty Gainsborough bride of 1981 was just a photographic memory on someone's mantelpiece. Similarly, Shy Di, the 'Gosh, Golly, Help, Panic!' Princess of a decade earlier, had been totally banished from her life – and so had the embarrassing Squidgy. On show in this jewelled temple was a woman of Substance who outwardly sparkled like the magnificent sapphire, encircled with diamonds, which shone from her seven-strand pearl choker. To best display the massive gem, she had selected a figure-hugging short-sleeved dress of midnight blue with a scooped neckline. If Charles was The Thinker, Diana in this phase of her metamorphosis was The Presence, an unmissable figure who glowed with an aura that was electrifying.

The stylish event had been organised with almost military attention to detail by Rosa Monckton, Tiffany's managing director and wife of the *Spectator* editor, Dominic Lawson. Rosa had promised her royal guest that no one, not even key members of her staff, would be warned that she was coming.

Clearly having decided that this birthay was a milestone in her new life, Diana was cramming high-society events in between her official duties. She was sending signals to anyone who cared to notice that even a novice Mother Teresa could also enjoy the finer things that life had to offer. Earlier in the day she had led local dignitaries through the narrow alleys of the Ely housing estate in Cardiff to open a new playground and, aware that feelings were running high about a local man murdered by vandals, she had instructed a policewoman to place a bouquet of flowers at the spot where the tragedy occurred. The Work done, Diana had transformed herself for the Tiffany's bash, where she greeted old chums in a voice that showed none of the exaggerated inflections she had mastered for her public speaking.

Rosa, whose grandfather, the first Viscount Monckton, had drafted King Edward VIII's abdication speech and actually led him to the microphone to make it, remained constantly at her side. But she gave no sign that she was in the company of one who some considered a royal outcast. On the contrary, Rosa was noticeably proud that Diana saw her as a close and trusted friend.

A winning smile on her face, the Princess towered over the diminutive Hong Kong Governor Chris Patten as his daughter Laura bowed her head and curtsied low between showcases displaying life's greater luxuries. Pausing on the stairs to take another look at the painted male model, Diana returned to the ground floor, which was now seething with anticipation. There she greeted such social luminaries as the actor Derek Nimmo, the actress Sian Phillips, the inventor Sir Clive Sinclair, the Marquess of Blandford's sister Lady

Henrietta Spencer-Churchill and Lady Edith Foxwell. Rosa led the Princess to a screened off area at the back of the salon and when one guest tried to follow, Diana's tall but youthful-looking detective barred the way. it's security, Madam,' explained a member of staff, hastily briefed about what to say. 'Her Royal Highness is wearing an extremely valuable sapphire.' But it was doubtful that Diana's desire for a little privacy had anything to do with the fear of armed robbery. Now that she could establish her own boundaries, she liked some space for herself even in an exclusive setting like Tiffany's.

Behind the screen, Diana set up her court and awaited another royal arrival, Viscount Linley, who pressed through the throng with Lynn Wyatt, mother of Steve, at his side. Her hair smartly coiffed, the blonde Texas rose was a woman whose looks belied her sixty-three years, 'I am very impressed,' she told Linley as she took in the scene. Uncomfortably out of place in dinner jacket and black tie, he guided her past a line of waiters dressed in exotic eastern costumes and bearing bowls of strawberries and cream.

Trailing behind as though she had arrived quite by accident was Princess Margaret's prospective daughter-in-law, Serena Stanhope, so recently a new star in the royal tableau. She clutched at the lapels of her jacket to conceal the plunging neckline of the black cocktail dress she wore beneath it. The future viscountess had been left to find her own way through the partygoers to the screened off VIP suite.

The Ely estate in Cardiff was a world away as, two-by-two, the most celebrated guests were allowed briefly through a gap in the screen to pay homage to the Princess. The chosen few did not include another tall and slim blonde: Cazzy Neville, the girl whose hard work in consoling Prince Andrew over his broken marriage had marked her out as a potential royal rival for a brief time.

Dazzled by Diana's star, few of those assembled at Tiffany's spared a thought for her husband, who had tactfully left town before the birthday celebrations began. He had refused to respond in even the mildest way to the aspersions that had ripped his private world to shreds. His silence baffled and infuriated people who had watched his progress ever since he was born. 'Charles is behaving like a jerk.' Lady Edith Foxwell said bluntly. 'He should stand up and say, "I'm sorry about what happened, but I'm your future King." He has all those advantages, why not get up and say something?'

Through his chink in the parapet near Euston Station, Andrew Morton watched the Prince's movements with professional interest. 'Prince Charles lost a lot of ground both morally and in terms of his popularity with the Camillagate tape,' he said. 'Everything Diana had said to her friends was bloody well right because her suspicions have been vindicated about Camilla. But the strategy of the Prince of Wales camp is absolutely right. They hope that time will heal, that people will forget about it and that people will accept that this was just a late-night conversation between two lovers. That's what they are hoping, obviously, but there are a lot of people who just feel they won't forget about it.'

Frustrated as Charles's friends were by what they regarded as a character assassination carried out with his wife's connivance, they respected his wishes not to answer back in his defence. Serious charges, however, had been levelled against him as a husband, a father and a man, and no account of the tumultuous events of 1992-93 would have been balanced or complete without an honest response from someone who knew the truth as Charles saw it. One of his most intimate friends finally broke ranks to provide some informed guidance. She insisted, however, that she was not speaking at the Prince's instigation in answering a series of key questions put to her by the authors.

Did Diana attempt suicide by throwing herself down a staircase at Sandringham when she was pregnant with William?

'I find it very hard to believe. Has anybody in history taken their own life by falling downstairs? Perhaps there was an attempt to attract attention which would tie in with the way this story was told for publication.'

Did Charles ever produce his diary during their honeymoon, only for photographs of Camilla to fall out in front of Diana?

'Again, you only have her word for it. But it would be so out of character for him that I would be very, very surprised if there was any truth in it. As he was travelling, there is always the possibility that he might have been carrying some pictures of a number of his friends. But I am very, very suspicious about this story, partly because I know that in the time leading up to the marriage and for quite a long time into it he did everything he could to try and make it work.

'Diana, on the other hand, did very little. For example, I learned not only to cook but also to fish so that I could be with my husband during his recreational activities. It's important to do things out of the house and build up the relationship that you had before marriage. You know, you can say, "Isn't that upstream wind a killer?" and you're sharing an experience with your man.

'So I think he tried very hard to include her in many ways and a lot more effort could have been made on her part. If you know that your man likes fishing and shooting, his liking for those things doesn't suddenly end when you walk up the aisle, especially if you've got other responsibilities like he has. It's not enough to just sit round a dinner table chattering – those outdoor activities are very important.

'They are also very private moments. You are not just out of the public eye but out of the house and away from the staff. It's terrific quality time. Standing in a grass butt in the hills for hours waiting for the pheasants to rise is a wonderful time for two people in their kind of position to be together and relax. But she never wanted to be part of that, she made no effort and I find that very sad. Polo, fishing, hunting and shooting are his interests and she always knew that. I haven't seen any marriage work in these circles where the wife hasn't shared the husband's activities.'

Diana has let it be known that her grandmother Lady Fermoy warned her of 'difficulties' if she married Charles. Do you know anything of this?

'Lady Fermoy was a very nice lady and of course she might have warned her granddaughter that marrying a man in his position would bring special problems. When Charles asked her to marry him, he said: "You must understand that it will not be an easy life and I must ask you to think very carefully before you give me your answer." But there is no doubt that she'd set her cap at him and she wasn't going to be put off even though it might be for her own good.

'Several years ago Tina Brown wrote an article in *Vanity Fair* which was headlined *THE MOUSE THAT ROARED*. Tina told me at the time that the article would have London in uproar and that her name would be mud for pointing out that Diana was beginning to change. But how right Tina was. It was the first indication that this shy, sweet, gentle girl had changed.'

Diana's friends, talking with her approval, said that Charles used cufflinks with the two letter 'C's intertwined and that they had been a gift from Camilla. Did they ever exist?

'I've certainly never seen them, but if they ever did exist what makes her think they were from Camilla? They could have been his own initial repeated. How did she know they were from Camilla? Did she find a card? Does she go round constantly opening boxes and picking up telephone extensions overhearing conversations? If your paranoia is such that you want to believe bad of someone, you will always find something that confirms your suspicions. She is supposed to have picked up a telephone and heard him talking to Mrs Parker Bowles during a Mediterranean cruise. Well I'm not going to go into details of how their telephones work, but believe me that's just not possible.'

Diana's messengers say that she sees Clarence House as the 'font of all negative comment' and that the Queen Mother drives a wedge between her and the Royal Family. What is your opinion of that?

'Queen Elizabeth is one of the wisest, most intelligent ladies I have ever come across. I know her very, very well and there has been no greater supporter for anyone than she has been. She has always put the monarchy before her own life. Anyone would be very fortunate to have the benefit of her advice, but of course it's no good if you're not going to listen to it.'

Diana is said to have overheard a conversation Charles was conducting from his bathtub in which she claims that he said, 'I will always love you' and that he was talking to Camilla. True or false?

It sounds like the fantasy of an unwell mind. Yet again you only have her word for it.'

Diana is also said to have confronted Camilla at her sister Annabel Elliot's fortieth birthday party and asked her to leave Charles alone. Did it happen?

'Something did happen that night. I'm sorry, I can't tell you what. We will just have to leave it there, I'm afraid.'

Diana's confidant James Gilbey told Andrew Morton: 'She thinks he is a bad father, a selfish father, he will never compromise. That's why she gets so sad when he gets photographed riding with the children at Sandringham.' What comment would you make on that?

'A classic example of what we are talking about here was the photographs taken of Harry at some car racing event just the other day. The Prince of Wales does not arrange photo calls for the media to show whether he's a good father or not. I think he is an extremely good father. I can tell you that he loves those boys very, very much and in the past he has wanted to spend more time with them than he has been allowed to.'

Is it true that Prince Philip wrote an angry letter to Diana?

'That is nobody else's business. What you have to ask yourself is, "Why has she made this an issue?" What is the point in making public that kind of information?'

Another biographer says that Prince Charles broke down in tears when Camilla's father Bruce Shand gave him a dressing down about their relationship.

'Was the biographer there? To my knowledge Bruce has never said this took place and I find it very hard to believe that a man who has been brought up with such self-control as Charles has would suddenly burst into tears in the manner prescribed. It is highly unlikely to say the least.

The same author claims that Charles and Camilla slept together at Buckingham Palace two nights before he married Diana. True or false?

'I have to reiterate that before and after the marriage, Charles worked at it very hard at making it work and did nothing to endanger it.'

Has Diana ever admitted to Charles that she cooperated with Morton?

'I very much doubt it.'

It would appear that Diana felt the need to get certain things published when she learned that there was a danger that the recording of her intimate telephone conversation with James Gilbey might be made public. What is your reaction?

If that is so, then she obviously felt the need to control what was going on for her own purposes. But to make it appear that Charles was behaving badly at a point when he was doing everything he could to make marriage to her work, is unforgivable. This woman is just trying to create an image for herself at the expense of her husband – it's wicked.

'What makes me cross is that since all the fuss blew up it has been said that there were two camps and this one was saying this and that one was saying that. Those of us close to him said nothing because that was the way he wanted it. He has behaved like a true gentleman.

It doesn't take a genius to see that she has used the media. The obvious example is the way all the newspapers were tipped off that she was going round to Carolyn Bartholomew's house at a time when the book came out. Knowing that there were photographers waiting outside, she gave her that kiss. What greater lengths could you go to in order to sanction all the things that had been said against her husband – in her name – than that?

'He is just not the sort of person to respond to that kind of character assassination. He believes that if you are happy with yourself, satisfied that you have done what you can, then you will be seen for what you are and you don't have to put on an act.'

Nor is Diana without other critics who mistrust the lead she is giving. Marcelle d'Argy Smith of *Cosmo* said: 'I think she is very dangerous for women because the signals are very clear – grow up tall, look good and you can marry a prince. It is the non-working, tall blonde syndrome and there are millions of them in different guises. Some are Susan Sangster, some are Diana – but they are all the same woman. She might personally be nice but that's not the point. Take this thing about charity work. Millions of people do charity work but they actually do it, they mop up the spit and the sick. Millions of women in this country do all the schlepping and carrying for the elderly and the sick. I just find it odd that we need this goddess figure.'

DIANA was among only friends when she sat down to enjoy her birthday dinner. The low key event was staged in a private room at the Ivy, one of theatreland's most popular restaurants on the border of Soho and Covent Garden. She ended a hearty meal by slicing into a pink-iced birthday cake. At her side was a man who knew all about food – Simon Slater, owner of two West London restaurants she favoured from time to time, Launceston Place and Kensington Place.

Initial reports almost inevitably linked Diana with Slater, a bespectacled figure in the Philip Dunne mould.

But the restaurateur was more interested in one of the seven other guests, Kate Menzies, heiress to the £37 million newsagents fortune. A former girlfriend of David Linley, Kate had been introduced to Diana by Fergie who told her that Diana needed some social life while Charles was away. Subsequently Kate had taken over Fergie's job as the Fixer finding suitable dinner parties for the Princess to attend and discreet escorts to accompany her.

Across London, the Yorks were staging another episode in the bizarre chapter of their own failed union. Just three days after Buckingham Palace had announced that their separation was permanent and intimated that an early divorce was on the cards, Andrew and Fergie turned up at Carlyle Square in Chelsea appearing for all the world like a pair of blissfully happy newly-weds.

The Duchess always enjoyed a party and Sir David Frost's annual shindig for some of the nation's most high profile citizens was an occasion which pleased her. Politicians including Lord Owen, Lord Tebbit, Norman Lamont and William Waldegrave rubbed shoulders with showbusiness stars Sean Connery, Michael Palin, Terry Wogan and Sir John Mills.

No one ventured to ask Fergie about the overall financial settlement Johnny Bryan had helped work out for her with the Queen's lawyers. Reports of it varied between £1 million and £4 million, but if Princess Ferguson (as Sarah Kennedy liked to refer to her) was as disappointed with the pay-off as the commentators claimed, she was not allowing it to spoil her evening.

Another contentious issue was whether she would still be addressed as Her Royal Highness after a divorce. Constitutional experts argued that although the Queen could technically strip her of the HRH title, she was likely to keep it unless she remarried. 'Notably unstuffy,' wrote one observer, 'she prefers to introduce herself as Sarah anyway.' Nothing could have been further from reality: the woman whose father insisted on being addressed as Major Ronald Ferguson long after he had left the Army, wallowed in the grandeur that marriage had bestowed on her. Her behaviour may have been closer to that of the much maligned Essex Girl of popular disdain, but Fergie even insisted that Johnny Bryan refer to 'Her Royal Highness' when discussing her with others.

No one was standing on such ceremony, however, as beaming Fergie, wearing a pink jacket over her short white party dress, chatted amiably with Frost and his wife Lady Carina before crossing the specially sealed-off square to greet David Linley and his bride-to-be. By now, Serena Stanhope was getting into the swing of the travelling royal circus.

Of all the complex family problems facing the Queen, the relationship of Andrew and Fergie was the most baffling. She knew through her intelligence sources that Fergie was still entertaining Johnny Bryan, but her son continued to make every effort to remain a loyal husband and doting father although his wife had humiliated him once again with her demand that the separation should be made formal. Even while she was applying pressure on Buckingham Palace to discount a reconciliation, Fergie insisted that she and Andrew should appear in public as if all was well. Princess Beatrice's school sports day was an ideal opportunity for her to demonstrate that, while she had her freedom, she also had her husband on hand whenever required.

It had been fifteen months since they went their separate ways and yet Andrew and Fergie still put on a convincing display of Happy Families. Andrew picked up Princess Eugenie to watch Fergie run barefoot in the mothers' race and then removed his jacket to compete against the fathers. They achieved a mixed bag of results: the Duchess won her heat in the mothers' event but an unfit Duke struggled to come third in his race after picking up a pole he was meant to dodge. Beatrice came in last in her hula-hoop race despite cries of encouragement from Eugenie. The Queen cannot have been the only one to wonder what awful secret condemned them to live apart when, on that afternoon in June, they looked happier to be with each other than many of the parents still united by their marital vows.

'I just take every day as it comes,' the Duchess told viewers of ITN in yet another attempt to explain her actions, 'I love being with my children as much as I can be now, which is much more than I used to be which is great for the children because they see me more and that works very well, so that's good. Andrew and I speak every day and it's very important that we do to keep that friendship.'

What had happened, she said, had made her 'very much more thoughtful, very much more aware of trying to control my spontaneity a little bit so I won't fall into the awful great big Pooh traps in which the ramifications are too much for me to cope with.'

Returning to a familiar theme, she added: 'I have made huge faults *(sic)*. Don't we all make mistakes? Everyone's got to live and learn, get on with life. My life is very much just seeing each day how it is, helping people as much as possible, looking after my girls.

Hopefully in the months to come the laughter and the joy will come springing back into it.'

ON the night of Tuesday, 9 June, Diana had knelt in prayer with Mother Teresa at Kensington Palace. Afterwards, Mother Teresa would say only: 'She was as I know her,' but the canny missionary was well aware that her royal protégée was in need of guidance about what lay ahead.

Neatly side-stepping Royal Ascot, the Princess drove herself from the splendour of Kensington Palace to Refuge, a hostel in West London for battered wives. Installed as its patron, she had been visiting the hostel for eighteen months, giving money to help fund operations ever since she discovered that depleted finances threatened the sanctuary with closure. Sandra Horley, the director of Refuge, was as proud of the royal association as she was grateful for it: 'She is one of the country's most influential people. Her support shows that stopping domestic violence is a worthwhile cause. It boosts the morale of women who are trapped in their homes and feel isolated and rejected, and reduces the stigma attached to their problems.'

In a more private capacity, she might have added that Diana needed her meetings with the women every bit as much as they needed her support. They had, in a sense, restored her to normality. That Saturday morning, Diana joined in a group therapy session, sharing her own problems with the other female victims of failed relationships as she had on a number of previous occasions.

This time, however, things were different. She and the other women had agreed to the discussion being filmed for Channel 4's *First Sex* programme. While the cameras whirred, Diana confessed that her own life was flooded with negative thoughts. If at times she sounded more counsellor than counselled, then the TV presence was almost certainly to blame. To Sandra Horley, who was leading the group, she said: 'When I came here last time, we did a group session and you asked all the ladies to name something positive they'd done in the week and it was quite a stumbling block for some of us. People had to really think. If you asked what negative aspects there had been you would have been flooded. Because it was positive we all had to think hard. Don't you remember?' She asked one woman: 'Don't you think it's positive coming here and sharing something

341

which has been hurting for so long?' and turning to another, added: 'We do, don't we?'

When one girl stumbled over a word to describe how different she felt from her friends, Diana came up with one that was close to her own feelings: isolated. Then, turning to another woman, she demonstrated how she remembered their stories by saying: 'Last time, you were saying one minute he'd be hitting you and the next he'd be crying. Then you'd have to be the mother, having been the abused wife beforehand. You remember saying that?' Before she left the shelter, everyone involved was sworn to secrecy about the programme which was to be shown a few nights later.

The Buckingham Palace Press Office went out of its way to let it be known that Diana's venture had the full support of Her Majesty's courtiers. A spokesman stressed that it would be 'unwise' to read anything sinister into her support for a battered wives' group, adding: 'The Princess helps leprosy victims and AIDS victims without suffering from either disease.' The Work did much to boost the caring image which Mother Teresa had helped her to foster, if you want self-esteem, do something estimable' had proved to be a solid piece of advice.

Not everyone who came in contact with Diana considered her views as valid as Sandra Horley. The film producer Michael Winner said: 'I think she is as nutty as a fruit cake but I admire her because she carries eccentricity to its extreme and I don't mind that. She has got this marvellous front she puts on and she has a wonderful volatile girl behind it. She really is two people, a female Jekyll and Hyde. That's what she is, I know she is. I know people and I am categorical about this. The other side (of her) which has been hinted at is this very, very emotional erratic behaviour, this very wild behaviour – almost maniacal. I think she plays a part every time she is out in the public arena. She is playing a role and I think she plays it brilliantly.'

Winner concluded: 'Of course there is heartache underneath it. She married a man who was cold and indifferent to her and she was quite a warm-hearted person. I feel it was unfortunate because I think he thought he was doing his duty and she thought she was getting a husband. It is understandable that she became what she became.'

There were indications that the new Diana might be due in part to a secret return to the healing hands and therapeutic thoughts of

Stephen Twigg, who had been sacked by Buckingham Palace in spectacular fashion the previous summer. Already worried about his influence over the Princess, the courtiers had been horrified to read his highly paid account of how she was faring just a year earlier.

'The solution to the royal marriage problem is likely to be a lot quicker than we think,' he told writer Shirley Flack just an hour after leaving the Princess's side at Kensington Palace. 'Diana is ready to take charge of her life for the first time. The problem must not be allowed to disappear through indifference. She is in perfect shape – the best she has been. She has, in fact, never been healthier, never been stronger emotionally, nor more able to deal with the turbulent events of her life. Diana is a balanced, healthy and mature young woman.'

To the alarm of the Palace secretariat, Twigg had given credence to the stories about his client's attempted suicides by referring to them as cries for help, it could happen to anyone. In getting to that point, in realising and acknowledging that there was a problem, she had the courage to seek help. When she came to me, it was very clear that there was a problem and I was aware from the moment I began working on her that these deep problems were based on attitudes and beliefs in her psyche.' Describing the framework he established for her recovery, Twigg commented: 'She entered into that with me specifically to work her way out of the hole she had dug herself. A hole dug unknowingly because it came from her background, her experience before she was married and during her marriage.'

It seemed inconceivable that she could ever return to his care after such a high profile dismissal by the Palace itself and yet a year later Matthew Freud, his former public relations adviser, admitted that the sacking was 'partially a diplomatic move of Diana's'. A source had told Freud that two or three months after ending the association, Diana might have quietly re-engaged the therapist. 'My guess is that she has ... I think that's quite likely,' he said. When Twigg was asked if it were true his royal client had indeed returned to him, he became suddenly modest. 'I've got no comment to make about that,' he told the authors.

Three days before Diana was to leave for what had been billed as The Suffering Tour of Africa, Lady Fermoy had died at her home in Eaton Square, aged eighty-four. The loss of her kind though not uncritical granny meant that Diana had to let go of another link with the past. They had mended a rift which followed the separation. 'Ruth has been appalled by what she sees as Diana's refusal to put duty before her own wishes,' a close friend said at the time. 'She feels that Diana ought to have accepted the Queen's suggestion that she and Charles should appear in public and lead separate private lives, rather than officially separate.'

Along with her brother and sisters, Diana showed no inclination to attend a belated party at the Paris Ritz to celebrate Raine Spencer's engagement, and the most royal guest at Raine's bash turned out to be the heir to the defunct French throne, Prince Henri of Orleans. The event, costing £25,000, was staged in the shadow of Dame Barbara Cartland's ominous warning that her daughter's marriage to the Count Jean-Francois de Chambrun might not have a happy ending.

Diana had no such reservations. None of the Spencer children attended the civil ceremony at Westminster Register Office or the blessing which followed in a church two days later. Even Dame Barbara, emerging from the tiny sixteenth-century Holy Trinity Church in the village of Cold Ashton near Bath, said that she was only there 'because I got into trouble for missing Johnnie Spencer's funeral.' Reporters covering Diana's arrival in Zimbabwe were told that she cared less about Raine's nuptials than Dame Barbara. 'The Princess was very amused by a reference to Raine which read, "To call her a dog's dinner would be to provoke widespread outrage among canine nutritionists," ' an aide said, possibly with Diana's agreement. 'As far as she is concerned, Raine is no longer the Countess Spencer and she is very glad to see the back of her.'

While Charles discussed the latest twists in the royal saga with the Queen over lunch at Highgrove, his wife was being feted in Harare. Disabled children performed a musical welcome and the country's leader Robert Mugabe showered her with compliments. 'When you have a visit from a noble person like Princess Diana, naturally you feel elated,' gushed the former Marxist. 'She brings a little light into our lives.'

Diana's entourage said that the Princess was quite happy to go along with the experiment of separate duties and separate courts while reserving the right to divorce if things didn't work out. Speaking openly from the Prince of Wales' office, Commander

Richard Aylard emphasised the couple's complementary roles. 'There will be occasional big national events and family things,' he said, 'but they are separated so I wouldn't expect them to go back to doing joint events on a regular basis. The important thing is for him to get on with his public life and for the Princess to get on with hers. Far from the competitiveness which newspapers suggest, I think they are rather complementary. The country probably benefits from having two people working in that way.'

He was cleverly outlining something that Britain had never had before – two figureheads on the throne with widely different interests and viewpoints, able to span the horizons in a broad manner as no individual could. Charles and Diana had already demonstrated on a State visit to Portugal and the ceremonial occasion in Liverpool that they could tolerate each other's company in public. They had become rather good as a working partnership, even though their personal relationship had been damaged beyond repair. Like all seasoned music hall double acts, they were learning that the best way to stay together was to go their separate ways at night.

Charles now accepted that Diana had the box office appeal the Windsors had been losing until he invited her to join the Family. Parallel roles would enable him to concentrate on the issues close to his heart. Similarly, Diana realised that there were causes which were way beyond her scope. Human suffering would always be a noble vocation but the look of towns and cities and the state of the environment were also matters that had to be addressed if the First Family were to serve society properly.

As the Queen might rule for a further twenty years at least, any really long-term solution was out of the question. Queen Victoria had lived to the age of eighty-one, Queen Mary died just short of her eighty-fifth birthday and the Queen Mother, though frail, was in her ninety-fourth year.

'The Queen has given no indication that she will step down,' said Andrew Morton. 'Any constitutional historian, anybody who is close to the Queen or anybody close to Buckingham Palace all say the same thing: she is never going to abdicate. My own caveat to that would be that if the Queen Mother or the Duke of Edinburgh predecease the Queen, there may well be some pressure from government or from inside the Royal Family for the Queen to adopt a more matriarchal role and allow Prince Charles to take on a lot more of the ceremonial duties.'

On a personal level the Palace went out of its way to persuade journalists that the separation was no more than that. Following a suggestion from Margaret Holder in the *Daily Star* that they might divide Diana's jewels 'with the divorce', she found herself being contradicted by Geoffrey Crawford of the Palace Press Office. 'You couldn't possibly have said that you know they are going to divorce,' he said. 'You know they don't hate each other. It is absolutely untrue — the couple are very fond of each other.'

Furthermore, intelligence was also being received that the Queen had made it clear to both Charles and Andrew that she saw no need for either of them to divorce. There was a strong suggestion that, if they sought permission to end their marriages, she might well refuse it. 'In the past, as in the case of Princess Anne, she has only agreed to a divorce in the Family where one of the parties wished to re-marry,' said a highly placed Palace source, 'I don't see any reason for her to change that stance.'

It was just possible that if Charles and Diana stopped looking critically at each other and began to look positively in the same direction, their parallel lives might one day converge. Though this seemed a distant mirage, it was the best the Windsors could hope for. In the meantime, Charles proved to the world that he was not averse to fighting back.

When the Queen gathered her depleted flock at Balmoral in August 1993, Charles seized the chance to play a role he had previously spurned. More from a sense of duty than a desire to challenge his wife, he agreed to appear in a TV documentary with his sons. The programme would celebrate the twenty-fifth anniversary of his investiture as Prince of Wales, which falls on 1 July, 1994 – the same day as Diana's thirty-third birthday. While the Princess enjoyed a break on the Indonesian island of Bali, the TV cameras were rolling on the shores of Loch Muick near the Balmoral Forest. The unscripted scenes provided the most intimate pictures ever taken of Charles with William and Harry, disproving the belief that he was an uncaring father. Just as significantly, they showed that the princes not only enjoyed his company, they revelled in it.

Charles knew he would be accused of playing Diana at her own propaganda game but he didn't give a damn. He had finally nailed for all time her lie, the one that had wounded him more than any other.

In the words of Charles's loyal supporter: 'She is a sick lady – I know that and he knows that and he has tried to help her.' Whenever the friend was tempted to judge Diana too harshly, however, she thought back to a night in November 1982 and remembered the scenes at Kensington Palace. 'What happened that night was absolutely devastating,' she said, it changed my view about Diana.'

The Princess, who was only twenty-one, had given birth to William less than five months earlier. Desperately trying to regain her figure, she had tried to stick to a rigid diet. But the ravages of bulimia coupled with post-natal depression had triggered the greatest crisis thus far in her marriage. 'Sudden changes of mood are the best way to recognise post-natal depression,' Sir George Pinker, the gynaecologist who delivered William, said at the time. 'The mother becomes very depressed and tearful and miserable.' Diana had been so upset that she pulled out of the royal party attending the annual Festival of Remembrance at the Albert Hall. Prince Charles whispered to officials that his wife was unwell and would not be attending. But Diana arrived unexpectedly just as attendants were removing her chair from the Royal Box.

Vastly intrigued, royal watchers kept their eyes on the royal couple throughout the performance. It was unheard of for a member of the Family to turn up late once apologies had been offered on their behalf. For much of the festival, Diana's head was bowed and she clung protectively to her husband's arm. Ever since that night eleven painful years ago, Charles had known that Diana's Nightmare would be his own for as long as he lived.

18

DIANA'S SECRET LOVER

'For three years I was THE man in her life'
James Hewitt

THROUGHOUT the tribulations of royal exile, Diana prayed that
the truth about her dangerous liaison with James Hewitt would
remain secret. The Princess's reputation with an adoring public
depended largely on the belief that she was the purely innocent
victim of a heartless husband. For that reason, disclosure of her love
affair with an amorous Army officer threatened her as nothing else
could.

However, Diana knew full well on the morning of 2 October 1994
that the myth of the Perfect Princess was about to come to a
shattering end. With callous disregard, Hewitt had betrayed her trust,
assailed her honour and exploited her fame. She was understandably
furious – and very frightened.

Never had Catherine Soames seen her friend so upset as they drove
in the Princess's new green Audi convertible to Romenda Lodge, the
Duchess of York's rented home in Surrey, on that cold, bright
Sunday. Fergie was later to impart that the Princess was spitting
blood from the moment she crossed the threshold.

As a soldier and a gentleman, Hewitt had sworn that he would
never divulge the confidences of his friendship with the Princess of
Wales. Not to anyone, not at any price. He was, he maintained, the
soul of discretion in matters of the heart. Her secrets were safe with
him.

Hewitt had kept his word until the bidding reached six figures, at
which point, like a badly drilled squaddie, he had executed an
embarrassing about-turn which infuriated his friends, delighted his
enemies and destroyed Diana's credibility at a stroke. Not for
nothing was Hewitt known to friends as 'pompous and arrogant'; a
man who 'keeps his compass in his trousers.' Now, however, he
seemed to be thinking only of his wallet.

By the time Diana arrived at Romenda Lodge, half the country knew from that morning's papers that she had been unfaithful to Prince Charles while they were still living under the same roof as husband and wife. Hewitt had confided to the *News of the World* that he and Diana had enjoyed a three-year love affair, that she had considered leaving Charles to live with him, and that he had passionate letters in his possession to prove it all.

As Diana swept in, Fergie knew from her own experiences that the Princess's anger was actually a mask to cloak the fear that was gnawing inside her. Nor was Fergie oblivious to the heavy irony of the situation. So often the butt of scandal herself, the tables had been neatly turned and, for once, Diana was in the hot seat. Here, sitting down to lunch with the sister-in-law she had called the Redhead, the Princess knew that her own Miss Goody-Two-Shoes image had been demolished for ever. No longer was she the unblemished wife of an adulterous husband: she was an adulteress herself and now the world was starting to learn the shocking truth of her darkest secret. It was a bitter moment.

'I was madly in love with her and helped in so many ways,' Hewitt was quoted as saying over coffee in a suite at the Sheraton Hotel in Knightsbridge. 'For three years I was THE man in her life. It got so serious I was warned to stay away from her.' At another meeting, in the nearby Basil Street Hotel, *News of the World* executives asked the former cavalry officer point-blank if he had ever made love to Diana. 'Yes,' he had replied.

At a third meeting, Hewitt had even let a reporter glance at the bundle of Diana's letters. They were 'intimate, affectionate' letters, the paper was able to record. 'Bet you'd love to get your hands on them,' teased Hewitt. 'I haven't shown them to anyone. I have just got to weigh up the consequences. I could be done for high treason and sent to the Tower.'

Hewitt was now telling a story about his relationship with Diana which was anything but 'entirely innocent', the words he had previously chosen to describe it. The big question the reporters had to answer was: If he was lying then, was he telling the truth now? He had already made £100,000 from the *Daily Express* earlier in the year for a turgid account of his friendship with Diana in which he told journalist Anna Pasternak nothing more scintillating than that the Princess had shared washing-up duties at his mother's cottage in

Devon. He had claimed that he met Diana at a party in 1987 and, when she told him she had lost her nerve about riding, he had volunteered to give her lessons to restore her confidence. They had struck up an easy rapport, he said, and become close friends until he heard in his gut 'the warning bell of the fear of getting too close.'

Hewitt said that Diana had stayed at his mother Shirley's house at Ebford near Exeter before he left for service in the Gulf War on Boxing Day 1990. She had been the perfect house guest, he said, 'a great mucker inner, who would do the washing-up and help out.' Using her pet name Dibbs, Diana had written to him frequently while he was a tank commander on active service in the Gulf and had sent him food hampers.

Undeterred by such trivia, Ms Pasternak had stuck to her task of debriefing the now jobless ex-Army officer and the results of her research had been accepted for publication in a book entitled *Princess in Love,* which was being rushed into print amid great security. Even as Diana drove Catherine Soames (the former wife of Charles's friend Nicholas Soames) back to London, she knew that the book would be going on sale throughout Britain the following morning. Ever since they had split up, Diana had suspected that the dashing though duplicitous Hewitt would betray her, and her withdrawal into princessly purdah the previous December had been motivated by that fear. At the time, most people had believed that she was leaving public life over publication of photographs which had been taken secretly of her working out in a London gym. Now the real reason for her sudden exit had emerged. For Diana, it had already been one hell of a year and it was getting worse with each passing day.

The only heartening development from the Princess of Wales's point of view was that Charles had finally admitted his affair with Camilla in a TV interview to accompany the documentary which marked the twenty-fifth anniversary of his investiture as Prince of Wales. He had conceded that he did indeed have a close relationship with Camilla, but insisted that he had been unfaithful only after his marriage to Diana had irretrievably broken down. The confession was an attempt to re-establish his position in the eyes of his future subjects, but it merely had the effect of making Diana seem the wronged party once again.

In the aftermath of the Camillagate scandal, Charles had realised he was a marked man. Literally hundreds of journalists were monitoring his movements twenty-four hours a day in the hope of uncovering some fresh indiscretion. The point at issue was whether or not Charles had forfeited his place in the succession by having an affair with a married woman. Not a few people in the media, politics and the clergy were arguing noisily that the heir apparent was unfit to rule.

The vanguard was led by the Venerable George Austin, Archdeacon of York, who said bluntly: 'When Charles took his solemn marriage vows years ago he promised to be faithful to his wife. He very quickly began to break those vows. It puts a big question mark against the vows to God he would take at his Coronation. The question arises about his trustfulness to make those vows as King.'

There were also fears among some Anglican bishops that Charles might actually marry Camilla after his divorce, if he married a divorcee he would have to renounce the Crown,' one stated emphatically.

Deeply wounded, Charles authorised Nicholas Soames to rebut the insinuations. 'To be King is not an ambition – it is a duty,' thundered the portly Soames. 'That duty will pass at the appropriate moment to the Prince of Wales. It is not like waking up in the morning and saying, "I want to be an engine driver". It simply doesn't work like that.'

This riposte stated Charles's constitutional position unequivocally, but it failed to take into account something that Soames and others close to Charles knew only too well: the infuriating duality of his character. The Prince of Wales was on the one hand an obedient heir who was born to rule and who was motivated mainly by duty. But on the other hand Charles Windsor was a private man who had broken one of the taboos of his royal birthright and, like Edward VIII before him, was now driven by a forbidden love. In the first role, he was very much his sovereign mother's son while in the second he resembled his great-uncle, who had thrown it all away for Wallis Simpson. The question was: Would Charles make the same sacrifice?

'Charles is very loyal to his friends and doubly so to Camilla,' said one who knows him well. 'She means too much to him to be dismissed from his life.'

As the controversy raged over 'the Crown or Camilla', Charles knew he had to protect his dignity and his sanity. One of the measures he took was to assume a new identity which would enable him to conduct what remained of his private life without constant surveillance and the threat of exposure. Long experienced in the art of deceiving the Press, he had adopted Stephen Langton, an unexceptional English name, as a cover. Without arousing suspicion, Stephen Langton could book tables for dinner at discreet restaurants or tickets for unpublicised evenings at the theatre and buy goods from stores which accepted credit cards as payment for telephoned orders. The harmless ploy proceeded undetected for months, giving Charles the degree of freedom he needs as a man caught between the wife he has rejected and the lover he still desires.

Charles was known to have kept secretly in touch with Camilla despite the furore over their relationship, and he was reported to be meeting her at friends' homes in Gloucestershire. After all she had endured, Camilla needed some attention long before Charles acknowledged their love on television. She looked haggard and thin, and she had started chain-smoking cigarettes, 'It would be absolutely unnatural if [the scandal] had not had some effect,' said Lord Patrick Beresford, a friend of the Parker Bowles family. 'But she does not let it show. She manages to be her cheerful self whenever I see her.' Confirming that he and his wife would stay together, Andrew Parker Bowles said: 'She's perfectly all right. Everything is all right between us.'

However, Camilla's sister-in-law, Carolyn Parker Bowles, heightened the speculation when she said: 'Everyone knows Camilla and Andrew have an arranged marriage. Ever since they married, they have had a fairly free life together, which suits them both.'

In truth, Camilla was no longer prepared to remain a lonely figure hiding in the shadows. To reclaim her own place in society, she had accepted an invitation to attend a memorial service for the Earl of Westmorland at the Guards' Chapel, Wellington Barracks, fully aware that Diana would also be there. The risks were obvious. Camilla knew she would be sharing centre stage with the Princess no matter how far apart they might be seated and that the Press would, once again, make unflattering comparisons between herself – and the royal superstar. 'The Princess has never accepted that her husband's relationship with Camilla is over,' said a friend. 'She can, however, live with it.'

In the event, the two women studiously avoided even eye contact, but the encounter seemed to signal a decline not only in Diana's social standing but in herself. Camilla's presence was stark proof that it was the mistress who had the backing of the Royal Family while she had become an embarrassing pariah. She was also worried about James Hewitt. At thirty-six, his job prospects in civilian life were uninspiring and he needed money to maintain his gallivanting lifestyle.

Even the stimulating company of other handsome young men hadn't been enough to prevent Diana's private world from falling to pieces. The day before the Camilla experience, she had dashed away from another engagement in tears, her distress being passed off as a migraine headache. On other occasions, blue eyeliner covered up the telltale signs of sobbing. The symptoms of her bulimia had resurfaced in the form of a mounting hysteria over the reality of her exposed position. Self-pity set in.

Her private life often consisted of nothing more exciting than watching television at Kensington Palace or chatting to friends on the phone. If she went out, it was to the cinema or to dinner with trusted girlfriends. Her male companions included reliable old friends such as Simon Slater, William van Straubenzee and Dr James Colthurst. The paparazzi stalked her every move, hoping to catch her with a new beau. But remarrying wasn't high on Diana's list of priorities.

The Princess had been only seven years old when her parents' unhappy marriage was dissolved in 1969. Her mother Frances had married her lover Peter Shand Kydd that same year, but that marriage also failed and the couple were divorced in 1990, just as Diana's own marriage was breaking down. For that reason alone, Diana had her suspicions about second marriages. Frances now spent most of her time living quietly on the remote Isle of Seil by Oban in Scotland. In her soulful moments, Diana wondered whether she might end up in some similarly isolated location, her beauty and her fame eroded by time. It is a bleak prospect.

Embattled and embittered, Diana had neither the reserves nor the willpower to withstand the Arctic chill of the Windsor freeze-out and all it entailed, especially with regard to her children. The hardest lesson that she has learned about life without Charles is that their sons are, first and foremost, princes of the royal blood.

Diana has already instilled in them the belief that their father's difficulty in expressing his emotions owes as much to his education at Gordonstoun and Timbertop as it does to the Royal Family's traditional reserve. While the Palace old guard would have the boys develop in their father's image, Diana is concerned that this would make them as flawed as she believes Charles to be. She wants William to go to Eton, one of the more enlightened public schools.

Throughout their lives, William and Harry have been torn between the vastly different styles of their parents. Charles, whose progress through life has been dominated by royal protocol, public schools and the strict discipline of the Navy, is the ultimate old-fashioned father. He dresses his sons in fogeyish suits and ties and takes them fishing and shooting.

But Diana, the former kindergarten teacher who loves music, dancing and sunshine holidays, prefers things to be more relaxed. When the boys are out with her – more usually in an amusement park than a Scottish castle — they dress in jeans and baseball hats and are encouraged to enjoy themselves. Since the break-up, the battle for William's heart in particular has become more serious. He has been used like an artillery piece on Charles and Diana's battleground.

The Palace decided that it was time for this to stop. The key tactic in the strategy mapped out for Charles's resurrection during 1994 was for him to be seen with William not as a weekend father but as the central figure in his life. No matter how much Diana might push herself into the public eye as his mother, she could never compete against the power of the Palace. One of the Queen's commands was that William should be presented to the public as Charles's son and heir, crushing the theory that the crown might pass directly to her grandson. The more William was pictured on outings with his father, the more Diana's resolve started to crumble. She was never far from a nervous breakdown during the painful weeks that followed that distant encounter with Camilla.

Only the uninitiated were fooled when she tried to make a joke of it in a hastily revised speech at a charity function, declaring, 'Ladies and gentlemen, I think you are very fortunate to have your patron here today – I was supposed to have my head down the loo for most of the day.' Her enemies at the Palace saved their smiles for the line that was supposed to be more serious: if it's all right with you, I thought I might postpone my nervous breakdown.'

When the Palace had tightened its squeeze on her headline-making activities, Diana had called in the Prime Minister. John Major assured the Princess that he regarded her as the best thing to happen to the Royal Family in generations. To Diana, it seemed as though she might have regained some ground, but even while she smiled and waved, they took away her detective, her chauffeur and a planned trip to Russia. The day Ken Wharfe, her official protector and personal friend, was reassigned to other duties, Diana knew she was fighting a losing battle. Despite working out with Carolan Brown to maintain her figure and listening to pep talks from her friends, she was, in the words of one of them, 'shattered and overstressed'. Without her sons at her side she felt naked, and no amount of walkers could make up for the loss.

With the Hewitt threat of disclosure hanging over her head, her decision to step aside and leave the stage to Prince Charles was accelerated by the loss of her closest friend, Lucia Flecha de Lima. After three years in London as Brazilian ambassador, Lucia's husband Paulo-Tarso was posted to Washington in a similar role. Diana drove to Heathrow for an emotional farewell with Lucia in the VIP lounge. 'She was obviously upset but there was no sign of tears,' said an airport official. Even more isolated without her 'second mother', Diana planned her escape with renewed purpose. She consulted her diary and ringed a date in early December 1993.

In contrast, a newly confident Charles actually seemed to be enjoying his freedom. He had come to believe that his infidelity had been thrust upon him by his wife's unreasonable behaviour, and his guilt over bringing her into the Royal Family in the first place became bearable when he realised that they were both victims of what had amounted to an arranged marriage. Once he accepted that married life was only a trigger to a disturbance buried deep down in Diana's psyche and not the cause of it, he was able to stop blaming himself. After a couple of false starts, Charles found that the best way to deal with Diana was to avoid her unless it was absolutely essential for them to be in the same place at the same time. As he had a busy schedule, this wasn't difficult. For instance, he contrived to be in Turkey on the day of Viscount Linley's wedding to Serena Stanhope at which Diana was one of the royal guests.

The Prince looked younger and smiled happily as he went about his duties with an added spring in his step. He delivered a hard-hitting speech at Oxford in which he attacked the 'unmentionable horrors' perpetrated by Saddam Hussein in Iraq and elsewhere in the Middle East. Aided by the Palace public relations machine, his image-building efforts started to bring unexpected results.

A poll of one thousand people commissioned by *Tatler* showed that the public's perception of Diana was markedly changing, at least in the upper levels of society. In answer to the question, 'Do you think the Princess of Wales is a victim or a manipulator?' only thirty-eight per cent declared her a martyr while forty-four per cent decided she was a monster. Eighteen per cent couldn't make up their minds. Asked for her opinion, Madonna had replied unhelpfully: if I'd been in a situation like hers I would have slit my wrists.' Bruce Oldfield, one of Diana's favoured designers, said: 'She is a modern young woman seeking a modern way out of a tricky situation. She is stuck between the devil and the deep blue sea. She holds the trump card in the form of the two boys, but it's a no-win situation.'

Diana knew in her heart that she had already played her trump card for the last time. Her dilemma was how to slip out of the limelight without leaving the impression that her massive popularity had finally slipped away. Like a shop-soiled black knight on a broken-down charger, a New Zealander called Bryce Taylor unwittingly came galloping to the rescue.

The troubled owner of the L.A. Fitness Centre in the west London suburb of Isleworth, Taylor devised a reckless scheme to save his financial skin. He reasoned that unposed photographs of the best-known member exercising at his health club would be worth a not inconsiderable fortune. Although such a venture would cost the club Diana's patronage, the wave of publicity would more than compensate for the loss. Diana could not have dreamed up a more perfect scenario if she had written the script herself.

The melodrama had started as far back as the morning of 26 April, 1992. Looking her athletic best, Diana had donned a fetching turquoise Lycra camisole and matching cycling shorts before setting off for her regular workout. Peering through the Venetian blinds of his office window, Taylor witnessed the arrival of member No. 753 shortly after 9 a.m. He watched nervously as the Princess ran across the courtyard from the car park to enter his club.

Taylor had spent the two preceding weeks in his garden shed working on a wooden box which now contained the second-hand camera in which he had invested £1,824 for his dangerous enterprise. He had placed the camera into a black plastic binliner stuffed with builders' insulation wool to deaden the sound of its shutter before positioning the entire assembly into panelling which housed the electrical wires and plumbing running across the ceiling directly above a leg exercise machine. Eighty feet of pneumatic cable ran from the camera's shutter mechanism through the roof space and into the office where the anxious New Zealander hid the trigger to activate it.

He wiped his sweaty palms on his trousers as he watched Diana work out first on a rowing machine and then an exercise bicycle before moving on to the leg press. 'I slid the ceiling tile back and reached up and got hold of the air bulb,' he recalled later. 'My legs were trembling. I never felt so scared in my life. I took a deep breath and squeezed the bulb as hard as I could – I actually closed my eyes. My worst fear was that Diana would leap off the machine screaming and yelling to her detective about the hidden camera she'd spotted in the ceiling and all hell would break loose.'

Diana neither heard the camera's repeated clicks nor summoned her bodyguard as her image was captured on film. After only six frames of the thirty-six-shot film were exposed, the shutter jammed. Exchanging the camera for a new one, Taylor repeated the exercise on 4 May. This time Diana, in a patterned top and blue shorts, obligingly ran her fingers through her hair to give him a different sort of picture.

Six months later, Taylor sold both sets of pictures to the *Daily Mirror* and *Sunday Mirror* for a reported £100,000. The Mirrormen had no idea of how neatly they were playing into Diana's hands. The screaming started on Saturday night, 6 November, when copies of the first edition of the Sunday paper surfaced around the country. In the cover photograph the royal gymnast was seen astride the leg press, her elbows and knees wide apart. 'The stunning picture is part of a remarkable set,' boasted the caption. Fleet Street's other editors were unanimous in their censure of the tabloids for publishing the snatched pictures, particularly since the *Sunday Mirror* had taken pains to detail the subterfuge Taylor had employed in order to trick the Princess, who immediately expressed her 'distress and deep sense of outrage'.

The *Daily Mirror's* headline declaring *WE LOVE DI* alongside another stolen snap on its Monday morning front page did nothing to defuse the row. 'Features locked in concentration and biceps straining, Diana is a study in grim determination as she clenches the handles of the weight machine,' began the story.

The Princess appeared an even grimmer study of determination when she dispatched her lawyers to the High Court where they won an injunction against Taylor and the newspapers from further publishing, disclosing or supplying (that is, syndicating to defray their huge cost) the photographs. Lord McGregor, still chairman of the Press Complaints Commission, condemned the publication outright. In retaliation, the *Mirror* called him 'an arch buffoon' and chief executive David Montgomery pulled MGN out of the commission while the Royal Family, Parliament and the rest of Fleet Street united in a formidable alliance against his papers.

However mortified she may have been by the pictures, Diana knew that she had found the perfect scapegoat. On Friday, 3 December, she was due to deliver a speech at a lunch arranged by one of her causes, the National Head Injuries Association. The sun shone for just two hours the previous day but the dull, wintry weather would not have bothered Diana, confined as she was behind the Kensington Palace walls of apartments 8 & 9, drafting the address she planned to launch on an unsuspecting nation.

More than one purpose would be served by her oratory: Fleet Street needed to be taught a lesson and what better way than to make it report its own punishment?

Early in the day, she telephoned Ludgrove School to inform her sons of her intentions. By mid-morning, Fleet Street editors, TV and radio stations had been told that the Princess would be including an important announcement in her lunchtime speech. The Queen was informed and Her Majesty had made no attempt to dissuade her daughter-in-law from the course of action she had chosen. Prince

Charles made it clear that he saw no reason why she needed to make a personal statement at all.

As the details emerged of a Gallup poll which showed that Diana was, in fact, holding her lead over other royals in the popularity stakes (twenty-four per cent naming her their favourite royal against nineteen per cent for the Queen Mother, seventeen per cent for the Queen and just six per cent for Charles), the Princess was being driven from Kensington Palace to the Hilton in Park Lane. Dressed eye-catchingly as ever in a bottle-green velvet outfit by Amanda Wakeley, she strode into the hotel and was shown to the Grand Ballroom where 550 guest were already seated, eagerly awaiting her arrival. The master of ceremonies Lord Archer, himself a master of suspense, had already been briefed by Diana about her plans. She had only to pass the time by toying with a mozzarella salad, a bowl of consomme and a helping of Christmas pudding (she refused the main course of turkey), until Archer announced that Her Royal Highness wished to make 'a personal statement'.

'It is a pleasure to be here with you again,' she began uncertainly, 'sharing in your successes of the past year.' Gaining confidence, she praised her audience for giving her 'an education by teaching me more about life than any books or teachers could have done. My debt of gratitude to you all is immense. I hope in some way I have been of service in return.'

The strain of her three-hour wait showed as she continued: 'A year ago I spoke of my desire to continue with my work unchanged. For the past year I have continued as before. However, life and circumstances alter and I hope you will forgive me if I use this opportunity to share with you my plans for the future which now indeed have changed.'

Clearly referring to the *Mirror* pictures, she then dropped her bombshell: 'When I started my public life twelve years ago, I understood the media might be interested in what I did. I realised then that their intention would inevitably focus on both our private and public lives. But I was not aware of how overwhelming that attention would become; nor the extent to which it would affect both my public duties and my personal life, in a manner that has been hard to bear.'

As faxes were being dispatched to every one of her 118 charities explaining what her decision meant to them, Diana continued: 'At the end of this year, when I have completed my diary of official engagements, I will be reducing the extent of the public life I have led so far. I attach great importance to my charity work and intend to focus on a smaller range of areas in the future. Over the next few months I will be seeking a more suitable way of combining a meaningful public role with, hopefully, a more private life. My first priority will continue to be our children, William and Harry, who deserve as much love, care and attention as I am able to give, as well as an appreciation of the tradition into which they were born. I would also like to add that this decision has been reached with the full understanding of the Queen and the Duke of Edinburgh, who have always shown me kindness and support.'

Fighting back the tears, she concluded: 'I hope you can find it in your hearts to understand and to give me the time and space that has been lacking in recent years. I could not stand here today and make this sort of statement without acknowledging the heartfelt support I have been given by the public in general. Your kindness and affection have carried me through some of the most difficult periods and always your love and care have eased that journey. And for that I thank you from the bottom of my heart.'

When she sat down, Diana listened to a round of applause that lasted almost as long as her five-minute speech. The decision could not have been communicated more effectively and her husband had no need to question further why she had needed to make a public announcement.

It comforted Diana to learn that she was by no means the only royal with a guilty secret. Suddenly, the spotlight was turned glaringly on Princess Margaret when the spectre of her adulterous love affair with Robin Douglas-Home in 1967 came back to haunt her. Never again could Auntie Margo point the finger of censure at the Princess she had called 'insensitive and utterly selfish'.

When Margaret's son Lord Linley had told friends at a London dinner part that 'something's going to come out that makes everything else look like nothing', he was speaking with authority. Linley had lived all his adult life with his mother's dread that the love letters she had penned to the lovelorn pianist in her own hand on Kensington Palace notepaper would one day be made public.

The letters, last known to be resting in a New York safe, turned up in the possession of Noel Botham, the Soho publican and journalist who had befriended Douglas-Home back in the Sixties. Ten days before he killed himself, Douglas-Home had told Botham: 'I want you to promise me that one day, when the climate is right for it, the world will know my relationship with Princess Margaret was a serious one. We did talk about divorce and about us getting married. Make sure the world sees these letters. Remember I have given them away and you know who to.' Botham waited until 1994 before publishing them in his book *Margaret: The Untold Story,* explaining that 'the climate with the royals has now changed'.

Although the affair had lasted a mere thirty days, it had obviously affected Margaret deeply. In one memorable phrase, she likened her love to the passionate scent of new-mown grass and lilies.

The most romantic of the young royals, Prince Edward, followed every scene of the royal high drama with even greater detachment than before. He had a life of his own to lead and things were looking up. No longer benefiting from the Civil List, he had launched a new TV company called Ardent Productions and become its joint managing director.

However, Edward's love life was still less private than he would have preferred. When his secret Sloaney girlfriend emerged in public she turned out to be Sophie Rhys-Jones, a twenty-eight-year-old blonde business consultant. Born in Oxford, she had been educated at Kent College for Girls before embarking on a career in public relations. She had met the bachelor prince while working on a project for the Duke of Edinburgh's Award Scheme in the summer of 1993. 'Edward is so sure he has found the right girl that he wasn't even nervous when he introduced her to his mother,' said a friend.

In fact, the Queen was overjoyed that one of her sons seemed to have found happiness. Sophie's west London flat, inauspiciously near 60 Coleherne Court, the address Diana had shared with three flatmates before she made what she now called 'my bad decision' to marry Charles, was soon besieged in the traditional manner, making her life extremely difficult.

She spent evenings with Edward at his apartment at Buckingham Palace and weekends at his quarters at Windsor Castle. Both enjoyed tennis, skiing and nights at the ballet. Although Edward had followed a similar routine during previous romantic entanglements, there was a new maturity in the way he proceeded. He took the extraordinary step of issuing a statement to editors under the Ardent letterhead asking them to leave him and his sweetheart alone. It had little noticeable effect. As the royal juggernaut, with Diana firmly in the driving seat, rumbled ever closer to the edge of the precipice, the media recorded every twist and turn of the journey.

Nothing thus far has brought Diana greater embarrassment than the story of her infatuation with a married man, antiques dealer Oliver Hoare. She stood accused of plaguing Hoare and his French wife with some 300 nuisance telephone calls to their £2 million mansion home in Tregunter Road, one of London's most exclusive streets on the edge of Chelsea, Fulham and Kensington.

The calls, silent at first, had come in at the rate of twenty a week over a period of eighteen months, beginning in September 1992, three months before the official announcement of Diana's separation from Charles. But it was not until October 1993 that the Hoares decided to take action after the calls took on a more menacing tone.

Hoare's wife Diane was distressed when she picked up the phone and heard an unidentified female shout a stream of abuse down the line. An independent and strong-minded woman, Diane Hoare had had enough. She sent Oliver round to Kensington police station to report the matter. Born into the highest echelons of French society, Diane is the daughter of Baroness Louise de Waldner, a friend of both Prince Charles and the Queen Mother, who calls her Lulu. When the Prince had broken his arm playing polo, he was invited to her chateau near Avignon to recover.

Diane and Oliver had met in France in his art student days and when she worked at the Paris office of Christie's. They married on 27 May 1976 at Kensington register office. He was thirty and she was twenty-eight and they were already living together at Oliver's bachelor home in Kynance Mews, Kensington.

By the time the telephone calls started in 1992, the Hoares considered themselves as friendly with Diana as they were with Charles and his grandmother. By then one of the world's leading dealers in Islamic art – a rarefied sector of the art market where only the very richest can afford to indulge – Oliver heads the Ahuan gallery in Belgravia and their house in Tregunter Road is filled with treasures. *Harpers & Queen* described the couple as 'cultured and erudite' and they are familiar figures on the art circuit of receptions, auctions and exhibitions.

Once Oliver Hoare contacted the police, British Telecom placed an electronic tracing device on their telephone line. Activated by pressing digit one on the phone's dial, the tracer instantly establishes where calls are coming from if not, initially, who is making them. The tracer proved that some anonymous calls to the house in Tregunter Road were made from numbers to which Diana had exclusive access – her private line at Kensington Palace and her personal mobile phone – while others were made from the home of her sister, Lady Sarah McCorquodale.

The nuisance calls had come to an end following the personal intervention of a government minister, who contacted the Royal Household. Diana remained close friends with Oliver throughout and he contacted her immediately when, in summer 1994, it became known that details of the matter had been leaked to the Press.

Diana response was to contact Richard Kay, a friendly reporter on the *Daily Mail.* Kay was told to drive to a rendezvous with the Princess in a square close to Paddington Station, just five minutes drive from Kensington Palace. He did as he was told and soon after he arrived, Diana drove up alone in her Audi. 'Extremely distressed', according to Kay, she got into the front passenger seat of his car.

'They are trying to make out I was having an affair with this man or had some sort of fatal attraction,' she told him, referring to Oliver Hoare. it is simply untrue and so unfair.' Diana asked the reporter if he would mind taking her for a drive in his car: 'Then,' he wrote in his subsequent account, 'over several hours, she poured out her anger and unhappiness.'

'Somewhere, someone is going to make out that I am mad, that I am guilty by association, that the mud will stick,' Diana told him. 'I am bemused by this constant attention, a level of intrusion that I had reasonably thought would diminish.'

Knowing that Kay would report everything she said in his newspaper, she delivered a message to the nation: it is said that some people want me to return to the public stage – well, this is hardly going about it the proper way.'

She also let it be known that Oliver Hoare had acted as an intermediary when she and Charles were unable to agree details of their access to William and Harry – albeit, apparently, after the nuisance calls to Tregunter Road had stopped. Indeed, Hoare had telephoned her several times that very weekend. 'He is a friend,' said Diana. 'He has helped me and I have phoned him.'

Time and again, she denied making the nuisance calls, but if she offered any explanation as to how they were made from her telephones, then Kay's newspaper never reported it. Hoare was said to have shouted Diana's name at his silent tormentor once he had been informed of the origins of the calls. She was alleged to have responded: 'I'm so sorry, so sorry. I don't know what came over me.' But in her version to Kay, she shook her head in vehement denial and repeated 'No, no, not at all'.

'Do you realise that whoever is trying to destroy me is inevitably damaging the institution of monarchy as well?' she demanded. Who, the reporter asked her, would do such a thing? 'I know there are those whose wish is apparently to grind my face in it,' came the reply, 'I knew I could not rely on anyone sticking up for me, but nor could I allow such hurtful things to be said about me in silence any longer. What should I do, close my ears and eyes to it all?'

The police had traced some of the calls to telephone boxes in streets in the Kensington Palace area and when Kay asked if she had made those calls, Diana's answer was more than just curious: 'You can't be serious,' she said, 'I don't even know how to use a parking meter, let alone a phone box.' This sounded disingenuous to even Diana's most loyal supporters. Prior to becoming Princess of Wales, she had been a London motorist living in one of the city's busiest suburbs, yet she claimed that she had never even learned to put coins in a parking meter.

'I know everyone wants me to be having affairs and this man fits the bill, but it's not true,' explained Diana. 'Besides, if I were as obsessed as these calls would suggest, why would I have had supper with him a few weeks afterwards?' Diana had indeed dined with Oliver Hoare and Beatriz Flecha de Lima, one of Lucia's daughters, on 13 March, six weeks after the calls had ceased. She had been photographed at Oliver's side as he drove her back to Kensington Palace after the meeting. Just as Diana was recovering from the whole unpleasant episode, *Princess In Love* burst into print.

Before she left Kensington Palace for her morning workout at her new gym, the Harbour Club in Chelsea, Diana took a call from Richard Kay. According to a *Daily Mail* colleague, they discussed the imminent publication of Hewitt's ghosted memoirs. Diana acknowledged that she had written letters to him and said that she was going to demand their return. According to the newspaper, Diana also wanted it made known that she and Hewitt had never made love: 'He wanted to, but I never let it happen,' she maintained. 'His account is fantasy.'

But by now almost no one believed Diana. *Princess in Love* stripped the final fig leaf from her dignity, leaving her naked and cold in the marketplace. Anna Pasternak, an Oxford graduate with wild, wind-swept tresses and a penchant for deeply purple prose, is related to the author of the Russian classic *Dr Zhivago* but her own fragrant literary style might have made even Mills & Boon blush.

Buckingham Palace dismissed the book as 'grubby and worthless' but Hewitt had sworn an affidavit testifying that everything he had told Ms Pasternak was the truth. According to Hewitt, he and Diana had first made love in her own bed at Kensington Palace, and later in her four-poster bed at Highgrove as well as her bathroom there, in a poolhouse at Althorp and in his bedroom at his mother's house in Devon. In Ms Pasternak's version, the cavalry officer held nothing back. The betrayal was everything that Diana had feared it would be.

Captain Hewitt (for now it was revealed that he had failed his exams and was not entitled to be called major) had disclosed to Ms Pasternak that he had been hooked from the first moment he had met Diana. They had ridden together in the royal parks in early morning sunlight and at sunset, and she persuaded the posse of police and officials that always flanked her to hold back or disappear altogether.

According to Hewitt, Diana enjoyed being able to talk to him as a friend for he was not in awe of her. It had been in the barracks after a crisp morning ride that she confided to him that her marriage had been falling apart for years. The media speculation that it was a sham was true and she and Charles were leading virtually separate lives. She felt more undermined than supported by people closest to her, even Fergie. 'I am surrounded by people but so alone,' she had said. Even when they did not meet, they spoke on the telephone at least once a day. Diana sought her eager swain's advice on her clothes and he listened to her rehearse the speeches she was to deliver at public engagements.

The setting for Diana's seduction of her new friend and riding instructor could not have been more regally romantic. She invited him to a candle-lit dinner in her apartment at Kensington Palace and, after they had drunk champagne and feasted on roast beef followed by apple tart and cream, in a room heavy with the scent of his favourite lilies, she had sat on his lap and they embraced. Without uttering a word, Diana had led him to her bedroom.

There was no danger of them being disturbed by her husband. Even when he was at the Palace, Charles slept alone in a separate suite of rooms. After they had made love, Diana had lain in Hewitt's arms and wept before falling asleep. Unafraid of his nakedness, the young lothario eventually went to her bathroom and put his clothes back on, pausing only to inspect the cluster of photographs of William and Harry around her wash basin and along the side of her bath. Hewitt said that he returned to the bedroom to 'kiss her awake'. He told her how beautiful she was and how she made his heart sing, which presumably removed any fears she might have been entertaining that he might have lost his respect for her. Some time after 2 a.m., he had left Diana's apartment and driven from Kensington Palace to his flat in nearby South Kensington.

In the following months, their affair gathered momentum. They met in low-profile restaurants and at prearranged rendezvous points. When Hewitt was posted to a barracks near Windsor Castle, they made use of Windsor Great Park's wide open spaces for early morning rides. Their evenings were spent in the Wales's apartment at Kensington Palace, where Hewitt said their love affair continued to blossom.

They also met once a month at Highgrove, where at night Hewitt would tread carefully along the corridor to join Diana in her creamy bedroom, three rooms from his own. Taking advantage of Charles's absence, they made love in her four-poster, but he rose early so that William and Harry, who slept in the next room, did not bound in and discover them in bed together.

Hewitt claimed Diana had grown to hate the house, believing that it was where Charles and Camilla had spent their happiest moments. Now, in the company of her own lover, she came alive in it. At breakfast, in front of the staff, they played the part of hostess and guest, although Hewitt believed that Nanny Barnes had guessed their secret. They never kissed in front of the children, who enjoyed the military tales their 'Uncle' James would tell them.

In the early evenings, Diana and James would sit catching the perfume of the thyme walk in Charles's herb garden or the scent of the overhanging roses. After they had bathed and changed, they would sit watching television and reading magazines, scanning the pages of *Country Life* to pick out homes they would fantasise about living in together.

As 1988 arrived, Diana knew that she must face a meeting with Hewitt's mother. James related that he asked Shirley if he could bring a girlfriend home for the weekend. Was it anyone she knew, his mother enquired? The Princess of Wales, said the Life Guard. When his mother asked which bedroom she would be sleeping in, he told her that she would be using his own and there was no further discussion on the matter.

In the company of Ken Wharfe, Diana and her libidinous soldier spent the first of several weekends in the pretty cottage. They walked on the beaches of Exmouth and Budleigh Salterton and picnicked together on Dartmoor, Diana often wearing a damson-coloured Puffa jacket he apparently gave her as a present. Hewitt would sometimes take Wharfe to the local pub, leaving open pages of Tennyson and Wordsworth or Shakespearean sonnets for Diana to read. In the evenings around an open fire, they would all chat for hours before James and Diana said goodnight and retired to his room, whey they indulged their passion in two single beds pushed together. They assured each other of undying love and each said how much they needed each other.

They went also to Althorp, where Diana introduced Hewitt to her father, her stepmother Raine and her stepgrandmother, Dame Barbara Cartland. Once again, Diana took her willing lover by the hand one hot night, leading him to Earl Spencer's poolhouse for a session of love-making. 'Nobody will find us,' Hewitt claimed she whispered in his ear.

When he was dispatched to the Gulf War, Hewitt said that Diana sent not only food hampers, but also Turnbull & Asser shirts . . . and those passionate, intimate letters. On his return, a member of the Highgrove staff was sent to meet him and he was bundled into the boot of a car to be transported secretly back through the gates of Charles's home.

The affair ended almost as suddenly as it had begun. According to Hewitt, Diana 'withdrew' and 'distanced herself from her old circle'. Strengthened for a new life that had to exclude him, she had loved him enough to leave him. She just walked away.

On the day that *Princess in Love* was published, Ms Pasternik appeared on TV, saying: 'I decided to tell this story because it was too beautiful a love to remain secret.' Elsewhere, she claimed that 'theirs was a love that arose through force of circumstance,' adding that she hoped the book would contribute to 'a proper understanding of and sympathy for Princess Diana.' Somehow, Diana managed to maintain her sense of humour. 'I'm going straight home to bed with a bowl of cereal,' she told late-night revellers at a champagne party she attended.

Hewitt was branded 'a rat' and 'a traitor', and his name was posted ignominiously on the gates of the Life Guards' barracks in London and Windsor, marking him as a disgraced former member of the regiment and barring him from the officers' mess, which he had hitherto enjoyed visiting. On the day of publication Diana lunched with two elderly and highly respectable ladies, Lady Rees-Mogg, wife of the former *Times* editor, and Lady Weinstock whose husband was head of GEC, both of whom could both be relied upon not to raise the matter.

Opinion pollsters, though, interrogated the public on the issue and their survey showed that exactly half of those questioned thought that Diana's standing had been harmed by Hewitt's revelations, and forty-eight per cent thought it would harm the monarchy. However, fifty-three per cent still blamed Prince Charles for the breakdown of the marriage compared with ten per cent who held Diana responsible.

With divorce remaining the only sane option for the royal casualties, Charles and Diana prepared to send out separate Christmas cards for the second year running. In the photograph of her 1993 card, Diana had struck the formal pose of a very regal King Mother with a royal prince stationed at either side: William dutiful and serious, Harry admiring her majestic profile. 'We three', as Diana called them, were photographed against the formal backdrop of an eighteenth-century tapestry at Kensington Palace. The message Diana seemed to be sending out to the world then was that she was still a force to be reckoned with, even though she was leaving the Royal Family. To emphasise the point, she had dropped the royal crest in favour of the Spencer family's coat of arms. Just like 1993, the year now passing into history had turned into an *annus terribilis,* and Diana needed her young princes as never before. They would not let her down.

The princes were devastated when their own father invaded the Royal Family's privacy – more than any dreaded tabloid had ever dared – to confirm to the world that he had never loved Diana, that their marriage had been a disastrous sham from the start and that the wedding had taken place only after Prince Philip had pressured him into proposing to save Diana's honour. 'Frequently I feel I'm in a kind of cage, pacing up and down in it and longing to be free,' Charles had written in a letter to a friend in 1986. 'How awful incompatibility is, and how dreadfully destructive it can be for the players in this extraordinary drama. It has all the ingredients of a Greek tragedy. I never thought it would end up like this. How could I have got it all so wrong?'

This letter was among a batch of private correspondence which Charles handed over to Jonathan Dimbleby for inclusion in a new biography on his life. But by betraying his own family in this way, the Prince appeared more like the Duke of Windsor than a Greek hero.

When he had first arrived at Ludgrove School, William walked into the kitchen and spied a picture of his mother which some wag had stuck on to the door of the refrigerator. One of the staff, a young woman, had tried to cover it up, thinking it might seem disrespectful in the eyes of her son. But her alarm was misplaced. William marched straight up to the photograph and beamed proudly at his beautiful mother. 'It's all right,' said the future King. 'She looks jolly nice.'

He and Harry would always love Diana no matter what anyone else might think.

HARRY
THE PEOPLE'S PRINCE

CHRIS HUTCHINS

PRINCE Harry is the most interesting – indeed the most exciting - member of the Royal Family and this no-holds-barred biography tells his story for the first time. Son of the late Princess Diana – the most famous woman on Earth – and Prince Charles, the next king, and brother of William, the king after that, he is determined to live by his mantra: 'I am what I am'. From a childhood overshadowed by his parents' troubled marriage and scarred by the tragic death of his mother, to his brilliant public performances at the Queen's Diamond Jubilee celebrations, the London Olympics and his brother's wedding, this book charts the remarkable journey of a young man with an extraordinary destiny. It also reveals details of his extraordinary love life, telling for the first time what caused his affair with Cressida Bonas to collapse. The author has enjoyed unparalleled access to a wide variety of people whose lives Harry has touched: senior aides, humble members of palace staff, aristocrats, bodyguards, school friends, comrades-in-arms . . . and old flames. They piece together the tale of a young man who admirably has created a life so different from the one set out for him by what he describes as 'an accident of birth'.

'Warm-hearted. Brave. But at times recklessly impulsive. A new biography gives a fascinating psychological insight into the forces that shaped Harry, the playboy Prince.'

Daily Mail.

ABRAMOVICH

DOMINIC MIDGLEY AND CHRIS HUTCHINS

'An incredible story' – *Mail on Sunday*; 'Well researched and fluently written' – *The Times*; 'Draws a picture of a man of immense ruthlessness, nerve and charm . . . offers a Vanity Fair of Russian oligarchy' – *The Spectator*; A superb insight into the Chelsea boss . . . a must read for both football fans and business tycoons' – *Sunday Business Post*; 'A well-researched investigation into the life and times of Chelsea's owner' – *World Soccer*; 'The first sustained effort to uncover the making of Chelsea's oligarch' – *Guardian*'; 'Authors Dominic Midgley and Chris Hutchins go to commendable lengths to tell the story' – *Sunday Times*; 'Where this book sets itself apart is in its quest to discover Abramovich's true identity. Interviews with his childhood friends, neighbours and teachers in Russia offer an original perspective on the man while access to the informed such as Boris Berezovsky, his one-time mentor, provides a picture of a canny dealmaker and consummate politician' – *The Times*'; 'Most fascinating account . . . should be read by anyone not just with an interest in sport but also in business and in politics' – *Press and Journal*.

FERGIE CONFIDENTIAL

CHRIS HUTCHINS & PETER THOMPSON

IT SEEMS that almost every week Sarah Ferguson - the Duchess of York, known to one and all as Fergie - makes headlines with her efforts to re-brand herself and explain her troubles. There are the weight-loss problems, the ongoing differences with the Royal Family and her financial difficulties. But how did it all start? It seemed like a fairy-tale come true when Sarah married the Queen's favourite son, Prince Andrew, and became one of the best-known women in the world. She was feted wherever she went – and she went everywhere. But the Duchess's world was to come crashing down in spectacular fashion.

We all heard the rumours, now here's a book that sets out the facts about all the scandals. Finally, the explosive truth from two experts – CHRIS HUTCHINS, the writer who broke the palace-rocking story of Fergie's risqué liaison with handsome Texan Steve Wyatt, and PETER THOMPSON, a former editor of London's *Daily Mirror*, the paper that ran the sexy St. Tropez stories of Fergie and her "financial advisor" Johnny Bryan. The book also details her often-tempestuous relationship with Princess Diana and how both women decided to end their marriages.

ATHINA:
THE LAST ONASSIS

CHRIS HUTCHINS & PETER THOMPSON

BY way of light relief as Greece continues to stand face-to-face with financial meltdown, it is well worth visiting the story of Athina Onassis Roussel, who became the richest little girl in the world when she inherited unimaginable wealth from her heiress mother, Christina Onassis. This compelling book explores the legend of Athina's grandfather, the shipping magnate Aristotle Onassis, and examines the legacy that became Athina's extraordinary birthright as The Last Onassis. No 20th-century saga features more great names than that of the Onassis dynasty; the Kennedys - including JFK and his widow Jacqueline, who became Onassis's second wife - the opera diva Maria Callas who longed to be the third; and Prince Rainier and Princess Grace, with whom he fought a celebrated feud for control of Monte Carlo. The cast list is endless: the Hollywood stars Elizabeth Taylor, Richard Burton, Marilyn Monroe and Greta Garbo, the politicians Sir Winston Churchill and Richard Nixon, the tycoons Stavros Niarchos and Howard Hughes and the FBI chief J. Edgar Hoover.

THE BEATLES: MESSAGES FROM JOHN, PAUL, GEORGE AND RINGO

CHRIS HUTCHINS

This is the inside story of the Beatles by a writer who knew them from the Hamburg days and was with them through the height of Beatlemania. He relates the secrets of their lives on the road and at home, and tells the full story of the night he took them to party with Elvis Presley and its astonishing consequences. John's secret shrine to a Beatle who died; the night Bob Dylan came to call; the Hollywood siren John mixed a most unusual cocktail for. It's John, Paul, George and Ringo as you have never read about them before ...

GOLDSMITH MONEY, WOMEN AND POWER

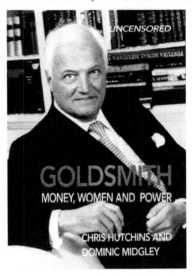

CHRIS HUTCHINS & DOMINIC MIDGLEY

The inside story of Sir James Goldsmith's elopement with the teenage daughter of a Bolivian multi-millionaire . . . The incongruous friendship between his second wife and his last mistress . . . The daring business deals that made him a billionaire . . . How Richard Branson pushed him into his own swimming pool and was told he was no longer a welcome guest . . . Lady Annabel Goldsmith's fascinating relationship with Princess Diana . . . The sad tale of the eldest son living in Central America . . . The niece who made her name in soft porn films . . .The full story of his £20-million push for political power . . . And an Indian doctor's account of how he tried in vain to help Goldsmith in his battle against cancer.

MR CONFIDENTIAL

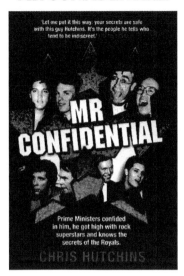

'Let me put it this way, your secrets are safe with this guy Hutchins. It's the people he tells who tend to be indiscreet.'

MR CONFIDENTIAL

Prime Ministers confided in him, he got high with rock superstars and knows the secrets of the Royals.

CHRIS HUTCHINS

CHRIS HUTCHINS

ELVIS Presley, Princess Diana, Elton John, the Beatles, Tom Jones, Fergie Duchess of York, Richard Branson – they all figure in this extraordinary book of revelations. Previously untold stories of royals, celebrities and the occasional politician are all relayed in this rich and unrivalled mix of anecdotes by the master.

Chris Hutchins is a journalist and author. For more than a decade his *Confidential* column chronicled the lives of the rich and famous and was featured in three national newspapers. Think of a moment in popular culture in the last three decades and the chances are that Hutchins either covered it or got caught up in it.

At one time he also operated the UK's most successful music PR company, shaping the careers and sharing the lives of Tom Jones, the Bee Gees, Eric Clapton and many other international stars. As a writer on the *New Musical Express,* he toured the world with the Beatles and took them to meet Elvis Presley who became his friend.

ELVIS MEETS THE BEATLES

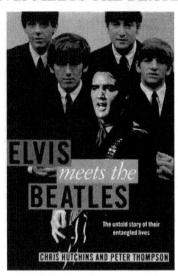

CHRIS HUTCHINS & PETER THOMPSON

HOW did John Lennon, Paul McCartney, George Harrison and Ringo Starr ever get to America in the first place? How did Elvis Presley, a poor boy from the Tennessee backwoods, arrive in Hollywood? Full of previously unpublished detail, this book is a rare focus on the lives and careers of five of the most famous entertainers ever. It converges on the night the greatest summit in rock 'n roll history took place and no one is better equipped to tell the story of that night than Chris Hutchins for not only was he the only writer there, he set the meeting up! When they first met in a Hamburg night club in 1962 John Lennon asked Hutchins if he ever thought he'd be able to meet the man they called 'the King'. The writer from the *NME* said he would try and arrange it – one day . . . That day came in August 1965 when Hutchins - after cultivating a friendship with Presley's legendary manager Colonel Tom Parker and by then on tour with the Beatles - took the group to Elvis's home to party. Collaborating with fellow author Peter Thompson, Hutchins has written this detailed and uncompromisingly frank account of what happened that night – and the strange events that followed. It's packed with rock 'n roll stories.

Lightning Source UK Ltd.
Milton Keynes UK
UKOW05n1325161216

290204UK00001B/23/P